A special offer just for you…
The ETA/Cuisenaire® Manipulative Starter Kit

The most powerful combination of hands-on and overhead materials designed to get teaching mathematics off to a great start!

Manipulative Starter Kit Includes:

24 Hardwood Color Cubes
50 Plastic 2-color Counters
24-piece Plastic Fraction Circle Set
1 Set of 74 Cuisenaire® Rods
4 Transparent Overhead Spinners
50 Colorful Overhead Counters
96-piece Overhead Pattern Block Set
1 pair each Red, Green, and White Dice Set
2 Flexible Plastic Mirrors
7-piece Plastic Tangram Set
1 25-piece Plastic Geoboard

ETA®
Cuisenaire

EXPANDING THE UNIVERSE OF LEARNING™

Teaching mathematics today means using a variety of manipulative materials to help children understand math concepts. The ETA/Cuisenaire Manipulative Starter Kit offers a selection of the most widely used manipulatives and overhead projector materials in classrooms today, and at a huge savings!

The Manipulative Starter Kit is your opportunity to learn how eleven different materials are used to introduce math concepts from kindergarten to eighth grade. A 92-page resource book, *Start with Manipulatives*, by Rosamond Welchman-Tischler, comes complete with a handsome three-ring binder to encourage addition of classroom notes and information from other resources. This clearly-written, concise guide begins with an overview of each manipulative, then focuses on its pedagogical usefulness, indicating which math concepts are most appropriately taught with each model.

Equipped with this excellent resource—and using the manipulatives from the kit—

you will have everything you need to teach mathematics with methods and materials that support the standards set by the National Council of Teachers of Mathematics.

What makes the Manipulative Starter Kit so popular?

"The Manipulative Starter Kit gives pre-service teachers the tools to accurately model math concepts. The kit also allows them to study at home and allows for individual investigation."

Dr. Steven Wilkinson
Assistant Professor of Mathematics
Northeastern State University

"This kit has become a critical component of our mathematic. methods and materials course: early childhood and elementar pre-service teachers. In many instances, students truly understand mathematical concepts for the first time."

Dr. Claire Graham
Framingham State College

www.etacuisenaire.com

WD0600D

Teaching Elementary and Middle School
Mathematics

Raising the Standards

Laura S. Sgroi

State University of New York, New Paltz

WADSWORTH

THOMSON LEARNING

Australia Canada Mexico Singapore Spain United Kingdom United States

WADSWORTH

THOMSON LEARNING

Education Editor: Dan Alpert
Associate Development Editor: Tangelique Williams
Editorial Assistant: Keynia Hardley
Marketing Manager: Becky Tollerson
Marketing Assistant: Ingrid Hernandez
Project Editor: Trudy Brown
Print Buyer: Mary Noel
Permissions Editor: Joohee Lee

Production Service: Johnstone Associates
Text and Cover Designer: Harry Voigt
Copy Editor: Judy Johnstone
Illustrator: The Clarinda Company
Cover Image: Lisl Dennis, The Image Bank
Compositor: The Clarinda Company
Text and Cover Printer: Courier Kendalville

Printed in the United States of America
1 2 3 4 5 6 7 04 03 02 01 00

ISBN 0-534-50875-8

Wadsworth/Thomson Learning
10 Davis Drive
Belmont, CA 94002-3098
USA

For more information about our products, contact us:
Thomson Learning Academic Resource Center
1-800-423-0563
http://www.wadsworth.com

International Headquarters
Thomson Learning
International Division
290 Harbor Drive, 2nd Floor
Stamford, CT 06902-7477
USA

UK/Europe/Middle East/South Africa
Thomson Learning
Berkshire House
168-173 High Holborn
London WC1V 7AA
United Kingdom

Asia
Thomson Learning
60 Albert Street, #15-01
Albert Complex
Singapore 189969

Canada
Nelson Thomson Learning
1120 Birchmount Road
Toronto, Ontario M1K 5G4
Canada

To
Richard, Allison, Elizabeth, and Kate
and to
The Community of Learners at
Pound Ridge Elementary School

Contents

Preface xv

1 New Standards for Learning and Teaching Mathematics 1

The Goals of Mathematics Education 3
The Nature of the Pre-K–2 Learner 5
Teaching the Young Child 6
Teachers of primary-grade children . . .
must be aware of the "whole child" 7
should integrate their instruction 8
should engage them in active as opposed to passive activities 9
should provide small-group activities that allow discussion
and interaction 9
Strength in Numbers: Communication 13
Teachers of primary-grade children . . .
should keep in mind the interests of their students when planning
lessons 13
need to provide a range of activities to meet the various developmental
needs of their students 14
Teaching Children Aged 8–13 16
Cooperative Learning 16
Teachers of intermediate-grade children . . .
should involve them in logical investigations 18
should involve them in investigations of other cultures 18
Summary 25

2 Standards for Number and Numeration 31

Planning for Instruction 32
Factors Affecting the Mathematical Achievement of Students 36
Time on Task 36
Wait Time 36

Gender Issues 37

Multicultural Issues 37

Curricular Issues 39

Constructivism in the Mathematics Classroom 39

Cognitively Guided Instruction 40

Strength in Numbers: Problem Solving 43

Performance-Based Assessment 43

Number and Operation for Grades Pre-K–2 45

Performance-Based Assessment: One-to-One Correspondence 47

Observing, Describing, Classifying 48

Use of Number 48

Performance-Based Assessment: The Cardinal Use of Number 52

The Hindu-Arabic Number System 53

Strength in Numbers: Chip Trading in Other Bases 58

Number and Operation for Grades 3–5 61

Performance-Based Assessment: Classification 63

Number and Operation for Grades 6–8 64

Prime and Composite Numbers 67

Estimation 67

Strength in Numbers: Rectangular Arrays for Prime and Composite Numbers 68

Summary 69

3   **Standards for Whole Numbers: Addition and Subtraction** 75

Operation for Grades Pre-K–2 76

Basic Facts of Addition and Subtraction 80

Properties of Whole-Number Addition 82

Basic Facts Strategies 82

Guess My Rule 83

I Have . . . Who Has . . . ? 83

Cover-Up 84

Salute 84

Add 'Em Up 85

Bingo 85

Computer Programs 86

Performance-Based Assessment: Basic Addition and Subtraction Facts 86

Strength in Numbers: Magic Squares 87

Addition and Subtraction of Multi-Digit Numbers 88

Estimation and the Commutative and Associative Properties 89

Forming Multiples of Ten 89

Rounding 91

Front-End Estimation 91

Powers-of-Ten Blocks and the Standard Addition Algorithm 92

Alternative Algorithms for Whole-Number Addition 93

Partial-Sums Algorithm 94

Powers-of-Ten Blocks with the Standard Subtraction Algorithm 95

Alternative Algorithms for Whole-Number Subtraction 98

Equal Addends Subtraction 98

Counting-Up Subtraction 99

The Spreadsheet as a Problem-Solving Tool 99

Strength in Numbers: Problem Solving 103

Performance-Based Assessment: Multi-Digit Addition and Subtraction 105

Strength in Numbers: Alternative Subtraction Algorithm 106

Summary 106

4   **Standards for Whole Numbers: Multiplication and Division** 111

Operations of Multiplication and Division 111

Number and Operation for Grades 3–5 112

Properties of Whole-Number Multiplication 113

Basic Facts of Multiplication and Division 115

Basic Facts Strategies 115

Even-Odd 119

Two Over 121

Multiplication Cover-Up 122

Salute 122

Bingo 124

Patterns 124

Computer Software 125

Strength in Numbers: Problem Solving 126

Performance-Based Assessment: Basic Multiplication and Division Facts 127

Multiplication and Division of Multi-Digit Numbers 128

Estimation and the Distributive and Associative Properties 128

Powers-of-Ten Blocks with Standard Multiplication Algorithm 129

Alternative Algorithms for Whole-Number Multiplication 133

Lattice Multiplication 134

Russian Peasant Multiplication 135

Performance-Based Assessment: Multi-Digit Multiplication 135

Strength in Numbers: Alternative Algorithms for Multiplication 136

Manipulatives with the Standard Division Algorithm 136

An Alternative Algorithm for Whole-Number Division 136

The Subtraction Method of Division 137

Number and Operation for Grades 6–8 139

Estimation 140

Rounding to Multiples of Ten 140

Rounding with Compensation 140

Estimating Quotients 141

Using Multiplication and Division to Solve Problems 142

Summary 144

5 **Standards for Geometry** 149

Geometry and Spatial Sense for Grades Pre-K–2 150

The Contribution of Research 150

van Hiele Level 0: Visualization 150

van Hiele Level 1: Analysis 152

van Hiele Level 2: Informal Deduction 152

van Hiele Level 3: Formal Deduction 152

van Hiele Level 4: Rigor 153

Observation, Description, and Classification 154

Performance-Based Assessment: Combining Shapes 155

Connecting Geometry to Other Mathematical Ideas 158

Strength in Numbers: Tangrams 159

Geometry and Spatial Sense for Grades 3–5 161

Performance-Based Assessment: Line and Rotational Symmetry 167

Computer Software 167

Summary 169

6 **Continuing the Study of Geometry** 173

Geometry as Measurement 173

Geometry and Spatial Sense for Grades 6–8 173

Performance-Based Assessment: Perimeter 176

Performance-Based Assessment: Area 177

Angle Measurements 178

Guided Discovery 180

The Relationship Between Surface Area and Volume 186

Geometric Drawing Utilities 191

Strength in Numbers: LOGO 194

Other Computer Software 198

Transformational Geometry 199

Geometry and Spatial Sense for Grades 6–8 199

Performance-Based Assessment: Transformations 202

Strength in Numbers: Conjectures 203

Summary 203

7 **Standards for Extending the Number Line** 207

Number and Operation for Grades Pre-K–2 and 3–5 209
  Models and Concepts of Fractions and Decimals 210
    Performance-Based Assessment: Naming Fractions 213
    Performance-Based Assessment: Equivalent Fractions 216
Adding and Subtracting with Fractions and Decimals 219
Number and Operation for Grades 3–5 219
Estimating Sums and Differences of Rational Numbers 225
  Strength in Numbers: Tangrams and Fractions 225
Linear Measurement 228
Measurement for Grades Pre-K–2 228
Measurement for Grades 3–5 230
    Performance-Based Assessment: Linear Measurement 232
  Strength in Numbers: Linear Measurement 234
Summary 235

8 **Standards for Multiplication and Division of Fractions and Decimals** 239

Multiplying and Dividing with Fractions and Decimals 239
Number and Operation for Grades 6–8 239
    Performance-Based Assessment: Multiplying Decimals 244
    Computer Software 248
  Percents 248
Measurement of Mass and Volume 250
Measurement for Students in Grades 6–8 251
    Performance-Based Assessment: Identifying Appropriate Measures 257
Proportional Thinking 259
    Performance-Based Assessment: Proportions 261
Summary 263

9 **Standards for Patterns and Relationships** 267

Simple Patterns, Functions, and Algebra 267
  Strength in Numbers: Problem Solving 269
    Performance-Based Assessment: Even and Odd Numbers 270
  Relationships 270
    Performance-Based Assessment: Identifying Relationships 273
  The Relationship Between Variables and Problem Solving 274
More Complex Patterns, Functions, and Algebra 277
  Computer Software 280

Number Theory in Context 280
Performance-Based Assessment: Prime Factors 281
Divisibility 285
Divisibility by 2 285
Divisibility by 4 285
Divisibility by 8 285
Divisibility by 3 or 9 286
Integers 286
Strength in Numbers: Divisibility by 11 287
Operations on Integers 288
Addition 288
Subtraction 289
Multiplication and Division 290
Performance-Based Assessment: Integers 291
Computer Software 294
Geometric Patterns 294
Multiplication of Whole Numbers and Binomials 296
Solving Equations with One Variable 299
Summary 300

10   **Standards for Data Analysis, Statistics, and Probability** 305

Graphing and Data Analysis 305
Focus Areas for Grades Pre-K–2 306
Physical Graphs 306
Bar Graphs 306
Data Collection and Representation 309
Strength in Numbers: Combinations 310
Using Graphs to Assess Children's Knowledge 313
Performance-Based Assessment: Placing Graphs in Contexts 314
Using Data to Solve Problems 315
Line Graphs 317
Measures of Central Tendency 317
Introducing Concepts of Chance 318
Representing Probability as a Fraction 319
Probability for Grades 3–5 320
Performance-Based Assessment: Equally Likely Events 323
Tree Diagrams 325
Computer Software 327
Summary 329

11   Further Investigations into Data Analysis, Statistics, and Probability 333

Focus Areas for Grades 6–8 333

Data Collection 334

Histograms, Line Graphs, and Circle Graphs 335

Performance-Based Assessment: Graphs 340

Graphing 341

Simulations 344

Strength in Numbers: Hanging Bar Graph 344

Plots: Box-and-Whisker and Stem-and-Leaf 345

Performance-Based Assessment: Plotting 347

Using Data to Make Decisions 347

Theoretical and Experimental Probability 348

Independent Events 349

Permutations and Combinations 351

Strength in Numbers: Pascal's Triangle 352

Summary 355

Appendix A   Masters 359
Appendix B   NCTM Summary 367
Index 383

Preface

This book is for teachers—and prospective teachers—of children from preschool through grade 8. It is designed to help you understand how young children learn mathematics and how you can teach mathematics successfully. It is based on the belief that before you can become a confident and competent teacher of mathematics you must first become a competent and confident learner of mathematics. To support you in this, I offer several features:

- **Strength in Numbers.** These are adult-level mathematical problems and investigations designed to help you learn more mathematical content as you solve an unfamiliar problem.

- **Interdisciplinary Lesson Plans.** A model can be a powerful way to communicate complex information, so Chapters 2 through 11 each include two interdisciplinary lesson plans of varying grade levels. The lesson plan outline introduced in Chapter 2 is used consistently throughout the text.

- **Activities.** To translate theory and research into classroom practice, I have included hundreds of classroom activities for grade levels Pre-K through 8. These activities often require manipulatives and are designed to help prospective and current teachers understand the difference between *telling about* mathematics and *doing* mathematics.

- **Journal Reflections.** Writing about what you are reading and learning can serve two functions: it can help you learn more—you come to understand more about the content through the process of writing about it—and it can provide an opportunity to reflect on the issues and connect them to your own life. For these reasons, every Activity is followed by a Journal Reflection. These are questions or writing prompts to help the reader consider cognitive, affective, cultural, pedagogical, mathematical, and equity issues on a deep and personal level.

- **Performance-Based Assessment.** Teachers already have a lifetime of experience with standardized short-answer, multiple-choice, fill-in-the-blank, and other paper-and-pencil tests. A form of assessment with which you may be less familiar, especially in a mathematical context, is performance-based assessments. At appropriate points in

Chapters 2 through 11, sample performance-based assessments appear. Scoring rubrics are occasionally included, and readers are encouraged to compare the advantages and disadvantages of performance-based assessments with more traditional forms of assessment.

It is important to stress that this book is grounded in documents published by two major professional organizations, the National Association for the Education of Young Children (NAEYC) and the National Council of Teachers of Mathematics (NCTM). The NAEYC's position paper on developmentally appropriate practices is discussed in detail in Chapter 1 and is used as a basis for all Pre-K–2 activities throughout the book, and the NCTM *Principles and Standards for School Mathematics* (2000) informs the entire book. At appropriate points, this textbook includes direct quotes and recommendations from each of these documents.

This book is unusual in that it does not address problem solving in a separate chapter. I believe that relegating problem solving to a distinct chapter implies that there are significant aspects of teaching and learning mathematics that do *not* involve problem solving. I disagree with that idea. Mathematics, in its essence, is the process of posing and solving problems. Therefore, every chapter includes Strength in Numbers, Activities, and Journal Reflections, within which problem-solving skills, strategies, and heuristics are addressed both explicitly and implicitly.

Chapter 1 offers a brief historical overview of the reform movement in mathematics education, discussing the contribution of various seminal documents. Findings about the nature of young learners lead to a consideration of developmentally appropriate practices for children from birth to age 8, and for children from ages 8 to 13. The chapter pays attention to factors affecting the mathematical achievement of students and introduces the concepts of constructivism and cognitively guided instruction.

Performance-based assessments first appear in Chapter 2. This chapter also addresses mathematical thinking skills, the concept of place value, and number and numeration activities for students in each of three groups: grades Pre-K–2, 3–5, and 6–8. The reader will recognize these groupings as those suggested by NCTM's *Principles and Standards*. The chapter ends with activities for estimating both continuous and discrete quantities.

In Chapter 3, the reader is asked to become engaged with the concepts of addition and subtraction. Attention is paid to activities and strategies for helping children remember the basic facts. The chapter discusses using manipulatives to model the operations, and both standard and alternative algorithms are included. One section is devoted to the use of spreadsheet programs as problem-solving tools.

Chapter 4 follows a structure similar to that of the previous chapter, focusing on the operations of multiplication and division. The chapter includes properties of multiplication that will help children develop facility with this operation. Again, both standard and alternative algorithms are illustrated and investigated.

Geometry is discussed explicitly in Chapters 5 and 6, although geometric understandings permeate the book. These chapters address the considerable body of research on children's geometric development and make explicit connections between geometry and other areas of mathematics such as operations on number, measurement, probability, and patterns and functions. Such applications of geometrical concepts as origami and tangrams can be found here. Transformational geometry is included, as well as a section on using LOGO and geometric drawing utilities to learn how to think geometrically.

Chapter 7 extends the treatment of the number line to include fractions, decimals, and linear measurement. Chapter 8 goes even further to include percents and the measurements of volume and mass. Proportional thinking as a form of problem solving closes the chapter.

Chapter 9 investigates the relationship among patterns, functions, and algebra. The chapter introduces the concept of a variable and considers its role in solving problems. Number theory concepts are addressed in context. Rules for divisibility appear, and the reader is invited to solve the problem of why the rules work. Earlier work on the four basic operations is extended to operations on integers, and the set model helps the reader both learn the concepts and how to teach the concepts. The chapter makes connections to geometric patterns and introduces the use of manipulatives to multiply binomials and solve simple equations.

Chapters 10 and 11 are devoted to data analysis, statistics, and probability. The chapters present gathering, displaying, and analyzing data, as well as measures of central tendency. They address such probabilistic concepts as equally likely events, simulations, independent events, the fundamental counting principle, and permutations and combinations. The reader is invited to use Pascal's Triangle to solve problems.

The comparatively small number of chapters in this book is deliberate. Readers are invited to make connections readily among the various topics taught in the elementary and middle schools, and to feel confident and competent as they continue the journey as both learners and teachers of mathematics.

Finally, I am grateful to the reviewers who responded with helpful suggestions as this book was being prepared: Joseph A. Baust, Murray State University; David L. Brown, Texas A & M University, Commerce; Karen S. Brown, Indiana Wesleyan University; Margaret S. Carter, Elizabeth City State University; John A. Craven III, Queens College, City University of New York; Lisa A. Friel, Mesa State College; Neal Grandgenett, University of Nebraska, Omaha; Regina Halpin, Mississippi State University; Mary Hamm, San Francisco State University; William D. James, Cameron University; Vince Mahoney, Iowa Wesleyan College; Ruby Midkiff, Arkansas State University; L. Diane Miller, Middle Tennessee State University; Emma M. Owens, Clemson University; Fred R. Parker, Henderson State University; Clyde Paul, Southwest Missouri State University; Ava Pugh, University of Louisiana, Monroe; Douglas Roebuck, Anderson University; Helene J. Sherman, University of Missouri, St. Louis; Martha Poole Simmons, Alabama State University; Donald Zalewski, Northern Michigan University.

1

New Standards for Learning And Teaching Mathematics

Teaching mathematics to elementary school children is a complex and demanding task. It is also a satisfying and joyous task. And it is a task that requires you to be, simultaneously, both a learner and a teacher of mathematics.

Many of us remember learning mathematics as if it were solely a series of procedures for obtaining a precise numerical answer to a word problem or a computational example. If we were accurate and fast, we liked mathematics because we were successful. Whether the liking followed from the success or the success from the liking is not certain. But if we were not successful, we disliked mathematics, because we could never get the answer fast enough or accurately enough.

As an adult, you have likely come to realize that mathematics comprises much more than a process of following procedures to obtain numerical answers. That's the good news! But the challenge remains for you to gain confidence in your ability to learn mathematics, and competence in teaching mathematics to children, whether the subject excites or dismays you. Working through this text, you may find you are learning some aspects of mathematics for the first time. Or, you may find yourself *re*learning mathematics in ways you never imagined. Ideally, you will find yourself learning mathematics through the eyes of the children you teach.

Learning mathematics thoroughly is essential if you are going to teach it. Obviously you cannot teach what you don't know, and you cannot teach well what you don't understand. My goal is to help you understand enough about mathematics, and the ways in which children learn mathematics, so that you can begin your journey as both a learner and a teacher of mathematics. It will, in fact, be a lifelong journey. Teaching is a complex endeavor, and no one excels quickly. So, as you work through this book, don't panic! It will take time for you to develop the skills, understandings, and disposition of a good teacher. This is merely one of the first steps.

You are entering the teaching profession at an auspicious time. The dawn of the twenty-first century is an exciting time to be involved in mathematics education. Many mathematics educators are recommending intriguing innovations, such as writing to learn, cooperative learning, learning through children's literature, learning through problem solving, learning based on manipulatives, and learning with the aid of technology. These approaches differ greatly from the focus of mathematics education during the 1970s, which was marked by a strong emphasis on basic computational skills that is commonly referred to as "back to basics." The decades of the eighties and nineties saw the innovations just mentioned, and these new approaches are still being enhanced and refined today.

The preeminent professional organization of mathematics educators in this country and Canada, the National Council of Teachers of Mathematics (NCTM), has been the impetus for many of these sweeping changes in curriculum, pedagogy, and assessment of school mathematics. It is possible to trace much of the current thrust of mathematics education to *An Agenda For Action,* a document published by NCTM in 1980. This document highlighted the importance of problem solving in the curriculum. At the end of the seventies, there was a growing concern among mathematics educators that a knowledge of basic skills, while important, was not sufficient. It did students little good to be able to compute $5649 \div 7$ if they did not also know that this was an appropriate way to determine how many weeks there are in 5649 days. While this example does not illustrate problem solving as it will come to be defined in this text, it does indicate that, in addition to knowing how to compute, students need to know when the computation is appropriate. *An Agenda for Action* argued that choosing a suitable strategy in a given situation is an important problem-solving skill (NCTM, 1980).

An equally important publication was *Everybody Counts: A Report to the Nation on the Future of Mathematics Education* (1989), which was issued by the National Research Council. This report emphasized the concept that achievement in mathematics is strongly linked to the amount of time devoted to its study:

> Three of every four Americans stop studying mathematics before completing career or job prerequisites. Most students leave school without sufficient preparation in mathematics to cope with either on-the-job demands for problem-solving or college expectations for mathematical literacy. Industry, universities, and the armed forces are thus burdened by extensive and costly demands for remedial education. Our country cannot afford continuing generations of students limited by lack of mathematical power to second-class status in the society in which they live. It cannot afford to weaken its preeminent position in science and technology (p. viii).

The National Research Council subsequently encouraged equal access to rigorous mathematics courses for every child in order to bring all students, no matter what their background, to achievement at accepted levels for our society. *Everybody Counts* stresses that we have been educating students to take their place in the industrial age, while we should be educating them to take their place in the electronic age.

The ideas and recommendations contained within *An Agenda for Action* and *Everybody Counts* were expanded and elaborated upon in the 1989 publication of the NCTM *Curriculum and Evaluation Standards for School Mathematics.* According to the authors, there were at least three reasons for the codifying of standards, " . . . (1) to insure quality, (2) to indicate goals, and (3) to promote change" (NCTM, 1989, p. 2). As a justification for setting standards for school mathematics, the authors write:

> Today's society expects schools to insure that all students have an opportunity to become mathematically literate, are capable of extending their learning, have an equal opportunity to learn, and become informed citizens capable of understanding issues in a technological society. As society changes, so must its schools (p. 5).

The Standards, as they have come to be known, have had a significant impact on the mathematics education community. Many conferences, publications, research efforts, textbooks, and in-service training sessions have been devoted to disseminating the Standards and translating their philosophy into specific classroom practices. Two related NCTM publications have contributed to bringing the reforms of the Standards to teachers and learners: the *Professional Standards for Teaching Mathematics* (1991) and the *Assessment Standards for School Mathematics* (1995). These publications, available from NCTM, can contribute significantly to your development as a mathematics teacher. The first, *Professional Standards,* contains classroom vignettes that provide a glimpse into the mathematics classroom. The second, *Assessment Standards,* addresses assessment from four vantage points: (1) monitoring student progress, (2) making instructional decisions, (3) evaluating student achievement, and (4) evaluating programs. In addition to these documents, NCTM has published a series of booklets called *The Addenda Series,* which contains exemplary grade-level lessons along with suggestions that can help teachers to incorporate the spirit of the Standards into their instruction.

In recognition of the dawn of the new millenium, and in celebration of the tenth anniversary of the Standards, NCTM has refined and updated its concepts and philosophy in *Principles and Standards for School Mathematics,* also known as *Standards 2000* (1999).

This textbook will use the *Principles and Standards* in investigating methods of teaching elementary school mathematics. This chapter introduces you to the broad structure of *Principles and Standards.* Since it is equally as important that you understand *how children learn* mathematics as it is that you understand *techniques of teaching* mathematics, the nature of the learner in kindergarten through eighth grade will be addressed. Teaching does not occur in a vacuum. The individual children in your classes will strongly influence both what you teach and how you teach it.

The Goals of Mathematics Education

Principles and Standards articulates a philosophy of mathematics education and specifically addresses issues of curriculum and teaching, learning, and assessment in each of four grade bands: grades Pre-K to 2, 3 to 5, 6 to 8, and 9 to 12. The Standards begin by listing five general goals for all students who study mathematics. Before reading any further, jot down several goals you think are appropriate for the mathematics students you will teach. How would you answer a parent who asked what you were trying to accomplish in that year? What do you think are the most important components of a school mathematics program? Look at your list. Does it contain topics and ideas similar to the five goals from *Principles and Standards* (p. 15) that follow? Students should:

1. Learn to value mathematics.
2. Become confident in their ability to do mathematics.
3. Become mathematical problem solvers.
4. Learn to communicate mathematically.
5. Learn to reason mathematically.

You may have noticed that these goals do not narrowly focus on specific skills, but on broad dispositions toward learning mathematics. The aim of these goals is for students to learn to *think* mathematically and appreciate mathematics, rather than to perform specific computations. The ability to think mathematically has become critical in light of the powerful and affordable calculators and computers accessible to students today. As students and schools need to devote less time to purely mechanical tasks, the mathematics curriculum can be broadened to pay greater attention to such topics as logic, problem solving, number theory, patterns, geometry, measurement, statistics, and probability. For example, a typical question on perimeter in a 1970s fifth-grade textbook would have been:

■ What is the perimeter of the accompanying figure (Figure 1.1)?

In a contemporary fifth-grade textbook, you might see the topic of perimeter addressed in the following way:

■ Using a centimeter ruler, sketch a hexagon with a perimeter of 36 centimeters. Can you do this in another way? Can you sketch a hexagon with a perimeter of 36 centimeters having two sides of one length and the remaining four sides of another length? (Take a moment and try this yourself.)

There are several differences between the first question and the second. When answering the first question, a student could arrive at the correct answer without really understanding the concept of perimeter because adding all of the numbers is the only reasonable thing to do. In addition, there is only one correct answer. If only the answer is required, and not the steps taken to arrive at the answer, the teacher has no way to interpret an incorrect answer. Did the student fail to understand the concept of perimeter, or was a simple computational error made?

The second question, in contrast, requires active involvement on the part of the student and the accurate use of a measuring device to answer the question. Since a sketch is required as part of the answer, it is possible for the teacher to assess incorrect responses. It will be clear if the error was made in

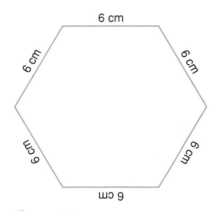

Figure 1.1

computation, if the student did not know the meaning of either *hexagon* or *perimeter,* if the student did not use the measuring device correctly, or some combination of these. In addition, several correct answers are possible. Questions such as these are typically called "open-ended" to indicate that there are many different ways to answer them. There is a progression in the line of questioning from a fairly simple task to more difficult ones. After reviewing the student drawings, the teacher might choose to pursue related topics such as the concept of a regular polygon, symmetry, or the number of hexagons that can possibly be drawn if the sides are limited to whole-number lengths. The teacher might then explore contexts in which the given question might arise, such as in determining the length of framing material required to frame a hexagonal mirror or the amount of binding required for a hexagonal rug.

The Nature of the Pre-K–2 Learner

Understanding how children from pre-kindergarten through grade 8 learn mathematics requires a thorough knowledge of child development. With this foundation, you will be able to teach in a developmentally appropriate manner.

Early childhood describes the ages of birth to 8 years, according to the National Association for the Education of Young Children (NAEYC). In this section we will look at ages 4 to 8 years because this is when most children are beginning their formal school experience. These ages cover pre-kindergarten, kindergarten, and first, second and (sometimes) third grades, or what are commonly referred to as the primary grades. Many people believe 4- to 8-year olds are in the preoperational stage of cognitive development (which is generally accepted to begin at 18 months to 2 years). At the ages of 7 or 8 years, most children move into the concrete operational stage of cognitive development. These labels, *preoperational* and *concrete operational,* were coined by the famous Swiss psychologist Jean Piaget. Over a period of many years, Piaget and his Geneva colleagues conducted clinical interviews with hundreds of young children. The children were asked to perform various tasks while they were observed and questioned by the interviewer. As a result of these interviews, Piaget identified stages of development that all children appear to pass through as they grow. While actual ages at which children achieve the levels vary from child to child, the order of progression through the stages is invariable. Piaget's stages of cognitive development are summarized here:

- *Sensorimotor stage* (birth to approximately age 2). In this pre-verbal stage of development, children learn about the world through their senses. Since children cannot yet symbolize the things around them with words or symbols or pictures, they have only direct experiences with the world. Objects that are covered with a cloth cease to exist for the children in this stage, even if the covered object is in full view.

- *Preoperational stage* (approximately ages 2 to 7). This stage marks the beginning of symbolic behavior because this is when language begins. However, children's understanding of the world is dictated

Figure 1.2

by their sensory perceptions. The number of flowers in a broad, shallow vase is judged to be "more" than the same number clustered in a tall, narrow vase because there *appear* to be more of them in the dispersed arrangement.

- *Concrete operational stage* (approximately ages 7 to 12). Children are now able to **conserve.** They understand that a number of items (or a given length, or a given volume) is conserved, or invariant, despite appearance and arrangement. A nonconserving child, when shown the arrangement of buttons in Figure 1.2, would say that the second row contains more buttons. A conserver would understand that they both contain the same number, but that the second row of buttons is more widely dispersed. An understanding of conservation requires an understanding of **reversal.** That is, a child who conserves understands that if the ten buttons in the second row are spread out, they can also be pushed back together and will once again resemble the top row. This concept of reversal is critical for an early understanding of operations on numbers. A preoperational child, lacking an understanding of reversal, may not be able developmentally to understand that if $3 + 2 = 5$, then $5 - 2 = 3$, and $5 - 3 = 2$.

- *Formal operational stage* (usually from ages 11 or 12). Children in this stage are no longer tied to the actual object or a representation of the object in order to think about it. They can conjecture, hypothesize, and think according to the rules of logic. Children trust their judgments, as opposed to their perceptions, when reaching conclusions about the world.

You have probably studied Piaget's stages of cognitive development in earlier courses. Now you are learning how an understanding of these stages can help you prepare to teach mathematics to school-age children. As you work with this text, engage in some of the suggested activities with children of various ages. Ask the children to explain why they are doing or thinking certain things. Ask them to "think out loud." Their answers will constantly remind you that children do not understand the world in the same ways that adults do.

Teaching the Young Child

In other courses on early childhood education, you have likely discussed the issue of developmentally appropriate practice. In 1988, the National Association for the Education of Young Children published a position statement entitled *Appropriate Education in the Primary Grades* that described the nature of the young child and the significance of developmentally appropriate practice for primary classrooms. Briefly, **developmentally appropriate practice** takes into consideration the age and developmental level of the child and focuses all curricular and pedagogical concerns on this information. The position statement issued by the NAEYC contains principles of appropriate practice for primary-age children. However, the concept of developmentally appropriate practice applies to all children. You may notice, as you read through the next few pages, that many of the recommendations made by the NAEYC have merit for both primary-age and older children. Although the classroom activities included here are focused on grades Pre-K–2, it is not difficult to imagine how each recommendation might be implemented in grades 3 to 8. After addressing the principles of appropriate practice for primary-age children, we will then discuss those for children in the middle and upper elementary grades. Throughout all of the discussions for grade levels from Pre-K though 8, you will see the common threads of respect for the individual learner, attention to actively engaging the learner, and encouragement of the learner to make sense of mathematical situations and problems.

We now turn to the implications for instruction in primary grades of the NAEYC position paper on developmentally appropriate practices, addressing each statement from a mathematical perspective and offering related activities.

Teachers of primary-grade children must be aware of the "whole child."

Young children are developing rapidly in many areas. They are experiencing growth in the social, physical, cognitive, and emotional realms. Even if schools try to stress cognitive development exclusively, they may still find aspects of these other developmental areas interfering with the children's ability to learn. For instance, a child who is having difficulties relating socially to other children in the class will feel ostracized and may have trouble functioning in the group setting. A child whose fine-motor coordination is delayed may have difficulty stacking blocks, putting together puzzles, or using a measurement instrument. These social and physical difficulties may prevent the child from attaining a cognitive understanding of the concepts that could otherwise be developed through these activities. When faced with a situation where a child is experiencing difficulty learning, it is useful for teachers to explore the possibility of several causes for the child's academic difficulties.

This book offers sample classroom activities to connect the NAEYC position statements to classroom practice. Following each Activity is a Journal Reflection. It contains a question or statement related to the Activity that is designed for you to reflect upon and then write about in your personal journal. Writing about new ideas and perplexing problems is one method of learning. If you go back and reread some of your journal entries from time to time, it will help you to monitor your own progress.

People of all ages learn best by becoming actively involved in the learning process. The sample classroom activities here are designed to involve you

Activity 1.1

Sand Numerals

Lesson: Individual

Children are asked to choose their favorite number from one to ten, then draw the numeral to fill an 8.5 × 11 sheet of paper. Using a glue stick to trace the numeral, and then sprinkling colored sand on the paper, they create a sand numeral. After the glue has dried, children are encouraged to close their eyes and trace the sand numeral. When displaying their numeral to classmates, children tell why that number is their favorite, and contribute to a classroom stack of blocks containing their number. This activity attends to the "whole child" because it encourages development in the emotional realm (the choice of a favorite number), the physical realm (the creating and tracing of the numerals), the cognitive realm (the association of the correct number of blocks with the numeral), and the social realm (the display and explanation to the class).

Journal Reflection

Think back to your earliest memory of learning in school. Does your memory indicate that your teacher had some understanding of educating the "whole child"? Why or why not?

intellectually in seeing the connections between educational theory and classroom practice. Whenever possible, try the activities with children (Activity 1.1). You may, in fact, be required to participate in classrooms as part of your teacher-preparation courses. If not, try to work with some neighborhood children, with your own children, or with children who attend an after-school program in your area.

Teachers of primary-grade children should integrate their instruction.

Because young children have a natural exuberance and curiosity, their investigations invariably lead quickly from one thing to another. A walk through the park when the leaves are falling may lead children to investigate the changing colors of the leaves, the shortening days of autumn, the hibernation of animals as winter approaches, and the temperature drop as the seasons change. All of these areas of investigation span the traditional school disciplines of language, science, math, and art. It would be artificial to separate these areas in a primary classroom.

In keeping with the NAEYC tradition of position papers, NCTM has issued a position statement, "Interdisciplinary Learning," in the February 1995 issue of *Teaching Children Mathematics*. If you have not yet become acquainted with this journal, now is a good time. Each February, a focus issue is published to deal in depth with one particular topic. The cited issue was devoted to communication in the mathematics classroom. As a student, you can become a member of NCTM at half of the professional cost by calling 703-620-9840, or consulting the NCTM website at *www.nctm.org*.

Activity 1.2

Planting Seeds

Lesson: Group Learning

On a nature walk, children investigate plants that grow in their area. Afterward, they sketch plants identified along the way. Given a choice of three, children choose seeds they wish to plant. Before the planting, the teacher leads the children in describing and classifying the seeds/plants by such attributes or characteristics as color, shape, symmetry/asymmetry, and need for water or light. When the seeds are planted in transparent cups, the concept of one-to-one correspondence can be introduced: for every hole there is a single seed, and for every single seed there is a hole. Because the cup is transparent, children can observe the formation of the root structure.

As the seedlings begin to sprout, they can be measured and their growth charted in a line graph. The amount of water used to nourish them can be measured and recorded. Older children may wish to perform simple experiments by varying the amount of water, sunlight, and soil used for each plant. When the plants have grown to a substantial height, they can be sketched and the parts labeled. This activity integrates social studies (plants indigenous to the region), science (nature walk), art (sketches of the plant), and mathematics (counting and classifying the seeds, measuring the growth and the water, charting the results).

Journal Reflection

How might you connect the measurement and growth of plants to the measurement and growth of children in a first-grade class? Do you think the connection is appropriate? Why or why not?

Activity 1.2 illustrates how the disciplines of language arts, social studies, science, mathematics, and art can be addressed in a motivating lesson for young children.

Teachers of primary-grade children should engage them in active as opposed to passive activities.

Developmentally, young children's understanding of their world is tied to their physical experience with that world. They understand that, when building a tower of blocks, the broader blocks must go on the bottom for support. Young children come to this understanding as a result of building many towers of blocks and observing the results. Primary-grade children find it more exhausting to sit quietly for long periods of time than they do to build, draw, manipulate, or create. Activity 1.3 provides the opportunity to get involved physically with the learning.

Teachers of primary-grade children should provide small-group activities that allow discussion and interaction.

Critical to a child's development are the ability to communicate and the ability to understand another's point of view. Research (Elkind, 1981) suggests that, when children engage in conversation with peers and teachers, both their reasoning skills and ability to express themselves are enhanced.

Activity 1.3

Creating Quadrilaterals

Lesson: Individual or Small Group

A geoboard is a manipulative device used in elementary schools. It is a wooden or plastic square, covered at regular intervals with pegs or nails, around which rubber bands are stretched. Some geoboards are depicted in Figure 1.3.

Distribute a geoboard and rubber bands to each child. Invite the children to use a single rubber band to create a closed, four-sided figure on their geoboard. Define this four-sided figure as a quadrilateral. Ask students to volunteer to share their quadrilaterals with the class. This can be done by having the children hold up their own geoboards for the class to see, or by having the children, one at a time, reproduce their quadrilateral on a transparent geoboard placed on an overhead projector. Ask each child to write a justification of why his or her shape is indeed a quadrilateral.

Courtesy of Gary Goldberg

Figure 1.3

(continued)

Teachers can initiate or prolong conversations with children by asking appropriate questions and by commenting in such a way that children are encouraged to verbalize their experiences. For example, a neutral and open-ended comment is "Tell me about your drawing (building, game, story, problem . . .)." The phrase "Tell me about. . ." does not permit a yes/no answer and is neither approving nor disapproving in nature. Rather, it affirms the teacher's interest in the child and the child's work.

Activity 1.3 (continued)

Creating Quadrilaterals

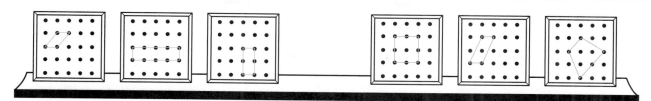

Figure 1.4

Next, choose some of the geoboards and separate them into two groups by arranging them along a chalk ledge. One possible basis for the separation into two groups is shown in Figure 1.4.

As you can see, these quadrilaterals have been separated into two groups based on the number of pins in the interior of the quadrilateral. Those on the left contain zero pins in the interior, while those on the right contain one or more pins. Without revealing the basis for sorting the quadrilaterals, invite students to place their geoboards on the chalk ledge in the appropriate group. You will be able to tell if the children have understood the basis for sorting by where they place their geoboards. After several children have an opportunity to participate, repeat the activity with a different basis for the sorting. Possible bases for sorting quadrilaterals include those with only right angles vs. those with other angles, those with four equal sides vs. those with sides of different lengths, those with only horizontal and vertical sides vs. those that contain other than horizontal

or vertical sides. After it is clear that students understand the activity, invite a student to initiate a sorting according to his or her own reasoning. The rest of the class can be challenged to identify the basis for the student's sorting.

This activity encourages the child's active participation as each shape is created on the geoboard and as the students sort the geoboards. One of the advantages of using geoboards is that all children are able to create shapes that appear precise and accurate, with straight sides. In addition, the geoboard allows children to alter responses easily without being hampered by erasures. The activity can be repeated several times by asking students to construct a variety of triangles, pentagons, objects that fly, or symmetrical figures.

Journal Reflection

How might you deal with a child who used the rubber bands in an inappropriate way?

Classroom organization can engender conversation between and among children. When provision is made for small centers of learning where three or four children can choose an activity that interests them, the stage is set for children to converse among themselves. As children engage in a common activity like that of Activity 1.4 with a small group of their peers, the opportunity exists for comments and questions to be shared and discussion to ensue.

Activity 1.4
Rod Structures

Lesson: Small Group

Cuisenaire rods are manipulatives commonly used in elementary mathematics classrooms. The rods were developed in Belgium during the 1950s by George Cuisenaire to illustrate various concepts and operations on fractions. They have since found many other applications. These manipulatives are packaged as a set of ten colored rods ranging in length from one to ten centimeters, all one centimeter in width (Figure 1.5). The rods pictured here have been labeled with their color initials, as will all other depictions of

Figure 1.5

Photo used with permission from ETA/Cuisenaire ®, Vernon Hills, Illinois.

Figure 1.6

rods shown in this text. The colors of the rods, in order, and their corresponding initials are white (w), red (r), light green (g), purple (p), yellow (y), dark green (d), black (k), brown (n), blue (e), orange (o).

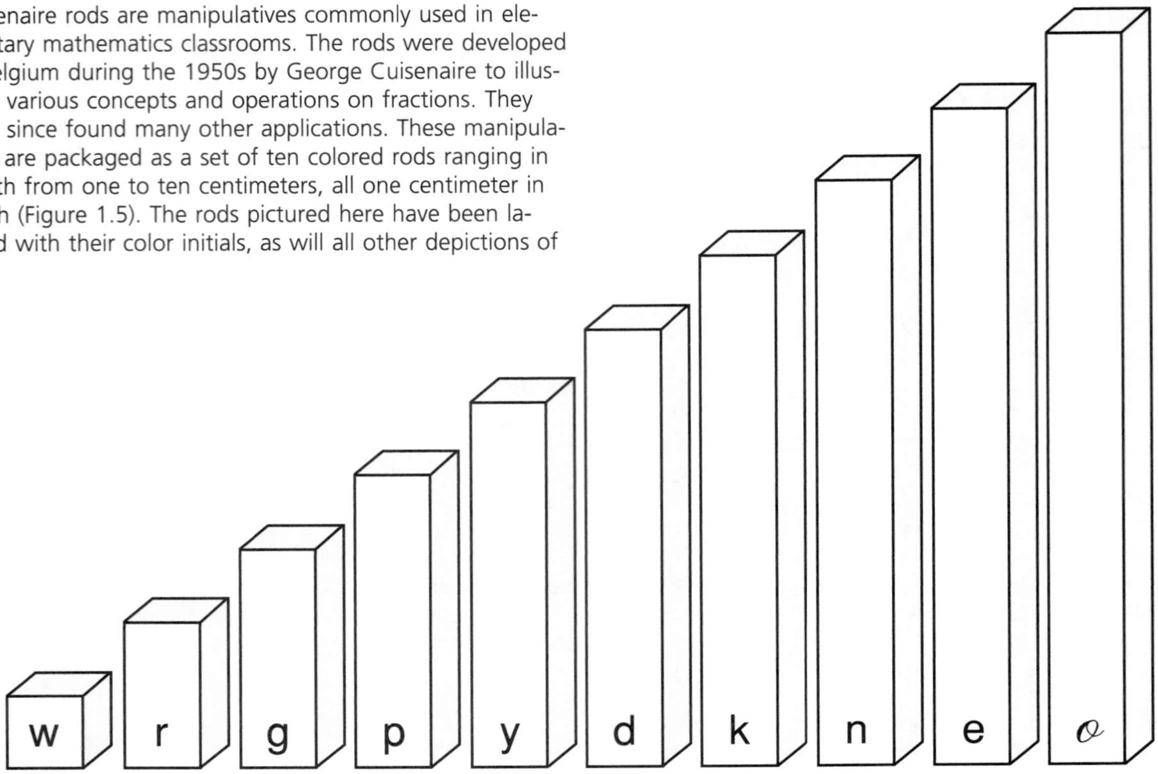

In a small-group setting, equip each child with a sufficient number of Cuisenaire rods (Figure 1.6), typically, 70–80 per student. Invite them to create their own structure, perhaps according to some topical theme. For example, if the class is currently engaged in a study of types of houses, the children can be invited to build a house. If the class is studying transportation, students can be invited to build a vehicle. Encourage children to discuss their creation with peers by making a comment like "Kate, why don't you tell your friends about your house (car, boat, etc.)."

Journal Reflection

Do you think Cuisenaire rods are appropriate for a child with color blindness or a color deficit? Why or why not? What would you do if a student in your class has a visual deficit?

Strength in Numbers

Communication

Strength In Numbers boxes are designed to engage you, the adult learner, in some mathematical activities. These activities are only valuable if you actually do them, as opposed to simply reading about them. Most of them will require you to work with one or more classmates.

Groups of Two

With a book propped between you to shield the view, one partner builds a structure with a given number of Cuisenaire rods. This person then verbally directs the other partner in replicating the structure. After a given period of time, the partners switch roles and repeat the activity.

- What words did you use to communicate the placement and location of the rods? Were some words more effective than others?
- Was there a difference in the nature of the activity after the roles were switched? To what do you attribute this difference?

- Did you find it more difficult to be the receiver or sender of instructions? Why do you think this is so? What does this suggest to you as you assume the role of teacher?

Various constraints can be placed on the activity. For example, the number of rods can be varied, limits may be placed on the number of questions allowed, or communication can be restricted to builder only. This activity can be extended by having a third person act as a transmitter of all communications between the sender and the receiver.

Upon the completion of the building and replication, generate a list of words used during the activity. Which of these words are mathematical terms with precise meanings and which of them are everyday words? As a class, discuss ways in which the communication between partners could have been made more accurate or efficient.

Teachers of primary-grade children should keep in mind the interests of their students when planning lessons.

When you begin to teach keep in mind that, although *you* get older every year, your kindergarten students are five years old year after year. Always remember that children do not see the world the way adults do. You can learn about subjects of current interest to children by listening to their conversations and observing their play. These topics of interest can then be used to motivate a lesson, or as themes that span several lessons.

Typically, children are most interested in the things that surround them. Children who live in a rural area are likely to have a high level of interest in farms, plants, and outdoor activities. Urban children are probably interested in their neighborhood, various modes of urban transportation, and landmarks that may be found nearby.

One of the ways to connect topics studied in school to the personal lives of children is to plan for the children to share a common experience (Activity 1.5). This can take the form of a class trip to a local natural-history museum to begin a unit on dinosaurs, a trip to a greenhouse to begin a unit on plants, a trip to an apple orchard to begin a unit on apples, or a trip to a local

Activity 1.5

Pumpkins

Lesson: Small Group or Whole Group

As Thanksgiving approaches, capitalize on the holiday interest to explore pumpkins. If you can, begin with a visit to a farm where the children can pick their own pumpkins, or visit a greengrocer where the children can choose their own pumpkins. You will need at least one pumpkin for each group of 4–5 children.

Begin by asking the children to describe their pumpkins. By your example, introduce them to words such as *smooth, sphere, stem, curved, heavy,* and so on. Next, invite the children, working in groups of four or five, to classify the pumpkins in their group according to some characteristic. For example, children may choose to classify the pumpkins according to big/small, smooth/bumpy, stem/no stem, all orange/orange and green, or tall/short.

Subsequent lessons can focus on estimation and counting. Choose a large pumpkin, and have the children estimate the number of its seeds. This is an opportunity for children to practice the verbalization and symbolization of numerals. After cutting open the pumpkin so that the children can see the number of seeds, ask them to make a second estimate.

Remove the seeds and involve the children in counting them. Give each child a small paper cup and invite them to fill their paper cups with ten seeds. When all the seeds have been placed in cups, the children can skip-count by ten to arrive at a total number of seeds. The actual number is then compared with the original estimates. This is an opportunity to reinforce the concepts of greater and less by comparing an estimate with the actual number (175 would be greater than the actual count of 121).

Further extensions can include an introduction to the concept of circumference through actual measurement; to weight, through actual weighing; and the naming of geometric shapes that might be used in transforming the pumpkin into a jack-o-lantern.

Journal Reflection

List as many mathematical concepts as you can that might be explored through this activity. Compare them to a "Scope and Sequence" chart for a second-grade mathematics textbook. (This is a chart listing all the topics addressed in the textbook. It is frequently found in the front of the Teacher's Edition.) Describe how you might integrate an activity like this with the textbook.

restaurant to begin a nutrition unit. Studies of foreign countries and cultures are usually postponed until children are older and are making the transition from preoperational to concrete operational thinking. Concrete operational thinking marks the beginning of other-centeredness in children. They begin to develop the ability to see things from another's perspective, and they become interested in things that are not a part of their immediate world.

Teachers of primary-grade children need to provide a range of activities to meet the various developmental needs of their students.

Meeting the needs of all the children in your class will be a continuing challenge regardless of the ages of the children you teach. It is particularly critical, however, when you teach young children. As a first-grade teacher, you might have children in your class who are nonconservers, children who are in transition from preoperational to concrete operational thinking, and children who are firm conservers. The developmental levels of the children will indicate their readiness to understand an abstract concept such as place value.

Understanding place value requires an understanding that ten ones is equivalent to one ten, and that the connection can be reversed: that is, one ten can be traded or regrouped into ten ones. A nonconserving child will have a great deal of difficulty understanding this concept. Nonconservers make sense of the world based on their perceptions. Since ten white Cuisenaire rods that are spread out *look like* more than one orange Cuisenaire rod, nonconservers perceive them as more.

Piaget maintained that children cannot be changed from nonconservers into conservers by direct instruction. Each child is functioning at a personally appropriate developmental level, and each child will move from preoperational thinking to concrete operational thinking when he or she is ready to do so. Providing activities that are stimulating for children at a variety of developmental levels makes teaching young children difficult, but also satisfying and rewarding (Activity 1.6).

Activity 1.6

Measuring Height with Unifix Cubes

Lesson: Small Group or Whole Group

Unifix cubes are small, interlocking plastic cubes with a ¾-inch square base (Figure 1.7). They can be used for a variety of numeration and measurement activities. An illustration of these cubes is shown below:

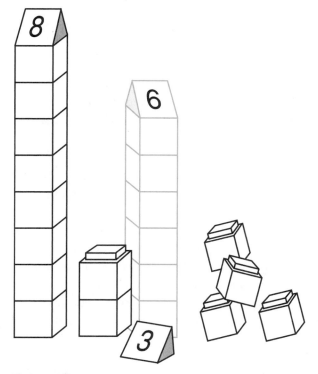

Figure 1.7

After removing all the white Unifix cubes, invite the children to build a tower of cubes that is as tall as they are. This is easily done by asking the children to lie on the floor or stand against a blackboard or wall and mark their height with a piece of chalk. Three different investigations follow. Some children will be able to do all three investigations; others, only one or two.

1. Have three or four children compare the lengths (or height) of their towers of Unifix cubes. If the towers have been laid flat on the floor, make sure that they are all aligned on the same baseline (Figure 1.8). (In Figure 1.8a, two towers of the same height are shown lying on the floor. In Figure 1.8b, the same two towers are moved in such a way that the base of one is higher than the base of the other. Nonconserving children, even if they observe the towers being moved from position a to position b, will judge tower b as taller. For this reason, when measuring height or length with young children, it is important that the objects share a common baseline.) When the children compare the heights of the towers in their group, invite them to identify the tallest (or longest) tower, the shortest tower, and any towers who heights fall between the two extremes. Encourage them to verbalize such statements as "Kathryn's tower is shorter than Jose's tower" or "Trinh's tower is taller than Rosa's tower."

2. Invite the children to count the number of Unifix cubes in their tower, and write the numerals on a card. Again, working in groups of three or four, have the children compare the numbers to determine greatest and least. Help the children understand the connection among the tallest tower, the tallest child, the greatest numeral, and the greatest number of cubes.

(continued)

Activity 1.6 (continued)

Measuring Height with Unifix Cubes

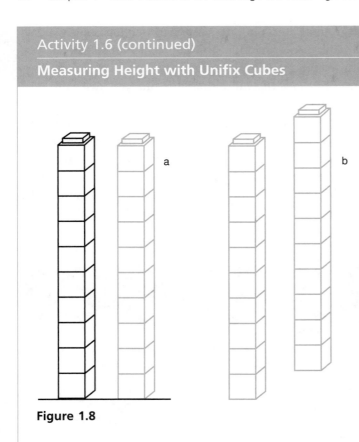

a

b

Figure 1.8

3. Ask the children to lay out their towers on the floor, replacing every tenth cube with a white cube. Invite the children to count the number of cubes by tens (by focusing on the white cubes) and add any cubes that remain. When the children write this number in numerals, emphasize the connection between the number of white cubes and the numeral in the tens place, and between the number of remaining cubes and the numeral in the ones place.

This activity, depending on how far it is carried, is appropriate to children at many developmental levels. Nonconservers can easily engage in the first activity, while the third activity will only make sense to conservers. Children who have achieved conservation are better able to understand that nine tens represents nine groups of ten ones, or ninety ones.

Journal Reflection

One of the real challenges of teaching children lies in recognizing and meeting the needs of each individual child, especially since most children and their needs are very different. Discuss how you might be sensitive to both the needs of a nonconserver and the needs of a firm conserver in you second-grade class.

Teaching Children Aged 8–13

All of the suggestions for teachers of young children apply to teachers of older children. *All* children should be actively involved in their own learning. *All* children should learn in a classroom where their individual needs are met. *All* children should have the opportunity to learn in small groups and to interact with their peers. But teachers of middle and upper elementary grades need to be aware of the developmental characteristics of children from about ages 8 to 13. Cognitively, children of these ages are becoming able to think logically and abstractly. Socially, they are developing a sensitivity to the perceptions others hold of them; they are becoming less egocentric and more able to see a situation from another's perspective. These characteristics make middle to upper elementary-grade students interested in working in cooperative groups, and interested in learning about other cultures. What follows is a discussion of cooperative group learning linked with classroom activities specifically designed for children of ages 8 to 13, or what we will now refer to as intermediate-grade children.

Cooperative Learning

Cooperative learning is an alternative approach to the traditional whole-class instruction/discussion technique often used in the mathematics classroom. *Principles and Standards* state "The classroom is a community of mathematical inquiry and the students are participants in that community, striving toward mapping and understanding mathematical ideas, norms, and rules. This view of learning presumes that a part of the process involves interactions with others as a means of testing out mathematical ideas, learning to evaluate the thinking of others, and develop mathematical reasoning skills" (p. 34).

Much has been written in recent years concerning both the cognitive and affective outcomes of cooperative learning. Prominent researchers such as Neil Davidson (1985, 1990) , David and Roger Johnson (1987, 1990), Shlomo Sharan (1984), and Robert Slavin (1983, 1987, 1989, 1990) have reported positive results in studies conducted to examine the outcomes of cooperative learning environments. Marilyn Burns, writing in *Cooperative Learning in Mathematics: A Handbook for Teachers* (Davidson, 1990), speaks of the overall positive effects of good cooperative learning environments:

> Students' learning is supported when they have opportunities to describe their own ideas, hear others explain their thoughts, speculate, question, and explore various approaches. To provide for this, learning together in small groups gives students more opportunities to interact with concepts than do class discussions. Not only do students have the chance to speak more often, but they may be more comfortable taking the risks of trying out their thinking during problem solving situations in the setting of a small group (p. 25).

Just what constitutes a cooperative learning experience may differ from classroom to classroom. In his study of cooperative learning, Robert Slavin (1989) underscores two important components in a successful cooperative learning environment: individual accountability and group goals. The concept of *individual accountability* means that each student is asked to make some contribution to the group effort. In some cooperative activities, the individual tasks are the same for all members of the group; in others, each member works on a different aspect. Individual students then bring to the group their findings and results, sharing strategies and refining plans.

The group is also given some *collective goal,* which may be in the form of a problem for investigation and/or solution. The members of the group are asked to collaborate using the information and skills developed in the individual component of the activity. Spencer Kagan (1990), in his article "The Structural Approach to Cooperative Learning," raises the issue of positive and negative interdependence in cooperative vs. competitive structures:

> One of the most common structures teachers use is the competitive structure called Whole-Class Question-Answer. In this arrangement, students vie for the teacher's attention and praise, creating negative interdependence among them. That is, when the teacher calls on one student, the others lose their chance to answer; a failure by one student to give a correct response increases the chances for other students to receive attention and praise. Thus, students are set against each other, creating poor social relations and peer norms against achievement (1990, p. 12).

In discussing cooperative learning structures, Kagan states the importance of positive interdependence, where students work together for the good of all. The goal in a cooperative group setting is not to succeed where another has failed, but to work together so that all can succeed. This positive interdependence is incorporated into the structure of many cooperative learning models. Kagan offers fifteen such models, each with a different function, approach, and use. In this chapter, we will examine three cooperative learning models within a mathematical context. Additional cooperative learning models will be introduced throughout the text.

Activity 1.7 is designed to illustrate the cooperative learning model of *numbered heads together* (Kagan, 1990). It also includes a four-step problem-solving heuristic with which you are probably familiar from an earlier course. We strongly urge you to join with several of your classmates to perform these tasks in a cooperative setting rather than merely reading about them.

Teachers of intermediate-grade children should involve them in logical investigations.

The special characteristics of intermediate-grade children, their increasing ability to think logically and abstractly, their concern with peer relations and getting along with others, and their need to be actively involved in the learning process all suggest that children of these ages would benefit from learning in a cooperative group setting. Here is an example of a logical investigation that asks children to compare geometric arrangements of shapes. This investigations takes place within the context of the cooperative group model called numbered heads together.

Notice that there are three important components in the preceding activity: individual accountability, group goals, and positive interdependence. The positive interdependence can be seen in the structure of the numbered-heads-together model. All students will need to understand the concepts because any student could be chosen to represent the work of the group. This is appropriate for children in the intermediate grades because it actively involves them in group work and logical thinking.

Teachers of intermediate-grade children should involve them in investigations of other cultures.

Recall that, as children move through primary and into intermediate grades, they are evolving from an egocentric perception of the world to a more other-centered view. They realize that the moon does not follow them when they are traveling in a car at night! They begin to realize that other people may have different experiences and live different lives than they do. This awakening of interest in other people and their lives leads naturally to a study of other cultures.

For this reason, the elementary social-studies curriculum typically follows the progression of studying the family, the community, the native

Activity 1.7

Dominoes

Lesson: Numbered Heads Together

The class is arranged into heterogeneous groups of four students, with each student assigned a number from one to four. Ask each group to "put their heads together" to develop the definitions requested in the following activity on polyominoes. Polyominoes are figures composed of two squares (dominoes), three squares (triominoes), four squares (tetrominoes), and so on. At the end of the allotted time, the teacher calls a number between one and four. Students with that number then present their group's answer.

- Examine the following statements and accompanying Figure 1.9:

This is a domino: This is not a domino:

These are triominoes: These are not triominoes:

These are tetrominoes:

These are not tetrominoes:

Figure 1.9

Develop a definition for a domino, triomino, and tetromino. Based upon these definitions, define a pentomino and draw the complete set of pentominoes.

Understand the Problem

You are given a set of diagrams. The sketches on the left show figures that are polyominoes. The sketches on the right show figures that are not polyominoes. You are to determine the important characteristics of dominoes, triominoes, and tetrominoes in order to arrive at a definition of each. Then, you are asked to extend your understanding by writing a definition of pentominoes and sketching each of them.

Devise a Plan

Within the cooperative group, members examine the sets of figures. Look for characteristics that are present in the positive examples on the left and are not present in the negative examples on the right. Either reach a consensus on a definition, or have each member write a definition and present it to the group. The latter technique affords each member some reflection time to formulate individual definitions. Having individuals write their definition first assists in the clarification process because the definition must be expressed so that it is understood by all members of the group. Once the definitions are developed and agreed upon, and patterns and relationships established, the task of defining and creating the set of pentominoes can commence.

Carry Out the Plan

Assume that each person writes a definition, the definitions are read and discussed, and then a collective definition is agreed upon.

- A **domino** is an arrangement of two congruent connected squares that share a complete side. One such arrangement is possible.

Figure 1.10

- A **triomino** is an arrangement of three congruent connected squares each sharing at least one complete side. There are two unique triominoes.

Figure 1.11

- A **tetromino** is an arrangement of four congruent connected squares each sharing at least one complete side. There are five possible tetrominoes.

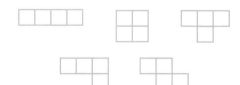

Figure 1.12   (continued)

Activity 1.7 (continued)

Dominoes

- A **pentomino** is an arrangement of five congruent connected squares each sharing at least one complete side. There are twelve possible pentominoes.

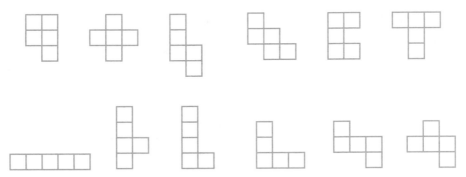

Figure 1.13

Look Back

Pentominoes have an interesting characteristic. When put together, they can be made to form several different rectangles. Try to form some rectangles with the pentominoes you have discovered. How will you determine the dimensions of the possible rectangles? What is the area of each rectangle?

Build upon your knowledge of geometry throughout this activity. As a group, write a definition of a **hexomino**. Cite three positive examples of hexominoes and three negative examples of hexominoes.

Journal Reflection

How would you respond to a member of a group who monopolizes the activity? How would you respond to a student who is disengaged?

---

country, and then other countries of the world. It is appropriate to connect this progression to the mathematics curriculum, and involve intermediate-grade children in historical investigations of the mathematics of other cultures. Activity 1.8 shows one way that such an investigation can take place within the context of a cooperative group lesson.

Teachers of intermediate-grade children should integrate their lessons.

Recently, the education profession has come under the criticism that school subjects are taught in isolation and children are not helped to see the connections that exist among the various subjects they are studying. The critics argue that if schools did a better job of connecting areas of the curriculum student interest would be heightened, and issues dealt with in a school setting would more closely resemble issues dealt with in the real world, where problems are often complex and interrelated.

One way that teachers have begun to integrate mathematics and language arts is by using children's literature. Mitsumasa Anno is the well-

Activity 1.8

Historical Investigation

Lesson: Jigsaw, Cooperative Learning

This is one of many different versions of the jigsaw approach. In this model, each group member becomes an expert on a particular topic, then teaches the rest of the group. The groups' knowledge can then be assessed through individual or group activities.

The class is arranged into heterogeneous groups of three. Each group member is to research a different numeration system: Babylonian, Mayan, or Egyptian. Each group member is to examine these systems in light of the symbols used and the presence or lack of a place value system. Resources include:

- Boyer, Carl. *A History of Mathematics.* Princeton, NJ: Princeton University Press, 1989.

- Eves, Howard. *An Introduction to the History of Mathematics.* Orlando, FL: Saunders, 1990.

- Katz, Victor J. *A History of Mathematics: An Introduction.* New York: HarperCollins, 1993.

- Kline, Morris. *Mathematics and Western Culture.* London: Oxford University Press, 1953.

- National Council of Teachers of Mathematics. *Historical Topics for the Mathematics Classroom.* Thirty-First Yearbook. Washington DC: NCTM, 1969.

- http://emmy.NMSU.edu/~history/

Each group member researches one system and then teaches the others. As a group or individually, students then compare the systems . Are they place-value systems? What limitations do they have? How do they compare with our base-ten system? Why might they have fallen into disuse? Which is the most similar to our Hindu-Arabic system? Which is the least similar?

As you can see from this activity, the final questions can only be answered by understanding the three components individually researched; hence, the activity reflects the two important cooperative learning characteristics of individual accountability and group goals. This activity also has important characteristics that make it developmentally appropriate for intermediate-grade children. It actively involves children in a group setting, it integrates such areas of the curriculum as mathematics, history, and art, and it introduces children to other cultures.

Journal Reflection

Discuss how you think a knowledge of the history of mathematics can influence a child's understanding of mathematics.

known author of beautifully illustrated children's books; these books often deal with mathematical themes, since Anno was trained as both an artist and a mathematics teacher. In his book *Anno's Hat Tricks* he introduces the reader to the concept of if-then logic. Activity 1.9 has been inspired by this book.

A cooperative model like think-pair-share allows for maximum involvement of the students in the class. When whole-class discussions are held, only one student out of thirty can contribute to the discussion at one time. Quiet students are frequently left out. In addition, students whose primary language is not English may hesitate to engage in class discussions.

Pairing students gives every student in the class an opportunity to contribute to the discussion. You may find that small-group discussion has increased the confidence of quieter students, making them more likely to contribute to the whole-class discussion.

In their book *Circles of Learning: Cooperation in the Classroom,* Johnson and colleagues (1990) make an attempt to dispel several myths about cooperative learning. Take a moment to imagine the kinds of objections that might be raised by parents, teachers, or school administrators about cooperative learning.

(text continues on p. 24)

Activity 1.9

Problem Solving

Lesson: Think-Pair-Share, Cooperative Learning

This flexible model of cooperative group instruction incorporates individual reflection into its structure. The teacher can arrange heterogeneous groups of four, and then pair off members within the groups. A particular topic or point of discussion is introduced by the teacher. Each student is asked to reflect on the task at hand. Then, a discussion takes place between two members of a pair, who subsequently share with the other pair within their group of four. This sharing can also take place on a whole-class level. The following cooperative activity demonstrates this simple method.

You will need three students to act as volunteers, and five hats or construction-paper models of hats, two white and three black.

Problem One

Begin with two students and two hats, one white and one black. (You should make clear to the class how many hats in all and how many of each color will be used at the beginning of each problem.)

■ While the two students are hiding their eyes, place a hat on each student's head, and hide the extra hats. Each student should be able to see the color of the other student's hat, but not the color of his or her own. The problem posed to the class is, can students tell the color of their own hat?

Think: Since there were two hats to begin with, one black and one white, if Student A can see a black hat, then he must be wearing a white hat. The same reasoning allows Student B to identify the color of her hat.

Pair: Compare your reasoning with that of your partner, and together decide upon a mutually acceptable solution.

Share: Join with another pair, and share your solution and the reasoning behind your solution. If called upon, share this solution with the class.

Problem Two

Begin with two students, and three hats, two black and one white. Place one of each color on the students, as

shown. The problem posed to the class is, can each student tell the color of his or her own hat?

Think: Both students can tell their hat color, *if* they are asked to identify their hat color in a specific order. For example, student A can tell that he is wearing black, since there was only one white hat to begin with, and he can see his partner wearing it. Student B can only tell what color she is wearing if she first hears student A identify his color. Since she can only see one black hat on his head, she could be wearing either black or white. But when she hears him identify his own color, she knows he must have seen a white hat on her head, and thus she knows what color she is wearing.

Pair: Compare your solution with your partner's, and agree upon one solution.

Share: Share your solution with another pair, perhaps acting out the problem to settle any disagreements. If called upon, share the solution with the class.

(continued)

Problem Three

Begin with three students and five hats, three black and two white. The problem posed to the class is, can each student tell the color of his or her own hat?

Think: Once again, the colors of the hats can be identified, *if* the questions are asked in a specific order. Imagine that Student A is asked to identify the color of his hat, but says that he is unable to do that. Since there were three black hats and two white hats to begin with, and since he can see two black hats, his hat could be either black or white. When the same question is posed to Student B, she thinks for a moment, and also says that she is unable to identify her hat color. The only way that student A could have identified his own hat, she reasons, is if he saw two white hats. Since he was unable to identify his hat color, he must have seen *at least* one black hat, and he may have seen two black hats. Since she knows that Student C is wearing black, she reasons that her own hat could be either black or white. At this point, student C should be able to identify her hat color. Do you see why? If Student B

had been able to identify her hat color, it would mean that she saw a white hat on the head of Student C. (Remember, there had to be at least one black hat. The only way she could have identified her own hat would have been if she saw a white hat, and realized that her hat was the black one.) Since she couldn't identify her own hat, she must have seen a black hat on the head of Student C. This reasoning allows student C to correctly identify the color of her hat as black.

Pair: Compare your solution with your partner's, and agree upon one solution.

Share: Share your solution with another pair, perhaps acting out the problem to settle any disagreements. If called upon, share the solution with the class.

Journal Reflection

Imagine that a parent questioned your use of a book such as *Anno's Hat Tricks* in a sixth-grade math class. How would you justify the series of activities described above?

Here are objections anticipated in *Circles of Learning,* along with how those objections might be answered:

- *Students need to learn how to be competitive because the world is a competitive place.*

On the contrary, many people believe that the best parts of our world are its aspects of interdependence. A good example of this growing interdependence can be seen in the movement toward a global economy. Global politics has several examples of cooperation, such as the United Nations and NATO. Disasters occurring in the far reaches of the globe are met with an outpouring of aid from many different countries.

- *Able students are hurt by cooperative group activities.*

Johnson, Johnson and Holubec make the following comments in their attempt to dispel this popular myth:

> We and others around the country have conducted numerous studies comparing the achievement of high-, middle-, and low-achieving students in cooperative, competitive, and individualistic learning situations. The high-achievers working in heterogeneous cooperative groups have never done worse than their counterparts working competitively or individualistically, and often they do better (pp.130–31).

In addition to benefiting intellectually, I believe that students of all ability levels benefit socially from working with one another. All students deserve the opportunity to develop skills of leadership, communication, and negotiation.

- *Cooperative learning treats all learners in the same way.*

A cooperative learning situation can be structured to encompass and address the needs of a variety of ability levels within the group. For example, in a jigsaw approach, students can be given material at varied levels of sophistication. In other models, the number of problems to be solved can reflect the ability level of the group and a flexible grading system can be employed. Cooperative learning activities need not "teach to the average student" as whole-class activities often do. The assignments can reflect the make-up of the group. Students can be working on different problems, but they can still assist each other in discussing the hows and the whys of the activities in question.

- *Giving a group grade is an unfair grading system.*

There are a variety of approaches that can be used in grading. For example, the entire collaborative effort can receive one grade that has two components: an individual grade and a group grade. The individual grade is based on the outcomes of the individual accountability activity. Depending on the activity, it could be worth 50% of the total grade. The group grade is a single grade based on the level of achievement of the group goal. This component can also be worth 50% of the entire grade. The sum total of the points allotted for the individual and group activities determines the total grade awarded for the cooperative activity. This scoring system addresses the grading of the activity itself. There are other scoring systems that focus on the use of the cooperative learning experience and the exams themselves. A student can receive an individual grade on an exam in addition to a group grade on the exam. This group grade is the average of the grades of each group member. The exam grade that is recorded can be the average of the individual grade and the group average.

Johnson and the others (1990) offer another alternative. Prior to the exam, the group, in consultation with the teacher, can set a benchmark for success on the exam. If the average grade for the group members surpasses the benchmark, each member receives some preset bonus points which are added to the individual grade.

There are many models of grading. The most important question you can ask yourself has to do with your perception of the *purpose* of assigning a grade. Why are you giving students this information? If the purpose of the grade is to inform students of the quality of their work in comparison to that of the whole class, it makes sense to grade everyone's work according to the same criteria. If the purpose of the grade is to inform students of the individual progress they have made, it makes sense to grade a student's work in relation to previous work. Issues of assessment and evaluation will be addressed in greater depth throughout this book. Each chapter will examine assessment activities and practices appropriate for each topic.

We do not mean to imply that cooperative learning is a panacea for all of the problems facing elementary education today. It is one of many possible ways to organize a classroom. It is discussed at length here because you may not have had experience with cooperative learning when you were an elementary student, and because it is currently receiving a great deal of attention. In my experience, cooperative learning theory has much to offer both teachers and learners of mathematics. Part of becoming a successful teacher lies in developing a sufficient repertoire of techniques so that you have several options when faced with a particular class and a particular topic on a particular day.

Summary

This chapter introduced you to documents that have shaped the way educators currently approach mathematics teaching and learning. Most recent is the NCTM *Principles and Standards,* which is made available to members of National Council of Teachers of Mathematics. As a full-time student, you can become a member of NCTM for a reduced fee. The NCTM website is *www.nctm.org.*

Chapter 1 addressed developmentally appropriate teaching practices for children. Implicit in the concept is the understanding that different stages of childhood development require different learning situations. The chapter reviewed Piaget's sensorimotor, preoperational, concrete operational, and formal operational stages of cognitive development. Conserving is a developmental signpost of the concrete operational stage, which ranges from ages 7 to 12; its appearance announces a new level of abstract thinking that is essential to understanding mathematics beyond the concrete level.

The position statement of the National Association for the Education of Young Children (NAEYC) was addressed in some detail. Further information about NAEYC can be obtained from their website at *www.naeyc.org*.

Finally, the chapter addressed the role of cooperative learning in the mathematics classroom. When students work in cooperative settings, both group goals and individual accountability are practiced.

Extending Your Learning

1. Examine a third-grade mathematics textbook from the 1980s and one from the 1990s. Compare and contrast the two texts. Do you see specific evidence that the 1990s text was influenced by the 1989 publication of the NCTM *Standards?* Count the number of pages that deal primarily with problem solving in each of the books. Is there a difference? Did your findings surprise you?

2. Write a letter to parents or guardians that you might send home on your first day of teaching third grade. Describe your year's mathematical goals for their child based on your understanding of the NCTM *Principles and Standards.*

3. Go to the library and examine one copy of *Arithmetic Teacher* from the decade of the seventies, the eighties, and the nineties (after April 1994, this journal was reissued as two separate journals, *Teaching Children Mathematics* and *Mathematics Teaching in the Middle School*). Describe the similarities and differences among the three journals. Focus on implicit assumptions about the nature of mathematics and the nature of mathematics teaching.

4. The NCTM *Principles and Standards* state that "[A] challenging pedagogical task for teachers is finding ways to connect new mathematical ideas to the understandings and experiences that students bring to the classroom" (p 28). List ten situations that are relevant to elementary school students. Suggest mathematical connections that might grow out of each situation.

5. Spend a few hours in the children's section of a library. Look for children's books that deal with mathematical themes, either explicitly or implicitly. Begin to develop a file of annotated bibliographies of these books. You may wish to connect this investigation to similar ones you are doing in a language-arts methods course.

6. Go to visit a mathematics class in a local elementary school or preschool. Do you see any practices that are in keeping with suggested reforms in school mathematics? Do you see any practices that are developmentally appropriate? Write a summary of practices you noted that fall into either or both of these categories.

7. Investigate museums or exhibits in your area that could be visited by an elementary school class and then serve as the basis of a mathematics unit or lesson. Write up specific information about the site (hours of operation, location and phone number, cost, possible connections to mathematics). Share this information with your classmates.

8. Visit your college library. Determine how many journals there deal with issues in the field of education. Examine at least ten different journals. Write a descriptive summary of each journal you examine, pointing out the strengths and weaknesses as you perceive them. Share this information with your classmates.

9. Determine if your state or locale has a mathematics education professional organization. Write to that organization and the National Council of Teachers of Mathematics, 1906 Association Drive, Reston, Virginia 22091–1593, or access their website at *www.nctm.org* and request membership information. Become a member! There is no better way to keep informed about conferences, institutes, and new trends in the field of mathematics education.

10. Interview a local principal, curriculum coordinator, or other school administrator. Ask the educators to articulate the goals in mathematics for students in their school or district. Ask about characteristics and backgrounds sought when hiring new teachers. You may wish to invite three or four local administrators to serve on a panel discussion on "Mathematical Needs for the Twenty-First Century," "Issues of Multiculturalism in the Elementary School Classroom," or "The Move Toward Manipulative-Based Mathematics Instruction."

Internet Resources

www.nctm.org
The official website for the National Council of Teachers of Mathematics. Information is provided about membership, journals, conferences, and publications.

www.naeyc.org
The official website for the National Association for the Education of Young Children. In addition to information about conferences, resources, and accreditation, the website provides links to early-childhood research reports.

www.nmsa.org
The official website of the National Middle School Association, a group devoted to improving the educational experiences of young adolescents (ages 10 to 15). Information about membership, conferences, and resources is provided.

www.enc.org
The website of the Eisenhower National Clearinghouse for Math and Science Education. It offers information about summer research opportunities for teachers, exemplary instructional programs, and will allow you to search for K–12 math and science curriculum resources.

www.illuminations.nctm.org
This website is offered by NCTM as a support resource for *Principles and Standards*. It includes teaching strategies, opportunities for professional growth, and a searchable, interactive version of *Principles and Standards*.

Bibliography

Anno, Mitsumasa and Akihiro Nozaki. (1985). *Anno's hat tricks.* New York: Philomel.

Baroody, Arthur J. *Children's mathematical thinking.* (1987). New York: Teachers College Press.

Baroody, Arthur J. *A guide to teaching mathematics in the primary grades.* (1989). Boston: Allyn & Bacon.

Boyer, Carl. *A history of mathematics.* (1989). Princeton: Princeton University Press.

Bredekamp, Susan (Ed.). (1987*). Developmentally appropriate practice in early childhood: Programs serving children from birth through age eight.* Washington, DC: National Association for the Education of Young Children.

Brooks, J. G., and M. Brooks. (1993). *The case for constructivist classrooms.* Alexandria, VA: Association for Supervision and Curriculum Development.

Burns, Marilyn. (1990). The math solution: Using groups of four. In Neil Davidson (ed.), *Cooperative learning in mathematics: A handbook for teachers* (pp. 21–46). Menlo Park, CA: Addison-Wesley.

Copeland, Richard W. (1970). *How children learn mathematics.* New York: Macmillan.

Curcio, Frances R., and Susan Folkson. (1996). Exploring data: Kindergarten children do it their way. *Teaching Children Mathematics 2*(6).

Davidson, Neil. (1985). Small-group learning and teaching in mathematics: A selective review of the literature. In R. Slavin, et al. (eds.), *Learning to cooperate, cooperating to learn* (pp. 211–30). New York: Plenum.

Davidson, Neil (Ed.). (1990). *Cooperative learning in mathematics: A handbook for teachers.* Menlo Park, CA: Addison-Wesley.

Elkind, David. (1981). *Children and adolescents: Interpretive essays on Jean Piaget.* New York: Oxford University Press.

Eves, Howard. (1990). *An introduction to the history of mathematics.* Orlando, FL: Saunders.

Folkson, Susan. (1995). Who's behind the fence? Creating a rich learning environment with a nontraditional problem. *Teaching Children Mathematics 1*(6).

Garrison, Leslie. (1997). Making the NCTM Standards work for emergent English speakers. *Teaching Children Mathematics 4*(3).

Johnson, David, Roger Johnson, and Edythe Johnson Holubec. (1990). *Circles of learning: Cooperation in the classroom* (3rd ed.). Edina, MN: Interaction.

Johnson, David, and Roger Johnson. (1987). *Learning together and alone: Cooperative, competitive, and individualistic learning* (2nd ed.). Englewood Cliffs, NJ: Prentice-Hall.

Kagan, Spencer. (1989/1990). A structural approach to cooperative learning. *Educational Leadership 47*(4).

Karp, Karen. (1994). Telling tales: Creating graphs using multicultural literature. *Teaching Children Mathematics 1*(2).

Katz, Victor J. (1993). *A history of mathematics: An introduction.* New York: HarperCollins.

Kline, Kate. (1999). Helping at home. *Teaching Children Mathematics 5*(8).

Kline, Morris. (1953). *Mathematics and Western culture.* London: Oxford University Press.

Lemme, Barbara S. (1998). Putting math into routine classroom tasks: Some ideas for teams in cooperative-learning structures. *Teaching Children Mathematics 4*(5).

McCracken, Janet Brown. (1987). More than 1,2,3 . . . the real basics of mathematics. Brochure 575. Washington, DC: National Association for the Education of Young Children.

National Association for the Education of Young Children. (1988). Testing of young children: Concerns and cautions. Brochure 582. Washington, DC: Author.

National Association for the Education of Young Children. (1988). Appropriate education in the primary grades. Brochure 578. Washington, DC: Author.

National Council of Teachers of Mathematics. (1995). Position statement on interdisciplinary learning pre-K–4. *Teaching Children Mathematics 1*(6).

National Council of Teachers of Mathematics. (1989). *Curriculum and evaluation standards for school mathematics.* Reston, VA: Author.

National Council of Teachers of Mathematics. (1969). *Historical topics for the mathematics classroom.* 31st Yearbook. Washington DC: Author.

Schwartz, Sydney L., and Anna Beth Brown. (1995). Communicating with young children in mathematics: A unique challenge. *Teaching Children Mathematics 1*(6).

Sharan, Shlomo. (1984). *Cooperative learning in the classroom: Research in desegregated schools.* Hillsdale, NJ: Lawrence Erlbaum.

Slavin, Robert. (1989/1990). Research on cooperative learning: Consensus and controversy. *Educational Leadership 47*(4).

Slavin, Robert. (1989). *Cooperative learning: Theory, research and practice.* Englewood Cliffs, NJ: Prentice-Hall.

Slavin, Robert. (1987). Cooperative learning in the cooperative school. *Educational Leadership 45*:7–13.

Slavin, Robert. (1983). *Cooperative learning.* New York: Longman.

Williams, Connie K., and Constance Kamii. (1986, November). How do children learn by handling objects? *Young Children,* pp. 23–26.

Zanger, Virginia Vogel. (1998). Math storybooks. *Teaching Children Mathematics 5*(2).

2

Standards for Number and Numeration

Growing children need a language-rich environment, with ready access to books, magazines, posters, signs, and letters. They need us to read, speak, and listen to them and they need to be encouraged to communicate through reading and writing. Raising a child in a mathematically rich environment is equally important to the child's developing numeracy. A mathematically rich environment can be created in a classroom by having a large number of attractive materials available. Chapter 1 described a number of popular materials—Unifix cubes, Cuisenaire rods, counters, Geoboards—and we will look at many more in the course of this book. But simply surrounding a child with mathematical manipulatives is not sufficient for the development of numeracy; the child must become engaged with the materials. How to foster this engagement will become clear as the chapter unfolds.

The structure of this chapter will be replicated throughout the rest of the book. To help you experience the mathematics reform movement first-hand, each chapter presents one of the Standards at the appropriate grade levels, performance-based assessment activities appropriate to that Standard, one or more sample lesson plans, and several Strength in Numbers activities. If you are going to engage children in solving problems by writing about them, if you are going to focus children on the big ideas in mathematics, if you are going to introduce children to mathematics as an intellectually satisfying and absorbing way to make sense of things—then you yourself must have that experience. Remember that people learn best and remember most when they connect new knowledge to past understandings. Therefore, as you read, ask yourself the following questions:

- What does this remind me of?
- What surprises me? What doesn't?
- What do I agree with? What do I disagree with?
- What connections exist between learning mathematics and learning social studies? Language? Science? Art? Music?
- What connections exist between theories of learning and development and the ways I will teach children mathematics?
- How can my own experiences as a learner of mathematics positively influence my development as a teacher of mathematics?

Planning for Instruction

When you observe a master teacher, it appears that the lesson flows effortlessly, almost instinctively. Actually nothing could be further from the truth. Every veteran teacher was once a beginner who went through years of development to achieve the fluency you are observing. In the beginning, all teachers spend many hours writing *lesson plans*. As the name suggests, these are detailed plans for the teacher to follow when teaching a lesson. When you are practice teaching, you will realize that one of the most difficult aspects of teaching is having to think on your feet—while still focusing on the time, the temperature of the room, the behavior of the students, the question you were just asked, the question you want to ask, the development of the lesson, and the child who just told you he was going to be sick. For all of these reasons, and then some, it is necessary for teachers to have thoughtful and detailed lesson plans carefully constructed in advance. Teaching a lesson is a skill that is rehearsed before it is implemented.

There are almost as many different forms of lesson plans as there are books on pedagogy. The lesson plan offered here is simple and generic. You may wish to expand upon it as you gain experience, but it is a good starting point for developing skill in lesson writing. Basically, a lesson plan answers three questions:

- What am I going to teach?
- How am I going to teach it?
- How will I assess the students' learning?

You can approach the writing of a lesson plan just as you would approach any problem to be solved. First, make sure you understand what is needed; then, develop and implement a plan (discarding and refining as you go along); finally, review to make sure you have accomplished your goals. The lesson plan outline on page 33 is adaptable to many different kinds of lessons. The sample lesson plan that follows on pages 34 and 35 answers the three important questions set forth above:

- What am I going to teach? Answered by the concept, topic, and student objective sections.
- How am I going to teach it? Answered by the materials, motivation, and procedures sections.
- How will I assess the students' learning? Answered by the assessment section, which in this lesson requires the teacher to note which students can successfully skip count by two and how far they are able to continue the pattern. Recording this information is important because it helps the teacher to decide what future activities are appropriate for each student.

As this text unfolds, I will include two sample lesson plans in each chapter. These lessons are interdisciplinary and are designed to help you connect the theories of teaching with classroom practice.

Lesson Plan Outline

Grade _____   **Concept** _____

Topic _____

Student Objectives _____

_____

_____

Materials _____

_____

Motivation _____

_____

_____

_____

_____

_____

_____

_____

_____

_____

Procedure _____

_____

_____

_____

_____

_____

_____

_____

Assessment of student learning _____

_____

_____

_____

References _____

_____

Journal entry _____

_____

_____

_____

Lesson Plan

Here is how this lesson plan format looks for the topic of skip counting on the first-grade level.

Grade 1   **Concept** Number and Numeration

Topic Skip Counting by Two

Student Objectives After completing this lesson, students should be able to

- Recognize the numerical skip counting pattern for two
- Continue a skip counting pattern by two that has been begun for them.

Materials Overhead calculator, large class-size calendar, red chalk, blue chalk.

Motivation Tell the following story to the class.

At camp four children were bored, sitting in their tent on a rainy afternoon. The counselor stopped by to suggest a game. She told them the object of the game was to try to count to ten before she clapped her hands three times. The first child began 1, 2, 3, 4, 5, 6 . . . but only got to six before the third clap. The second child counted very fast, but only got to seven before the clapping was over. The third child laughed so hard that he could only get out the words one. . . . two. . . . before he collapsed with laughter.

Would anyone here like to try it?

(Allow several students to attempt the task. Clap quickly enough so that none are successful.) But, do you know what, boys and girls? The fourth child said five words, and managed to say them all before the counselor finished counting. Everyone agreed that the fourth child won the game. What five words do you think were said?

Procedure

1. Have students offer suggestions as to what words might have been said by the fourth child. 2. Assuming none are successful, have students observe while you use the following keystroke sequence on an overhead calculator.

$$AC + 2 = = = = =$$

Repeat the keystroke sequence a second time and ask the class to say the numerals out loud as they appear in the calculator display. Explain to the students that this was how the fourth child won the game.

(continued)

The reform movement in mathematics education is encouraging teachers to do less direct instruction and more activity-based lessons that engage children in constructing their own knowledge. Whole-class lessons, where children sit and listen quietly while the teacher talks for a prolonged period of time are not appropriate for young children, and are not in keeping with what we have come to understand about how children learn mathematics.

Lesson Plan (continued)
Here is how this lesson plan format looks for the topic of skip counting on the first-grade level.

3. Ask two students to come up to the board. Give one red chalk and the other blue. Ask one student to write the numeral 1 and the other student to follow it with a 2. Have them alternate writing the numerals to 10. Ask the class what they see. Possible answers will be:

■ There's a pattern. First one color, and then the other. The pattern repeats. First there a red numeral, then a blue, then a red, then a blue . . .

■ There are five red numerals and five blue numerals. The next numeral will be 11, and it will be red.

4. Explain to the class that this pattern shown by the numerals is called skip counting. Ask the students why they think this is so. Possible answers will be:

■ Because you skip some numerals when you count.

■ You skip every other numeral.

5. Focus the attention of the class on the large calendar. Have the students practice skip counting by two while referring to the calendar.

Assessment Ask the students to use a red and a blue crayon to generate vertical columns of numerals as they skip count by two. Adding-machine tape is useful for this. Point out the repetitive nature of the pattern. Note which students can accurately skip count by two and note how high they are able to do so.

References Frank, Alan R. Counting skills—A foundation for early mathematics. *Arithmetic Teacher 37*(1), 14–17.

Journal entry To be filled in by the teacher upon completion of the lesson, it will contain suggestions for improving the lesson and ideas for extensions. This part of the lesson plan is critical, although it is completed after the lesson is taught. It is useful for teachers to get into the habit of reflecting on the lessons they have taught. For example, this journal entry might suggest following the lesson with a music lesson on rhythmical patterns, or an art lesson on stringing beads in an AB AB AB AB . . . pattern.

An alternative to a whole class, teacher-directed lesson is to organize the classroom around **learning centers** or **learning stations.** Within this structure, children can take ownership of their own learning and begin to develop autonomy and independence by being encouraged to choose activities that interest them. A typical kindergarten classroom could have four stations set up on any given day. One station might contain an art activity;

a second might contain books chosen according to a certain theme plus writing materials; a third station could involve children in block play, and the fourth station might be focused on mathematics. Learning centers are designed so that, once the teacher has explained how the center operates, the children can engage in the activity independently. This frees the teacher to focus on one of the centers and engage in direct instruction and assessment with a small group of children from the class. A sample mathematics station might involve the teacher and four children with a basket of Unifix cubes. The teacher asks the children to use the cubes to model an addition story. For example, the children are told that Jose puts three apples in a basket and Susan puts two more apples in a basket. They are asked to show this using the Unifix cubes. Observing the children as they manipulate the cubes, the teacher asks them how many apples are now in the basket and how they know. Depending on the ability of the children, the teacher tells more stories, some of which involve subtraction. An extension of this activity would be for children to make up their own stories and model them with the cubes.

As the children leave the math table to engage in another activity, the teacher invites another group of children to work with the Unifix cubes. It is useful for the teacher to record the children's performance with notes on index cards or stickies. The cards or notes can later be filed alphabetically.

Factors Affecting the Mathematical Achievement of Students

Obviously all students do not achieve at the same level in mathematics. Some of the variables that affect students' mathematical achievement can be addressed by the classroom teacher, and we now turn to those aspects of classroom practice.

Time on Task

It might seem common sense that, the more time you spend on a task, the better you will become at it. In fact, there is a significant body of research to indicate that increased time spent studying mathematics—both increased time within a school day and increased years of study in high school and college—positively affects mathematics achievement (Fisher, et al., 1978).

As a classroom teacher, you can ensure that an adequate amount of time is spent on mathematics every day, and that both your students and their parents understand the importance of a formal study of mathematics every year the students are in school. This is especially important when students reach high school and mathematics becomes an elective. Unfortunately, while many schools require high school students to study English and social studies for four years, few require four years of mathematics.

Wait Time

A well-known researcher, Mary Budd Rowe (1973, 1974, 1978), studied the average time teachers waited for a response after asking a question of a student; surprisingly, the average "wait time" was less than one second. Following this recognition of the fast pace of the typical classroom, teachers were encouraged to pause for several seconds after posing a question, to give the students time to think and to prepare a response. When teachers increased their wait time to five seconds after articulating a question but before inviting a response, more students raised their hands to offer answers, and the cognitive level of student responses increased.

Teachers can train themselves to wait an adequate amount of time before asking a student to answer a posed question by silently counting to five after they have asked it. In addition, if teachers also wait before they respond to a student's answer, the student will very often continue to add to and refine the original answer.

Gender Issues

Regardless of the teacher's gender, research shows most teachers have more interactions (both verbal and nonverbal) with their male students than their female students. Teachers, on average, praise males more frequently, monitor their work more closely, and tend to criticize them more. This research finding has been replicated across countries and across socioeconomic groups (Brophy & Good, 1974; Becker, 1981; Greib & Easley, 1984; Hart, 1989; Leder, 1987, 1989, 1990; Fennema, 1990; Walden & Walkerdine, 1985). In addition, female students are more often asked low-cognitive questions while male students are more often asked challenging, high-cognitive questions (Leder, 1987, 1990).

Teachers can try to mitigate these realities by becoming aware that they might unconsciously favor one group over another. Some teachers mentally target five or six student each day, carefully attending to these students and monitoring their progress. By changing the target group each day, they feel confident that each child receives special attention at some point throughout the week. Other teachers keep a class roster on their desk, and make a tally mark next to the name of each child who has been questioned or answered a question during the day. Thus the teacher can see patterns and guard against having some children receive a disproportionate amount of attention while others are ignored.

Another important point, especially for female teachers, is that all children need to see positive role models. Children ought to see teachers who enjoy teaching and doing mathematics, who are confident about their ability to understand and help others understand mathematics, and who are willing to expend time and effort in the pursuit of mathematical knowledge.

Multicultural Issues

The term *multicultural education* means different things to different people. I believe that multicultural education requires schools to encourage a knowledge of, and respect for, the diverse backgrounds that students and teachers bring to a classroom. It is no secret that members of a subordinate culture are likely to be at a disadvantage in the dominant setting. The advantages often ascribed to the dominant culture include (a) a sense of belonging to the mainstream, (b) ease of functioning in the school culture, and (c) shared language, goals, and values with those who are in positions of power and authority. The disadvantages of the subordinate group include (a) difficulty understanding the structure and values of the school culture, (b) difficulty when instruction is not in the native language, and (c) the sense of being different, and therefore suspect.

There are several steps that teachers can take to further the goals of multicultural education in their classrooms (Dean, et al, 1993):

- *Incorporate authentic and student-centered assessment strategies.* Children from a different culture are often at a serious disadvantage in a formal testing situation. Linguistic differences can lead to confusion, and certain assumptions made by the dominant culture can unfairly penalize some students. For example, a question that asks for the total number of legs twelve chickens have depends on the knowledge that chickens have two legs each, which an urban child, familiar mostly with dogs and cats, might not have. (In each of the subsequent chapters, I will offer alternative assessment activities to help to mitigate these cultural differences.)

- *Develop an appreciation for, and a sensitivity to, other cultures.* The study of holiday traditions can be broadened to include those from many different cultures, especially those cultures represented by children in the class. In your capacity as a role model, you need to be scrupulous in avoiding stereotypes and eager to learn about and appreciate cultures other than your own.

- *Develop pedagogical strategies that encourage the inclusion of all students.* In addition to cooperative learning, which will receive considerable attention in this textbook, we will also discuss such inclusionary classroom practices as journal writing, the use of manipulatives, and writing-to-learn problem solving.

- *Encourage connections with the home.* Many parents welcome the opportunity to read to (or with) their children. However, the same does not always hold true for doing mathematics. Not all parents are comfortable about their ability to engage in mathematics with their children, and many of them avoid mathematics in their own lives. Sometimes parents simply need to be guided in what to do to help their children with mathematics. To address this, the book *Family Math* was published by the Lawrence Hall of Science in Berkeley, California. This book offers specific mathematical activities appropriate for parents and caregivers to share with their children. Many schools have begun to sponsor family math sessions in the evenings or on weekends as a way to encourage parental involvement.

  At one family math night, the school district provided translators to allow for the full participation of families whose primary language was not English. This sensitivity to other cultures is most important as we begin the twenty-first century. Statistics predict that by the turn of the century in the United States 1 out of every 3 residents will be nonwhite (Good & Biddle, 1988). There are school districts in the United States today where the children who compose the student body speak dozens, if not hundreds, of different languages.

It is not possible to prepare teachers fully for every student they will teach. Your students will bring to class an enormous variety of ethnic, religious, linguistic, cultural, physical, and cognitive characteristics. As this book unfolds, we will offer specific pedagogical strategies that are appropriate for a wide variety of students. It is a truism of teaching that each child is an individual with unique strengths and needs. As a professional teacher you need to develop strategies for meeting those needs.

Curricular Issues

During the mid-1990s, an important international study was undertaken to determine the mathematics and science achievement of students in fourth, eighth, and twelfth grade (or final year, secondary school). It involved more than 500,000 students from forty-one nations. The study covered curriculum, teaching practice, textbooks, and even the lives of students and teachers. Published in 1999, the Third International Mathematics and Science Study (TIMSS) has important things to say to those beginning their teaching career. When the United States is compared with other nations that include our major trading partners, we do not fare well.

> At the fourth grade, the U.S. students were above the international average in both science and mathematics. In the eighth grade, U.S. students scored above the international average in science and below the international average in mathematics. At the end of secondary schooling (twelfth grade in the U.S.), U.S. performance was among the lowest in both science and mathematics, including among our most advanced students. (National Center for Educational Statistics, 1999)

Findings of significance for elementary and middle-school teachers is that the fourth-grade mathematics curriculum in the United States contains more topics than those of other countries; the eighth-grade mathematics curriculum is less focused and less advanced, being comparable to the seventh-grade curriculum of other countries. Thus, it has been said that the mathematics curricula in the United States are a mile wide and an inch deep!

As you plan your mathematics curriculum, keep this research in mind. In some ways, less is more. Teaching fewer topics, but teaching them more deeply and over a longer period of time, might serve students better than the current model. These decisions, of course, cannot be made in a vacuum, and have implications for teachers of the grades that precede yours and teachers of the grades that succeed yours. You may find it beneficial to enter into a discussion with all of the stakeholders about how the curriculum should be distributed among the grade levels.

Constructivism in the Mathematics Classroom

Piaget distinguished among at least three different types of knowing. He said that children can have *physical* knowledge, as when they realize through trial and error that a stable tower of blocks can be constructed only if the larger blocks are used to form the base and the smaller blocks are placed on top.

Figure 2.1

Figure 2.2

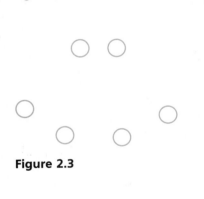

Figure 2.3

Figure 2.4

2 + 4 = ?

4 + 2 = ?

6 − 2 = ?

6 − 4 = ?

He said that children can have *social* knowledge, as when information is socially transmitted to them. For example, when a child knows that her birthday is August 21 or that her phone number is 555–1234, that knowledge has been imparted by someone else. Last, children can develop *logico-mathematical* knowledge through interaction with the world. Logico-mathematical knowledge develops when children interact with their environment and try to make sense of the data they perceive. For example, a teacher might read to the class *Ten Black Dots* by Donald Crews. This counting book has simple illustrations that show different arrangements of black dots, from one to ten. To assist the children in actively creating their own understanding of, say, the number six, the teacher might give each child six plastic disc counters, all of which are the same color (bingo markers work well). It is important to use discs of the same color because it is the number of discs that is the focus, not their color.

Using a sheet of paper of contrasting color, the children are invited to arrange the discs in several different patterns. A child might create the arrangement of discs in Figure 2.1 and explain that six can be the slide in the playground. Another child might arrange the discs as in Figure 2.2, explaining that six can be a caterpillar crawling along the ground. Another child might say that six can be a happy face, and arrange the discs as in Figure 2.3, but some children might respond that the arrangement shows 2 + 4, with two dots used for the eyes and four used for the smile. An arrangement of dots that looks like Figure 2.4 might be described as flowers growing in a garden, and can be used to model 3 + 3.

In a constructivist classroom, children actively attempt to make sense of situations, and the teacher moves from a role as disseminator of information to one as initiator and guide of mathematical investigations. *Constructivism*, which is generating a great deal of interest in mathematics education, is based on the idea that, while we have long taught mathematics as if it were social knowledge, we should have recognized that it is logico-mathematical in nature.

For the elementary classroom teacher, this means we need to involve children actively in their own mathematical learning. For example, it is common to see pages in a second-grade mathematics workbook that deal with "fact families." The pages would typically consist of a large number of example sets like those in the margin.

While the page is clearly intended to highlight patterns and the inverse relationship of addition and subtraction, it would be possible for a child to work mindlessly through a page like this with little or no understanding of the concept, and with little or no retention of the number facts. Activity 2.1 is constructivist in nature, and thus in greater synchrony with the NCTM Standards.

Cognitively Guided Instruction

Cognitively guided instruction (CGI) was developed by researchers at the University of Wisconsin (Fennema, et al., 1988). This view of mathematics teaching and learning bears some similarities to, and is philosophically congruent with, the concept of constructivism. A basic tenet of CGI is that

Lesson: Individual

This activity requires two-color counters (small discs, red on one side, yellow on the other) or dried beans that have been darkened on one side with a marker. Each child gets five counters or beans, shakes them (an empty film container works well for this), and tosses them onto the desk. If the beans spill out as in Figure 2.5, for example, the child writes the appropriate number sentence, $2 + 3 = 5$, in the notebook. This activity is repeated a number of times.

Figure 2.5

Alternately, the information could be recorded in graphical form on a worksheet like that of Figure 2.6. Such a completed worksheet, or one created on the board by the whole class, could provide the basis for discussion of such questions as:

- What combination came up most often?
- What combination came up least often?
- How many times altogether were the beans tossed? How do you know?
- Did anyone get a combination that is not shown here?

This activity is mathematically richer, more interesting, and open to much greater discussion than the sample page from a workbook. It can also be repeated many times throughout the year, as the number of beans is varied. One way you can build the children's confidence is by involving them in activities similar to those they have done in the past. As they connect the present situation with prior learning, it imparts a sense of familiarity and competence. This need to connect new knowledge to prior knowledge is one of the tenets of constructivism.

Journal Reflection

How might you include parents and caregivers in an activity like this one?

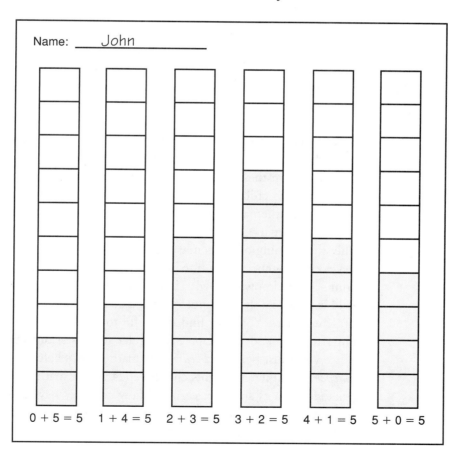

Name: John

$0 + 5 = 5$ $1 + 4 = 5$ $2 + 3 = 5$ $3 + 2 = 5$ $4 + 1 = 5$ $5 + 0 = 5$

Figure 2.6

teachers must understand the thinking of students in order to respond appropriately in guiding subsequent instruction. This primacy of teachers' knowledge as the basis for instructional decision making is echoed in *Principles and Standards,* when it states

> More than any other single factor, teachers influence what mathematics students learn and how well they learn it. Students' mathematical knowledge, their abilities to reason and solve problems, and their self-confidence and dispositions toward mathematics are all shaped by teachers' mathematical and pedagogical decisions (p. 30).

A similarity between constructivism and CGI is the belief, stated in Activity 2.1, that children learn when they are able to link new knowledge to existing knowledge. Three main ideas structure CGI:

- Mathematics instruction should be based on an understanding of the ways in which each individual learns.

- Mathematics instruction should grow out of knowledge of how children naturally develop mathematical ideas.

- In order for learning to occur, children's minds need to be actively engaged in solving problems.

Research has shown that, compared with a control group, teachers who spent one month during the summer being trained in CGI focused more on word problems and less on problems dealing with number facts, paid closer attention to the processes students used to arrive at their solutions, and encouraged the use of a wider variety of problem-solving strategies (Koehler & Grouws, 1992). What significance does this research have for you as a classroom teacher? It suggests that you should spend time observing and listening to students as they work to solve problems, and then use the information obtained from these observations to inform your instruction. It suggests that you treat each child as a unique learner of mathematics. It also suggests that, the more mathematics you learn, the better you will be able to teach it.

In summary, constructivism and CGI are concepts that inform not only the learning of elementary school children but also *your* learning as a developing teacher. As you work through this course, it is important that you connect new knowledge with knowledge developed in previous courses or field experiences. It is essential that you actively involve yourself in the activities presented here. You may find it helpful to take notes on cards, keep a double-entry notebook, or participate in regular study sessions with your colleagues. Since you must become a *learner* of mathematics before you can become a *teacher* of mathematics, this chapter ends with a mathematical activity appropriate for you as an adult learner. Many activities have been designed for your participation as part of a cooperative group. This experience will be useful as you begin to engage children in cooperative group settings.

Strength in Numbers

Problem Solving

Cooperative Group Model: Think, Pair, Share

Working in pairs, try to solve this problem. Use the following problem-solving steps, made famous by George Polya.

Understand the Problem

Make sure you read the problem carefully and understand what the problem is asking. Restate the problem in your own words and repeat it to your partner to ensure that you both understand it.

Devise a Plan

Together, create a tentative a plan that you think will help you arrive at a solution. Sometimes after a plan is carried out it is found to be unsuccessful. In this case, an alternate plan must be devised.

Carry Out the Plan

Implement the plan, thinking out loud with your partner as you go. Be aware that the plan may need to be altered, or even discarded, if it does not succeed in helping you reach a solution.

Look Back

Go back to the original problem. Does your answer make sense? Is it the only possible solution? Is it the best possible solution? Might you have arrived at this solution using another strategy?

- An ant is trapped inside a cube having dimensions of 10 cm on each side. The ant is at one corner of the cube, and the food is at the diagonally corner (Figure 2.7). What is the shortest path that the ant can take to reach the food?

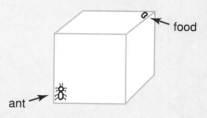

Figure 2.7

After each pair has had an opportunity to solve this problem, two pairs join to discuss alternative solutions and strategies. Then have a whole-class discussion. *Hint:* Most people believe the shortest path to be 30 cm (along three edges) or approximately 24 cm (along one edge and diagonally across a face). However, there is a shorter path. If you're having trouble seeing it, imagine what the cube would look like if it were opened up and laid flat.

Performance-Based Assessment

Probably you remember taking tests, both teacher-made and standardized, when you were an elementary school student. Mathematics educators have become dissatisfied with many aspects of those tests. For years teachers have been disturbed that students who can accurately compute a numerical example (12% × 223) do not know how to compute the tip in a restaurant or approximate the discounted price at a shoe sale. Students seemed unable to connect skills learned in the classroom with problems in the real world.

Standardized tests have been criticized for being culturally and linguistically biased toward the dominant group. For example, if English is not your native language, how much of your performance on a mathematics test is dependent upon your language skills? If a question on a mathematics test asks you how many saucers are needed for five cups, is that testing your knowledge of one-to-one correspondence or your cultural knowledge that coffee can be served in mugs or in cups and saucers? In addition, standardized tests provide a snapshot of a student's responses on a single day. This conflicts with our understanding of learning as an ongoing process that surges ahead at some points and stabilizes at others. One of the biggest criticisms leveled at standardized tests is that they provide the teacher with no information about what the child was thinking when answering a particular question. A classic problem on a standardized mathematics test for young children might instruct *Mark the circle under the picture that shows a square inside a triangle.* How should an incorrect response to this question be interpreted? Does the child know how to mark the circle? Can the child identify a square? Can the child identify a triangle? Does the child know the meaning of *inside?* All of these answers must be yes if the child is to respond correctly. Further, a teacher may not know which items were missed by which children, having been provided only a composite score. As a second-grade teacher, for example, you might simply be informed that Mary Ann received a grade-equivalent score of 2.3 on math concepts.

Not knowing what was answered incorrectly by each child, or why, prevents the teacher from altering the curriculum or the instruction to remediate any difficulties. Yet this is the primary goal of assessment: to obtain adequate information for future curricular and instructional planning. These weaknesses of testing have led educators to suggest many different types of assessment instruments, including *performance-based assessments.* A performance-based assessment requires students to put knowledge to use to perform a specific task or solve a problem. Sometimes a teacher observes or interviews a single child during an assessment task. For example, in lieu of the test item requiring the child to *Mark the circle under the picture that shows a square inside a triangle,* a teacher might call her kindergartners, one at a time, over to a table during free play time. With a variety of paper cutouts or blocks displayed on the table, the child is asked to point to the square, point to the triangle, and so on. If the child is able to identify the shapes, the teacher asks the child to draw a square inside a triangle. By directly observing each child's performance, the teacher is able to identify any difficulties.

As you can see, it would not be possible to assess the performance of every child in the class at one sitting. This type of assessment is meant to be ongoing. Typically, teachers rotate through the class, changing the topic being assessed on a weekly or biweekly basis. This necessitates that the teacher assess the mathematical performance of approximately five children each day, a manageable number. Because the assessment is ongoing, the teacher can monitor the progress of each child over time, and not be limited to information from a few isolated occasions.

On a different type of assessment task, the teacher might even ask for clarification. Suppose a second-grader was asked to solve the following problem, written by one of her classmates:

■ "If each tiger has 99 stripes, how many stripes do 4 tigers have?"

When the child promptly replied "396," the teacher asked the child to explain how she knew that was the answer. The child explained that if the tigers each had 100 stripes, there would have been 400 stripes in all. Since the tigers only had 99 stripes each, 400 is 4 stripes too many. The child counted backwards to obtain the answer of 396.

Listening to this explanation, the teacher is given significant insight into the child's problem-solving skills, mental math skills, and number sense. Also, if the child had been unable to solve the problem, the teacher could have simplified the problem on the spot to one involving four tigers with 9 stripes each. The point is not simply to determine who is able to solve the problem correctly, but to obtain information about the problem-solving and mental math abilities of each and every child. This information is valuable as the teacher plans out the next week's or the next month's lessons, both for the whole class and for individual children.

It is important for the teacher to devise some efficient method for recording information obtained from performance-based assessments. A typical grade book does not allow the necessary space. Some alternatives include large index cards kept in alphabetical order, a binder with separate sheets devoted to each child, or a computer file for each child. Each entry should be dated, and the context of the interaction noted, whether individual-conference, small-group, or whole-class setting. This textbook includes suggestions for performance-based assessments throughout.

Number and Operation for Grades Pre-K–2

According to the NCTM *Principles and Standards,*

Mathematics instructional programs should foster the development of number and operation sense . . . In grades pre-K–2, all students should

■ Count fluently with understanding and recognize "how many" in small sets of objects;

■ Understand the cardinal and ordinal meaning of numbers in quantifying, measuring, and identifying the order of objects;

■ Connect number words, the quantities they represent, numerals, and written words and represent numerical situations with each of these;

■ Develop an understanding of the relative magnitude of numbers and make connections between the size of cardinal numbers and the counting sequence;

■ Develop an understanding of the multiple relationships among whole numbers by comparing, ordering, estimating, composing, decomposing, and grouping number, including beginning understanding of place value; (pp. 108–109)

Arithmetical skills of real importance a generation ago have become less so because of recent technological advances. Looking at a mathematics textbook from several decades ago, you are struck by the emphasis on complex, mental computation. Before the widespread availability of calculators, the ability to "do figures" in one's head was an important business skill. The ability to perform accurate and speedy mental computations was emphasized in school because it was useful in real life. As we begin the twenty-first century, however, mental computation is becoming less and less important. Readily available low-cost calculators can quickly and accurately perform computations formerly done mentally or with a pencil. This does *not* mean that children no longer need to develop skill in mental computation or that they no longer need to know basic facts. Take a minute to think about which of the following mathematical tasks you have performed over the last two weeks. Then note which you performed using paper and pencil, which required electronic technology, and which you did mentally.

In addition, indicate if a precise answer was necessary or if estimating was sufficient.

■ Determine the unit price of an item in the grocery store.
■ Balance your checkbook.
■ Determine the length of a trip.
■ Use a table to determine the cost of an item or service.
■ Read a timetable.
■ Determine monthly loan payments on a large purchase.
■ Perform multi-digit calculations.
■ Arrange objects or create objects for an artistic composition.
■ Use mathematics in the context of a sport or physical activity.
■ Determine how many calories or grams of fat were in a food item.

If you are like many students I have taught, you were probably surprised by the large number of mathematical tasks you performed mentally and the small number of tasks that required a precise answer using a pencil or calculator. Because the ability to perform mental estimation has become increasingly important, helping children develop number sense has become critical.

Number sense can be defined as a feel for numbers, strong estimation skills, a sense of competence and confidence when working with numbers, and the development of individual, creative strategies to perform computations. A first-grade student who says that "Six plus seven must be more than ten, since six plus four is ten and seven is more than four" has good number sense, while a second-grader who arrives at the answer in the margin and is untroubled by the fact that it does not have good number sense.

$$\begin{array}{r} 45 \\ + 7 \\ \hline 412 \end{array}$$

A concept that is important for children to understand when they are beginning to develop number sense is the concept of *one-to-one correspondence*. This means that, when objects are being enumerated, for every object there is a numeral and for every numeral there is an object. Included in this concept is the idea that each object is counted once and only once, that all objects are counted and none are skipped over, and that the last numeral spoken serves two functions. The last numeral refers both to the final object in the set, and also to the total number of objects in the set. Children who understand one-to-one correspondence are able to count in a *rational* manner as opposed to a *rote* manner. Rational counting means that children can accurately enumerate a set of objects, while rote counting may produce any of several errors: objects may be left out, objects may be double-counted, or a child may make errors in the sequence of numerals that are spoken.

Activities 2.2 and 2.3 can help to develop the concept of one-to-one correspondence.

Performance-Based Assessment: One-to-One Correspondence

At snack time, ask a child to set out enough cups and napkins for the children at each table. Note if the child simply puts a cup and napkin in front of each chair, regardless of the number of children present that day, or if the child counts up the number of children, parcels out that number of cups and napkins, and then distributes them. While both actions indicate an

Activity 2.2

Anno's Counting Book

Lesson: Individual

This counting book by Mitsumasa Anno (1975) is unusual in several respects. It devotes a two-page spread to a beautifully detailed illustration of each of the numbers from 0 through 12 (while most counting books only deal with the numbers from 1 to 10). The numbers are connected to the months of the year; for example, the page for the numeral 5 shows a springtime scene in a country village that could be expected to be seen in the month of May. In the illustration, there are five buildings, five evergreen trees, five vehicles, five people; even the clock in the tower reads 5 o'clock. As the book moves through the counting numbers and the months of the year, there are illustrations of stacked blocks along the side of the page to correspond to the number being represented. The page for twelve,

for example, is a winter scene, and has a stack of 10 blocks and two additional blocks shown on the side of the page.

This book contains no words, and thus encourages children to verbalize what they see in the illustrations. After reading the book to the class, encourage the children to draw their own illustration for a favorite number and then share it with the class.

Journal Reflection

Discuss your view of the teacher's role in presenting this book to a class. Should the teacher lead a discussion, ask focused questions, point out number representations, facilitate children's own discoveries, move to the sidelines and allow free exploration, or something else?

Activity 2.3

Anno's Counting House

Lesson: Whole Group
In this counting book by Anno (1981), ten boys and girls move, one at a time, from a house on the lefthand side of each double page to a house on the righthand side. If the children in the class are given ten counters, they can keep track of the movement of the boys and girls in the book by sliding the counters, one at a time, across their desk. As an extension of this activity, older children can symbolize the movement of the children by writing number sentences such as:

$$10 + 0 = 10$$
$$9 + 1 = 10$$
$$8 + 2 = 10, \text{ etc.}$$

A useful attribute of Anno's books is that he often includes notes to adults where he explains the mathematical concepts implicit in the book and suggests how the reader might help children better understand them.

Journal Reflection
Anno recommends that, after the book is read to children front to back, it then be read back to front. What do you think about this?

---

understanding of one-to-one correspondence, the second method is more sophisticated. If the child shows no understanding of one-to-one correspondence and does not lay out enough items or lays out too many, resist the urge to interfere. At snack time, the children lacking cups or napkins will make that known, or alternately children may comment that there are too many supplies. Allow the child who set the table to solve the problem.

Observing, Describing, Classifying

Three thinking skills that are important to children's mathematical development are the skills of observing, describing, and classifying. These skills are also critical to children's language development and to their development of scientific understandings. Thus they deserve a great deal of attention. A commonly available manipulative that can be utilized to help children develop these skills is a set of attribute pieces (Figure 2.8). *Attribute pieces* are a set of plastic or wooden blocks whose faces are in the shapes of triangles, squares, rectangles, and circles. These pieces vary in color (usually red, blue, green and yellow) in size (large and small) and in thickness (thick and thin). You can see that there are four different characteristics, or attributes, that can be used to describe each piece: color, size, shape, and thickness. Sorting is one of the simplest ways a child can use attribute pieces. Activity 2.4 deals with sorting, Activity 2.5 encourages accurate description, and Activity 2.6 presents categorizing.

Uses of Number

As you structure your teaching to help children develop one-to-one correspondence, the ability to count rationally, and the ability to observe, describe, and classify, it is also helpful to have children use numbers in each of the three ways

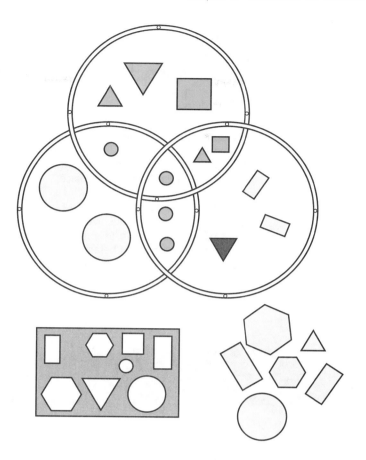

Figure 2.8

that adults use numbers; in the cardinal, ordinal, and nominal sense. When numbers are used in the *cardinal* sense, they are used to enumerate groups of objects. Several activities have already been suggested for using counting books to help children understand the cardinality of numbers. In addition, you may wish to use Activity 2.7 to make number boxes for your classroom.

Activity 2.4

Sorting

Lesson: Individual

Children are given a set of attribute pieces plus several sheets of paper or mats of contrasting color. They are asked to put the pieces that belong together on the paper or mats. Typically, young children will initially sort the pieces by color. If a child successfully sorts the pieces based on one attribute, invite the child to sort in a different way. A more advanced basis for sorting is one that utilizes two or more attributes; for example, a child might place all of the red triangles on one mat, all of the blue squares on another, and all of the yellow circles on a third.

Journal Reflection

What strategies might you use to help a child who does not appear to sort from any consistent or recognizable basis?

Activity 2.5

Describing

Lesson: Whole Group

The teacher or a student chooses one attribute piece and hides it. The class is invited to ask yes/no questions in order to identify the hidden piece. For example, children might ask "Is the piece red?" "Is the piece a square?" "Is the piece thick?" When the activity has been repeated many times over several days, you might want to tally the number of questions needed before a piece is successfully identified. Challenge the students to identify the piece using the fewest number of questions possible. This activity encourages the development of listening and memory skills, as the children try to remember what previous answers have already revealed about the piece.

Journal Reflection

What materials, other than attribute pieces, could be used for this activity? What do you see as the advantages and disadvantages of each material?

Activity 2.6

Classifying

Lesson: Whole Group

Using large loops of yarn, place attribute pieces in the loops according to some predetermined basis. For example, one loop might look like Figure 2.9. Invite a child to chose an attribute piece from the box and decide to place it either inside or outside the loop. When several children have succeeded at this task, encourage the children to articulate the rule for classification. In Figure 2.9, the rule would be that straight-sided red pieces belong in the loop.

This activity can be simplified by labeling the loop with cards reading RED and STRAIGHT SIDES before the children

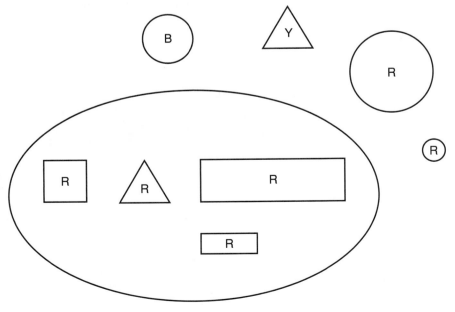

Figure 2.9

(continued)

Activity 2.6 (continued)

Classifying

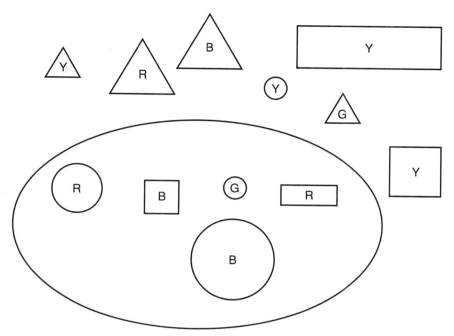

Figure 2.10

attempt to place their piece. It can also be extended and made more difficult by using negative classifications. For example, how would you describe the rule governing the placement of the pieces of Figure 2.10?

Journal Reflection

Did you identify the classification rule as NOT YELLOW and NOT TRIANGLE? Are any other descriptions justifiable?

Activity 2.7

Number Boxes

Lesson: Whole Group

In a sturdy shoe box that has been covered with plain paper, place between 0 and 20 small, visually appealing objects. You may wish to use polished rocks, brightly colored plastic milk caps, or small animal figures. The numeral and the number word that corresponds to the number of objects in the box are carefully written on both the outside and the inside of the box top. When children work through learning centers, a selection of these boxes could be available at a table.

Children could be encouraged to chose a box and practice counting the objects contained within it. If paper and pencils are made available, the children can also practice reproducing the numerical symbol for the number of objects in the box.

Journal Reflection

Why is it important to have the numeral written on the box top and to have paper and pencil available to the child?

Performance-Based Assessment: The Cardinal Use of Number

Display approximately thirty identical blocks on the table. Invite the child to show you 5 blocks, then 12 blocks, then 9 blocks, then 20. Typically, kindergartners should be able to count accurately up to 10 blocks, while first-graders should be able to identify a group of up to 20. Observe if the child uses any grouping strategies, which indicates a developing number sense. For example, are groups of five or pairs of blocks formed by the child?

If this task appears to be too simple for the child, have the child use the blocks to act out a simple addition or subtraction problem. For example, ask the child to keep 6 blocks and give 5 blocks to you. Now ask how many blocks you both have together.

When numbers are used in the *ordinal* sense, they indicate placement in a series. Activity 2.8, developed by Nancy McCormick Rambusch, gives children the opportunity to practice using numbers in both the cardinal and ordinal sense.

Numbers are used in the *nominal* sense when they name someone or something. For example, a football player whose jersey bears the numeral 72 is simply named by that numeral. The 72 does not identify his order on the team, or his age or his weight or his height. An example that may have more meaning to young children is a toy robot referred to as XL5249, or a film robot named R2D2. In each of these cases, the numerals in the names do not have any significance other than the fact that they name the robot.

Activity 2.8

Put and Take

Lesson: Pairs

You will need between 5 and 10 identical plastic bowls or baskets and approximately fifty monochromatic plastic counters. The activity consists in having two children follow directions on a series of index cards. The directions should be something like this:

> Put 3 in the 1st.
> Put 4 in the 5th.
> Put 2 in the 2nd.
> Take 2 from the 1st.
> Take 1 from the 2nd.

The cards should be constructed so that, at the end of the series of 20 to 30 cards, no counters are left in any of the bowls. This is called the "control of error," and is a way for the children to verify that they have played the game correctly.

It is important that the cards be used in order, or a child may be put in the position of having to take counters from an empty bowl. This can be managed by threading a metal ring through the top corner of the cards, so their order is invariant. It is equally important that the children agree between themselves as to which bowl will be considered the "first."

Journal Reflection

Why do you think that the directions indicate that the bowls and the plastic counters all be the same color?

4
8
12
16
20
24
28
32 . . .

In addition to using manipulatives to develop number sense, children can also use calculators to appreciate the patterns and regularities of our number system. Many teachers have found it valuable to give young children markers, calculators, and rolls of adding-machine tape to explore number patterns. The children are encouraged to begin skip counting by any number, and to record the repeated displays of the calculator on the roll of adding machine tape held sideways. The result, a lengthy roll of recorded numbers like those in the margin can be used to focus a class discussion about patterns in our number system. Children become excited about the never-ending series of numbers, and feel grown-up when writing down such big numbers. Many children continue with this activity over a period of weeks, taking their number series into the thousands. Activity 2.9 can be used to introduce children to the CONSTANT feature of a calculator.

The Hindu-Arabic Number System

One of the ways that students can develop number sense is by understanding the nature of our Hindu-Arabic number system. It is generally believed that the Hindus invented the numeration system we use today and that the Arabs introduced it into Europe. Unlike the Egyptian and Roman systems, the values in the Hindu-Arabic system are not a function of the individual symbol alone, but of the symbol in conjunction with its place. For example, in the Roman system, three is represented by III, thirty by XXX, and three

Activity 2.9

The Constant Feature of the Calculator

Lesson: Whole Group

Most calculators have a feature that allows for the repeated addition or subtraction of a certain number. For example, the following question can be posed to children:

- If I begin skip counting by 3, will I eventually say the number 51?

The following calculator keystroke sequence will allow the children to answer that question.

AC + 3 = = = = = = = . . .

If the calculator has a CONSTANT key, usually marked with the letters CONS or K, the following keystroke sequence is used:

+3 CONS 0 CONS CONS CONS CONS CONS. . . .

Pressing the "0" key after +3 CONS makes the calculator begin counting at 0. It is possible to have the calculator begin counting at any number. And if the keystroke sequence began with a − instead of a +, the calculator would have repeatedly subtracted instead.

Journal Reflection

Do you think it is desirable for children to have the calculator display large numbers such as 3,299 in the above activity? Explain your reasoning.

hundred by CCC. In each instance, the value is determined by totaling the values of the three symbols.

In the Hindu-Arabic system, three is represented by 3, thirty by 30, and three hundred by 300; The same symbol is used in each case, but its *placement* is different. Depending on where the 3 is placed, it can have a value of 3 ones, 3 tens, 3 hundreds, and so on. A system where the value of a digit is determined by its place is said to be a place-value system. Place-value numeration systems are based on a grouping principle. This principle allows for greater efficiency when dealing with large quantities of items. Without symbols standing for groups of items, a representation of the quantity two thousand, seven hundred nine could require two thousand, seven hundred nine symbols!

Children sometimes ask why our numeration system bases its grouping on ten. Although we cannot be sure, it is most likely because human beings have ten fingers. When early humans were enumerating objects, they probably counted on their fingers. When they reached ten, they ran out of fingers, so some other object was used to represent the ten that had already been counted. Activity 2.10 allows children to simulate the process that early humans may have experienced when counting.

One of the critical aspects of our numeration system is that the grouping is reversible. In other words, after a group of ten is formed, it can once again be broken down into ten individual ones. An understanding of this reversibility is important if children are to understand the concepts of adding and subtracting with regrouping, topics that are typically introduced in second or third grade. Unfortunately, teachers cannot be

---

Activity 2.10

Counting

Lesson: Individual

Children are invited to scoop from a bowl as many dried beans as can be held in one hand. Returning to their desks, they are to count out ten of them and then make a slash mark. This process is continued until it is no longer possible to make a group of ten. Loose beans are then notated by small circles. Children exchange papers with their partners and invite the partner to interpret their markings. For example, a paper that looks like Figure 2.11 would represent 24 beans.

Figure 2.11

Journal Reflection

Would you ever play this game by having the children make a slash mark for every group of five beans? Why or why not?

sure that all of their second- or third-graders understand this concept. If you can, actually do this experiment with children who are 6, 7, or 8 years of age. Having this first-hand experience is more valuable than simply reading about it.

Show the child a drawing of some children, say, three boys and five girls. Ask the child to count the number of boys, the number of girls, and the number of children in all. It is reasonable to expect that most children of this age would be able to perform these tasks accurately. Then ask the child "Are there more girls or more boys?" Again, it would be reasonable to expect an accurate answer. But when you ask "Are there more girls or more children?" a child who has not yet achieved reversibility will respond that there are more girls. When asked "More girls than what?" the child will say "More girls than boys." Even if the question is repeated and even if you stress that you want to know if there are more girls or more children, a child who cannot reverse will continue to say that there are more girls than boys, as opposed to more children than girls.

Piaget and other theorists believe that children who have not yet achieved reversibility cannot *simultaneously* keep in mind both the logical class (children) and the sets that compose the logical class (boys and girls). Most children do achieve reversibility by age 7 or 8, but by that time they may have already been asked to perform many formal tasks in school involving the symbolic regrouping of ones into tens and tens back into ones.

The danger in having children symbolically manipulate tens and ones before they truly understand the concept of regrouping is that they may begin to believe that mathematics does not make sense. They find themselves in a situation where what they think and understand differs from what the teacher thinks and understands. Succumbing to a higher authority, the child mentally shrugs and imitates what the teacher thinks, whether or not it makes sense. When children stop thinking of mathematics as a way of making sense of things, they stop learning mathematics.

A manipulative that can help children develop an understanding of the place-value nature of our number system is a set of *base-10 blocks,* or *powers-of-ten blocks.* These blocks are modeled on the "golden bead" materials invented by Maria Montessori, an idea that was later adapted by Zoltan Dienes in his "Dienes blocks." Base-10 blocks are a *proportional* place-value model (Figure 2.12) because each piece is built in a proportional size. Notice that the ten "long" is ten times the size of the unit block, and the hundred "flat" is ten times the size of the long, and the thousands "cube" is ten times the size of the flat.

Activity 2.11, which uses base-10 blocks, can help children develop an understanding of the concept of regrouping; the activity also illustrates the concept of reversibility.

Activity 2.12, chip trading, which also illustrates the nature of our Hindu-Arabic system of numeration, makes use of a *non-proportional*

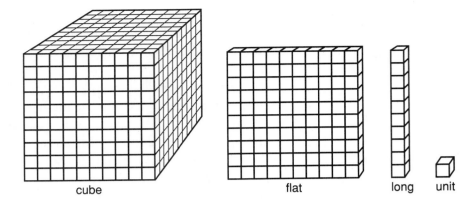

Figure 2.12

Activity 2.11

Building a Flat

Lesson: Pairs

Distribute a die or a number cube and one flat, ten longs, and 20 units to each pair of children. Taking turns, each child tosses the number cube and places that many units on top of the flat. Play continues, with ten units being exchanged for one long whenever possible. When the entire flat is filled with ten longs, the activity is played in reverse. This time, when the number cube is tossed, the child removes that number of units. This will require repeated exchanges of one long for ten units.

When the children have had considerable experience with this concrete activity, it can be extended by having them symbolically record the process. For example, if there were two longs and three units laid out on the flat (Figure 2.13) and the child tossed a 4, the child would record 23 + 4 = 27.

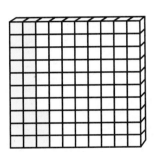

Figure 2.13

This symbolic recording of the process mirrors the procedure followed for addition and subtraction with regrouping, which will be dealt with at greater length in Chapter 3.

Journal Reflection

Why is it important that children also play this game in reverse?

Red	White	Blue

Figure 2.14

place-value model. Three different colored chips—perhaps red, white, and blue—are needed, along with a spinner or a number cube showing the numbers 1, 2, and 3. An activity board like that of Figure 2.14 is also used. This activity is valuable for children, because it gives them practice in trading for equivalences. This concept of equivalence is one of the "big ideas" in elementary school mathematics. As they move through elementary school, children will learn that 10 ones are equivalent to 1 ten, that

Activity 2.12
Chip Trading

Lesson: Pairs

Each pair of children will need six blue, six white, and three red chips, plus the game board and a number cube or spinner. Play begins by tossing the cube or spinning the spinner. The number appearing on the spinner or number cube represents the number of blue chips that can be placed on the board. Whenever three blue chips accumulate, they must be traded in for one white chip. Likewise, when three white chips accumulate, they must be traded in for one red chip. Students work in pairs, alternating turns, until three red chips are accumulated.

Just as Building a Flat can be played in reverse, so also can Chip Trading. Once three reds have been accumulated, the number tossed or spun represents the number of blue chips to be taken away. You can see that this version of the activity will require a red chip to be traded for three whites, and a white chip to be traded for three blues, before any blue chips can be taken away.

Journal Reflection

Describe some similarities and some differences between this activity and Activity 2.11. Do you see one of the activities as being more valuable than the other? Explain.

10 centimeters are equivalent to 1 decimeter, that 30 minutes are equivalent to ½ hour, that ⅔ is equivalent to %, that 50% is equivalent to 0.5 which is equivalent to ½, and so on. Chip trading also illustrates the structure of our number system.

The "magic number" that determines when a trade is necessary is arbitrary and can be changed according to the goal of the activity. Many teachers like to begin playing the activity in base-3, since most children can look at up to three objects and know how many there are without actually touching and counting them. This ability, called *subitizing*, helps the activity move along quickly. However, occasionally playing the activity in base-5 or base-6 is useful, since the point of this activity is to give children practice in trading for equivalences. It is important for children to realize that the steps followed in chip trading are the same regardless of what number is the magic number, or, in adult language, regardless of what base defines the activity. The accompanying "Strength in Numbers" activity shows some of the characteristics of our Hindu-Arabic number system that are implicit in chip trading.

A non-proportioned place-value model that has been in use for hundreds of years is the Chinese abacus. The following lesson plan introduces second- or third-graders to the place-value concepts implicit in an abacus.

(text continues on p. 61)

Strength in Numbers

Chip Trading in Other Bases

Cooperative Group Model: Jigsaw

Each group member plays Chip Trading individually in one of four bases: base 3, base 4, base 5, and base 10. Each player will need a different chance device, depending upon the base: for base 3, a spinner or number cube with the numerals 1, 2, and 3 is needed; for base 4, the spinner or number cube should show the numerals 1, 2, 3, and 4; for base 5, the spinner and number cube should show 1 through 5; for base 10, 1 through 10.

After everyone has had the opportunity to play several games of Chip Trading, each member is to determine the value of red chips and white chips in terms of the number of blue chips necessary to obtain them. Since one blue can be obtained by tossing a 1 regardless of the base in which the trading takes place, the value of blue will always be 1. Arrange the data in the following chart:

Base	Red	White	Blue
3			
4			
5			
10			

What patterns do you see? Can you represent the value of each color in terms of x raised to some power where x is the base defining the trade? Do you see how this information relates to base-10 blocks? Discuss these questions with your group members before continuing.

You probably noticed that the completed chart could have been expressed in the following way using exponents:

Base	Red	White	Blue
3	3^2	3^1	3^0
4	4^2	4^1	4^0
5	5^2	5^1	5^0
10	10^2	10^1	10^0

This may suggest to you that the base-10 blocks pictured in Figure 2.6 can be used to represent each of the entries for base-10. In base-10 blocks, the unit block represents 10^0, which has a value of 1. The long block represents 10^1, which has a value of 10. The flat block represents 10^2, which has a value of 100. These blocks are also commercially available in other bases, as is illustrated in Figure 2.15.

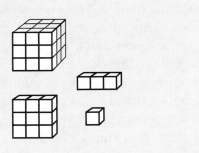

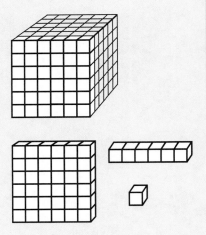

Figure 2.15

Grade 2–3   **Concept** Number and Numeration

Topic Representing Numerals on the Abacus

Student Objectives After completing this lesson, students should be able to

• Represent numerals up to 3 digits on the abacus

• Build their own abacus

Materials abacus, index cards, string, beads, markers

Motivation Share the following information with the children.

For about 800 years, Chinese people have used an abacus to help them count, add, subtract, multiply and divide. The Chinese call the abacus a *suan pan*, which means "counting board." Here is an example of a Chinese abacus. (Teacher should display abacus.) The beads on the bottom part of the abacus, called the Earth beads, stand for 1. The beads on the top part of the abacus, called the Heaven beads, stand for 5. Watch while I count to ten on the abacus. (Figure 2.16).

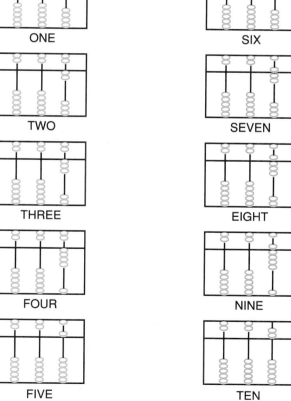

Figure 2.16

(continued)

Lesson Plan (continued)

There are other ways to show 10 on the abacus. Can anyone figure it out? (10 can be shown with 1 Heaven bead and 5 Earth beads in the ones column; 2 Heaven beads in the ones column, each representing 5; or 1 Earth bead in the tens column, representing 1 ten (Figure 2.17).

Figure 2.17

Procedure

1. Distribute a sheet like Figure 2.18 to students. Encourage them to supply the Hindu-Arabic numeral for the first four abacus displays.

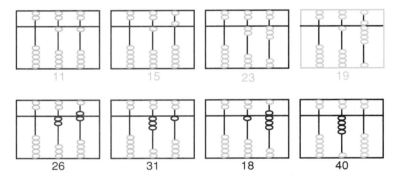

11   15   23   19

26   31   18   40

Figure 2.18

Invite them to sketch in the appropriate beads for the next four abacus displays. Solutions are included here. 2. Offer instructions for the children to create their own abacus (Figure 2. 19). Begin by stringing

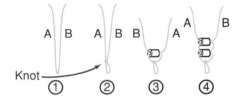

Figure 2.19

7 beads on each of four strings. On each of these strings, 2 beads will be the Heaven beads and 5 beads will be the Earth beads. The Heaven beads should be a different color than the Earth beads. Follow the illustrated steps to string the beads. Use a hole punch to punch four holes opposite one another along each of the long sides of an index card. Insert the ends of the strings into these holes and secure on the back with tape. Each child can now use a personal abacus to represent

(continued)

Lesson Plan (continued)

numbers. 3. Challenge the children to use the abacus to add the following pairs of numbers:

	12	23	26	17
	+12	+14	+5	+26

(The process for finding these sums on the abacus is deliberately left to the reader.)

Assessment Invite the children to represent four 3-digit numbers of their own choosing on their abacus, and then to sketch this representation on a blank abacus pattern. Have the children write the corresponding Hindu-Arabic numeral under each abacus pattern.

Reference Zaslavsky, Claudia. *Multicultural Math.* New York, Scholastic Professional Books. 1994, pp. 31–34.

Journal Entry After teaching this lesson, note your comments and suggestions for the future.

Number and Operation for Grades 3–5

In *Principles and Standards,* the first Standard is devoted to number and operation. Under this heading, for grades 3–5, it is recommended that

> Mathematics instructional programs should foster the development of number and operation sense so that all students understand number, ways of representing numbers, relationships among numbers, and number systems. . . . (p. 155)

To help students become facile with representing numbers, some teachers begin each math class with a warm-up exercise like that of Activity 2.13.

Part of learning to appreciate mathematics is developing a sense of playfulness with numbers. While students are often playful with language, especially when writing poetry, and while they are often playful with form

Activity 2.13

Today Is . . .

Lesson: Whole Group

Depending on the day of the month, the teacher might begin math class by announcing "Today is September 18th. In how many different ways can you represent the number 18?" Depending on the age and level of experience of the students, the responses can vary from "6 × 3" to "1 ten and 8 ones" to "100 − 82" to "Two more than the square of four." To add to the challenge, teachers may choose to say

"Today is the 125th day of school. In how many ways can you represent the number 125?"

Journal Reflection

There are several ways to represent numbers. These include pictorial, numerical, and verbal descriptions. How would you encourage students to make use of several of these different ways as they respond to the above questions?

Activity 2.14

Calendar Math

Lesson: Individual

Distribute a blank 7 × 5 grid to students. Using a current calendar, have the students find their birth month and fill in the numbers of the days, as shown in Figure 2.20. Invite the students to trace a 3 × 3 square around any nine numbers on their grid, provided that no small squares are blank. Pose the following questions to students (the reader is invited to answer these questions, too!):

- What is the sum of the three numbers in the center row?
- What is the sum of the three numbers in the center column?
- Do your answers surprise you? Why or why not?
- Make a prediction about the sum of the three numbers in each diagonal. Did your prediction hold true? Can you explain the relationship among the four trios of numbers that you have worked with so far?
- What do you think will happen if you trace a 4 × 4 square? What relationships do you predict will exist? Can you find any relationships in the 4 × 4 grid that don't exist in the 3 × 3 grid, and vice versa?
- How would your answers vary as you change the location of the traced squares?
- How do these relationships translate to a 10 × 10 grid of the first 100 numbers?
- What do you think would happen if the grids were filled in with consecutive even numbers instead of the counting numbers? How about consecutive odd numbers?
- What additional questions can you pose for your classmates?

Journal Reflection

In language arts, students are encouraged to make predictions about the plot or characters in a book they are reading, as a way of helping them become involved in the unfolding of the story. What do you think is the purpose of having students make predictions in mathematics?

Sun	Mon	Tues	Wed	Thurs	Fri	Sat
		1	2	3	4	5
6	7	8	9	10	11	12
13	14	15	16	17	18	19
20	21	22	23	24	25	26
27	28	29	30			

Figure 2.20

and color and design in art class, they are not often playful with numbers. Activity 2.14 encourage students to experiment and play with numbers, and to use that experience to offer conjectures about numbers and their relationships to one another.

As students expand their understanding of our number system, they need to become aware of the attributes of numbers. A nonthreatening way to have students develop their understanding of attributes in general is to revisit attribute pieces (see earlier Activities 2.4, 2.5, and 2.6). At the middle elementary level, students will engage in a more sophisticated analysis of pieces that belong and pieces that don't. This experience will help them develop skills of logical reasoning. Activity 2.15 is designed to help students reason about shared characteristics.

Performance-Based Assessment Classification

Display four or five empty cereal boxes. Ask the child to tell you which one doesn't belong in the group, and why. Choose boxes that allow the question to be answered in several ways. For example, perhaps one box pictures fruit with the cereal, perhaps one cereal is a hot cereal, or perhaps one shows a cartoon character on the front of the box. If the child is able to identify one box as "not belonging, " ask if there is another box that might not belong, and why. Continue probing until the child is unable to identify any other discrepant box. For children who are unable to identify any box as not belonging, give them an easier, narrower task, such as choosing from four red blocks and one blue block. As they become successful at such gross classifications, offer them tasks requiring more refined distinctions.

Activity 2.15
Shared Attributes

Lesson: Individual

In this activity, students are presented with two groups of attribute pieces that share an attribute. The yarn loops are arranged in such a way as to overlap the shared pieces (Figure 2.21).

Students are to identify the attributes that define each loop, and then name the common characteristic shared by the pieces that belong to both groups. In Figure 2.21,

the left loop encloses green pieces, while the right loop encloses circular shapes. Pieces that are both green and circular belong in the overlapping section.

Journal Reflection

Offer a numerical example of the above concept, such as a loop containing multiples of 7, and an overlapping loop containing even numbers. Explain how your numerical example is related to this activity.

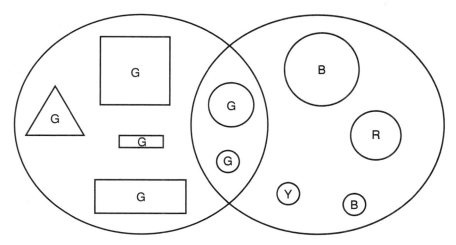

Figure 2.21

The Strength in Numbers activity with attribute blocks is designed to give you some firsthand experience with attribute pieces and to help you develop skill in deductive logic.

Strength in Numbers

Attribute Blocks

Groups of Two

Working with a partner, arrange the attribute pieces side by side in such a way that they form a "one-difference train." A one-difference train is composed of attribute pieces that differ from adjacent pieces by only one attribute. For example, if the first piece in the train is a large, blue, thick square, the second piece could be a small, blue, thick square, but it could not be a small, red, thick square. If it were small, red, thick, and a square, it would differ from the first piece in more than one way, and would not belong in a one-difference train, but a two-difference train.

Try to use all of your pieces in your train. To challenge yourself, try to make the train form a complete loop, like a wagon train. This will necessitate the final piece differing from the first piece by only one attribute. After you have experienced building a one-difference train, try a two-difference, a three-difference, and a four-difference train. After completing this activity, reflect on the logic you used. Was this activity more difficult than you expected? When you were building the three-difference train, how did you chose each subsequent piece? Did you think that it had to be different in three ways, or did you think that it had to be the same in *only one* way? Which of the trains was the easiest to build? Why?

Number and Operation for Grades 6–8

The NCTM *Principles and Standards* state that, in grades 6–8, all students should

- Develop an understanding of large numbers, including the use of benchmarks to comprehend their magnitude;

- Use number-theory concepts (e.g., factors, multiples, prime factorization, relatively prime numbers) to solve problems . . .

- Develop and refine strategies for estimating . . . . . use estimations as a means to check the reasonableness of results (pp. 216–17).

As students enter the upper elementary grades, their interest increases in the things around them. They become more interested in current events, more interested in organized sports events, and more interested in their own place in the larger world. This provides the teacher with a valuable opportunity to connect mathematics to things that interest students in grades 6 through 8. In these grades, it is appropriate to expand the study of the Hindu-Arabic number system to larger numbers. For example, depending on the season, each child can keep a record of the gate attendance of their favorite football, basketball, hockey, or baseball team. These realistic numbers require students to become familiar with hundred-thousands and millions. Figure 2.22 shows the names of the place values for larger numbers. The following lesson plan addresses the topic of place value for grades 6, 7, and 8.

Name	Symbol	Value
One thousand	1,000	One thousand ones
One million	1,000,000	One thousand thousands
One billion	1,000,000,000	One thousand millions
One trillion	1,000,000,000,000	One thousand billions
One quadrillion	1,000,000,000,000,000	One thousand trillions
One quintillion	1,000,000,000,000,000,000	One thousand quadrillions

Figure 2.22

Lesson Plan

Grades 6, 7, 8   **Concept** Place Value

Topic The role of the grouping in a place-value system of numeration.

Student Objectives After completing this lesson, the students should be able to. . .

- imagine and articulate different ways of grouping objects that enable enumeration of those objects.
- write a children's book that communicates this idea.

Materials a copy of *The King's Commissioners* by Aileen Friedman (1994), counters, markers and paper appropriate for the creation of a children's book.

Motivation Read *The King's Commissioners* to the class. This book tells the story of a king who has many commissioners in his kingdom. When he asks two assistants to count how many commissioners he has in all, they each use a different grouping principle. One assistant counts 23 groups of two and 1 more; the other counts 9 groups of five and 2 more. The king doesn't understand how to interpret these enumerations, so his daughter helps him. She has all of the commissioners line up in rows of ten. This results in 4 rows of ten with 7 more. She then explains how this arrangement allows for the simple counting up of 10, 20, 30, 40, and 7 more makes 47. She also shows how 23 groups of two and 1 more, and 9 groups of five and 2 more, also result in a total count of 47.

Explain to the students that this book is written for a younger audience. Their task is not simply to listen and enjoy the story, but to analyze how the author explains concepts such as place value and the grouping principle in a way that is understandable.

Procedure

1. Invite the students to discuss how the author and illustrator communicate the concept of enumerating the commissioners by the creation of equal groups. Suggest that the students pay careful attention to the way the illustrations are used to show tallies of equal groups. Ask students to suggest other ways the commissioners could have been grouped, and to discuss advantages and disadvantages of each. 2. Read to the students the three pages of notes "For Parents,

(continued)

Teachers, and Other Adults" that appear at the end of the book. Ask them to explain the connection between the arrangement of commissioners in rows of ten and the way that the number forty-seven is written in Hindu-Arabic numerals. 3. Ask the students to hypothesize what our system of numeration would be like if humans had four fingers on each hand. Ask them to predict how the commissioners would then be grouped. 4. Invite each group of four students to take 47 counters back to their desks, and to arrange them in rows of eight. Explain how the 5 groups of eight with 7 left over corresponds to the way in which forty-seven is written in base-8 (57_8). Suggest that each group write the base-8 numerals from 1_8 to 57_8 to show how the commissioners might be counted if the people in the kingdom had eight fingers. 5. Invite each group to write their own version of their story. After the students have had the opportunity to work through the writing process on their stories, have the students bind and illustrate the stories. It would be enjoyable for the students to visit a second-grade class and share their books.

Assessment of Student Learning The cogency and lucidity of the books produced by the students will give you a good indication of their understanding of place value. You might also wish to have students arrange the counters in groups of seven and write the numerals from 1_7 to 65_7.

References *Math by all Means: Place Value* by Marilyn Burns.

Journal Entry In this section, you might comment that using stacks of Unifix cubes to form the groups of 7 or 8 made the concept of base clearer to the students. You might also record some organizational suggestions for ways in which the book writing could be facilitated.

It is important for students to have some understanding of the magnitude of a million. This can be accomplished by connecting units to thousands and then transferring this connection to thousands and millions. For example, pose the following problem to the students:

- "If I put $1.00 in this box every single day, how many years would it take me to save $1000.00?"

Begin by having the students estimate that it would take approximately three years to save this amount, since it would be possible to save more than $300.00 per year. The following keystroke sequence (which assumes an integer-divide key) allows for an accurate answer:

$$\text{AC } 1000 \text{ INT} \div 365 = 2 \ 270$$
$$\text{Q} \qquad \text{R}$$

This solution is interpreted as 2 years and 270 days. Invite the students to represent this answer in several different ways, such as approximately 2 years and 9 months, or 2¾₂ years.

If the calculator lacks an integer-divide key, the following keystroke sequence can be used to obtain a quotient and a remainder:

$$\text{AC } 1000 \div 365 = -2 = \times 365 = 270$$

Now pose the following question:

- "If I put \$1000.00 in my box every single day, how long would it take me to save \$1,000,000.00?"

Again, ask the students to estimate this answer. Most students do not immediately see the connection between the two questions, and underestimate the time needed to save \$1,000,000.00. This is likely because they underestimate the magnitude of \$1,000,000.00. After the students have had sufficient time to solve the problem, point out to them that just as it takes one thousand ones to make one thousand, it also take one thousand thousands to make one million. Ask the students to predict how long it would take to save one billion dollars, if one million dollars were saved every day.

Prime and Composite Numbers

In the middle grades, it is appropriate to distinguish between two sets of positive integers—the set of prime numbers and the set of composite numbers. The next Strength in Numbers activity will help you understand the difference between these two classifications. Further investigations of prime and composite numbers will appear in Chapters 9 and 10, which deal with Patterns and Relations.

Estimation

Recall the earlier discussion about ways people use mathematics in their daily lives. It became clear that in many real-life contexts an estimated answer is sufficient. It is important that students develop strong estimation skills, especially since they will likely be using calculators to perform multidigit computations. Rather than relying completely on the calculator answer, students should be encouraged to estimate the answer first. This guards against gross errors caused by inaccurate keystroke entries.

Students should be encouraged to estimate in many contexts. Later chapters that deal with operations on numbers offer specific estimation strategies. But before that, students can experience estimating both continuous and discrete quantities. A continuous quantity is measured, while discrete quantities are counted. For example, while the volume of a glass of water is measured, a dozen glasses are counted. While the weight of a book is determined by placing it on a scale, the number of pages in the book is determined by counting them. Students need experiences with both continuous and discrete contexts because that reflects their real world. Activity 2.16 gives students the opportunity to estimate continuous quantities. Activity 2.17 provides students with the opportunity to estimate discrete quantities. Most real-life estimation is based on experience and number sense. It is important

Strength in Numbers

Rectangular Arrays for Prime and Composite Numbers

Cooperative Group Model (Pairs): Think-Pair-Share

Obtain approximately twenty-five color tiles for each person. These tiles are small plastic squares, 1 inch on each side. One person is assigned the numbers from 1 to 12 and the other is assigned the numbers from 12 to 24. Each person is to determine how many different rectangular arrangements are possible with the given number of tiles. For example, with four tiles, it is possible to make the arrangements show in Figure 2.23.

Figure 2.23

Think: Each partner records the dimensions of the rectangles that can be made with each number of tiles. Is it possible to predict the dimensions and the number of rectangles that can be made with 25 to 35 tiles?

Pair: With your partner, arrive at some generalizations about this activity. Do you see that you have determined the factors of each number from 1 to 24? Look closely at the rectangles that could be made with 2, 3, 5, 7, 11, 13, 17, 19, and 23 tiles. In each of these cases, only two rectangles could be formed. For example, with eleven tiles, only a 1 × 11 rectangle and an 11 × 1 rectangle could be formed. This is another way of saying that these numbers, 2, 3, 5, 7, 11, 13, 17, 19, and 23 have two distinct factors, themselves and 1. Numbers having this characteristic are called **prime numbers.**

Students often think that 1 is a prime number. But how many rectangles could be formed with one tile? Since 1 does not have two distinct factors, but has only one factor, itself, it is not considered to be a prime number. In fact, one is considered to be neither prime nor composite.

Share: Discuss your findings with another pair of students, or with the whole class. Include in your discussion different ways that elementary school students can investigate the difference between prime and composite numbers.

Activity 2.16

Estimating Distance and Time

Lesson: Whole Group

Take the students out to the playing fields. Ask each of them to mark off the distance they think they can run in 10 seconds. Using a stopwatch, allow students to sprint for 10 seconds and then compare their performance with their estimate. Ask students to repeat the process to see if their estimating ability improves.

Next, ask students to estimate how long it will take them to run a given distance, say, 50 meters. To avoid showcasing students who excel at physical activities, you can vary the activity by having students run a three-legged race, a wheel barrow race, a relay—or even run backwards.

Journal Reflection

How might you strengthen your own estimation skills of distance and time? How might you help students strengthen theirs?

Activity 2.17
Estimating Quantities

Lesson: Whole Group

Display a large transparent plastic bag filled with popcorn. Allow students to handle and examine the bag as they attempt to estimate the number of popped kernels in the bag. Have the students write down both their estimate and the method they used to arrive at it. For example, students might estimate the number of popped kernels in a single layer, then multiply that amount by the estimated number of layers in the bag. Alternately, students might envision the bag broken into smaller congruent regions, estimate the number of pieces in that region, and multiply by the number of regions. Some students might even base their estimate on past experiences.

The object of having students write down both their estimate and their strategy is to encourage reflection on methods of estimation. You may wish to give students the opportunity to refine their estimates after a small number of popcorn kernels is removed from the bag and counted.

Journal Reflection

Brainstorm five realistic contexts in which discrete estimation skills would be valuable.

to provide a variety of experiences so that students can develop better estimation skills.

Summary

The important concepts introduced in this chapter can be categorized as mathematical, developmental, and pedagogical. A mathematical concept is the place-value system of numeration, where the value of a digit is dictated by its place. While our Hindu-Arabic system of numeration is clearly a place-value system, other systems (the Roman system, for example) are not. Another mathematical concept is that of the ordinal, cardinal, and nominal uses of number. A further concept is one-to-one correspondence, which is necessary to understanding the cardinal use of number.

The important developmental concept of reversability holds that unless children are ready physically and mentally to decompose a ten into 10 ones, and also understand that this process can be reversed, then they are not yet ready to understand the concept of place value.

Several pedagogical issues were addressed in this chapter. The outline for writing lesson plans was designed to help you answer three questions: What am I going to teach, and why? How am I going to teach it, and why? and How will I know what students have learned? The lesson plan outline was then utilized to structure a specific lesson for children.

The principle of constructivism informed this chapter. Constructivism suggests that mathematical understandings cannot be *taught* to the students, but can only be *constructed* by the students themselves. Learning mathematics is not a process of listening carefully and remembering, but of thinking about problems and solving them on your own. The related initiative of cognitively guided instruction was used to help you think about how children learn mathematics.

Individual performance-based assessments were offered as alternatives to paper-and-pencil assessments of what children know and can do. Attribute pieces were used to show how children might develop the thinking skills of observing, describing, and classifying. Both proportional (base-10 materials) and nonproportional (Chip Trading game) models of our Hindu-Arabic system of numeration were presented.

Finally, this chapter and the chapters that follow will make more sense to you if you have the opportunity to apply the concepts you are reading about. Look for ways to work with children in both formal and informal settings. Observe children, ask them questions, try to understand how they learn and how they think. As you reflect on your observations, reflect also on how *you* learn and how *you* think. The best preparation for becoming a teacher of mathematics is to become a learner of mathematics.

Extending Your Learning

1. Distinguish between proportional and nonproportional place-value models and offer several examples of each. Describe their advantages and disadvantages. If you had to chose one place-value material for your elementary-grade classroom, which one would it be? Why?

2. Determine the base-10 value of each chip-trading board in Figure 2.24.

3. In your own words, describe the philosophy of performance-based assessment. Reflect on assessment experiences you have had, such as a driver's license road test, that are performance-based. What are some advantages and disadvantages of using performance-based assessments in the classroom?

4. Develop a list of at least five contexts that have meaning for students in grades 6 through 8 that involve the use of large numbers. Develop a visual, mnemonic, and/or manipulative device that will help students remember the place-value names that were illustrated in Figure 2.10.

5. Using the format presented in this text, write a lesson plan for children in kindergarten to help them understand the concept of one-to-one correspondence.

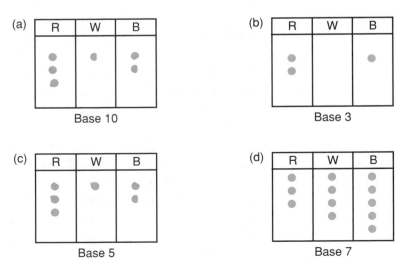

Figure 2.24

6. Assign three students the task of bringing to class items that can be used to estimate distance, volume, or quantity. After each student has had the opportunity to write down an estimate, have someone measure *part* of the distance or volume or count out *some* of the objects. Now, allow students to refine their estimate. Repeat this process during two subsequent classes, with different students bringing in different objects. Did the estimation skills of the students improve after these three class sessions?

7. Explain how our system of recording time can be viewed as a base-60 numeration system. How might the appearance of an analog clock change if our system of recording time was changed to a base-10 system?

8. A teacher-made version of base-10 materials can be made at little cost. Save the perforated strips torn from the edges of computer paper. Cut them into smaller strips of ten holes each. These strips are the equivalent of a "long," which is a model for ten. Arrange ten of these on a square of dark-colored cardboard or oaktag. This is the equivalent of a "flat," which is a model for 100. Little, individual holes can be used to represent units. If these materials are developed in quantity, each child can have an envelope of proportional place-value materials for modeling numbers and various operations on numbers. Make as many sets as you can. The same effect can be obtained at a slightly higher cost by gluing red kidney beans to tongue depressors, arranging ten such tongue depressors to form a hundreds flat, and using loose beans to represent units.

9. Obtain a copy of *How Much Is a Million?* by David Schwartz. Use this book to write a lesson on large numbers for students in grades 3 to 5. As part of your lesson, include a performance-based assessment.

10. Invite someone who is facile with an abacus to come to class and offer a demonstration. Compare the speed and ease of the abacus with the speed and ease of a calculator. What are the advantages and disadvantages of each?

Internet Resources

http://archives.math.utk.edu/k12.html
An extensive database containing the following headings: lesson plans, software, topics in mathematics, and others.

http://falcon.jmu.edu/~ramseyil/math.htm
Part of a larger Internet library. Provides information on math history, professional organizations, puzzles and games, lesson plans, and curricular resources.

http://forum.swarthmore.edu/
An extensive website, containing such features as "Ask Dr. Math," "Problems of the Week," lesson plans, discussion groups, "Teacher 2 Teacher," and many links to other mathematics education sites.

www.census.gov/
The U.S. Census Department website. Provides a rich source of real data.

www.ipl.org/youth/
A very helpful and broad website produced by the Internet Public Library Youth Division. The connection to "Math Whiz" leads you to many valuable resources, including a website on building and using an abacus.

www.timss.org/
A source of information on the Third International Mathematics and Science Study, an analysis of the math and science achievement of students in 41 countries.

Bibliography

Anno, Mitsumasa. (1977). *Anno's Counting Book*. New York: HarperCollins Children's Books.

Anno, Mitsumasa. (1982). *Anno's Counting House*. New York: Putnam.

Becker, J. (1981). Differential treatment of females and males in mathematics class. *Journal for Research in Mathematics Education* 12:40–53.

Bird, Elliott. (1999). What's in the box? A problem-solving lesson and a discussion about teaching. *Teaching Children Mathematics* 5(9).

Bloom, Stephen J. (1994). Data buddies: Primary grade mathematicians explore data. *Teaching Children Mathematics* 1(2).

Bright, George W., and Karl Hoeffner. (1993). Measurement, probability, statistics, and graphing. In Douglas T. Owens (ed.), *Research ideas for the classroom: Middle grades mathematics,* p. 91. New York: Macmillan.

Brooks, Jacqueline Grennon, and Martin G. Brooks. (1993). *The case for constructivist classrooms*. Alexandria, VA: Association for Supervision and Curriculum Development.

Brophy, Jere, and T. L. Good. (1974). *Teacher-student relationships: Causes and consequences*. New York: Holt, Rinehart and Winston.

Burns, Marilyn. (1994). *Math by all means: Place value*. Sausalito, CA: Math Solutions Publications.

Carle, Eric. (1987). *The very hungry caterpillar*. New York: Philomel.

Cohen Ira S., and Joan Fowler. (1998). Create assessments that do it all. *Mathematics Teaching in the Middle School* 4(1).

Conway, Kathleen D. (1999). Assessing open-ended problems. *Mathematics Teaching in the Middle School* 4(8).

Crews, Donald. (1986). *Ten black dots*. New York: Mulberry Books.

Dean, Ann V., Spencer J. Salend, and Lorraine Taylor. (Fall 1993). Multicultural education: A challenge for special educators. *Teaching Exceptional Children* 26(1): 40–43.

De La Cruz, Yolanda. (1999). Reversing the trend: Latino families in real partnerships with schools. *Teaching Children Mathematics* 5(5).

Fennema, E., Carpenter, T.P., and Lamon, S.J. (Eds.) (1988). *Integrating research on teaching and learning mathematics*. Madison: Wisconsin Center for Education Research.

Fennema, E., Carpenter, T.P., and Peterson. P.L. (1989). Learning mathematics with understanding: Cognitively guided instruction. In Jere Brophy (ed.), *Advances in research on teaching*. Greenwich, CT: JAI Press.

Fennema, E., J.S. Hyde, M. Ryan, and L. A. Frost. (1990). Gender differences in mathematics attitude and affect: A meta-analysis. *Psychology of Women Quarterly* 14:299–324.

Fisher, C., et al. (1978). *Teaching and learning in elementary schools: A summary of the beginning teacher evaluation study*. San Francisco: Far West Laboratory for Educational Research and Development.

Frank, Alan R. (1989). Counting skills: A foundation for early mathematics. *Arithmetic Teacher* 37(1):14–17.

Friedman, Aileen. (1994). *The King's Commissioners*. New York: Scholastic.

Goldsmith, Lynn T., and June Mark. (1999). What is a standards-based mathematics curriculum? *Educational Leadership* 57 (3).

Good, Thomas, and Bruce J. Biddle. (1988). Research and the improvement of mathematics instruction: The need for observational resources. In Lawrence Erlbaum Associates, *Effective mathematics teaching* (pp. 114–142). Reston, VA: National Council of Teachers of Mathematics.

Greib, A., and J. Easley. (1984). A primary school impediment to mathematical equity: Case studies in rule-dependent socialization. In M.W. Steinkamp and M. Maehr (eds.), *Advances in Motivation and Achievement: Vol. 2. Women in Science,* pp. 317–62. Greenwich, CT: JAI Press.

Hart, L.E. (1989). Classroom processes, sex of student, and confidence in learning mathematics. *Journal for Research in Mathematics Education 30*:242–60.

Kline, Kate. (1998). Kindergarten is more than counting. *Teaching Children Mathematics 5*(2).

Koehler, M.S., and Douglas Grouws. (1992). Mathematics teaching practices and their effects. In Douglas Grouws (ed.), *Handbook of research on mathematics teaching and learning.* New York: Macmillan.

Leder, G.C. (1987). Teacher-student interaction: A case study. *Educational studies in mathematics 18*:255–71.

Leder, G.C. (1989). Do girls count in mathematics? In G.C. Leder and S.N. Sampson (eds.), *Educating girls: Practice and research,* pp 84–97. Sydney: Allen & Unwin.

Leder, G.C. (1990). Gender differences in mathematics: An overview. In E. Fennema and G.C. Leder (eds.), *Mathematics and gender,* pp. 10–26. New York: Teachers College Press.

Mikusa, Michael G. (1998). Problem solving is more than solving problems. *Mathematics Teaching in the Middle School 4*(1).

National Center for Educational Statistics. (1999). Highlights from TIMSS. NCES 1999-081. Washington, DC: U.S. Department of Education, Office of Educational Research and Improvement.

National Council of Teachers of Mathematics. (1995). *Assessment Standards for School Mathematics* (working draft). Reston, VA: Author.

Parker, Diane, and Anthony Picard. (1997). Portraits of Susie: Matching curriculum, instruction, and assessment. *Teaching Children Mathematics 3*(7).

Rowe, Mary Budd. (1978a). *Teaching science as continuous inquiry.* New York: McGraw-Hill.

Rowe, Mary Budd. (1978b). Wait, wait, wait. *School Science and Mathematics 78,* pp. 207–216.

Rowe, Mary Budd. (1974). Wait-time and rewards as instructional variables, their influence on language, logic and fate control: Part I, fate control. *Journal of Research in Science Teaching 11*:81–94.

Schwartz, David. (1985). *How much is a million?* New York, Scholastic.

Sgroi, Laura A., et al. (1995). Assessing young children's mathematical understandings. *Teaching Children Mathematics 1*(5).

Shirley, Lawrence. (1995). Nominals: Numbers as names. *Teaching Children Mathematics 2*(4).

Stenmark, Jean Kerr, Virginia Thompson, and Ruth Cossey. (1986). *Family math.* Berkeley, CA: Lawrence Hall of Science.

Stenmark, Jean Kerr (Ed.). (1991). *Mathematics assessment.* Reston, VA: National Council of Teachers of Mathematics.

Tang, Eileen P., and Herbert Ginsburg. (1999). Young children's mathematical reasoning: A psychological view. In Lee V. Stiff (ed.), *Developing mathematical reasoning in grades K–12.* 1999 Yearbook of the National Council of Teachers of Mathematics. Reston, VA: NCTM.

Van Leuvan, Patricia. (1997). Young women experience mathematics at work in the health professions. *Mathematics Teaching in the Middle School 3*(3).

Walden R., and V. Walkerdine. (1985). Girls and mathematics: From primary to secondary schooling. Bedford Way Papers 24. London: London University, Institute of Education.

Wilcox, Sandra K., and Marie Sahloff. (1998). Another perspective on concept maps: Empowering students. *Mathematics Teaching in the Middle School 3*(7).

Zaslavsky, Claudia. (1994). *Multicultural mathematics,* pp. 31–34. New York: Scholastic.

Standards for Whole Numbers: Addition and Subtraction

$$\begin{array}{r} 2678 \\ -1899 \\ \hline \end{array} \qquad \begin{array}{r} 597 \\ \times 362 \\ \hline \end{array} \qquad 23{,}276 \div 532$$

The current reform movement in school mathematics has caused many teachers to question the role of computational skill in the elementary school curriculum. Why, they ask, should large portions of class time be devoted to practicing computational procedures such as those in the margin when inexpensive calculators can perform these operations accurately and quickly? Rather, they argue, the teacher should work toward helping students understand the procedures and the situations in which they will use these procedures. In addition, many would argue that children should be encouraged to invent their own methods of dealing with numbers, since a personally invented algorithm is more understandable to a student than an inherited algorithm.

Although computation, or the emphasis on procedures, has in the past been the predominant element of the elementary school mathematics curriculum, teachers and other mathematics educators are now struggling to determine the appropriate emphasis as the reform movement makes us reexamine what we teach and how we teach it.

Some teachers and mathematics educators defend the curricular emphasis on numerical computation by claiming that procedural skill is an aspect of mathematical literacy, often referred to as *numeracy,* and by stressing the cumulative nature of mathematical knowledge. They claim that it is impossible to teach children how to perform the long-division algorithm if they do not already know how to multiply.

Hiebart and Carpenter (1992) write:

> One of the longstanding debates in mathematics education concerns the relative importance of conceptual knowledge versus procedural knowledge or of understanding versus skill. . . . The debate has often been carried out in the context of proposing instructional programs emphasizing one kind of knowledge over the other. The prevailing view has see-sawed back and forth. . . . we have not made great progress in our understanding of the issue. Perhaps a first step in understanding how procedural and conceptual knowledge contribute to mathematical expertise is to agree that the question of which kind of knowledge is most important is the wrong question to ask. Both kinds of knowledge are crucial. A better question to ask is how conceptual and procedural knowledge are related. (pp. 77–78)

The authors go on to discuss the interrelatedness of these two aspects of mathematical knowledge. They point out that procedural skill allows students to develop a certain automaticity in their computation, that it highlights the patterns and consistency in our system of numeration, and that it allows for the efficient solution of routine problems. However, procedural skill unaccompanied by conceptual understandings results in students knowing *how* to multiply, but not always knowing *when* to multiply. A lack of conceptual understanding can also prevent students from placing the procedural knowledge into any sort of context. Students are unable to make connections among the various topics of mathematics, and this lack of cohesiveness makes retention of the procedures more difficult.

This chapter presents both the conceptual understanding of whole number computation, and also the teaching strategies that help children develop and retain procedural skill. I agree with Hiebert and Carpenter (1992) that ". . . all mathematical procedures are potentially associated with connected networks of information" (p. 78). We hope to make these connections clear to you, so that you, in turn, can make them clear to your students.

Operation for Grades Pre-K–2

According to the NCTM *Principles and Standards,* in grades Pre-K–2 all students should

- Understand different meanings of addition and subtraction of whole numbers and the relation between the two operations;

- Develop understanding about the effects of the operations on whole numbers.

- Develop and use strategies and algorithms to solve number problems;

- Develop fluency with addition and subtraction facts by the end of second grade;

- Compute using a variety of methods, including mental computation, paper and pencil, and calculators and chose an appropriate method for the situation;

- Recognize whether numerical solutions are reasonable. (pp. 109–110)

This book has been written from the assumption that you, and the children you teach, have access to a calculator. Although many teachers, administrators, and parents are apprehensive about allowing children free access to a calculator, the research does not support this reluctance. In 1986, Hembree and Dessart published a meta-analysis on the impact of calculator use in the classroom. A *meta-analysis* is the compilation of many previous research studies. After analyzing 79 such research studies, Hembree and Dessart concluded that regular use of a calculator does not harm the development of students' computational sills and that using calculators can enhance the development of reasoning and problem-solving skills. In addition, they found that ". . . students using calculators possess a better attitude

Activity 3.1

Mind or Machine?

Ask that two children volunteer for this activity. One child, representing MIND, has to perform all examples mentally. The other child, representing MACHINE, has to perform all examples using the calculator. Ask the rest of the class to predict who will give the correct answer more quickly, the mind or the machine. Then say the following examples out loud, one at a time: 5 + 6, 7 − 3, 2 × 5, 3 + 8. Of course, the child who is using the mind will be able to answer these examples before the child using the calculator has even punched in the correct numbers. Then, give this example: 267 × 873.

This activity is designed to illustrate to children that there are times when using a calculator makes perfect sense, and there are times, especially involving the recall of basic facts, when using a calculator is inefficient and time-consuming.

Journal Reflection

How would you answer the concerns of parents that using the calculator will prevent their children from learning the basic facts?

toward mathematics and an especially better self-concept in mathematics than non-calculator students. This statement applies across all grade and ability levels" (p. 96).

Many teachers and parents fear that if students are given free access to calculators, they will become dependent upon them. Activity 3.1 is designed to show students the appropriate and inappropriate uses of calculators.

Young children come to school with significant experience in putting things together and taking them apart again. They have built towers of blocks and knocked them down, they have put together puzzles and taken them apart, they have dressed and undressed dolls, they have assembled and reassembled train tracks and trains. Connecting the operations of addition and subtraction with these early experiences helps children to develop mathematical understandings.

When teaching children about addition and subtraction, it is important to recognize that there are several different *models,* or ways of thinking, about these operations. Addition can be thought of as the combination of discrete items, or as the combination of continuous quantities. When working from the model of addition as the combination of discrete items, individual countable objects such as plastic teddy bear counters or plastic chips may be used. Activity 3.2 utilizes an edible counting object.

Cuisenaire rods can be used to illustrate addition as the combination of continuous quantities. These colored plastic or wooden rods were invented during the 1950s by George Cuisenaire. There are ten different lengths of rods, from 1 cm to 10 cm, while all of the rods are 1 cm in width and depth. The rods are color coded; for example, every 5-cm rod is yellow and every yellow rod is 5 cm in length (Figure 3.1).

Activity 3.2

Fish in a Pond

Distribute ovals of blue paper and small paper cups containing about 10 little goldfish crackers to each child. Invite the children to act out the story as you tell it:

- "One day, two little goldfish went swimming in a pond. (The children remove two crackers and place them on the blue paper.) They were lonely all by themselves, so it made them very happy when three more fish came along. (Three more crackers are added to the pond. At this point, ask the children how many fish were in the pond at first, how many more came along, how many are there now.) Four fish wanted to look for rocks to hide behind, so they swam away. (The children are invited to eat four crackers. Again, questions such as how many were there at first, how many swam away, and how many are left can be

discussed.) The one little fish was sad to be all alone, so she called for three of her friends to join her in the pond. . . ."

Continue in this fashion until there are no crackers left. On subsequent occasions, the activity can be repeated with a different number of crackers or in a different context, such as using raisins as ants that scurry away or stick pretzels as snakes that slither away. When children become comfortable with this activity, it can be repeated with a child volunteering to be the storyteller, and the other children in the class acting it out.

Journal Reflection

Describe how you might introduce the appropriate symbolic number sentences (such as 2 + 3 = 5) into this activity. Would you do so? Why or why not?

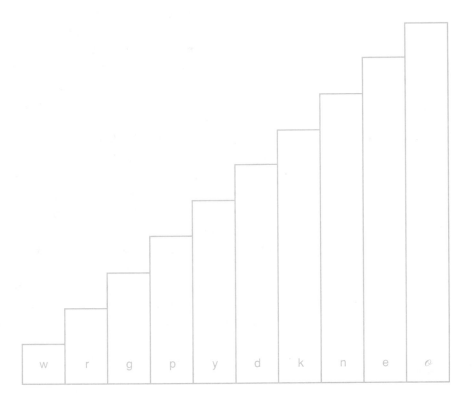

Figure 3.1

When introducing a new material to children it is important to give them several opportunities to explore the material before using it in a structured activity. Exploration activities with Cuisenaire rods might include building a structure or design, creating letters or numerals, or arranging them in a pattern. Discussions that accompany these activities provide the opportunity for children to communicate mathematically as they describe their patterns or buildings, and to use mathematical vocabulary such as longer, taller, repeat, match, inside, outside, increase, decrease, more, or less.

After some exploratory activities, Cuisenaire rods can be used to illustrate addition as the combination of continuous quantities by making "trains," as shown in Activity 3.3.

There are several models of subtraction, and children should be given experience with each of them. In the *take-away* model, a given number of items or a given quantity is diminished by the removal of some items or some amount. In encouraging the children to eat some of the crackers, Activity 3.2 was an example of the take-away model of discrete items. Activity 2.12, when chip trading was played in reverse, was also an example of the take-away model of subtraction, since the number tossed indicated the number of blue chips to be removed. Do you see why it is a discrete model of number?

A take-away model of continuous quantities involves the removal of some continuous amount from a larger amount. This is easily experienced by children when they play at a sand table or water table. The pouring from one size container to another, the scooping of sand or rice into piles, and the pouring from a pitcher into smaller cups or containers all involve children in the removal of continuous quantities. When children engage in these activities during "free play" in the classroom, they are not *just* playing. Rather, children's play and children's learning are one and the same thing.

Another model of subtraction is the *comparison* model. In this model, nothing is removed. Rather, two sets of items or quantities are compared, and the difference between them is determined. Activity 3.4 uses the comparison model of subtraction with discrete items.

Just as Cuisenaire rods can be used to model the addition of continuous quantities, they can also model the subtraction of continuous quantities. In Activity 3.5, students are given practice in answering the question "How much more?" When written numerically, this type of example is often confusing to first- and second-graders. It is referred to as the *missing addend* model of subtraction, and looks like this:

$$3 + ? = 7$$

Many young children believe that the number 10 belongs in the box. This is not surprising, since in all of their previous experience, whenever they saw two numbers and a "+" sign, they added the numbers together. Before introducing children to the missing addend model in a numerical form, encourage them to play "I wish I had."

Activity 3.3
Rod Trains

Lesson: Pairs

As an introduction to Cuisenaire rods, ask the children working in pairs to practice identifying the rods by touch. The first child stretches a hand overhead while the second child places a rod in that hand. By feeling the rod from end to end, the first child attempts to identify its color through touch alone. After several turns, the children trade places. Children usually discover that arranging the rods by size on their desk (a "staircase" arrangement) makes identification easier.

When the children have had several opportunities to freely explore the rods and to identify their colors, they can build "trains" (a train is an arrangement of rods end to end). When working with Cuisenaire rods, the following terms are often used:

two-car trains—trains composed of only two rods
three-car trains—trains composed of only three rods
one-color trains—trains composed of rods of only one color.

Invite the children to build as many two-car trains as they can that are as long as the dark green rod. Figure 3.2 illus-

trates the complete set of such trains. Do you notice the symmetry of this arrangement? If this set of rods were to be recorded numerically, it would look like this:

$$0 + 6 = 6$$
$$1 + 5 = 6$$
$$2 + 4 = 6$$
$$3 + 3 = 6$$
$$4 + 2 = 6$$
$$5 + 1 = 6$$
$$6 + 0 = 6$$

There are many concepts imbedded in this arrangement of rods. First, the concept of **compensation** is apparent. Since the sum remains constant, as the first addend increases, the second one necessarily decreases, to compensate. Second, the **commutative property** can be seen, since yellow and white make green, and white and yellow make green. Third, this activity has a **control of error.** This means that children can know when they have done something incorrectly without consulting the teacher. For example, it is obvious to a child that a train of purple and purple would not be as long as a dark green. If the child tried to put a such a train in this arrangement, it wouldn't fit. The discrepancy would be clear. Last, Cuisenaire rods are a **continuous** model of number. The dark green rod is six cm long. It represents the number 6, not because there are six of anything, but because it has a length of 6 cm. A material that illustrates a discrete model of six would require six individual items.

After each child has constructed a set of trains, discussion can begin about the concepts of *same as, as long as, equal to, more or less,* and *symmetry.* An appropriate extension would be to ask the children to predict if the set of two-car trains that are as long as the orange rod would be larger or smaller than the two-car trains that are as long as the dark green rod.

Journal Reflection

How would this activity differ if it were not limited to two-car trains? Do you think it would be a better activity? Explain.

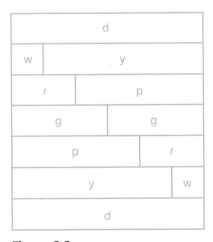

Figure 3.2

Basic Facts of Addition and Subtraction

After children have had substantial experience with the various models for the operations of addition and subtraction, it is important to give them practice in recalling the basic facts quickly and accurately. The basic addition/subtraction facts are defined as the 100 combinations from $0 + 0$ to $9 + 9$. These facts are considered to cover both addition and subtraction because, once children have learned that $5 + 6 = 11$, they can use this knowledge to determine that $11 - 5 = 6$.

Activity 3.4

Comparing Towers

Lesson: Pairs

Working in pairs, children are invited to take as many Unifix cubes as they can hold in one hand and then form the cubes into a tower. Each child should be offered only one color of cubes from which to grab a handful. (Since number, not color, is significant here, the color should be held constant so as not to distract from the focus on the number of cubes.)

When the towers have been formed, the height of the towers can be compared and the differences in height, as defined by the number of cubes, can be determined. Children must be encouraged to verbalize observations about their towers ("My tower is three cubes taller than my partner's tower.")

Journal Reflection

How could this lesson be extended by using the towers of Unifix cubes to create a realistic bar graph?

Activity 3.5

I wish I had . . .

Lesson: Pairs

The children work in pairs, with approximately 25 assorted Cuisenaire rods between them. One child chooses two rods and holds them up, saying, for example, "I have a red rod, but I wish I had a black rod. What other rod do I need?" (Figure 3.3). The partner, through physical experimentation, determines the rod that defines the *difference* between the red rod and the black rod—in this case, the yellow rod. The children play for several minutes, alternating between themselves.

Journal Reflection

This activity offers a tangible model for the number sentence $x + ? = y$, and answers the question, how much more than x is y? How would you help children understand the relationship between the rod activity and its numerical representation? Is it necessary for children to see this relationship?

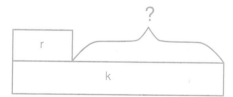

Figure 3.3

Properties of Whole-Number Addition

There are some properties of addition that will help children to understand the operation of addition:

- *The closure property of whole-number addition.* The sum of two whole numbers is itself a whole number. A set with this property is said to be *closed* under addition.

- *The commutative property of whole-number addition.* The order of the addends may be changed without changing the sum; that is, if *a* and *b* are both whole numbers, $a + b = b + a$. This property is useful when children are trying to master the basic facts. Understanding this property cuts in half the number of basic facts to be memorized.

- *The associative property of whole-number addition.* When combining two or more addends, the way in which the addends are grouped does not affect the sum; that is, if *a*, *b*, and *c* are whole numbers, then $(a + b) + c = a + (b + c)$. This property will be useful when children are learning to estimate sums and perform mental math. Rearranging addends often makes numbers easier to work with.

When helping children commit the basic facts to memory, practice sessions should be brief, frequent, and employ a variety of materials. The following are several activities that will help children remember the basic facts, after they have been introduced to the concepts of addition and subtraction.

Basic Facts Strategies

Take one minute and try to memorize this string of letters:

i p a t t f o t u s o a a t t r f w i s o n u g i w l a j f a

Most people who are successful at memorizing the letters do the same thing—they impose a structure on them. For example, some people break the string of letters into triples. Instead of trying to memorize 31 separate, isolated pieces of information, they focus on memorizing groups of three letters. Thus, they 'see' the letters as ipa / ttf / otu / . . . and so on. Others use the mnemonic device of making nonsense words. They might 'see' the letters as "I patt fotusa attr . . . and so on. What these strategies share is an attempt to ascribe meaning to something that appears to have no meaning, since it is much easier to remember meaningful pieces of information.

Attempts to commit these letters to long-term memory are typically unsuccessful since there is no apparent pattern or structure to the letters. However, if you were to realize that these are the first letters of the words in the Pledge of Allegiance, it would not be at all difficult for you to rattle off the letters, and to do so at any time in the future. Once the underlying structure becomes clear to you, the task of remembering becomes much easier.

If children can discover or be shown the structure underlying the basic addition/subtraction facts, committing them to memory is simplified. For example, the + 0 facts are the easiest to begin with, since children quickly see that adding 0 to a number does not change its value. This characteristic makes 0 the *identity* element in addition.

Moving to the + 1 facts, children recognize that the sum when adding 1 to a number is the very next number. Children find remembering the *double* facts (3 + 3, 4 + 4, etc.) easier than many others. The double facts can be connected to *near-doubles* in the following manner: "If 4 + 4 = 8, 4 + 5 must be one more than 8, since 5 is one more than 4."

Helping children realize that they can *make the nine a ten* when 9 is an addend is also a useful strategy. For example, when given the addends of 9 and 4, children are encouraged to mentally remove one from the 4 and give it to the 9 to make 10. The sum of 10 plus 3 (what is left from the original 4) is easily found.

Having introduced children to common strategies for finding sums and differences, encourage them to develop their own strategies for thinking about addition/subtraction combinations, and then ask them to share those strategies with the class.

Guess My Rule

The teacher, or a child acting as the leader, writes a rule on an index card and places it face down on the desk. As children in the class call out numbers, the leader mentally performs the operation described by the rule, and records the outcome in the following chart.

IN	OUT
5	12
1	8
3	10

When someone thinks he or she has discovered the rule, they challenge the leader by saying, in this case, "I think the rule is to always add 7." The child who has successfully identified the rule is the next person to be the leader. When children have learned multiplication, the rule can have two parts, such as "Add 3 and multiply by 2."

I Have . . . Who Has. . .?

This teacher-made game promotes listening skills and mental math, and can focus on a wide variety of mathematical topics. Begin with a stack of index cards, and mark the first card with a star. (This is done so that when the cards are distributed to the class you know which child should read a card first.) On the first card, write the following words:

I have 3. Who has two more than this number?

On the next card, write:

I have 5. Who has three less than this number?

On the next:

I have 2. Who has eight more than this number?

Continue to make cards until there are a sufficient number so that each child gets at least one. Keep a list of the numbers you have used to avoid having two cards begin with, for example, "I have 2."

The game is played by randomly distributing the cards to the class and having the child with the star read that card aloud. Whoever has the card that answers the first card then reads their card out loud, and so on. Children are encouraged to listen carefully and to mentally compute each addition or subtraction so they will know when to read their card. This game is adaptable to any age group and any mathematical topic by varying the content of the cards. Here is an example of a set composed of multiplication and division questions that could be used with a fourth-grade class:

I have 11. Who has twice that number?
I have 22. Who has that number minus 7?
I have 15. Who has three times that number?
Have 45. Who has that number divided by 9?
I have 5. . . . .

Cover-Up

This activity is adapted from the excellent book *Young Children Reinvent Arithmetic* by Constance Kamii (1985). Each pair of students is given the game board shown in Figure 3.4. Using two standard dice, the children take turns tossing the dice and covering up the sum of the two numbers that appear on the dice. When one player has covered a side completely, the activity is over. This activity can be expanded by using number cubes rather than dice, and changing the sums on the game board. This allows for the practice of higher sums if the numbers on the cube are, for example, 5 through 10. Also, the activity can be played by asking the children first to *cover* all the numbers and then *uncover* them as the sum is tossed.

Children quickly see that certain sums, especially 6, 7, and 8, are tossed more frequently than others. By giving them eleven markers, but allowing them to place the markers anywhere they wish, students are encouraged to experiment with probability concepts. For example, a child who places two markers on the numbers 6, 7, and 8, but no markers on 2, 11 or 12, should increase the chances of uncovering all of the markers. Do you see why?

Salute

This activity is adapted from another book by Constance Kamii, *Young Children Continue to Reinvent Arithmetic: Second Grade* (1989). It requires a deck of playing cards with the face cards removed, and three children. One child is the General, and the other two are soldiers. The cards are evenly divided and placed face down in two piles in front of the two soldiers.

Each soldier takes a card from the top of the pile and holds it against the forehead, as if saluting the General, so that only the other soldier and the General can see it. The General calls out the sum of both cards, and

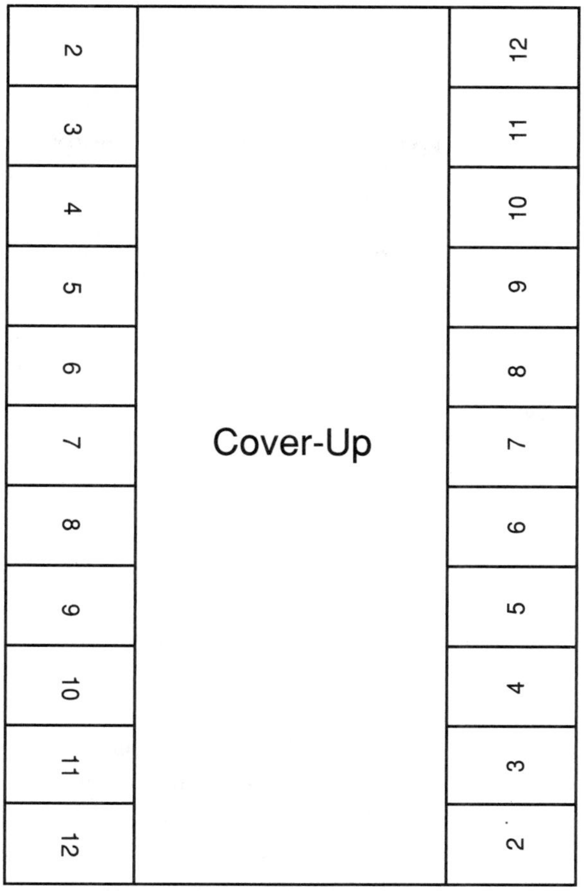

Figure 3.4

the first soldier to identify his or her own card keeps both cards. So, for example, if one soldier sees the other soldier holding a 4 and hears the General say 9, the reasoning is that his or her own card must be a 5.

Add 'Em Up
Two children evenly divide a deck of cards minus the face cards. They simultaneously turn over the top card from their own pile. The first person to call out the sum keeps both cards. This activity can be altered to help children practice subtraction facts by asking them to subtract the lesser number from the greater number and then call out the difference.

Bingo
Distribute a blank 4 × 4 matrix to each child (Figure 3.5). Ask each child to write the numerals from 1 to 16 randomly in the blanks. Create a deck of index cards bearing number sentences such as "3 + 7, " or "2 + 4 + 1," whose sums cover all of the numbers between 1 and 16. Have one child read out the number sentences while the other children cover the sums on their card.

This game can easily be adapted to subtraction by changing the number sentences on the cards to read "11 − 7" or "15 − 9."

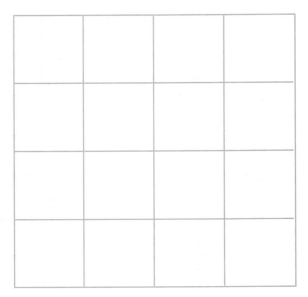

Figure 3.5

Computer Programs

There are many computer programs on the market that help children practice their basic facts. These include *Math Ace* (Magic Quest) and *The Flashcard System* (You and Me Products). In addition to software focused specifically on practicing the basic facts, there are software programs designed to develop a variety of mathematical understandings. *Millie's Math House* (Edmark) is recommended for children from preschool to second grade, and engages children in activities in the following areas: identification and comparison of size, identification of shapes, the completion and creation of patterns, number recognition from 0 to 30, number sentences—as well as practice with addition and subtraction facts.

Advantages to having children practicing basic facts with computer programs include (1) the infinite patience of the computer, (2) the privacy of no one else knowing when an error is made, (3) the opportunity for children to work on material suitable to their own level of expertise, and (4) the aspect of many programs that allows the teacher to monitor the progress of the children.

Disadvantages include (1) the lack of opportunity for the teacher to clear up any confusions, (2) the lack of opportunity for children to learn from each other, and (3) the repetitive nature of some programs, which can lead to boredom. However, recall the suggestions made a few pages earlier about helping children practice the basic facts. The practice sessions should be brief, frequent, and varied. If you keep these suggestions in mind, you can avoid many of these disadvantages.

Performance-Based Assessment: Basic Addition and Subtraction Facts

When assessing children's knowledge of the basic facts, it is important to determine the way they figured out the answer. If a child consistently relies only on memory, it would be useful to introduce that child to some strate-

Strength in Numbers

Magic Squares

Cooperative Group Model: Think, Pair, Share

Think: Using each of the numbers from 1 to 9 only once, where should they be placed in the empty Magic Square of Figure 3.6 so that each row, column, and diagonal adds up to 15?

Pair: After each person has had an opportunity to think about the placement of the numbers, work with a partner to try to solve this problem. Remember the steps of problem solving:

- Read the problem (and restate it in your own words to make sure you understand what is being asked).

- Devise a plan.

- Carry out the plan.

- Look back to verify that you have answered the question and to assess the method of solution.

Share: Join with another pair of students, or with the whole class, and analyze the different methods used by members of the class in solving this problem. For example: What number did you place in the grid first and where did you place it? Why? Did you use a calculator? Or, did you use another device to help you solve the problem? What combinations of numbers did you immediately discard? Why? If you were to present this problem to a fourth-grade class, what hints would you offer to them? (Hints are very useful in problem solving. They prevent children from becoming frustrated, and suggest a direction in which to proceed.)

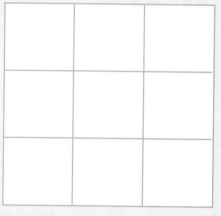

Figure 3.6

gies for thinking about sums and differences. If a child has trouble with facts involving sums greater than 10, it would be helpful to send some card or dice games home that can be practiced with an adult or older sibling.

Ask the child to solve the following problems and to explain how the answer was determined. Have a variety of materials available on the table, such as counters, Unifix cubes, paper and pencils, and Cuisenaire rods.

- Sally had 7 cookies. Jose had 4. How many more did Sally have? How do you know?

- Natasha had 9 baseball cards. She got 8 more. How many did she have altogether? How do you know?

- Danielle can swim 15 laps of the pool. David can swim 9 laps. How many more laps can Danielle swim? How do you know?

- Tom ran for 7 minutes. After a rest, he ran for 6 more minutes. For how long did he run in all? How do you know?

■ Kate had 16 valentines. She gave 5 of them away. How many did she have left? How do you know?

As the children work on these problems, pay attention to the methods they use to determine the answers. This information will help you to structure future lessons and activities. There are several methods you can use to record your observations of each child's performance. Some teachers carry a clipboard with self-adhesive address labels, recording the date and identity of a child on each label, and writing a few sentences of assessment. These labels are later transferred to alphabetized index cards or binder pages.

Another choice would be to write a summary of each child's performance, include any written samples of work produced by children in this setting, and file this away in a *portfolio*. Every item that is placed in a portfolio should be dated, with a brief explanation of the nature of the task and the setting attached. In this situation, for instance, the following note might be included:

3/6/00 Individual assessment conference. Four +/− problems given. Manipulatives available. Duration approximately 6 minutes. Student appeared confident, and successfully solved problems without hesitation.

Portfolios provide another means for teachers, students, and parents to understand a child's mathematical accomplishments. They can include teacher assessments (as described above), samples of students' work, students' assessments of their own work, and special projects. Additional discussions of portfolios and other methods of assessment will be included throughout this textbook.

Addition and Subtraction of Multi-Digit Numbers

Given the opportunity, children invent their own *algorithms,* or procedures, for addition and subtraction of numbers greater than 10. These invented algorithms are often performed mentally, and tend to rely on using numbers that are easy to work with. For example, a second-grader was asked to solve the following problem:

■ If I have 200 baseball cards and I give 3 away, how many do I have left?

$$\begin{array}{r} {}^{1}\ {}^{9} \\ 2\,{}^{1}\!\cancel{0}\,{}^{1}0 \\ -\ \ \ \ 3 \\ \hline \end{array}$$

When asked how she arrived at her answer of 197 cards, she explained "If I take 1 from 200, I have 199. If I take another 1 away, I have 198, and if I take 1 more away, I have 197 left." If this child had been shown the standard algorithm in the margin she would not have known the steps to solve it. And, seeing it in symbolic form, she would have been unlikely to utilize the mental procedure she chose.

This phenomena is widely recognized among teachers. Children are often able to solve problems presented in a meaningful (personal or realistic) context. However, if the identical numerical situation is presented on paper, they feel incapable of solving it. It is as if they stopped *thinking* about the numbers and groped for a rule instead. If they cannot recall or have never learned the appropriate algorithm, they are paralyzed.

All of this suggests that teachers should postpone instruction in standard algorithms until children have developed a strong number sense and have been convinced that there are many valid ways to solve almost every problem. While some mathematics educators argue that children should *never* be taught standard algorithms, I believe that standard algorithms, when used judiciously, can streamline computation and lend efficiency to children's numerical investigations.

Estimation and the Commutative and Associative Properties

Children need ample encouragement, and opportunity, to estimate sums and differences before using a formal algorithm to find a precise answer. Developing this habit of estimation strengthens number sense and prepares children for adulthood, when much of the "figuring" we do is mental estimation. Understanding some of the properties of whole-number addition can help children become efficient estimators, as shown in Activity 3.6.

Although estimating is part of the elementary school curriculum and is one of the NCTM Standards for whole-number computation, estimation skills are often taught out of context. Because of this, elementary school students do not always realize the many situations in which estimation is useful. For example, many people use estimation in the contexts of consumerism and data analysis. We mentally verify that we have enough money to pay for our groceries; we approximate the tip on a restaurant bill; we estimate the miles per gallon our car gets; we estimate home-run distances and football yardage.

The widespread use of calculators has increased the importance of estimation. It is very easy to make a keystroke error. Unless the calculator user has estimated a reasonable result, a grossly inaccurate answer can go unnoticed. It is impossible to check a keystroke sequence once it has been entered into the calculator unless it produces a paper strip or has a graphical display.

There are specific estimation skills that can be taught to children, although they often develop their own strategies based on a combination of these skills.

Forming Multiples of Ten

Children scan down a list of numbers, grouping together those that will form sums close to ten or a multiple of ten:

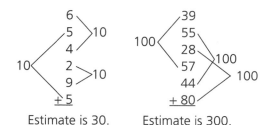

Estimate is 30.   Estimate is 300.

Activity 3.6

Commutative and Associative Properties

Lesson: Individual

Have each child chose two different Cuisenaire rods and form the possible trains (Figure 3.7). Then, ask each child to choose one additional rod, and again form all of the possible trains (Figure 3.8).

Next, ask the children to measure in centimeters the length of their three-car train. This may be done with a centimeter ruler or with orange and white rods. Have each child write the number sentences that correspond to the rods:

$$6 + 2 + 1 = 9$$
$$6 + 1 + 2 = 9$$
$$2 + 1 + 6 = 9$$
$$2 + 6 + 1 = 9$$
$$1 + 2 + 6 = 9$$
$$1 + 6 + 2 = 9$$

Figure 3.7

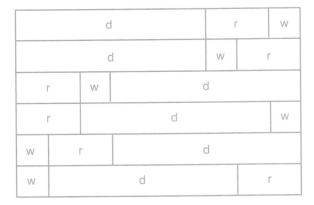

Figure 3.8

Repeat this activity using towers of fewer than ten monochromatic Unifix cubes. The do the activity using small paper cups filled with fewer than ten beans. Encourage the students to verbalize or write a sentence about this activity ("It doesn't matter what order the numbers were in. The answer was always the same.").

Journal Reflection

Why do you think this activity incorporates three different materials? What other materials might also be used?

Rounding

Each number is rounded to the nearest multiple of ten.

457 rounds to 500
209 rounds to 200
+ 34 rounds to 30
Estimated sum is 730

218 rounds to 200
− 98 rounds to 100
Estimated difference is 100

Front-End Estimation

This is a refinement of the rounding technique, appropriate for children in the fourth grade or higher. It is a two-step procedure that groups the largest place-value digits together and then combines this sum with an estimate of the remaining amounts:

1617   1 thousand + 5 thousand + 4 thousand = 10 thousand
5408   408 and 617 can form an estimate of 1000
+ 4966   966 can be rounded to 1000

The estimated sum is 10,000 + 1000 + 1000 = 12,000.

Activity 3.7 gives practice in estimation.

Activity 3.7

Making Predictions

Lesson: Whole Class

The teacher or a child writes down a two-digit target number, and then calls out a number from 2 to 9. The children are to predict if that two-digit number will appear in the display of a calculator that has been programmed to skip count by the number between 2 and 9 that was called out. Using the constant feature on a calculator, the children then verify their own predictions.

In this instance, the child can see that the sequence of digits resulting from the repeated addition of 4 does not include 21. It is important to elicit the reasons for the children's predictions. For example, one child might say that she did not think that 21 would appear because repeatedly adding 4 to zero always results in an even number, and 21 is not even. Another child might incorrectly think that 21 would

appear because it would appear in the skip counting sequence for 3, and three and four share many multiples such as 12 and 24.

This activity can be expanded to challenge older or more able children by beginning with a three-digit target number, or by having the skip counting begin with a number other than zero. The activity can be adapted for children who struggle by recording on the board or on chart paper each multiple as it appears in the calculator display. This helps the children to focus on the repeated patterns in the set of multiples.

Journal Reflection

How might this activity be adapted for a class that lacks calculators? What are some advantages of this adaptation? Some disadvantages?

Powers-of-Ten Blocks and the Standard Addition Algorithm

When children are ready to be introduced to the standard algorithms for addition and subtraction, modeling these operations with powers-of-ten blocks can be useful, as can introducing these algorithms in a realistic context. The following situation can be presented to children.

■ Imagine that a second-grade class is going to join their fifth-grade buddies for a party. If there are 28 children in the second-grade class and 27 children in the fifth-grade class, how many children will be at the party?

After children have had an opportunity to estimate an answer in their own way, they can be taught the standard algorithm involving *regrouping,* which is the process of trading 10 individual ones into 1 group of ten. Examine the representation of each of the addends with powers-of-ten blocks in Figure 3.9. When these blocks are combined, the result is 4 longs and 15 units. The 15 units can be regrouped into 1 long and 5 units, as shown in Figure 3.10. The final sum is 55. When preparing refreshments for the party, the children should plan for 55 children.

The standard algorithm for addition with regrouping looks like the one in the margin. Notice how the numerical procedure follows the manipulation of the powers-of-ten blocks. The 8 ones and the 7 ones are combined, and their sum is regrouped into 1 ten (which is then placed into the tens column) and 5 ones. Adding 1 ten plus 2 tens plus 2 tens results in a sum of 5 tens, for a grand total of 55. This answer should be close to the estimated total of children expected at the party. Activity 3.8 on page 94 give practice in regrouping.

$$\begin{array}{r} {}^{1}28 \\ +\ 27 \\ \hline 55 \end{array}$$

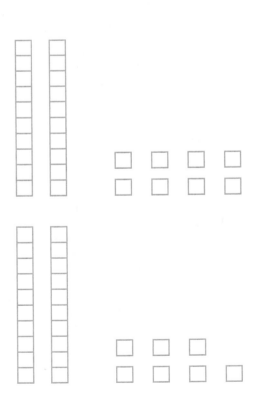

Figure 3.9

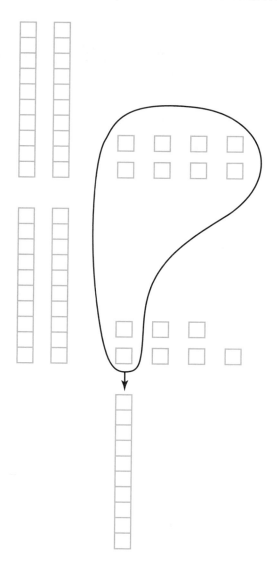

Figure 3.10

Alternative Algorithms for Whole-Number Addition

The regrouping algorithm is the way most children are taught to add numbers beyond single-digit basic facts. But it is not the only algorithm that can be used. There are a number of alternative algorithms that can be of use, especially for children with special educational needs.

Alternative algorithms represent another way to arrive at the answer, and they send the message that there are many different ways to perform an operation, each equally valid. This can be motivating for children who have not previously met with success. Alternative algorithms are also valuable for children who quickly master the standard algorithm. They can provide a challenging opportunity for children to figure out *why* each different algorithm always results in the correct answer. Here are two alternative methods for adding numbers.

Activity 3.8
The Dart Game

Lesson: Whole Class

Display the target of Figure 3.11 to the class. Then pose the following questions, encouraging the children to explain how they arrived at their answer:

- Is it possible to score 25 if you have three darts? How do you know?
- Is it possible to achieve an even-numbered score if you throw three darts and they all hit the target? How do you know?
- Is it possible to achieve an odd-numbered score if you throw two darts and they both hit the target? How do you know?
- Assuming two darts are thrown and hit the target, how many different scores are possible? What is the greatest possible score? What is the least possible score?
- Assuming three darts are thrown and hit the target, how many different scores are possible? What is the greatest possible score? What is the least possible score?

Journal Reflection

How would you assist a child who is having difficulty listing all the possibilities in the last two questions? How would you help a child develop a method to ensure that all combinations had been accounted for?

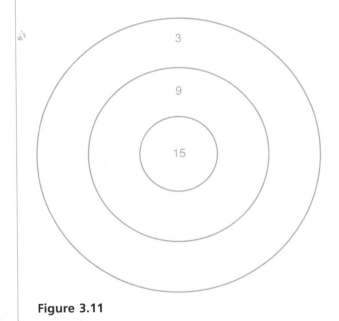

3

9

15

Figure 3.11

Partial Sums Algorithm

This algorithm finds the sum of each place value in turn, beginning with the leftmost, and then adds up each of these partial sums to arrive at the grand total. Since children learn to read by moving from left to right, many children find it more natural to find the sum in a written algorithm by working from left to right. Here are two examples.

■ Kate has read 17 Boxcar Children books. There are 19 more in the library that she hasn't read. How many books is this all together?

$$
\begin{array}{r}
17 \\
+\ 19 \\
\hline
20 \quad (10 + 10 = 20) \\
+\ 16 \quad (7 + 9 = 16) \\
\hline
36 \quad (16 + 20 = 36)
\end{array}
$$

There are 36 Boxcar Children books all together.

■ Geoffrey has 126 football cards. With his allowance, he buys 35 more. How many football cards does he have now?

$$
\begin{array}{r}
126 \\
+\ 35 \\
\hline
100 \quad (100 + 0 = 100) \\
50 \quad (20 + 30 = 50) \\
+\ 11 \quad (6 + 5 = 11) \\
\hline
161 \quad (100 + 50 + 11 = 161)
\end{array}
$$

Geoffrey now has 161 football cards.

Lattice Addition Algorithm

In this algorithm, each column is added separately, and the sum of each column is recorded in a box diagonally cut in half (hence the name "lattice" addition). When all of the boxes are filled in, the numbers are added along the diagonals. This adding along the diagonal performs the function of regrouping. Thus, it is not necessary to add, then regroup and add, then regroup as it is in the standard algorithm. Many children find this algorithm easier than the standard one.

■ In a certain school district, there are 3429 children. Following a consolidation with another district, 785 more children are admitted. How many children is this in all?

$$
\begin{array}{c}
3 \quad 4 \quad 2 \quad 9 \\
+\ \quad 7 \quad 8 \quad 5 \\
\boxed{\begin{smallmatrix} 0 \diagup 1 \diagup 1 \diagup 1 \diagup \\ \diagup 3 \diagup 1 \diagup 0 \diagup 4 \end{smallmatrix}} \\
4 \quad 2 \quad 1 \quad 4
\end{array}
$$

There are now 4214 children in the district.

Powers-of-Ten Blocks with the Standard Subtraction Algorithm

Children can be given the following situation:

■ Mrs. Dedrick began the year with 42 pads of drawing paper. By spring break, the class had used 29 pads. How many were left?

After children have had an opportunity to estimate and to use their own methods to achieve the answer, they can be introduced to the standard algorithm using powers-of-ten blocks. Examine how each number is represented in Figure 3.12.

Since 9 units cannot be removed from 2 units, 1 ten from the 42 needs to be regrouped into units, resulting in 42 being rewritten as 3 tens and 12 units, as shown in Figure 3.13. This allows the removal of 29 from 42, leaving 13. Thirteen pads of drawing paper were left.

Here is the standard algorithm for subtraction involving regrouping. This algorithm is referred to as the *decomposition algorithm,* since it involves

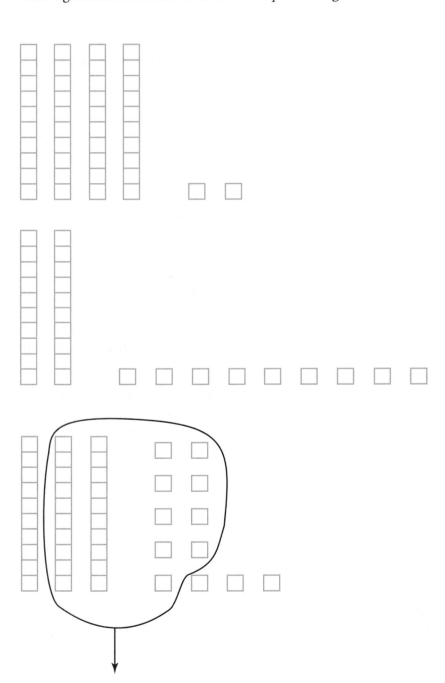

Figure 3.12

Figure 3.13

1 ten being decomposed into 10 ones, or 100 being decomposed into 10 tens.

$$\begin{array}{r} \overset{3}{\cancel{4}}\overset{1}{2} \\ -\ 29 \\ \hline 13 \end{array}$$

Notice how the paper-and-pencil algorithm mirrors the procedure with powers-of-ten blocks. Initially, subtracting 9 ones from 2 ones is not possible, necessitating the decomposition (or regrouping) of 1 ten into 10 ones. These 10 ones, added to the 2 ones that were already there, result in 12 ones. The subtraction is now possible.

A common error that children make when faced with an example of this type is to subtract the 2 from the 9, resulting in a solution that looks like this:

$$\begin{array}{r} 42 \\ -\ 29 \\ \hline 27 \end{array}$$

The frequency of this error underscores the need for children to get into the habit of estimating before solving algorithms. Even a rough estimate of this difference should be "a bit more than ten," alerting the child that an answer of 27 is suspect. Activity 3.9 give practice in subtraction.

Activity 3.9
Rotten Apple

Lesson: Pairs

Pair the children, then give each pair 15 markers, 14 of one color and 1 of another. The markers are lined up as shown in Figure 3.14, with the odd-colored marker on an end. Alternating turns, each child can remove 1, 2, or 3 markers at a time. The object of the activity is to force the other partner to take the "rotten apple," the odd-colored marker.

After they have had several opportunities to play, encourage children to develop a strategy that will enable them to win consistently.

Journal Reflection

Play this game with yourself or with a partner several times. At what point in the game can you tell who is going to win? Do you see the strategy that will allow you to tell almost from the beginning who will win? Articulate a general version of this strategy that can be used with any number of markers, and with rules that will allow any range of numbers of markers to be removed on each turn.

Figure 3.14

Alternative Algorithms for Whole-Number Subtraction

There are several different methods commonly used for subtracting. Depending on where you went to school, you may be familiar with one or more of them.

Equal Addends Subtraction

This algorithm is based on the concept that an equal amount added to both the minuend (top number) and subtrahend (bottom number) does not change the *difference* between the two numbers. Remember that subtraction is the operation that is used to determine the difference between two numbers. Consider this problem:

- The distance between Boston, Massachusetts and Memphis, Tennessee is approximately 1384 miles. If 795 miles are traveled during the first two days of a trip, how many miles remain?

$$
\begin{array}{r}
1\ 3\ 8\ ^1 4 \\
-\ 7\ 9\ 5 \\
_{10} \\
\hline
9
\end{array}
$$

Since 5 ones cannot be subtracted from 4 ones, make the 4 ones 14 ones and compensate by increasing the 9 tens in the subtrahend to 10 tens, as shown. Notice that the difference between the numbers is unchanged, since the minuend was increased by 10 ones, and the subtrahend was increased by 1 ten.

$$
\begin{array}{r}
1\ 3\ ^1 8\ ^1 4 \\
-\ 7\ 9\ 5 \\
_{8}\ _{10} \\
\hline
5\ 8\ 9
\end{array}
$$

Since 10 ones cannot be subtracted from 8 tens, make the 8 tens 18 tens, and compensate by increasing the 7 hundreds in the subtrahend to 8 hundreds. Finally, 8 hundreds can be subtracted from 13 hundreds, resulting in a difference of 589.

There are 589 miles remaining in the trip.

This algorithm is often easier for children with perceptual difficulties. Compare the visual appearance of the algorithm above with the standard decomposition algorithm shown here to see why.

$$
\begin{array}{r}
^{2}\ ^{17} \\
1\ \cancel{3}\ \cancel{8}\ ^1 4 \\
-\ 7\ 9\ 5 \\
\hline
5\ 8\ 9
\end{array}
$$

Another advantage of the equal addends method is that it is consistent. We *always* increase the minuend by ten of whatever place value it happens to be, and *always* compensate by increasing the subtrahend of the immediate next place value by one. This is in contrast to the decomposition method, where the place-value column in the minuend that is decomposed varies from example to example. Because we are so familiar with the decomposition method, we forget just how confusing it can be to children, especially with numbers like this:

$$
\begin{array}{r}
{}^{1}\,{}^{9}\,{}^{13}\\
2\,{}^{1}\!\emptyset\,\cancel{4}\,{}^{1}3\\
-\,1\,7\,8\,9\\
\hline
2\,5\,4
\end{array}
$$

Counting Up Subtraction

This alternative algorithm models the process used to count back change. Examine the following problem:

- A plot of land requires 762 feet of fencing to enclose it. If 183 feet of fence has already been erected, how much fencing remains to be installed?

762	Look at the subtrahend. Count to the next highest 10 and
− 183	record the number.
7	(183 to 190)
10	Count up to the next highest hundred (190 to 200)
500	Count up to the greatest place value (200 to 700)
+ 62	Count up to the minuend (700 to 762)
579	Find the sum of all of these differences,

There are 579 feet of fence that remain to be installed.

A big advantage of this algorithm, especially for children who have become convinced that they are incapable of learning subtraction, is that it allows you to subtract without subtracting. Notice that it was never necessary to know that $12 - 3 = 9$. Rather, the difference between the two numbers is determined by counting up from the lesser to the greater, a little bit at a time. When children become comfortable with this algorithm, they consolidate some steps (for instance, counting up from 200 to 762 in one step), and they perform almost all of it mentally. For these reasons, the counting-up algorithm is of practical value, and useful for children who are overwhelmed by the decomposition algorithm.

The Spreadsheet as a Problem-Solving Tool

Years ago, accountants kept their records in a book called a ledger. This ledger would list debits and credits in organized columns and rows. It was the job of the accountant to do all of the mathematics necessary to make sense of and connect the data recorded in the ledger. A computer spreadsheet is a technological tool that functions as an electronic ledger. In its simplest role, a spreadsheet can be used as an advanced calculator to organize and make sense of a set of data. Mathematics educators are finding that the spreadsheet can be a rich tool for problem solving at all levels.

Let's begin by examining the empty spreadsheet in Figure 3.15. Notice that the rows are labeled using numbers and the columns are labeled using letters. A particular location on the spreadsheet is identified by its lettered column and numbered row. For example, C5 is the location which

	A	B	C	D	E	F	G
1							
2							
3							
4							
5							
6							
7							
8							
9							
10							
11							
12							
13							
14							
15							

Figure 3.15

is at the intersection of column C and row 5. These locations are known as cells.

A *cell* is a location on the spreadsheet where a column and a row intersect. A cell can contain three different types of information; a label, a value, or a formula. A *label* is a word or phrase used for identification. It is often found as a column or row heading, or at some place in the display where an explanation of a calculated value is needed.

A *value* is a number. The degree of accuracy of this number can often be determined in the spreadsheet by defining the number of decimal places to be used. For example, if the spreadsheet is set for a degree of accuracy of 2, all entries will show two decimal places, and all calculations will be rounded to two decimal places.

A *formula* is a rule or command that instructs the computer to perform some preprogrammed function. Formulas can be formed by using the standard arithmetic functions (the four basic operations and square roots), or other functions that are defined by the particular program being used. But why use spreadsheets? What can this tool accomplish? Here is one answer.

> Spreadsheets allow the student to apply a variety of mathematics skills, both thinking and computing. A single spreadsheet can incorporate many mathematical topics and call on reasoning abilities that are rarely tapped in textbook problems. Initially, students may only use the technique of random trial and error by entering values in certain cells and then hoping for the best. But, as work continues with spreadsheet programs, haphazard guesses may lead to the development of systematic trial-and-error skills. The student enters a value, examines the results, then chooses another value based on the newly calculated display. The immediacy of the result encourages students to systematize their plan of attack by affording them the opportunity to reflect, review, and retry (Sgroi, 1992).

In the following example, the initial spreadsheet display is given to you, along with the generic formulas used to create the spreadsheet. Spreadsheet programs do differ. If you are transferring the spreadsheet from this text to your own spreadsheet files, you must first "translate" the commands given here into ones recognized by your software. Figure 3.16 presents a problem for which you can use your spreadsheet to model and determine a solution.

■ There are 20 animals in a barnyard. Some are chickens and the others are cows. Together, these animals have a total of 56 legs. Find the number of chickens and cows that can be in this barnyard.

	A	B	C	D	E	F	G
1							
2	Enter the number of cows in D2			0			
3							
4	Enter the number of chickens in D4			0			
5							
6	The total number of animals is			0			
7							
8	The total number of legs is			0			
9							
10							

Figure 3.16

Cells A2, B2, C2, A4, B4, C4, A6, B6, C6, A8, B8, and C8 all contain labels. In its present form, a zero is displayed in cells D2, D4, D6, and D8.

Figure 3.17 depicts the format of the spreadsheet. Cells D2 and D4 are value cells. The user moves the cursor to the cell and enters a value. Cells D6 and D8 are formula cells. Notice that an equal sign appears before each formula. (This symbol varies among software programs.) This symbol is used to show that the contents in the cells are formulas rather than values. The user enters a number of cows in D2 and a number of chickens in D4. The sum of these values appears in cell D6, and in this case, must equal 20.

	A	B	C	D	E	F	G
1							
2	Enter the number of cows in D2			0			
3							
4	Enter the number of chickens in D4			0			
5							
6	The total number of animals is			=D2+D4			
7							
8	The total number of legs is			=4*D2+2*D4			
9							
10							

Figure 3.17

	A	B	C	D	E	F	G
1							
2	Enter the number of cows in D2			8			
3							
4	Enter the number of chickens in D4			12			
5							
6	The total number of animals is			20			
7							
8	The total number of legs is			56			
9							
10							

Figure 3.18

The total number of legs appears in cell D8. The user can then experiment with different values until a pair is determined which yields the desired result. Figure 3.18 illustrates the solution to the problem.

Activity 3.10 contains a problem that can suitably, but not necessarily, be solved using a spreadsheet.

Activity 3.10

Bicycles and Tricycles

Lesson: Individual

■ A bike shop has 24 bicycles and tricycles on the show-room floor. Altogether there are 54 wheels. How many of the vehicles are bicycles and how many are tricycles?

Provide the students with counters, paper and pencil, or the format of the spreadsheet shown in Figure 3.19.

Journal Reflection

How might students systematize their trial-and-error guessing through the use of spreadsheets? How might you connect the use of tangible objects, such as counters, with the symbolic manipulation of a spreadsheet?

	A	B	C	D	E	F
1						
2	Enter the number of bicycles in D2			0		
3						
4	Enter the number of tricycles in D4			0		
5						
6	The total number of bicycles and tricycles is			=D2+D4		
7						
8	The total number of wheels is			=2*D2+3*D4		
9						
10						

Figure 3.19

Cooperative Group Model: Think, Pair, Share

Think: A coffee shop offers its customers the opportunity to mix four different types of coffee beans and create their own blend. French roast coffee costs $8.00 per pound. Mocha Java coffee costs $9.00 per pound. Columbian coffee costs $7.00 per pound. Hawaiian Kona coffee costs $10.00 per pound. Each type of coffee can be ordered in eighth-, quarter-, half-, or whole-pound quantities. The shop owner combines the desired types and amounts of beans, then grinds them. Rich stumbled upon a particular mix of these beans that he thoroughly enjoyed. Unfortunately, he cannot remember the quantities of each type. His old sales receipt indicates that his last purchase was a 1.5 pound bag of the special mix, which cost him $12 before tax. If you used a spreadsheet to determine a possible mix, would your solution be unique?

Pair: Use the spreadsheet of Figure 3.20 to model the situation and determine a solution. Figure 3.21 depicts the format of the spreadsheet. The formula SUM(cell:cell) finds the sum of the entries from the first cell name listed to the last cell name listed. The format of this command varies from one software program to another. Notice that an equal sign appears before each formula. This is used to show that the contents in that cell are formulas rather than values. Experiment with different amounts of each coffee type to attain the desired solution. You will find that the solution is not unique. Try to determine at least three different solutions.

Share: Discuss your methodology with the class. How did you organize your attempts? Once a solution was found, how were you able to use it in order to determine another solution?

	A	B	C	D	E	F
1						
2						
3						
4						
5	COFFEE	COST PER	QUANTITY	AMOUNT		
6	TYPE	POUND				
7						
8	FRENCH ROAST	$8.00	0.000	0.000		
9	MOCHA JAVA	$9.00	0.000	0.000		
10	COLUMBIAN	$7.00	0.000	0.000		
11	KONA	$10.00	0.000	0.000		
12		TOTALS	0.000	0.000		
13						

Figure 3.20

	A	B	C	D	E	F
1						
2						
3						
4						
5	COFFEE	COST PER	QUANTITY	AMOUNT		
6	TYPE	POUND				
7						
8	FRENCH ROAST	$8.00	0.000	=B8*C8		
9	MOCHA JAVA	$9.00	0.000	=B9*C9		
10	COLUMBIAN	$7.00	0.000	=B10*C10		
11	KONA	$10.00	0.000	=B11*C11		
12		TOTALS	=SUM(C8:C11)	=SUM(D8:D11)		
13						

Figure 3.21

Interdisciplinary
Lesson Plan

Grade 1   **Concept** Take-away model of subtraction

Topic Subtracting monetary amounts in a realistic context

Student Objectives After completing this lesson, students should be able to

• Illustrate the take-away model of subtraction using coins

• Identify the value of a penny

Materials 100 pennies, a copy of *Alexander, Who Used to Be Rich Last Sunday* by Judith Viorst.

Motivation Read *Alexander* to the class. Ask the children to describe ways they have spent their money, and suggestions they might offer Alexander to help him save some of his money.

Procedure Invite the children to sit in a circle in a carpeted area of the classroom, with a basket containing 100 pennies in the middle of the circle. Invite predictions about the number of pennies in the basket. Verify that there are, indeed, 100 pennies. 1. Ask the children to determine the value of 100 pennies. Verify that 100 pennies (or 100 cents) make a dollar. Invite the children to offer other combinations of coins that make a dollar, such as 10 dimes or 4 quarters. 2. Reread the book. Each time Alexander spends some money, invite a child to come up to the basket and remove the appropriate number of pennies. 3. At the end of the book, ask a child to verify that there are no pennies left in the basket, just as Alexander had no money left from his dollar.

Assessment Give each of the children 20 counters and have them write their own version of *Alexander, Who Used to Be Rich Last Sunday*. Make note of the number of items "purchased" by each child, and each child's accuracy in subtracting the appropriate amount from the total.

References *Alexander, Who Used to Be Rich Last Sunday*, Judith Viorst, Macmillan, 1978.

Journal Entry To be filled in by the teacher upon completion of the lesson. This section contains ways in which the lesson can be improved and ideas for possible extensions.

The teaching of the above lesson plan can easily be extended for older or more able children by varying the coins that are used. For example, the lesson can begin with 10 dimes, some of which are then traded for 10 pennies to allow the subtraction to take place. Do you see how this is a model of the process of subtraction with regrouping?

Alternately, the lesson can begin with four quarters (requiring a great deal of trading) or a dollar bill. If the children are adept with currency, the lesson can be done with paper and pencil, where each child writes down the numerical subtraction example that illustrates each purchase.

Performance-Based Assessment: Multi-Digit Addition and Subtraction

Distribute the following hypothetical student paper to the class. Ask each child to respond in writing about the accuracy or inaccuracy of each solution. Each child includes an explanation as to why the work was judged to be accurate or inaccurate, and corrects any errors.

- Evan has 63 marbles. Jacob has 39. How many more marbles does Evan have?

  63 −39 = 36   Evan has 36 more marbles.

- Allison earned $18 babysitting. Tony earned $25. Kate worked for an entire day and earned $33. How much money did the three friends earn all together?

  $18 + $25 + $33 = $76   The three friends earned $76 in all.

- Rosa sold 189 boxes of Girl Scout Cookies. Maria sold 211 boxes. How many boxes did the two girls sell in all?

  211 − 189 = 22   The girls sold 22 boxes in all.

The child who judged the first solution to be correct made the classic error of thinking that you can subtract the lesser number from the greater number, regardless of the position of the numbers. This child could be helped by being encouraged to estimate the difference before actually subtracting the numbers. In this case, a reasonable estimate would have been 20. It would also be helpful for all children to be encouraged to check their subtraction answers by adding the difference and the subtrahend to arrive at the minuend.

The second solution is correct. A child who judges it incorrect might have made an error in aligning the digits. This problem can be alleviated by having the child either turn lined paper sideways so that the blue lines form vertical columns, or by working on cm-square graph paper.

The third solution illustrates correct arithmetic, but an incorrect solution to the problem. The child who judges the given solution to be correct would be helped by being reminded of the four steps of problem solving: Read, Plan, Do, Look Back. This child did not pay sufficient attention to the Read or Look Back steps. To help the child understand what the problem is asking, encourage the child to rephrase or restate the problem. Some children are also helped to understand the problem by drawing a picture. After arriving at a solution, the child can be helped to pay attention to the

Look Back step by writing the answer in a complete sentence ("Rosa and Maria sold 22 boxes of cookies in all") and then assessing the reasonableness of the answer. This answer can be easily judged to be unreasonable, since each girl individually sold many more than 22 boxes.

Strength in Numbers

Alternative Subtraction Algorithm

This activity will be described within the context of the Numbered Heads Together model of cooperative groups. Recall that this model calls for heterogeneous groups of four students, each of whom is assigned a number from 1 to 4. The students work together to solve the problem, knowing that any one of them might be invited to explain the group's solution to the class.

Each student examines the alternative subtraction algorithm of Figure 3.22, called the Nine's Complement algorithm, as illustrated in example A, B, and C. Then, as a group, they apply the algorithm to examples D, E and F.

Now that you have determined *how* this algorithm works, determine *why* it works. To focus your investigation, answer the following questions:

- What is the mathematical significance of the movement of the 1 from the left-most column to the ones column? Will this number always be a one? How do you know?
- Is this another algorithm that allows you to subtract without actually subtracting?
- Do you see how the concept of an odometer might help you understand why this algorithm works?
- If you were to introduce this algorithm to students, what do you see as its advantages and disadvantages?

a)
$$
\begin{array}{r}
15 \\
-\ 6 \\
\end{array}
\longrightarrow
\begin{array}{r}
15 \\
+\ 93 \\
\hline
108 \\
+\ \llcorner 1 \\
\hline
9 \\
\end{array}
$$

b)
$$
\begin{array}{r}
203 \\
-\ 152 \\
\end{array}
\longrightarrow
\begin{array}{r}
203 \\
+\ 847 \\
\hline
1050 \\
+\ \llcorner 1 \\
\hline
51 \\
\end{array}
$$

c)
$$
\begin{array}{r}
15{,}683 \\
-\ 14{,}320 \\
\end{array}
\longrightarrow
\begin{array}{r}
15{,}683 \\
+\ 85{,}679 \\
\hline
101{,}362 \\
+\ \llcorner 1 \\
\hline
1363 \\
\end{array}
$$

d)
$$
\begin{array}{r}
652 \\
-\ 298 \\
\end{array}
$$

e)
$$
\begin{array}{r}
1001 \\
-\ 391 \\
\end{array}
$$

f)
$$
\begin{array}{r}
1952 \\
-\ 1527 \\
\end{array}
$$

Figure 3.22

Summary

There is an appropriate balance between focusing instruction on computational facility and focusing instruction on conceptual understanding and problem solving, and these goals are not mutually exclusive. You can help children learn and remember their basic facts by leading them to understand the nature of the operations of addition and subtraction. Children will become better problem solvers if they are confident about their ability to use numbers to reason about mathematical situations. This confidence grows out of facility with basic facts. A teacher must not decide between stressing computation or stressing problem solving. Rather, the challenge is to use both of these aspects of the curriculum to support each other.

This chapter presented different models for the operations of addition and subtraction. Addition is most often thought of as the process of combination, while subtraction can be thought of as the process of taking away, of comparing two quantities to find the difference between them, or of identifying the missing addend.

The standard algorithms of multi-digit addition and subtraction were modeled with powers-of-ten materials and given the names of regrouping (for addition) and decomposition (for subtraction). In offering alternative algorithms for both operations, the argument was made that alternative algorithms benefit children who are already facile with the standard algorithm by challenging them to figure out why the algorithms work. Alternative algorithms also benefit children who struggle with the standard algorithm by offering them an alternate process. Finally, alternative algorithms are valuable because they vividly illustrate that there are many valid ways to solve problems.

Extending Your Learning

1. Visit a primary or an elementary school. Look for materials, other than powers-of-ten materials, that can be used to model the processes of addition and subtraction for students. Discuss the pros and cons of each material.

2. Describe separate classroom activities that you would use to introduce the following concepts to children:

   - Addition as the combination of continuous quantities
   - The comparison model of subtraction using discrete quantities
   - The take-away model of subtraction using discrete quantities

3. Discuss specific reasons why, and specific examples of how, you would teach the commutative and associative properties of whole-number addition.

4. Write a sample letter to parents to obtain their assistance in helping children commit the basic addition/subtraction facts to memory. Include specific suggestions for activities that parents can do at home to help their children. Include in this letter your philosophy about the memorization of basic facts.

5. Examine a current second-or third-grade textbook to see if any alternative algorithms are included. Explain and justify your position on the role of alternative algorithms in the elementary school classroom.

6. Interview two or three people who attended elementary school in another country. Ask them to explain how they add and subtract. Do they use different algorithms than you do? Do they understand why their algorithm works?

7. Create a game that children can play to help them practice their basic addition/subtraction facts. Some possibilities are board games, card games, dice games, or spinner games. Ask some children to play the game. Does your game seem to achieve its goal? Why or why not? Do the children like the game? Why or why not?

8. Visit a local bookstore. Examine the books written for the general public that are designed to help children improve their ability to add and subtract. Critique these books. Would you recommend them to parents? Why or why not?

9. Write a lesson plan that integrates science and mathematics and addresses addition and/or subtraction concepts.

10. Write a lesson plan that integrates art and mathematics and addresses addition and/or subtraction concepts.

Internet Resources

http://ernie.wmht.org/trail/trail.htm
This website, a joint initiative between the Troy Public Schools and WMHT, a public radio station, is a cybertrail for K-5 teachers who are relatively inexperienced in using the web. It provides resources available on the web, links to elementary school home pages and student publishing on the web, and interactive student projects using the Internet. It has links to sites for children.

www.infotrac-college.com/wadsworth
This online library service, free with the purchase of this text, searches for and then displays on screen the full text of articles from more than 700 publications, including *Exceptional Children, Educational Leadership,* and the NCTM publication *Teaching Children Mathematics.* Currently, there are more than 700,000 articles contained within the service, which is updated daily.

www.pbs.org/teachersource/math/
This website, sponsored by the Public Broadcasting System, provides links to many sites of interest to elementary school math teachers.

www.sportsline.com/
This website provides current scores, standings, and other statistics from a variety of sports, including baseball, basketball, football, hockey, golf, tennis, and racing. This information can be used for creating realistic problems in the classroom.

www.gsn.org/
This website, Global School Network, is extensive and contains many links to other sites. Lesson plans are available, as well as student worksheets and activities that can be printed out directly from the website.

Bibliography

Bartek, Mary Marron. (1997). Hands-on addition and subtraction with the three little pigs. *Teaching Children Mathematics 4* (2).

Carroll, William M., and Denise Porter. (1999). Invented strategies can develop meaningful mathematics procedures. *Teaching Children Mathematics 5* (9).

Crews, Donald. (1986). *Ten Black Dots.* New York: Mulberry Books.

Curcio, Frances R., and Sydney L. Schwartz. (1998). There are no algorithms for teaching algorithms. *Teaching Children Mathematics 5*(1).

Drum, Randell L., and Wesley G. Petty, Jr. (1999). Teaching the value of coins. *Teaching Children Mathematics 5*(5).

Flashcard System. (1993). IBM Compatible. You and Me Products, PO Box 61488, Vancouver, WA 98666.

Hankes, Judith E. (1996). An alternative to basic-skills remediation. *Teaching Children Mathematics 2*(8).

Harris, Jacqueline. (1999). Interweaving language and mathematics literacy through a story. *Teaching Children Mathematics 5*(9).

Hembree, Ray, and Donald J. Dessart. (1986). Effects of hand-held calculators in precollege mathematics education: A meta-analysis. *Journal for Research in Mathematics Education 17*: 83–99.

Hiebert, James, and Thomas P. Carpenter. (1992). Learning and teaching with understanding. In Douglas A. Grouws (ed.), *Handbook of research on mathematics teaching and learning* (pp. 77–78). New York: Macmillan.

Isaacs, Andrew C., and William M. Carroll. (1999). Strategies for basic fact instruction. *Teaching Children Mathematics 5*(9).

Kamii, Constance. (1985). *Young children reinvent arithmetic: Implications of Piaget's theory.* New York: Teachers College Press.

Kamii, Constance. (1989). *Young children continue to reinvent arithmetic: 2nd grade.* New York: Teachers College Press.

Math Ace. 1993. IBM Compatible. Magic Quest, 125 University Ave., Palo Alto, CA 94301.

Millie's Math House. Edmark, PO Box 97021, Redmond, WA 98073-971.

Viorst, Judith. (1978). *Alexander, who used to be rich last Sunday.* New York, Macmillan.

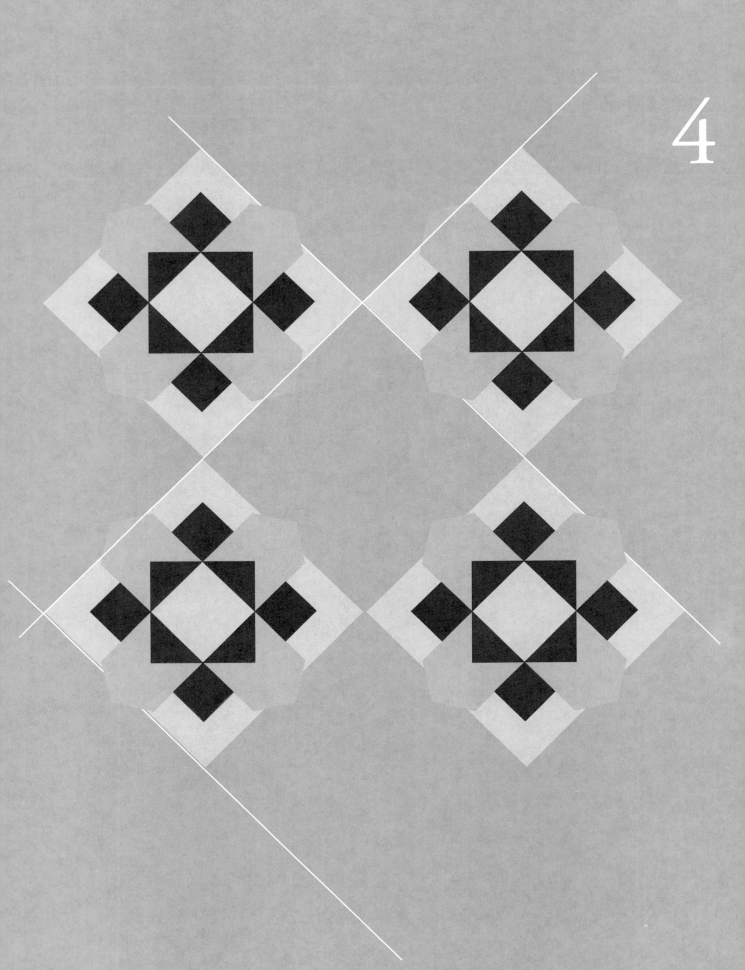

Standards for Whole Numbers: Multiplication and Division

Literacy educators agree that if children are not yet able to read by the time they have reached third grade, then they will have difficulties for the rest of their school careers. Similarly, children who have reached third grade and are not yet facile with the basic addition and subtraction facts will have difficulty with multiplication and division. Mathematics has often been described as a sequential discipline, and there is some truth in that description. One of the ways that children can understand multiplication is as the process of repeated addition, and division can be thought of as repeated subtraction. Understanding these connections is dependent upon understanding addition and subtraction in the first place.

On a more encouraging note, however, children who have had positive experiences learning mathematics in the primary grades enter the elementary and intermediate grades with confidence, enthusiasm, and curiosity about solving mathematical problems and engaging in mathematical activities. Many of the same thought processes—observation, description, classification, and analysis—will continue to be important as children begin to study the operations of multiplication and division.

Operations of Multiplication and Division

As children become interested in larger numbers and more complex mathematical situations, they naturally develop the need to use the operations of multiplication and division. For example, a child who receives three dollars a week for allowance and wants to know how much money can be saved by a certain day might take a calendar and count "3" for each week in question. Introducing the child to the use of multiplication in this context would be both timely and appropriate.

A child wishing to share a bag of candy hearts with friends would likely want to achieve an equal distribution. This would be a useful time to introduce the operation of division while pointing out its efficiency for equal sharing. This would also be a realistic context in which to deal with a remainder.

The operations of multiplication and division are usually introduced in third grade, as children become mathematically more sophisticated and their world expands to included greater numbers. There are at least three ways for children to think of the operation of multiplication and at least three different real-life contexts in which it is used: (1) as the process of repeated addition, (2) as an array, and (3) as a collection of equal groups. Following the excerpts from *Principles and Standards,* Activities 4.1, 4.2, and 4.3 illustrate each of these models of multiplication. Notice that they all employ number in the discrete sense. Different models of multiplication are addressed later in this chapter.

Number and Operation for Grades 3–5

According to NCTM *Principles and Standards,* in grades 3 through 5, all students should

- Understand the meaning of multiplication and division, including multiple representations—for example, multiplication as repeated addition or as an array
- Identify and use relationships between operations to solve problems—for example, 28×7 is equivalent to $(20 \times 7) + (8 \times 7)$, or $(30 \times 7) - (2 \times 7)$

Activity 4.1

Paper Plate Flowers

Lesson: Individual

Distribute a small paper plate to all of the children, and ask them to create a flower that contains exactly five petals. Some examples are shown here in Figure 4.1

Invite one child to come up to the front of the room to display a flower. Ask the children to determine the number of petals in all. Ask a second child to join the first child, and again determine the number of petals in all. Repeat with three children, then four, then five, and so on. After the children become comfortable with this process, invite a child to speak a complete sentence about the number of petals on, for example, three plates. When the child says "Three flowers with five petals each is 15 petals in

all," offer this symbolic version of the sentence:

$$5 + 5 + 5 = 15$$

3 groups of 5 is 15, or

$$3 \times 5 = 15$$

Again, repeat the above process until the children seem to be comfortable with it.

Journal Reflection

How would you use this activity to generate a written record of the five times table? Do you foresee any possible problems with your plan?

Figure 4.1

Activity 4.2

Planting a Garden

Lesson: Individual

Distribute twelve monochromatic Unifix cubes or other counters and one $8\frac{1}{2} \times 11$ sheet of green construction paper to each child. Explain to the children that you are planning a garden, and that the twelve Unifix cubes represent the plants you want to put in your garden. Ask them to arrange the cubes into *equal* rows on the construction paper so you can see how your garden will look. The following arrangements, or arrays, are possible:

```
x x x x   x x x x x x x x x x x x   x x x x x
x x x x                             x x x x x
x x x x
```

For children who are unsure if a 3×4 array is equivalent to a 4×3 array, simply have then rotate the construction paper 90 degrees to illustrate the equivalence. While there may be contexts in which you want 3×4 to be considered a different outcome than 4×3 (as in a probability context of tossing two dice), in this situation they should be considered equivalent.

To make the connection between the physical array and its symbolic representation, again ask a child to speak a sentence about one array. When the child says "Two rows with 6 plants in each row is 12 plants in all," write the following symbols:

$$2 \text{ rows of } 6 \text{ is } 12$$

$$2 \times 6 = 12$$

Journal Reflection

Do you think that doing this activity with inch-square graph paper as the background would be an improvement? Why or why not?

- Develop fluency with single-digit multiplication facts by grade 4 and use these facts to compute related problems efficiently—30×50 is related to 3×5, 300×5, and 15×100

- Develop and compare whole-number computational algorithms for each operation that are based on understanding number relationships, the base-10 number system, and the properties of these operations—and, by the end of grade 5, develop efficiency and accuracy in using these algorithms

- Develop and use computational estimation strategies based on an understanding of number concepts, properties, and relationships

- Choose appropriate computational procedures and tools—calculators, pencil and paper, mental computation, estimation—to solve problems (pp. 156–57)

There are several properties of multiplication that will help children understand it as an operation. Two of these, the associative property and the distributive property, will be introduced in a context where they are useful—that of mental estimation. Others will be discussed here.

Properties of Whole-Number Multiplication

- *The closure property of whole-number multiplication.* The product of two whole numbers is itself a unique whole number. A set with this property is said to be *closed* under multiplication.

Activity 4.3

Bears in their Beds

Lesson: Individual

Use a spinner divided into 6 sections or write the numbers from 0 to 5 (numbers larger than this become unwieldy) on a small wooden cube to provide a fair chance device. Distribute several pieces of newsprint to each child, along with at least 25 monochromatic Teddy Bear counters. Explain to the children that the first number you spin (or toss) tells them the number of beds to draw, and the second number tells them how many bears to put in each bed. Model spinning the number 3 and then the number 2 to result in an illustration such as that shown in Figure 4.2

Spin the spinner and call out the numbers to allow the children to fill in several sheets with "Bears in their Beds." Invite the children to write a number sentence on the bottom of each page to describe the illustration. The number sentence corresponding to the above illustration would be:

3 Beds with 2 Bears in each is 6 Bears, or

$$3 \times 2 = 6$$

After displaying the children's work, read them a favorite version of *The Three Bears*.

Figure 4.2

- *The identity property of whole number multiplication.* There exists a unique whole number, 1, such that for any whole number *a*, $a \times 1 = 1 \times a = a$.

- *The zero property of whole number multiplication.* For any whole number *a*, $a \times 0 = 0 \times a = 0$.

Because of the zero property of whole-number multiplication, many children think that there must also be an inverse relationship, and that any number divided by zero must result in a quotient of zero. This is not the case. Zero is excluded as a divisor in all definitions of division. If *a* and *b* are any whole numbers with *b* not equal to zero, and if $a \div b = c$, then $b \times c = a$ for some whole number *c*. If zero were not excluded from this definition, then $a \div 0 = c$ would imply that $0 \times c = a$. The zero property of multiplication states that 0 times any number is equal to 0. Therefore, $0 \times c = 0 = a$. This contradicts the given information that *a* could be any whole number. It is for this reason that division by zero is said to be *undefined*.

Sometimes children think that any number divided by 0 should equal 0, or that any number divided by 0 should equal that number itself. Examine what would happen if either of these statements were true.

$$a \div b = c$$

Let $a = 3$ and $b = 0$ Let $a = 3$ and $b = 0$.

If $3 \div 0 = 0$, then   If $3 \div 0 = 3$, then

0×0 must equal 3 3×0 must equal 3

Clearly, neither of these statements can be true, and thus division by zero is excluded from the definition of division.

Children typically use the operation of division in one of two contexts: (1) in the context of repeated subtraction, or (2) in the context of equal partition or sharing. In both of these contexts, a real-life situation often results in a remainder. It is not often that there are exactly enough cookies for everyone to have two, or exactly enough crayons to last throughout the year. Be careful to help children interpret remainders within the context of the situation. In this way, children are less likely to report that "four remainder two" cookie sheets are needed to bake the cookies, or that "six remainder three buses" are needed for transportation to the museum.

Activities 4.4 and 4.5 illustrate, in turn, the two models of division mentioned above, repeated subtraction and equal sharing. Notice that both involve using number in the continuous sense.

Basic Facts of Multiplication and Division

Many of the activities for practicing the addition and subtraction facts introduced in Chapter 3 can be adapted for the 100 multiplication and division facts (for instance, Guess My Rule and I Have . . . Who Has . . . ?). Additional adaptations are included here, along with some new games and activities. The same precautions mentioned earlier apply here: Children should fully understand the operations of multiplication and division before they are encouraged to commit the basic facts to memory, and practice sessions should be brief, frequent, and varied.

Basic Facts Strategies

If children understand the connections among the various times tables, they can often use their knowledge of one times table to generate another. For example, a child who knows the two times table can generate the four times table in the following way:

If two groups of six equals twelve,

X X X X X

X X X X X

then four groups of six would look like this:

X X X X X   X X X X X

X X X X X   X X X X X

and would equal two groups of twelve, or 24.

Activity 4.4

Watering Plants

Lesson: Whole Class

Display a pitcher containing 1500 ml of water. Have the following materials available: calculators, graduated cylinders, metric measuring cups, other pitchers and sources of water. Pose the following problem to the class:

- "If my plant requires 100 ml of water each day, how many days will this pitcher last?"

  Allow the students time to solve the problem. After the students have had ample opportunity to solve the problem, encourage them to share their solution and method with the class. Some comments might be:

- "We measured out 100 ml of water and poured it down the sink to see how many times we could do that. We were able to do it 15 times. That means that the water will last 15 days."

- "We used the following keystroke sequence on our calculators to see how many times we could subtract 100 from 1500:

  $\boxed{\text{AC}}$ −100 $\boxed{\text{CONS}}$ 1500 $\boxed{\text{CONS}}$ $\boxed{\text{CONS}}$
  $\boxed{\text{CONS}}$ $\boxed{\text{CONS}}$ $\boxed{\text{CONS}}$ . . . .

  We found out that we could subtract 100 from 1500 15 times before the display said 0."

- "We just knew that the water would last 15 days, because we knew that there are 15 one hundreds in 1500. Listen to the number *fifteen hundred*. You can tell that there are 15 one hundreds in that number."

Use this opportunity to introduce the two common symbolic means of recording this division problem:

$$1500 \div 100 = 15 \qquad 100\overline{)1500}^{\,15}$$

Each of these examples should be translated as "There are 15 100s in 1500." Avoid using the common but meaningless phrase "goes into." As you can see from this example, nothing is going into anything else. Rather, the students are faced with the problem of determining how many times a certain quantity can be removed from another quantity. Hence, this model of division is referred to as repeated subtraction.

Journal Reflection

Try to write two word problems that would illustrate for children the repeated subtraction model of division. In one word problem, use number in the discrete sense. In the other problem, use number in the continuous sense.

The eight times table can be generated from the four times table in the same manner.

In addition, children quickly realize that having a factor of zero always results in a product of zero, since no matter how many groups of zero you have, the result is always zero. This is an appropriate time to introduce 1 as the *identity* element in multiplication, by giving children many examples of multiplication with 1 as a factor. Children are able to generalize that one group of any number *N* always results in a product of *N*. In other words, multiplying by 1 does not change the value of a number.

If a multiplication chart like that of Figure 4.3 is displayed in the class, children can easily become overwhelmed. However, if you point out to the class that they know almost half of the chart before they even begin, they

Activity 4.5

Sharing Paper

Lesson: Small Group

Divide the class into groups and give each group 100 sheets of construction paper. Have the following materials available to the students: calculators, counters, paper and pencil. Pose this problem: "If I want to share this paper equally among the 28 people in this class, how many sheets of paper will each person get?"

After the groups have had an opportunity to solve the problem on their own, encourage them to share their results with the class. Some comments might be:

- "We drew 28 circles on a large sheet of paper. Then we made one mark in each circle to show that everyone can get one sheet. Then we did it again, and we did it again. So far, we had used up 84 sheets of paper. We didn't have enough to give everyone another sheet of paper, but we think that if we cut the leftovers in half, everyone can get another half, or

$3\frac{1}{2}$ sheets in all. There will be some half sheets left."

- "We put the number 100 into the calculator. Then we subtracted 28 and got 72. We subtracted 28 again and got 44. We subtracted 28 again and got 16. This means that everyone can get 3 sheets of paper and there will be 16 sheets left over."

- "We dealt out 100 counters into 28 groups, and realized that each person could receive 3 sheets of paper with 16 sheets remaining.

At this point, it is useful to model the symbolic representation of the above problem.

$$100 \div 28 = 3 \text{ R } 16 \qquad 28\overline{)100}\ ^{3\ R\ 16}$$

Journal Reflection

How would you use this problem to explain the concept of a "remainder" to children?

will feel reassured. Because of the predictability of the facts, generally children already know the 1, 2, 5, and 10 times table, and you can highlight these rows and columns as shown in Figure 4.4. Remind them that the commutative property cuts in half the number of facts to be committed to memory.

Some children find a chart helpful to envision the times tables. This can be done in two ways: (1) based on the equal groups model of multiplication, and (2) based on the array model of multiplication. In the first case, the chart might look something like the one pictured in Figure 4.5, on page 120. While it has been drawn to include only five groups of each set of objects, you may wish to create a larger one for your classroom that shows ten groups of each set of objects. Notice that there are no numbers written across the top of the chart. This is because the chart must be interpreted cumulatively, and cannot be read in the same way as the chart of Figure 4.3, which can be read both horizontally and vertically.

Another type of visual chart that is based on the array model of multiplication is shown in Figure 4.6, on page 121. Here, the cumulative arrays are built both horizontally and vertically. If you follow the third column down, for example, you can see a 1 × 3 array, a 2 × 3 array, a 3 × 3 array,

X	1	2	3	4	5	6	7	8	9	10
1	1	2	3	4	5	6	7	8	9	10
2	2	4	6	8	10	12	14	16	18	20
3	3	6	9	12	15	18	21	24	27	30
4	4	8	12	16	20	24	28	32	36	40
5	5	10	15	20	25	30	35	40	45	50
6	6	12	18	24	30	36	42	48	54	60
7	7	14	21	28	35	42	49	56	63	70
8	8	16	24	32	40	48	56	64	72	80
9	9	18	27	36	45	54	63	72	81	90
10	10	20	30	40	50	60	70	80	90	100

Figure 4.3

and so on. If you follow the third row across, you can see a 3 × 1 array, a 3 × 2 array, a 3 × 3 array, and so on. For an interesting account of children's creating their own chart of this type, see the article by Barbara Armstrong in the March 1995 issue of *Teaching Children Mathematics*.

Still another multiplication chart, given to me by a Russian colleague, is shown in Figure 4.7, on page 122. It uses a hundreds chart, but shows only the products of the factors from 1 to 10. This representation has the effect of focusing attention on the products of the 100 basic multiplication facts, and many students respond by commenting how few of them there actually are. Many composite numbers are the products of more than one set of factors. This information is communicated in the chart by the pairs of factors that are written above each product. Notice that 2*6 and 3*4 are both written above the 12, and that 2*9 and 3*6 are both written above the 18.

Another chart, also a gift from a Russian colleague, is a good deal more attractive than many of the multiplication charts. As you can see in Figure 4.8, on page 123, the times tables can be read either from the center toward the edges, or along one of the arcs from left to right. In the original, this chart is similar to the array chart shown in Figure 4.6 in that it makes use of color, but also because both charts show, for example, 64 things as the

X	1	2	3	4	5	6	7	8	9	10
1	1	2	3	4	5	6	7	8	9	10
2	2	4	6	8	10	12	14	16	18	20
3	3	6	9	12	15	18	21	24	27	30
4	4	8	12	16	20	24	28	32	36	40
5	5	10	15	20	25	30	35	40	45	50
6	6	12	18	24	30	36	42	48	54	60
7	7	14	21	28	35	42	49	56	63	70
8	8	16	24	32	40	48	56	64	72	80
9	9	18	27	36	45	54	63	72	81	90
10	10	20	30	40	50	60	70	80	90	100

Figure 4.4

product of 8 and 8. In the array chart, an 8 × 8 array contains 64 little cells. In the "peacock" chart, there are 64 little bars by the time the arc reaches the sector marked with the large "8."

Displaying these charts around the classroom and having children reproduce their own versions to be taken home can help children who have a strong visual sense to commit the multiplication facts to memory.

Even/Odd

This activity will help children learn something about probability as well as about the multiplication facts. Working in pairs, children are given two number cubes and a pencil and paper for keeping score. They are to choose between themselves who will get a point if the product tossed is even, and who will get a point if the product tossed is odd. Before beginning the activity, encourage the children to predict if they think the game is a fair game or an unfair game. A fair game is defined as one in which neither player has an advantage.

Any six numbers can be written on the cubes, depending on the times tables that you want the children to practice. The only caution is that the numbers should either be consecutive or be equally balanced between even and odd. (Do you see why?)

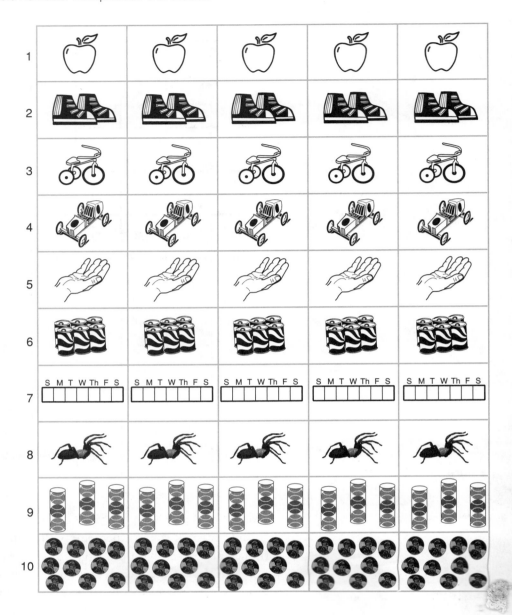

Figure 4.5

After several minutes of play, tally the class to see if the "even" person was winning or the "odd" person was winning. Invite the class to explain why the even person won consistently. Some children might try to count up, from a multiplication chart, the number of odd products and the number of even products. You can help children generalize to any set of numbers by constructing, with explanation, a tree diagram like that of Figure 4.9, on page 123, or by allowing for all possibilities like this:

$$E \times E = E$$

$$E \times O = E$$

$$O \times E = E$$

$$O \times O = O$$

Chart of arrays

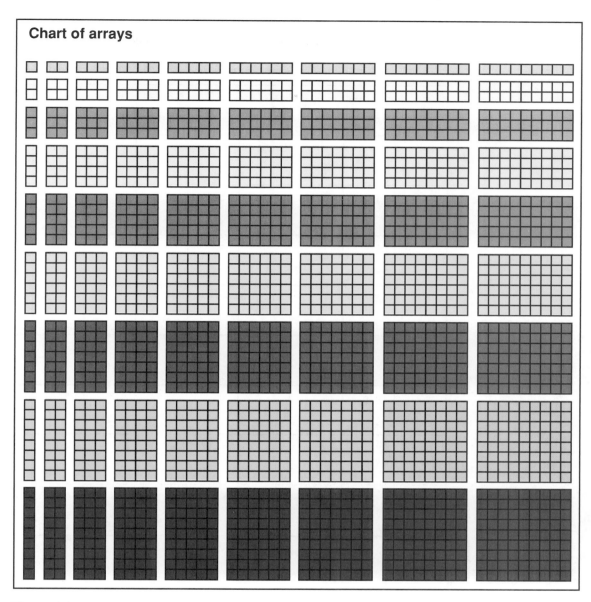

Figure 4.6

This activity illustrates to children that $\frac{3}{4}$ of the multiplication facts from 1 to 10 are even. If they are unsure if 7×8 is 55 or 56, they should realize that it is more likely 56. A more sophisticated analysis would lead the children to realize that if there is at least one even factor the product must be even, and that the only situation in which a product is odd is when *both* factors are odd.

Two Over

Two children evenly divide a deck of cards minus the face cards. They simultaneously turn over two cards each. The person with the highest product (obtained by multiplying the numbers on the two cards) takes all four cards. If the two pairs of cards both have the same product, each player turns over two more cards and again finds the product. The person who has the highest product this time takes all eight cards.

1	2	3	4	5	6	7	8	9	10	
1·1 1	1·2 2	1·3 3	1·4 2·2 4	1·5 5	1·6 2·3 6	1·7 7	1·8 2·4 8	1·9 9	1·10 2·5 10	10
	2·6 3·4 12		2·7 14	3·5 15	2·8 4·4 16		2·9 3·6 18		2·10 4·5 20	20
3·7 21			3·8 4·6 24	5·5 25		3·9 27	4·7 28		3·10 5·6 30	30
	4·8 32			5·7 35	4·9 6·6 36				4·10 5·8 40	40
	6·7 42			5·9 45			6·8 48	7·7 49	5·10 50	50
			6·9 54		7·8 56				6·10 60	60
		7·9 63	8·8 64						7·10 70	70
	8·9 72								8·10 80	80
9·9 81									9·10 90	90
									10·10 100	100

Figure 4.7

Multiplication Cover-Up

This game (adapted from Kamii, 1985) is similar to the addition version introduced earlier in the chapter 3. Here, the game board is adapted to accommodate the products obtainable from the factors of 1 through 6. If your goal is to practice the facts of higher numbers, the game board would have to contain the products obtainable from, for instance, the numbers 5 through 10.

Each pair of students is given the game board pictured in Figure 4.10 plus two dice or number cubes. The students take turns tossing the dice and covering up the product of the two numbers that appear on the dice, until one player has covered up a side completely.

Salute

This activity (adapted from Kamii, 1989) is played by three children, and requires a deck of playing cards with the face cards removed. One child is designated the General, and the other two "soldiers" divide the cards evenly between themselves in face-down piles. Each soldier selects the top card and

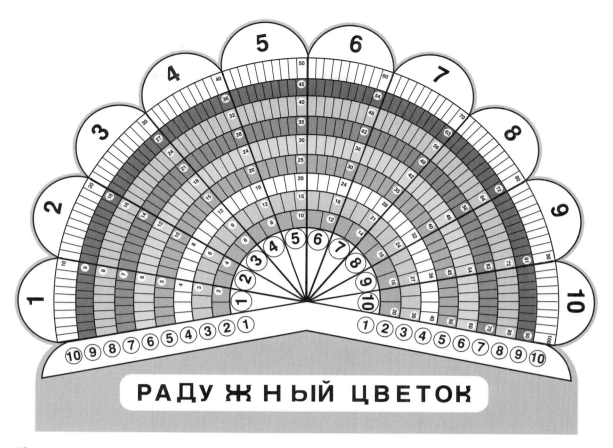

Figure 4.8

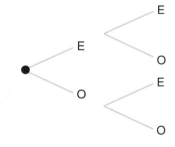

Figure 4.9

"salutes" the General by holding the card up against the forehead, so it can be seen only by the General and the other soldier. The General mentally multiplies the two numbers together and calls out only the product. The first soldier who correctly identify his or her own card takes both cards. For example, a soldier who sees the other soldier saluting with a 5 and hears the General say "40" reasons that he or she must be saluting with an 8, and quickly calls out "Eight!"

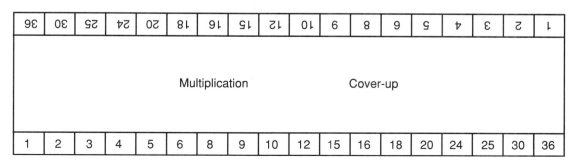

Figure 4.10

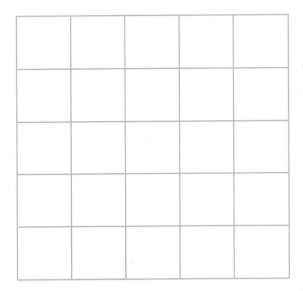

Figure 4.11

Bingo

Distribute a blank five-by-five matrix to each child, as shown in Figure 4. 11. Ask the children to choose 24 numerals randomly to fill in each blank cell, taken from the following list of the products of the 100 basic facts:

1	2	3	4	5	6	7	8	9	10
12	14	15	16	18	20	21	24	25	27
28	30	32	35	36	40	42	45	48	49
50	54	56	60	63	64	70	72	80	81
90	100								

Using a commercially available set of multiplication flash cards, or a spinner divided into ten sections to generate each factor, have a child call out a number sentence such as "5 × 8" until someone has gotten Bingo. It will be interesting to see if some children realize that certain products, such as 12, 16, or 24 are more likely to occur, and choose their numbers accordingly.

Patterns

Distribute a blank hundreds chart to each child. Ask the children to color in the multiples of a given number between 2 and 10. An example of what this would look like for the number 4 is shown in Figure 4.12. Encourage the children to describe any patterns they see. Some comments might be:

- ■ "All of the numbers are even."
- ■ "The numbers all end in a 2, 4, 6, 8, or 0."
- ■ "The numbers form diagonal lines."

These activities, designed to help children commit the basic multiplication/division facts to memory, are deliberately varied. Some are visual, some

1	2	3	4	5	6	7	8	9	10
11	12	13	14	15	16	17	18	19	20
21	22	23	24	25	26	27	28	29	30
31	32	33	34	35	36	37	38	39	40
41	42	43	44	45	46	47	48	49	50
51	52	53	54	55	56	57	58	59	60
61	62	63	64	65	66	67	68	69	70
71	72	73	74	75	76	77	78	79	80
81	82	83	84	85	86	87	88	89	90
91	92	93	94	95	96	97	98	99	100

Figure 4.12

are tactile, some are auditory, and some are a combination. By varying the content of the practice sessions, you allow for the possibility of certain activities appealing to certain children. Success in mastering the basic facts is important for future topics, such as multi-digit computation, and also for developing estimation skills.

Computer Software

When students use a software program, it gives them a private venue for reinforcing their knowledge—and one that can be infinitely repeated with infinite patience. One such program, *MindTwister Math* (Edmark), provides opportunities for students to estimate products and quotients, to solve problems, to perform mental math calculations, and to develop fluency with the basic facts. The *Mighty Math Calculating Crew* (Edmark) involves students in a simulation where they use multiplication and division skills to distribute essential supplies in an alien civilization.

As you work with children in a learning situation, observe them as they interact with computer software. What kinds of programs absorb them? What kinds of programs help them develop mathematical skills? What kinds of programs force them to become directly engaged in the activity, as opposed to passively hitting keys? Use some of the programs yourself. Deliberately enter an incorrect answer. Does the program merely label the

Strength in Numbers

Problem Solving

Cooperative group model: *Consensus Strategies* (Robertson, Graves, and Tuck, 1990)

In this cooperative group model, students work together on a problem. Each student uses a different strategy in an attempt to solve the problem. After each member of the group shares their solution and method of solution, the group comes to a consensus about the preferred problem-solving strategy.

Working in pairs, solve the following problem. Two strategies will be suggested to you. After each member of the pair has successfully solved the problem, discuss the advantages and disadvantages of each method of solution. Decide between yourselves on the preferred method. Share this decision with your classmates. Discuss any other possible strategies, and their advantages and disadvantages.

■ Three friends are at a sleep-over party. They decide to share a bowl of candy the following morning. During the night, one of the friends divides the candy into 3 equal shares, giving the one extra piece to her cat. She then hides her share and goes back to sleep. Later that night, another of the friends again divides what is left of the candy into 3 equal shares, giving the one extra piece to the cat. She also hides her share and returns to sleep. The third friend later awakens and does the same thing. The next morning, the friends divide what is left of the candy into 3 equal shares, again giving the one extra piece to the cat. What is the fewest number of pieces of candy that originally could have been in the bowl?

Method 1: Trial and Check

You can attempt to solve this problem by randomly choosing a number that can be divided by 3 with 1 remainder, and then working through the steps of the problem to see if this original number allows for the multiple sharings with-one-left-over. You may want to begin by setting some reasonable parameters for the numbers chosen. You may decide, for example, that it is unreasonable to think that there would have been fewer than 16 pieces of candy in the bowl originally, or more than 200.

Method 2: Work Backwards

This strategy focuses on a possible solution and then works regressively through the problem to see if the solution fulfills the requirements of the problem statement. For example, when the friends divide the remaining candies in the morning, the smallest individual share could be one piece of candy. This would mean that the third friend left 4 pieces of candy in the bowl before she went back to sleep. These four candies represent two equal shares, since one share was hidden and the extra piece given to the cat. This implies that there were 7 pieces of candy in the bowl (3 shares of 2 with 1 left over) when she awoke. Continue to work backwards through the problem to see if these numbers allow for the multiple sharings stipulated in the problem. If they do not, work backwards through the possibilities (a final share of 2 pieces, a final share of 3 pieces, and so on) to ensure that you have not skipped over the solution.

Reaching Consensus

Which of these two strategies or any other strategies you may have chosen do you think are most appropriate? Why? Do you think this problem is useful in an elementary classroom? Why or why not?

response as incorrect and supply the correct response, or does the program give you the chance to figure out the correct answer for yourself? As with any learning situation, the more actively involved the learners are, the more valuable the experience (see Strength in Numbers, opposite page).

Performance-Based Assessment: Basic Multiplication and Division Facts

Working in groups of four, each group will be given this problem to solve. Have calculators, counters, paper, and scissors available for student use. There are four steps involved in solving the problem and, while each student is primarily responsible for one of those steps, all of the students must agree on the way each step has been carried out.

■ A manufacturer has 18 congruent wooden disks and 76 identical metal chimes that can be used to make two types of wind chimes. The larger size requires 5 chimes attached to the disk. The smaller size requires 3 chimes. Using all of the chimes, how many of each type can be made?

Student 1: *Restate* the problem in your own words.
Student 2: Devise a *plan* for solving the problem.
Student 3: *Carry out* the plan.
Student 4: *Look back* at the original problem and evaluate the solution. If the solution is inadequate, indicate how, and offer suggestions for improvement.

After the students have had an adequate amount of time to solve this problem, have them each write down their contribution according to the four steps just outlined. For performance-based assessment activities such as this, teachers often develop a *rubric* or a *schema* for evaluating student performance in problem solving. Here is a sample rubric that can be used with the above problem, and with problem solving in general.

Restate

0 Complete lack of comprehension of the nature of the problem.

1 Partial understanding of the problem.

2 Full and complete understanding of what the problem is asking.

Plan

0 Plan is completely inadequate to solve problem.

1 Plan, if successfully implemented, will lead to partial solution of the problem.

2 Plan is appropriate, and, if successfully implemented, will lead to accurate solution of the problem.

Carry Out

0: Plan is inappropriately carried out due to mathematical errors or misunderstandings of the plan.

1: Plan is partially implemented, and leads to partial solution of the problem.

2: Plan is successfully implemented, and leads to successful solution of the problem.

Look Back

0: No attempt to analyze solution within the context of the problem.

1: Some attempt to analyze solution, but critical aspects are overlooked.

2: Complete and accurate analysis of solution.

Multiplication and Division of Multi-Digit Numbers

The same cautions about overemphasizing multi-digit computational algorithms that were discussed in the chapter on addition and subtraction also apply here. In a society where calculators are readily available and convenient, spending several months of each school year working exclusively on the four basic operations on multi-digit numbers does not make sense. Rather, it is beneficial to pay attention to children's own algorithms, to estimation strategies, to alternative algorithms, to appropriate uses of calculators, and to developing students' understanding of when it is useful to employ the operations of multiplication and division. We will address each of these topics, along with suggestions for helping children understand the standard computational algorithms.

Estimation and the Distributive and Associative Properties

The ability to estimate products and quotients is important. We perform mental estimates every time we approximate a sale price, when we approximate the price of a single item although it is advertised in multiple quantities, when we approximate the mileage of our car, or when we estimate a tip in a restaurant. It is possible to teach specific skills to help children become better estimators. One skill is to learn how to use the distributive and associative properties:

■ *The associative property of whole-number multiplication.* When multiplying more than two numbers, the way in which those numbers are grouped does not affect the product—for example, $(4 \times 6) \times 5 = 4 \times (5 \times 6) = 120$.

■ *The distributive property of whole-number multiplication.* For any whole numbers a, b, and c, $a \times (b + c) = (a \times b) + (a \times c)$. For example, $7 \times (10 + 2) = (7 \times 10) + (7 \times 2) = 84$. This property also holds true for subtraction. For example, $7 \times (10 - 2) = (7 \times 10) - (7 \times 2) = 56$.

Activity 4.6 illustrates how these skills may be demonstrated.

Activity 4.6

Mental Multiplying

Lesson: Whole Class

Supply each child with a calculator, and use an overhead one yourself. Explain to the children that you will call out two or more numbers. Everyone in the class, yourself included, will write down a mental estimate for the product of those numbers. Then, everyone will use the calculator to find the exact product, and the difference between the actual product and their own estimate. Keeping a running tally of how far from the actual product they were allows students to monitor the development of their estimation abilities. If the numbers 2, 5, and 7 were called out, the responses might be something like this:

- "I thought the answer should be 70, because 5 × 2 = 10, and 10 × 7 = 70.
- "I thought the answer should be 70 also, but I multiplied 5 and 7 to get 35, and then doubled it to get 70."

If the numbers 60 and 42 were called out, the responses might be something like this:

- "I estimated 240 because I thought that 6 × 4 was 24, so 60 × 42

should be close to 240. When I checked it on the calculator, I saw that I was way off. I forgot that I really had to estimate 6 × 10 × 4 × 10 since each number was in the tens place. I should have guessed about 2400."

- "I thought that the answer should be more than 2000, because 4 groups of 60 is more than 200, so 40 groups of 60 should be more than 2000."
- "I got the exact answer, because I knew that 40 groups of 60 were 2400, and 2 groups of 60 were 120, so I put them together to get 2520."

Repeated practice with numbers such as these will help children develop both their mental math skills and their estimation skills.

Journal Reflection

Think about opportunities in your own life to practice such mental estimation skills. Make an effort over the next several days to practice. Reflect on you performance. Was it adequate? How do you know? Could it be improved? How?

Powers-of-Ten Blocks with Standard Multiplication Algorithm

It is useful for students to see tangible models of the operation of multiplication before they are introduced to abstract algorithms. Powers-of-ten blocks can be used to model multiplication. When you are modeling multiplication with a single-digit multiplier, the repeated addition model works best. When modeling multiplication with a double-digit multiplier, the array model works best. Examine the following problem.

- "The art teacher ordered three packs of origami paper. Each pack contains 46 sheets. How many sheets of paper is that in all?"

After students have had an opportunity to estimate the answer, encourage them to solve the problem in any way that makes sense to them. Most students will likely add 46 three times. After the students have had the chance to share their methods with the class, explain that using the operation multiplication is another way to arrive at this answer. Since 3 × 46 can

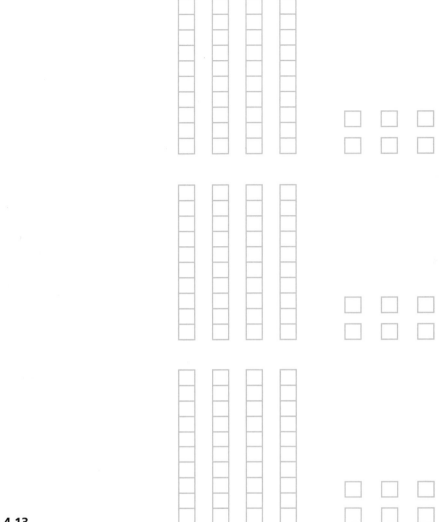

Figure 4.13

be interpreted as 3 groups of 46, model 3 groups of 46 with powers-of-ten blocks (Figure 4.13).

To find the total of three of these groups, assemble all of the unit cubes together and all of the longs together. Twelve longs can be traded in for one flat and two longs. Eighteen units can be traded in for one long and eight units. This results in a grand total of one flat, three longs, and eight units, or 138 (Figure 4.14). Now is an appropriate time to connect this model with a slightly expanded version of the symbolic algorithm.

$$
\begin{array}{r}
46 \\
\times\ \ 3 \\
\hline
18 \\
+\ 120 \\
\hline
138
\end{array}
$$

As you can see, in this algorithm the product of the multiplier and the ones column in the multiplicand is recorded separately from the product of the

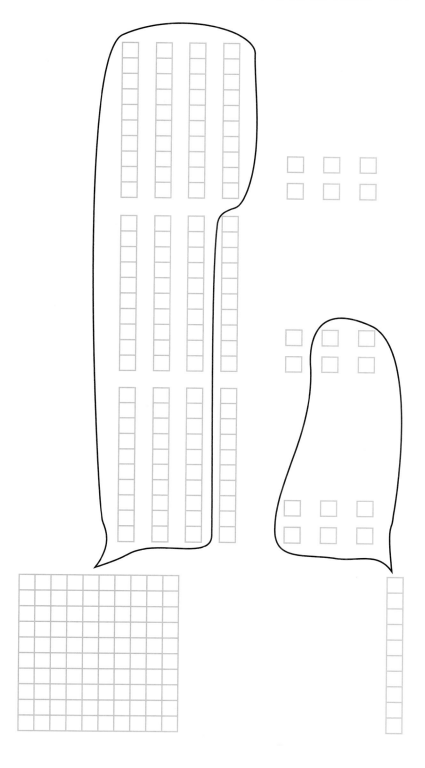

Figure 4.14

multiplier and the tens column in the multiplicand. In this way, the numbers mirror the process modeled by the powers-of-ten blocks. Another advantage of this expanded algorithm is that it stresses that multiplying the tens digit results in a product of 3 and 40 or 120, not the product of 3 and 4 or 12.

It is a short step to go from this expanded algorithm to the standard algorithm, by pointing out to students that any tens resulting from multiplying the ones digit in the multiplicand can be recorded *above* the tens digit in the multiplicand and added to the product of the multiplier and the tens digit in the multiplicand, as shown here:

$$
\begin{array}{r}
{}^{1}46 \\
\times\ \ 3 \\
\hline
138
\end{array}
$$

Thus, the students can see that the art teacher has 138 sheets of origami paper in all.

Powers-of-ten blocks will be used in a slightly different way to model multiplication with a double-digit multiplier. Examine the following problem:

■ "There are 24 children in a fourth-grade class. Their teacher has a budget of $14.00 per student to order math manipulatives. How much money is this in all?"

Again, it is important to encourage students to estimate the product of 24 and 14 and to explain how they arrived at their estimate. To illustrate the array model of this example, use powers-of-ten blocks to create a 24 × 14 array, as shown in Figure 4.15.

Fill in the array with the largest blocks possible. You can see that two flats can fit along with 12 longs and 16 ones. These blocks can be related to the multiplication algorithm in the following way:

$$
\begin{array}{r}
24 \\
\times\ \ 14 \\
\hline
16\ (4 \times 4) \\
80\ (4 \times 20) \\
40\ (10 \times 4) \\
+\ 200\ (10 \times 20) \\
\hline
336
\end{array}
$$

While it is not reasonable to expect children to create an array such as this each time they multiply, it is critically important that they see that the standard algorithm has its basis in an understanding of the concept of multiplication, and is simply a more efficient way to perform a task that can be performed in many different ways. The expanded algorithm shown earlier can easily be connected to the standard algorithm shown here simply by combining steps and recording any tens that result from multiplying the multiplier and the ones digit of the multiplicand *above* the digit in the tens column.

$$
\begin{array}{r}
24 \\
\times\ 14 \\
\hline
96\ (4 \times 24 = 96) \\
+\ 240\ (10 \times 24 = 240) \\
\hline
336
\end{array}
$$

Therefore, the teacher has $336 to spend on manipulatives.

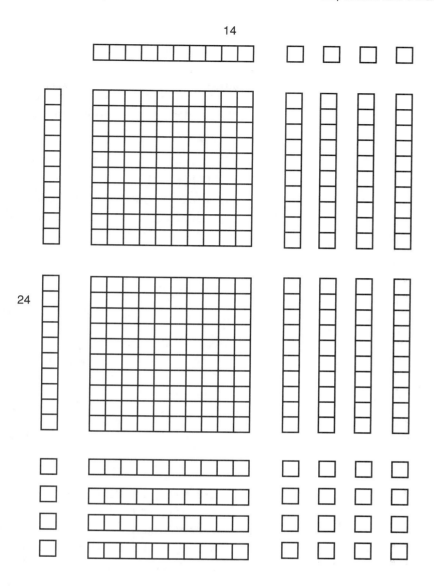

Figure 4.15

This algorithm is known as the *partial products* algorithm because it involves recording the partial products of 24 × 4 = 96 and 24 × 10 = 240 before arriving at the final product of 24 × 14 = 336.

Alternative Algorithms for Whole-Number Multiplication

There are two other important multiplication algorithms that children should be taught. One has the advantage of being visually more tightly organized, and the other avoids the need for memorizing the basic facts. While I support memorizing the basic facts, there are some children who truly struggle with committing the facts to memory. It is useful for them to know a method for multi-digit multiplication that allows them to be successful.

Lattice Multiplication

The lattice method of addition was introduced in Chapter 3. Lattice multiplication is very similar, as you can see from the following example:

- A certain school is budgeted to use 235 kilowatt hours of electricity per day. Based on this budget, what would be the total electricity consumption in one year?

An estimate of more than 70,000 kilowatt hours ($200 \times 350 = 70,000$) is reasonable here. The lattice used for this example will be a 3×3 lattice, since each factor contains three digits. This will not always be the case, since the dimensions of the lattice depend on the number of digits in the factors.

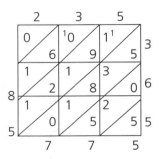

The school is budgeted to use 85,775 kilowatt hours of electricity per year.

Notice the characteristics of the lattice method of multiplication. The cells in the lattice can be filled in any order, and if children are interrupted while performing this algorithm, it is easy to pick up where they left off. The organization of the lattice also allows each individual product to be checked for accuracy.

After all the individual products have been recorded, the numbers in the lattice are added along the diagonals. This clear separation of the operations of multiplication and addition helps many children who get confused by the constant switching back and forth between multiplying the factors and then adding the regrouped numbers that goes on in the standard partial products algorithm. Finally, the lattice offers a simple organization of the digits. There is no danger of misaligning columns. Here are two other examples of lattice multiplication:

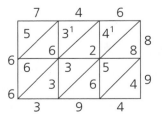
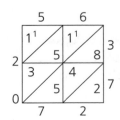

Russian Peasant Multiplication

This algorithm, used in many parts of Russia, is based on repeated doubling and halving of each factor. Study the following example.

- ■ Each of the 34 fourth-graders in a certain school read 16 books throughout the year. How many books were read in all?

A good estimate of the number of books would be 600 (30×20). Using the Russian peasant method, two columns are set up as follows:

$$
\begin{array}{rr}
34 & \cancel{16} \\
17 & 32 \\
8 & \cancel{64} \\
4 & \cancel{128} \\
2 & \cancel{256} \\
1 & +\,512 \\
\hline
 & 544
\end{array}
$$

Five hundred forty-four books were read in all.

Notice the characteristics of this algorithm. The numbers on the left are repeatedly halved. When an odd number is halved (as in the case of 17), only the whole-number portion of the quotient is recorded. The numbers on the right are repeatedly doubled. This process continues until the entry in the lefthand column is 1. Then, any righthand entry paired with an even number on the left is discarded. The remaining numbers in the righthand column are added to provide the product of the two original numbers. An interesting aspect of this algorithm is that it allows you to multiply multi-digit numbers without knowing the multiplication facts. The only skills needed are those of halving, doubling, and adding.

The Strength in Numbers activity on page 136 will give you the opportunity to think about why this algorithm works.

Performance-Based Assessment:
Multi-digit Multiplication

Distribute a circular from a local grocery store to each child. Instruct the children to plan one day's meals for a family of four, listing all of the items to be purchased and their prices. Based on this day's cost, they are to approximate the cost of feeding the family for one week.

The children's work can be evaluated according to the following rubric:

4 Child consistently shows an understanding of multiplication as a form of repeated addition, and uses the operation with accuracy and at appropriate times.

3 Child sometimes, but not always, shows an understanding of multiplication as a form of repeated addition, and uses the operation with accuracy and at appropriate times.

2 Child sometimes, but not always, shows an understanding of multiplication as a form of repeated addition, and sometimes uses the operation with accuracy.

1 Child rarely or never uses multiplication, and rarely or never uses it with accuracy.

Manipulatives with the Standard Division Algorithm

For fourth-graders, the gap between understanding that 24 ÷ 6 = 4 and understanding that 26 ÷ 6 = 4 R2 is a huge one. The first example is dependent on knowing a basic multiplication fact. The second requires an understanding of the *concept* of division. Recall that division can be thought of as a process of repeated subtraction or as a process of equal partition or sharing. Activity 4.7 is based on the model of division as equal sharing, and illustrates a way that students can be introduced in a concrete fashion to division with remainders.

Powers-of-ten materials lend themselves to modeling division with larger dividends, as shown in the Activity 4.8.

An Alternative Algorithm for Whole-Number Division

This alternative algorithm differs somewhat from others in that it is most useful as a means of introducing the division process and giving meaning to the standard algorithm. It would be cumbersome to use regularly, but it does have the advantage of demonstrating the repeated subtraction model of division.

Activity 4.7
Building Towers

Distribute 17 monochromatic Unifix cubes to each student. Invite the students to build congruent towers to show how many cubes each child would get if they were shared among 3 children. When students have built their towers, encourage them to verbalize that 17 cubes make 3 towers of 5 cubes each with 2 cubes left over.

Invite the students to build towers to share the cubes among 2 children, among 5 children, among 7 children, among 4 children, and so on. After each building episode, encourage the students to verbalize how many towers of how many cubes were built with how many left over, as modeled above.

After the students appear to be comfortable with this process (which may take more than one session), introduce the standard division symbolism by connecting it to the towers of cubes. For example, after having students distribute the 17 cubes among

4 towers, introduce the students to this symbolism:

$$17 \div 4 = 4 \text{ R}1 \qquad 4\overline{)17}^{\,4\,\text{R}1}$$

As you record each example, say "Seventeen cubes divided among 4 children gives each child 4 cubes with 1 cube left over."

Invite the children once again to build towers, but this time ask them to record the process symbolically, according to the above model.

Journal Reflection

Contrast this activity with a scenario where the teacher asks "How many times does 4 go into 17?" and encourages the children to answer the question by thinking of "Four times what number is close to 17?" Discuss the differences between these two approaches.

The Subtractive Method of Division

This method allows students repeatedly to subtract convenient numbers from the dividend and then total all the amounts that have been subtracted. In this example, since there are not 1000 three's in 1528, the student will see how many times 100 three's can be removed from 1528. When it is no longer possible to remove 100 three's, the student will then remove 10 three's if possible, and so on.

```
3 ) 1528 | 100
   −300
   1228  | 100
   −300
    928  | 100
   −300
    628  | 100
   −300
    328  | 100
   −300
     28  |   9
   − 27
      1  | 509R1
```

Activity 4.8

Sharing the Loot

With students working in groups of three, tell them the following story.

■ If I teach summer school this year, I will be paid $1528. I would like to use this money to open up bank accounts for each of my 3 children, so I can save for their college tuition. If I share the money equally, how much money will go into each of the 3 accounts?

Invite the students to represent $1528 with powers-of-ten blocks, and to use the blocks to illustrate an equal sharing of money. A reasonable estimate is that each child will get more than $500, since $3 \times 5 = 15$, and $3 \times 500 = 1500$.

The students will need to go through the process of trading in the thousands block for 10 flats and distributing the 15 flats. Then, they will need to trade the two longs for units (since two longs cannot be equally shared among 3 children) and distribute the 28 units. The students will discover that each child will get $509 and that there will be $1 left over. It will be interesting for you to see how the different groups deal with the leftover dollar. Will they attempt to share the dollar, or will they say it's for you to keep?

After each group has had the opportunity to act out the distribution of the money, say "Let me show you what this looks like with numbers":

```
      5 0 9    You couldn't share the
3) 1 5 2 8    thousands cube among 3
  −1 5 0 0    children, so you had to
      2 8    trade it in for 10 hundreds.
     −2 7    Then you shared the 15
      1    hundreds so that each
             child got 5. That's why
```

there's a 5 written in the hundreds column in the quotient. That left you with 2 longs and 8 ones. You had to trade the longs in for ones because you didn't have enough to go around. That's why there's a 0 in the tens column in the quotient. When you shared the ones, each child got 9. You can see the 9 in the ones column in the quotient. After you shared the ones, there was one remaining. So each child received $509 and there was $1 left over.

This explanation offers a justification for each step in the algorithm, and connects each step in the algorithm with a physical process that the students have just experienced. That sharing process could have been accomplished in exactly the same way with play money if the classroom in which you are working lacks powers-of-ten materials. You would need to provide a "bank" with extra hundreds and ones for the two trades that are necessary in this example.

Journal Reflection

Some teachers encourage their students to memorize the mnemonic device _Dad_ _Mom_ _Sister_ _Brother_ to help them remember to Divide, Multiply, Subtract, and Bring Down. What do you think about this?

After students have had ample opportunity to perform this algorithm, they can be introduced to the more streamlined standard division algorithm.

Many students have difficulty with the very first step in this algorithm when they have to estimate, in the following example, how many seventeens there are in 5400.

$$17 \overline{)5432}$$

One way to help children deal with this step is to have them use a calculator to generate the multiples of 17 down the side of the page, like this:

$$17 \times 1 = 17$$

$$17 \times 2 = 34$$

$$17 \times 3 = 51$$

$$17 \times 4 = 68, \text{ etc.}$$

This makes the algorithm less burdensome, and allows the child to concentrate more completely on the process of division.

Performance-Based Assessment: Multi-digit Division

Show the class a box of pretzels. Tell them that the box contains 180 pretzels, and you want to know how many pretzels each of the 28 students will get if the box is equally shared. The students' performances can be evaluated according to the following rubric:

4 Student understands problem, and takes appropriate steps to solve it. Answer is accurate and remainder is reasonably interpreted.

3 Student understands problem and has an appropriate plan, but implementation of plan contains some errors or inconsistencies.

2 Student has some understanding of the problem, but plan and its implementation is inappropriate or incorrect.

1 Student neither appears to understand the problem nor to know how to go about solving it.

Number And Operation for Grades 6–8

According to the NCTM *Principles and Standards,* in grades 6 through 8, all students should

- Understand and use the inverse relationships of addition and subtraction, multiplication and division, and square and square roots to solve problems.

- Select and use appropriate methods for computing from among mental arithmetic, estimation, paper-and-pencil, and calculator, depending on the situation at hand.

Estimation

Because your students live in a society where calculators are inexpensive and universally available, estimation skills take on increased importance. The estimation techniques that have already been introduced in this book can now be refined to deal with more complex cases.

Rounding to Multiples of Ten

Consider the following example:

■ A school auditorium has 52 rows. Each row contains 28 seats. Approximately how many seats are in the auditorium?

A quick method for estimating this product is to round each factor to the nearest multiple of ten. It will then be possible mentally to multiply the leading digits and annex the appropriate number of zeros.

$$52 \rightarrow 50 \quad 50 \times 30 = (5 \times 10) \times (3 \times 10)$$

$$\times\, 28 \rightarrow 30 \qquad = (5 \times 10) \times (10 \times 3) \text{ by the commutative property}$$

$$= 5 \times (10 \times 10) \times 3 \text{ by the associative property}$$

$$= 5 \times 3 \times (10 \times 10) \text{ by the commutative property}$$

$$= (5 \times 3) \times (10 \times 10) \text{ by the associative property}$$

$$= 15 \times 100$$

$$= 1500$$

Children can easily perform these steps mentally. The product of 52 and 28 is approximately 1500. Therefore, the estimated seating capacity of the auditorium is approximately 1500 seats.

Rounding with Compensation

In the preceding example, one factor was rounded up to a multiple of ten while the other was rounded down to a multiple of ten. The resulting estimate of 1500 was quite accurate, since the actual seating capacity of the auditorium would be 1456. If, however, both factors are rounded up, or both factors are rounded down, the estimated product might be less accurate. In that case, children should be taught to compensate by adjusting the estimated product. Examine what happens in these two examples.

■ Case 1: A toy maker sells sets of blocks that contain 275 blocks. If a school district orders 87 sets of blocks, how many blocks is this in all?

In this situation, both 275 and 87 are rounded up as follows:

$$275 \rightarrow 300$$

$$\times \quad 87 \rightarrow \times 90 \;\; (3 \times 9) \times (100 \times 10) = 27,000$$

Since both numbers were rounded up, we must adjust the estimated product. When attempting to adjust an estimate, focus on the greater of the two factors. Rounding 275 to 300 resulted in an additional 25 groups of 90 being included in the estimate. This can be seen by examining the distributive property as follows:

$$300 \times 90$$

$$(275 + 25) \times 90$$

$$(275 \times 90) + (25 \times 90)$$

The second of these two products represents the overage in the estimate of 27, 000. This product can itself be estimated and deducted from the initial estimate. Since 25×90 is approximately 30×90, or 2700, the initial estimate of 27,000 should be decreased by approximately 3000. The compensated estimate for the total number of blocks is 24,000. This compares favorably with the actual product of 23,925.

■ Case 2: An elementary school receives $72 in state aid for each of the 824 students enrolled in the school. Approximately how much state aid does the school receive in all?

Notice that both 72 and 824 will be rounded down. This will result in an estimate that is considerably less than the actual amount. Compensation can be made as follows:

$$824 \rightarrow 800$$

$$\underline{\times 72} \rightarrow \underline{\times 70} \; (8 \times 7) \times (100 \times 10) = 56,000$$

Again, focus on the greater of the two factors. Rounding 824 to 800 resulted in a loss of 24 groups of 70 from the initial estimate. Since 24×70 is approximately 20×70 or 1400, the initial estimate should be increased by 1400. The revised estimate for the total amount of state aid is 57,400. This is close to the actual amount of 59,328.

The greater the factors involved, the greater will be the possible margin between the estimate and the actual answer. For example, when finding an estimate for the product of 1234 and 643, you might round both factors down to 1000 and 600. Using this technique, the estimate would be 600,000, which doesn't come close to the actual product of 793,462. In cases such as this, you may need to use several steps of compensation before you reach an acceptable estimate. Remember, however, that if an accurate product is required with numbers of this magnitude, you should probably use a calculator.

Estimating Quotients

To estimate quotients, students must understand the pattern found when the divisor and the dividend are both multiples of ten. Activity 4.9 uses a calculator to help students recognize patterns.

Activity 4.9

Patterns in Division

Distribute calculators to each child, then present the following situation to students:

■ A certain school district has budgeted $560,550 for textbook replacement funds. If the school district has 7,112 students, about how much is this per student?

After discussing the rounding of each number to 560,000 and 7,000, have each child compute and record the quotient in each of the following examples:

$$560,000 \div 7000$$
$$56,000 \div 700$$
$$5,600 \div 70$$
$$560 \div 7$$

Invite the students to comment on any patterns they see. Their responses might be:

■ "All of the answers are 80."

■ "In each case, the first number contains two more digits than the second number."

■ "As you go down, the numbers get smaller and smaller."

Point out to the students that, beginning with the first line and in each subsequent line, both the dividend and the divisor were divided by 10. Since this division occurred in both the dividend *and* the divisor, the quotient remained unchanged. This information will help students estimate quotients, even if the divisor is a large number.

First, students need to round both dividend and divisor to a multiple of ten. Then, they should determine the greatest power of ten (10, 100, 1000, etc.) that divides both the dividend and the divisor. This power can be found by counting the number of zeros in each number. In the example above, 10,000 divides 560,000, but not 7,000. The greatest power of ten that divides both this dividend and this divisor is 1,000. Dividing both numbers by 1,000 results in both numbers having three fewer trailing zeros. It remains to divide 560 by 7, resulting in an estimated quotient of 80. Therefore, the school district has budgeted approximately $80 per student for textbook replacement.

Journal Reflection
When you were a student faced with a situation such as this, you may remember saying to yourself, "Cross off three zeros in the first number and three zeros in the second, and then divide." Would you say this to your students? Why or why not?

Using Multiplication and Division to Solve Problems

You will recall that the NCTM *Principles and Standards* recommends that students be given frequent opportunities to use the four basic operations to solve problems, and to chose for themselves the most appropriate tools for solving these problems. Here is a collection of problems that can be solved mentally, with paper and pencil, with technology, and with a wide variety of additional problem-solving strategies.

Take some time to work through these problems. This is a good opportunity to think about how you will make the transition from being a learner of mathematics to becoming a teacher of mathematics. Your first attempts to solve the problems will likely require you to think like a learner of mathematics. But, after you have successfully solved the problems, go back. Think about how you would teach a lesson involving that problem. One of the most challenging parts of teaching is realizing that you cannot learn for students, you can only teach them. How did your own experience of trying to solve the problems help you understand the role of the teacher in learning mathematics?

1. Geraldo purchased two tickets to a raffle. The tickets were numbered consecutively. The product of the ticket numbers is 65,792. The sum of the ticket numbers is 513. What are the two ticket numbers?

2. At Memorial Junior High School, all of the lockers have four-digit identification numbers that are consecutive even numbers. The product of two adjacent locker numbers is 2,088,024. The sum of the numbers is 2890. What are the locker numbers?

3. Use the digits 2, 3, 4, 5, and 6 only once to determine the indicated solution.

$$(\underline{\quad} \div \underline{\quad}) + [(\underline{\quad} \div \underline{\quad}) \times \underline{\quad}] = 12$$

4. A garage contains a number of bicycles, tricycles, and wagons. The total number of wheels on all of them is 44. How many of each type are there?

5. A warehouse contains 720 cartons of books. Can these cartons be placed in stacks 4 cartons high so that each stack contains an equal number of cartons? Can they be placed in stacks 5 cartons high? 6 cartons high? 7 cartons high? What is the greatest number of cartons that can be stacked so that each stack contains the same number of cartons and no stack is over 25 cartons high?

6. Find three whole numbers, none of which contain any zeros, whose product is 27,000.

7. When a coin collection is arranged in piles of 8, there are no coins remaining. When it is arranged in piles of 9, there are no coins remaining. When it is stacked in piles of 11, there are 7 coins remaining. What is the fewest number of coins that can be in this collection?

8. In a video game, points are awarded for capturing the following aliens:

eenie = 2 points

meanie = 3 points

meinie = 4 points

mo = 10 points

Interdisciplinary Lesson Plan

Grade 6   **Concept** Multiplication and Division

Topic Using Multiplication and Division in a Problem Solving Context

Student Objectives After completing this multi-day lesson, students should be able to

- Apply the operations of multiplication and division to real-life problem situations
- Organize information and make plans for a weekend trip, working within a given budget

Materials maps, calculators, brochures from local attractions, local bus or train schedules, the travel section from a local newspaper

Motivation Show slides, a video, or photographs from a trip you have taken. Invite the students to share their trip experiences, including field trips and trips to visit relatives or friends.

Procedure

1. After arranging the students into heterogeneous groups of four, explain that they are going to plan a hypothetical school trip for the four of them that will take place over a weekend. Tell the students that they have a budget of $500.00 to cover the four of them plus an adult chaperone, and that this budget must include transportation, food, accommodations, and any admission fees at their destination.

2. Provide the students with the necessary time and information to solve this problem. Tell them their final written report must contain the following information:

(continued)

Kate scored a total of 41 points, capturing more mo's than any other aliens. How many arrangements of captured aliens would result in this score? List these arrangements.

9. A jeweler charges $5.00 to open a link and $5.00 to close a link. How is it possible to have these four lengths of chain arranged into one continuous closed loop for $30.00 (Figure 4.16)?

10. What are the next three numbers in this pattern?

1, 1, 2, 3, 5, 8, 13, 21 . . .

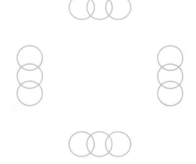

Figure 4.16

Summary

Multiplication can be thought of as the process of repeated addition, as a rectangular array, or as the process of creating equal groups. Division can be thought of as the process of repeated subtraction or as the process of equal

■ A description of their destination, including a statement about its educational, cultural, or historical significance.

■ Defensible plans for transportation and accommodations.

■ A map, drawn to scale, tracing the route that will be followed.

■ A detailed daily schedule.

■ A precise budget for each aspect of the trip.

3. Encourage the students to write the description of their destination as a group, and then have each individual take primary responsibility for one of the other components of the final written report.

4. Provide the opportunity for each group to present their report to the entire class.

Assessment The written reports should be assessed based on their inclusion of all components, their cohesiveness, and their appropriate use of mathematics. You may wish to allow the students to hand in draft forms of the final report to allow the opportunity for editing.

Reference *Professional Standards for Teaching Mathematics.* Reston, VA: NCTM, 1991.

Journal Entry Analyze this project. Try to determine which groups were most successful, and why. Ask permission of certain groups to share their projects with subsequent classes. If you keep the very best projects from year to year, the level of excellence will increase as students are motivated to surpass last year's projects.

sharing or partition. There are a number of strategies for helping children remember the basic facts and physical models for the processes of multiplication and division (powers-of-ten blocks).

A connection was made between the array model of single digit multiplication (4×3 as four rows of three objects) and the array model of multi-digit multiplication. This model, for instance, could be used to create a 23×16 rectangular array, and the product could be determined by finding the area of the enclosed rectangle (of dimensions 23×16) with powers-of-ten blocks.

This chapter described, illustrated, and explained alternative algorithms for multiplication and division.

Extending Your Learning

1. Obtain a copy of *The Doorbell Rang* by Pam Hutchins (Greenwillow, 1986). Use this book as a basis for writing an integrated lesson plan to introduce division to a third-grade class.

2. Create a classroom game to help children practice their basic multiplication and division facts. Using foam board or wood, and laminating any cards, will lend longevity to your game.

3. Visit a toy store. Examine commercial games (Monopoly, Chutes and Ladders, Tetris) that might provide students an opportunity to develop mathematical skills. Write a sample letter to parents that you might distribute at holiday time. Offer a justification for suggesting certain games for their children.

4. Obtain a menu from a local restaurant. Use it to develop a lesson on either multiplication or division concepts, or both. Include a rubric that can be used to assess students' learning.

5. Using graph paper or powers-of-ten materials, draw a rectangular array to model these products: 12×15, 21×9, and 13×13. In each case, connect the physical array with the appropriate numbers in the symbolic partial products algorithm.

6. Describe three classroom activities designed to introduce the following concepts to children:

   - the repeated addition model of whole-number multiplication
   - the repeated subtraction model of whole-number division
   - the sharing or partitive model of whole-number division

7. List ten real-life contexts that would appeal to students in grades 3, 4, or 5 in which multiplication and/or division are important. Briefly suggest how you would connect each context to the classroom.

8. Write an interdisciplinary lesson plan for the fourth or fifth grade that connects patchwork quilts to the array model of multiplication.

9. Discuss, with specific reasons and specific examples, how you would teach the associative and distributive properties of whole-number multiplication.

10. Write a sample letter to parents discussing the role of the calculator in basic computation. Include in this letter a statement of your philosophy on the use of calculators in the elementary classroom.

Internet Resources

www.aimsedu.org
This website is maintained by the AIMS Education Foundation (Activities for Integrating Math, Science, and Technology) and offers many suggestions for actively involving children in mathematical and scientific investigations. AIMS also publishes a periodical magazine that contains extensive lesson plans for math and science classroom activities.

www.aplusmath.com/
This interactive website is designed for children, with the expressed purpose of helping them to increase their skill and understanding of mathematics. Students can play games, print out practice sheets and answer keys, and get help with their homework by entering an example and an answer at this website.

www.mathgoodies.com
This website contains lesson plans for elementary school students, puzzles, advertisements, and useful information about home schooling. A newsletter is also connected with the site.

www.useekufind.com/learningquest/ tmfun.htm
A variety of puzzles and games appropriate for elementary and middle school students can be found at this website. In addition, the site provides links to several other related sites.

Bibliography

Anderson, Ann. (1995). Creative use of worksheets: Lessons my daughter taught me. *Teaching Children Mathematics 2*(2).

Armstrong, Barbara. (1995). Teaching patterns, relationships, and multiplication as worthwhile mathematical tasks. *Teaching Children Mathematics 1*(7):446–50.

Hembree, Ray, and Donald J. Dessart. (1986). Effects of hand-held calculators in precollege mathematics education: A meta-analysis. *Journal for Research in Mathematics Education 17*: 83–99.

Hutchins, Pam. (1986). *The Doorbell Rang.* New York: Greenwillow.

Kamii, Constance. (1985). *Young children reinvent arithmetic: Implications of Piaget's theory.* New York: Teachers College Press.

Kamii, Constance. (1989). *Young children continue to reinvent arithmetic: Second grade.* New York: Teachers College Press.

McIntosh, Allistair, Robert E. Reys, and Barbara J. Reys. (1997). Mental computation in the middle grades. *Mathematics Teaching in the Middle School 2*(5).

Philipp, Randolph. (1996). Multicultural mathematics and alternative algorithms. *Teaching Children Mathematics 3*(3).

Robertson, Laurel, Nancy Graves, and Patricia Tuck.(1990). Implementing group work: Issues for teachers and administrators. In Neil Davidson (ed.), *Cooperative learning in mathematics* (pp. 362–79). Menlo Park, CA: Addison-Wesley.

Sgroi, Laura. (1993). Mathematics as investigation. *New York State Mathematics Teachers' Journal 31*(1).

Sgroi, Laura. (1998). An exploration of the Russian peasant method of multiplication. In *The teaching and learning of algorithms in school mathematics: 1998 yearbook of the National Council of Teachers of Mathematics.* Reston, VA: NCTM.

Sgroi, Richard. (1992). Systematizing trial and error using spreadsheets. *Arithmetic Teacher 39*(7):8–12.

Simonsen, Linda M., and Anne R. Teppo. (1999). Using alternative algorithms with preservice teachers. *Teaching Children Mathematics 5*(9).

Spangler, David B. (1999). Ads that are BAAAD. *Mathematics Teaching in the Middle School 4*(4).

Vance, James H. (1998). Number operations from an algebraic perspective. *Teaching Children Mathematics 4*(5).

Standards for Geometry

Teaching geometry in the elementary school can be a very exciting and pleasurable experience. Geometry lends itself easily to integration with art, history, science, multicultural studies, and literature. It is the branch of mathematics that most visibly illustrates the beauty of mathematics, by emphasizing its symmetry, consistency, intricacy, patterns, and cohesion. Some children who struggle with the more computational aspects of elementary school mathematics find the study of geometry both interesting and satisfying. Including geometry as a major topic in your curriculum allows these children to feel mathematically successful. Also, with its emphasis on description, comparison, and classification, geometry is an appropriate vehicle for the development of thinking skills.

Unfortunately, geometry is often given inadequate attention in the elementary school curriculum. The study of geometry is often delayed until late in the school year, and then, it is given ". . . brief, cursory coverage" (Clements and Battista, 1992). This treatment comes from an image of geometry as an isolated topic to be "covered" or an unrelated set of definitions to be memorized. However, nothing could be further from the truth. According to Zalman Usiskin (1987), the "dimensions" of geometry that should structure the school curriculum include geometry as the study of the visualization, drawing, and construction of figures and as the study of the real physical world. Drawing and constructing figures and studying the world both play (or should play) an enormous role in the early childhood and elementary school curriculum. These topics allow for the active involvement of children in mathematics and satisfy children's curiosity about the world around them. Think back to your own experience in school. Did you enjoy building with blocks? Did you enjoy drawing? Did you enjoy exploring the natural world? If so, then you enjoyed geometry.

This chapter discusses the work of two pairs of researchers—Piaget and Inhelder, and Pierre and Dina van Hiele—for their insights on teaching geometry to children. As before, there are a large number of Activities for grades Pre-K–8, a few interdisciplinary lesson plans, and some Strength in Numbers activities that will allow you to engage in adult-level geometric investigations. Students of all ages learn mathematics best when they become actively engaged in its exploration, when they spend time solving problems and reflecting on their thinking, and when they mentally and physically play with materials and ideas. This is easy to do when you are studying geometry.

Geometry and Spatial Sense for Grades Pre-K–2

According to the NCTM *Principles and Standards,* all students in grades Pre-K–2 should

- Recognize, name, build, draw, describe, compare, and sort two- and three-dimensional shapes
- Recognize and locate geometric shapes and structures in the world
- Describe attributes and parts of two- and three-dimensional shapes
- Investigate and predict the results of putting together and taking apart shapes
- Recognize congruent and similar shapes
- Relate geometric ideas to number and measurement ideas (p. 121)

The Contribution of Research

Piaget and Inhelder (1967) sowed the seed that eventually flowered into constructivism when their clinical experiments led them to claim that children do not passively *absorb* knowledge about their world but actively *construct* it. This statement has great significance for the teaching of mathematics in general and for geometry in particular. In essence, it means that children come to understand the world around them by repeated active manipulations of their environment. We sometimes forget that telling children about something is not the same as teaching them. For example, sometimes teachers draw a figure like Figure 5.1 to help children see that triangles have three sides and three angles.

Figure 5.1

Then they point to each side of the triangle while counting out loud to 3, and they point to each angle as they count out loud to 3. Notice the role of the children throughout this demonstration; they are watching passively while the teacher points and counts. According to Piaget and Inhelder, this situation confuses social knowledge with logico-mathematical knowledge. Social knowledge (the days of the week, birthdays) can be transmitted to children by an adult. Logico-mathematical knowledge can only be *created* by the child. Activity 5.1 demonstrates how you might give children the opportunity to construct an understanding of triangles and quadrilaterals.

Two other researchers have had a significant impact on the teaching of geometry in elementary schools. The Dutch educators Pierre Marie van Heile and Dina van Heile-Geldof have developed a theory of the stages of geometric development that children pass through in a specified order (Crowley, 1987). According to the van Heiles, the geometric level at which a student is operating has less to do with the chronological age or maturation of the student and more to do with the student's experiences and instruction. This is an important point for teachers to recognize. It means that a child's geometric development can be enhanced by engaging in appropriate activities and thoughtful teaching. Here is a summary of the five van Heile levels. The first three have special importance for elementary school teachers.

van Heile Level 0: Visualization

For children operating at this level, geometric concepts and figures are seen as wholes. The child has no recognition of the component parts of shapes or

Activity 5.1

Triangles and Quadrilaterals

Lesson: Individual

Have available a supply of mini marshmallows or gumdrops along with toothpicks and coffee stirrers of various lengths. Give children the opportunity to construct two- and three-dimensional figures. Invite the children to verbalize any discoveries they make as they work with the materials. Some possibilities are:

- We made the tallest tower.
- I used eight toothpicks and eight gumdrops. My shape looks like a STOP sign.
- I wanted to make a diagonal in my square, but I only had toothpicks. The toothpick isn't long enough for a diagonal. I think I need a coffee stirrer.

After the children have had ample time to explore using the materials, invite them to take four toothpicks or coffee stirrers, or some combination of each, and four marshmallows or gumdrops. Ask them to construct a shape with these materials. Figure 5.2 shows some possibilities.

Encourage the children to describe their shape to the class. Here, in a meaningful context, you can introduce accurate vocabulary appropriate to the ages of the children (quadrilateral, simple, closed, convex, right angle, square, rectangle, kite, or trapezoid). While there is nothing wrong with young children calling a cube a "box," or an angle a "corner," modeling correct language allows the children gradually to develop a geometric vocabulary.

Ask some children to identify what shape might not belong. Some children might think that the square doesn't belong, because it is the only shape with four equal sides.

Others might think that the bowtie doesn't belong, because it has two "insides."

Invite the children to apply light pressure to the angles of the quadrilaterals to see if the shape can be changed. The children will discover that the quadrilaterals can be "squashed" by applying pressure. Now invite the children to remove one toothpick or coffee stirrer and one marshmallow and then rejoin the ends to make a new shape. Figure 5.3 shows the possible triangles.

Again ask the students to describe the shapes. Depending on the ages of the children, you might take this opportunity to introduce the terms *equilateral, scalene, isosceles,* and *right triangle.* Engage the children in a discussion of how the shapes are alike and how they are different, and which ones might not belong.

Once again, invite the children to apply light pressure to the angles, to see if the shape can be changed. This time, the children will see that the triangle is a stable shape that cannot easily be altered by outside force. For homework, ask the children to look around their homes and neighborhoods for examples of triangles that lend stability to structures. They can be found in swing sets, bridges, chairs, ladders, gazebos, and park benches. To extend this homework assignment for students in grades 3 or 4, challenge them to find a way to support a paperback book at least 15 cm above a table surface by using only a single sheet of paper.

Journal Reflection

Compare and contrast this Activity with the lesson where the teacher points to the sides and angles of a drawn triangle. What do you see as advantages and disadvantages of each?

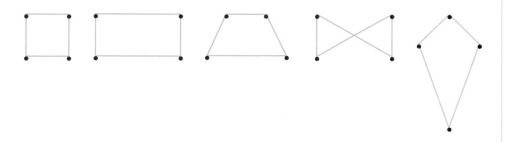

Figure 5.2

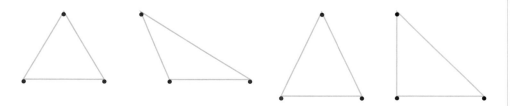

Figure 5.3

(a)

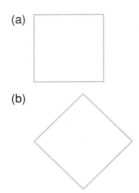

(b)

Figure 5.4

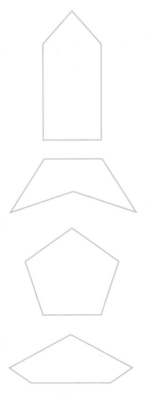

Figure 5.5

Figure 5.6

figures, but can only focus on them as complete entities. At Level 0, a child could recognize and identify a square, but perhaps only if the square were shown in its typical orientation with one side parallel to the floor (Figure 5.4a). When children at Level 0 are shown the square in Figure 5.4b, they might call it a "square turned on its point," or they might not even recognize it as a square. When asked *why* Figure 5.4a was a square, the likely response is "Because it looks like one!"

Figure 5.5 would also likely be called a square because its general appearance is "squarish," despite the fact that it lacks straight sides and right angles. Children who are functioning at this level of development should be engaged in block building, assembling puzzles, arranging shapes to form a design, or constructing tracks or roads for toy cars or trains.

van Heile Level 1: Analysis

At this level, through physical manipulation and analysis, children begin to recognize the properties of shapes. They begin to see shapes as being composed of constituent parts. Focusing on the number of sides and angles in a shape now becomes meaningful. It is appropriate to engage Level 1 children in description and classification activities that ask them to identify similarities and differences among shapes. If these children were shown the shapes in Figure 5.6, what do you think they might identify as similarities and differences? What shapes do you think they would label as "not belonging"? Why?

van Heile Level 2: Informal Deduction

Deduction is the process by which certain facts are found to follow necessarily from the acceptance of other facts. Deductive reasoning can be formal or informal, and at Level 2 students can understand informal deduction. Informal deduction allows conclusions to be drawn based on the acceptance of facts without the rigor of formal mathematical proof. During the process of observation and description, children have come to accept certain things as true. These truths, in turn, lead to the acceptance of other truths. At Level 2, students can begin to understand definitions of shapes and classes of shapes. A shape can be defined by the properties of its sides and/or angles. Students at this level should be able to understand and offer a formal definition of an individual shape and to identify the class of shapes to which it belongs. A hierarchy of shapes within each class can now be recognized (Figure 5.7).

van Heile Level 3: Formal Deduction

At Level 3, students are able to understand both informal and formal elements of the deductive reasoning process. Formal deduction incorporates the rules of logic and geometric proof and includes construction of proofs and creation of alternate proofs for theorems. This level of geometric reasoning is not generally reached by elementary school children, but Levels 3 and 4 are included here to give you a complete picture of the van Heile schema.

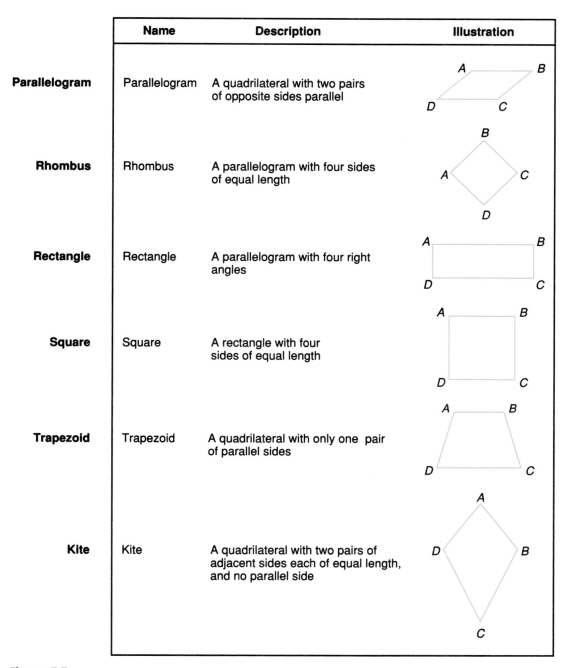

	Name	Description	Illustration
Parallelogram	Parallelogram	A quadrilateral with two pairs of opposite sides parallel	
Rhombus	Rhombus	A parallelogram with four sides of equal length	
Rectangle	Rectangle	A parallelogram with four right angles	
Square	Square	A rectangle with four sides of equal length	
Trapezoid	Trapezoid	A quadrilateral with only one pair of parallel sides	
Kite	Kite	A quadrilateral with two pairs of adjacent sides each of equal length, and no parallel side	

Figure 5.7

van Heile Level 4: Rigor

Students who are functioning at Level 4 are capable of understanding geometry in the abstract. They are ready to learn about non-Euclidean geometries, such as topology, and to compare and contrast them with each other.

What significance do the findings of Piaget and Inhelder and the van Heiles have for the classroom teacher? Both pairs of theorists strongly advocate that children spend a substantial amount of time working with geometric materials. Teachers, administrators, and parents need to become convinced that

Activity 5.2

Pet Enclosures

Lesson: Individual

Engage the children in a discussion of how to care for pets. Discuss meeting the basic needs of pets for food, love and attention, and fresh air and exercise. Explain to the children that you are planning to build an exercise yard for your dog, and that you need their help in deciding what shape to make it.

Distribute 10 popsicle sticks to each child, and invite them to design a yard for your dog. After the children have had an opportunity to experiment with the different possible enclosures, distribute construction paper and glue, and have them glue the sticks down to show their yard designs.

Chose some designs and discuss the similarities and differences. Point out two of the designs that look like Figure 5.8.

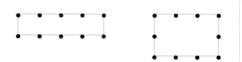

Figure 5.8

By using square pieces of paper placed inside each yard, model a tiling process that would demonstrate that four squares can fit in the first yard, but 6 squares can fit in the second, even though both yards had ten popsicle sticks around the outside.

Journal Reflection

The concepts of area and perimeter are difficult ones for many children. Describe two follow-up activities that can help children further explore these topics.

"playing" with blocks, puzzles, kits, beads, tiles, paper, and fabric is the child's way of learning about the things of the world. Activities such as these help children develop a strong spatial sense. There is evidence that spatial visualization is an important factor related to mathematical achievement (Fennema and Leder, 1990; Battista, 1990), and that males generally have a stronger spatial sense than do females. This suggests that engaging children in spatial tasks is beneficial to their mathematical achievement, and that developing *all* children's spatial sense can lead to greater equity in mathematics. Activity 5.2 provides students with an informal introduction to the concepts of area and perimeter.

Observation, Description, and Classification

The study of geometry can help children develop the thinking skills of observation, description, and classification. One of the ways you can help children become better observers is to ask them to reproduce a figure you have shown them. Activity 5.3 explains how this might be done.

In addition to developing skills of observation, encouraging children to articulate descriptions of geometric figures is an appropriate mathematical goal. Activity 5.4 gives children practice in describing figures, and in listening to others' descriptions.

Classification skills can also be developed within a geometric context. Pattern blocks are commercially available manipulatives that are versatile and appealing. They will appear several times throughout this chapter. Activity 5.5 shows how they can be used to develop skills of classification.

Activity 5.3

Show What You See

Lesson: Individual

You will need a transparent geoboard and an overhead projector. Equip the children with their own geoboards and a supply of rubber bands. Create a simple closed figure on your transparent geoboard and display it on the overhead projector for approximately 10 seconds. Turn off the projector and allow the children sufficient time to reproduce the figure on their own geoboard. Turn the overhead projector back on, and allow the children to compare their figure with the original. Repeat these steps several times, each time with gradually more complex figures.

Journal Reflection

Some children may become frustrated with the limited time the original figure is displayed on the overhead. What steps might you take to accommodate children who need more time to observe?

Activity 5.4

Show What You Hear

Lesson: Individual

This activity is similar to Activity 5.3, but instead of reproducing a figure that has been *shown* to them, the children reproduce a figure that has been *described* to them. Figure 5.9 shows what might be created by a child who hears the following description:

- "My shape has four sides. Two of the sides are 3 units long, and the other two sides are 1 unit long."

Figure 5.9

Of course, this is not the only shape that matches the spoken description. It is interesting for children to see the various possible interpretations of their descriptions, and to analyze each possibility to see if it actually matches the description.

Journal Reflection

Some children lack a strong enough auditory memory to allow them to listen to a three- or four-part description and then remember it long enough to reproduce the described shape. How could you adapt this activity to accommodate such children?

Performance-Based Assessment: Combining Shapes

Arrange a large sample of pattern blocks on a table. While the class is engaged in an alternate activity, call them, one at a time, to the table. Ask the children if they are able to create the hexagon shape out of red trapezoids? blue rhombi? green triangles? Some children may chose actually to place the shapes on top of a yellow hexagon to see if it can be done. Their performance can be assessed according to the following rubric:

3   Child can successfully create a hexagon from 2 trapezoids, 3 rhombi, and 6 triangles.

Lesson: Individual

You will need a standard set of pattern blocks that consists of six different shapes, with each shape a different color. Figure 5.10 illustrates the six pattern blocks.

Give the students sheets of paper to serve as mats, and invite them to "put the pieces together that belong together." The pieces could be sorted based on:

- Color/shape
- Number of sides
- Size
- Presence or absence of right angles

After the children have had an opportunity to sort the pieces, extend this activity by distributing the outline pictured in Figure 5.11. Invite the children to sort the pieces based on which ones can completely fill the outline and which ones cannot.

The first time children engage in this activity, you may want to say that only blocks of one color can be used at a time. After the children have had some practice, they will discover that combinations of several shapes can also be used to fill the outline completely. Children will discover that the yellow hexagons, blue rhombi, red trapezoids, and green triangles (and several combinations of these shapes) can all be used to fill in the outline, but that the orange squares and tan rhombi cannot.

Journal Reflection

What response would you offer to a child who questioned *why* it was so that some pieces could fill the outline and some could not?

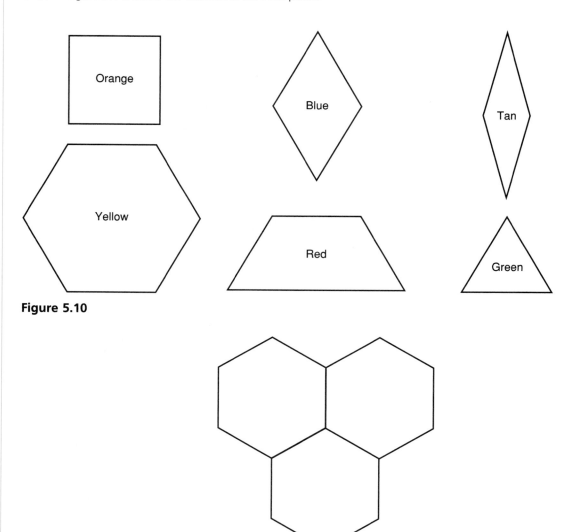

Figure 5.10

Figure 5.11

2   Child can successfully create hexagons from 2 of the 3 shapes.

1   Child can successfully create a hexagon from 1 of the 3 shapes.

0   Child is unable to create a hexagon from any of the 3 shapes.

Another material that can be used to develop children's spatial sense is the tangram. The *tangram* is an ancient Chinese puzzle composed of seven pieces that are cut from a square. Legend has it that the original tangram was created when a beautiful ceramic tile was dropped on the floor by a servant. Fearing his master's wrath, the servant tried to put the seven pieces back into the form of the original square. As he was manipulating the pieces, he discovered the enormous variety of shapes that could be made from the five triangles, one square, and one parallelogram.

Plastic tangrams are commercially available, but it is also possible to have children make their own tangrams from heavy paper by following these steps. (Justifications for the identification of each shape are included in parentheses.)

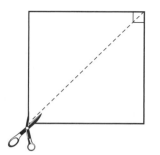

Figure 5.12

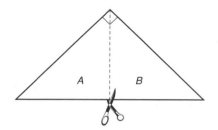

Figure 5.13

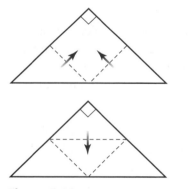

Figure 5.14

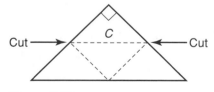

Figure 5.15

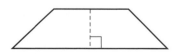

Figure 5.16

1. Begin with a square with sides of at least 20 cm. Fold along the diagonal so that opposite corners meet. Crease and cut along the diagonal, as in Figure 5.12. (The two shapes that result are congruent isosceles right triangles because they have two sides of equal length and one right angle. If they are placed over each other, they can be shown to be congruent.)

2. Fold one of the two triangles in half. Cut along this fold, as shown in Figure 5.13, and label the smaller triangles A and B. (Shapes A and B are congruent isosceles right triangles, for the same reasons as given in step 1. They are also similar to the original triangles since their angles are of equal measure and the lengths of their sides are in proportion.)

3. Put pieces A and B aside. Following Figure 5.14, take the other triangle and fold two of the vertices up to meet the third vertex, unfold, and then fold the top vertex down to meet its opposite side.

4. Unfold and cut along the horizontal dotted line (Figure 5.15). Label this shape C and set it aside. (Shape C is also an isosceles right triangle because it has two sides of equal length and one right angle. Is it also similar to triangles A and B? How do you know?)

5. Flatten out the remaining isosceles trapezoid. Fold the trapezoid in half, along its line of symmetry, as shown in Figure 5.16. Cut along this fold. (This shape is an isosceles trapezoid because it is a quadrilateral with one pair of parallel sides and 2 non-parallel sides of equal length. When this isosceles trapezoid is cut in half along the line of symmetry, two congruent right trapezoids result.)

6. Put one half aside. Fold the other half along the dotted line (Figure 5.17). Cut along this dotted line, and label the pieces D and E, as pictured. (Shape D is an isosceles right triangle. It can be shown

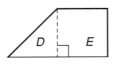

Figure 5.17

Figure 5.18

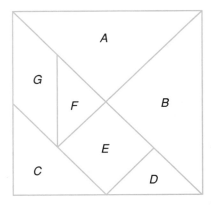

Figure 5.19

that the two sides that form the right angle are equal in length, because they are both as long as the sides of shape E. Because all sides of shape E are equal in length and because it contains four right angles, it is a square.)

7. Take the remaining right trapezoid and fold on the dotted line (Figure 5.18). Label these pieces F and G. Cut along the dotted line. (Shape F is also an isosceles right triangle because it is congruent to shape D. Shape G is a parallelogram because its opposite sides are parallel.)

8. All of the pieces that have just been cut out can be reassembled into a square like that of Figure 5.19.

In addition to forming a square with the seven tangram pieces, it is also possible to form several other standard geometric shapes. The accompanying Strength in Numbers activity (tangrams) challenges you to create these shapes, and to see how it is possible to transform one shape into another.

Connecting Geometry to Other Mathematical Ideas

One of the exciting things about teaching geometry is that it readily allows for mathematical connections. The reform movement in mathematics calls for greater coherency in mathematics curricula and greater attention to making mathematical connections apparent to students. According to NCTM's *Principles and Standards*:

> Many adults who recall their school mathematics experiences as less than satisfying see mathematics as a set of disconnected facts and procedures. . . . Conversely, mathematicians see their subject as both highly interconnected and cumulative. . . . It is important that students see the interconnections of ideas in the subject of mathematics . . . . (p. 29)

Currently, many states are developing core curricula for elementary schools that are built around several key ideas. A typical set of key ideas might resemble the topics on this list:

Key Idea #1: Mathematical Reasoning

Key Idea #2: Operations on Number

Strength in Numbers

Tangrams

Cooperative Group Model: Numbered Heads Together

Working in groups of four, each person is assigned one of the shapes of Figure 5.20, to be formed from all seven tangram pieces. Group members are asked to offer a justification as to why the shape they have created is a trapezoid, rectangle, triangle, or parallelogram.

After all of the members have had the opportunity to create their own shape and to share their informal "proof" of its identity, the members should reassemble as a group. Then, each member is asked to arrange the tangram pieces into three categories:

1. One large triangle
2. The other large triangle
3. A triangle, equal in size to both of the large triangles together, made up of the other five tangram pieces, as shown in Figure 5.21.

If the tangram pieces are thought of as falling into these three categories, it is possible to begin with the original square and form the trapezoid, rectangle, triangle, and parallelogram by moving only one or both of the two large triangles. Working as a group, the members are to determine how this can be done. Upon completion, one number will be chosen, and that person will be invited to share with the rest of the class the group's strategy for transforming each shape into another.

Combining the study of geometry with literature is a useful connection. Many illustrations of children's books are geometric in nature. Recently, several books have been written that use tangrams as both the theme and as the basis for the illustrations.

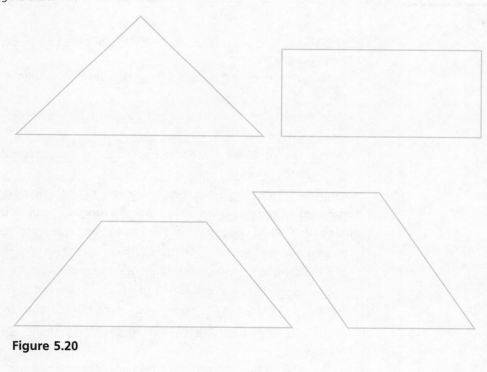

Figure 5.20

Figure 5.21

Key Idea #3: Geometry

Key Idea #4: Number and Numeration

Key Idea #5: Measurement

Key Idea #6: Probability

Key Idea #7: Patterns and Functions

Activities 5.6 through 5.12 are all developed around the theme of quilts. They address each one of these key ideas in turn, and are offered as a model for connecting the various topics of elementary school mathematics. These seven activities connect various mathematical topics within the theme of patchwork quilt designs. They are designed to appeal to students both visually and tactically, and to show students how mathematics can help people understand, make sense of, and appreciate the world.

The accompanying Interdisciplinary Lesson Plan connects spatial concepts with literature and provides children with an opportunity to create a book as a class.

Interdisciplinary Lesson Plan

Grade 3 or 4   **Concept** Spatial Visualization

Topic Tangrams

Student Objectives After completing this lesson, students should be able to

■ Create a figure from the seven tangram pieces according to a certain theme

■ Write two or three sentences explaining a transformation from one figure to the next.

Materials A tangram set for each student, paper, crayons, markers or paint, and a copy of *Grandfather Tang's Story* by Ann Tompert (1990).

Motivation Read *Grandfather Tang's Story* to the class. This book tells the story of two animals, the fox fairies, and their experiences as they transform themselves into different animals (the illustration of each is formed from a tangram) in an attempt to escape from predators. As the book is read, encourage the children to predict the identity of the animal resulting from each subsequent transformation.

Procedure

(1) Ask the class to describe the theme of the book. A possible response is that it tells about animals that magically become, for example, a goldfish to escape from a crocodile, or a turtle to escape from a hawk. Another possible response is that the book is about a grandfather telling a fairy tale to his granddaughter about animals that like to change shapes. (2) Have the class decide on a similar theme that can

(continued)

be used to create a class book. Possible responses are toys that change shape to try to please an unhappy child, superheroes who transform themselves in an attempt to defeat an enemy, or children who change shapes to remain hidden in a game of hide-and-seek. (3) Distribute to each child a tangram cut from construction paper or recycled file folders and allow the children ample time to explore with the materials. (4) Encourage the children to use their tangram to create a figure in keeping with the chosen theme, and then to glue the tangram pieces onto a large sheet of unlined paper. Ask them to write two or three sentences at the bottom of their paper that begin with this phrase: "Then the (toy, superhero, child, etc.) turned into a _____ to try to . . ." (5) Assemble all the individual sheets into a class book. Have the children decide on a title, and chose one figure to be used as a cover illustration. The book can be read to a first-grade class, and each fourth-grader can be paired with a first-grade buddy to create some tangram designs and a sentence or two describing the design.

Asessment Observe the children as they manipulate the tangrams. Note any child who appears to have difficulty. Assess the children's individual performance based on the tangram design and written work they produce.

References *Math and Literature,* Marilyn Burns, Math Solutions Publications, 1992.

Journal Entry This might contain practical suggestions or management ideas about the distribution of materials, the quality of paper or glue to use, etc., and it might also contain content-related reminders to use the lesson to introduce vocabulary words such as parallelogram, congruent, adjacent, and so on.

Geometry and Spatial Sense for Grades 3–5

According to the NCTM *Principles and Standards,* in grades 3–5, all students should

- Identify, compare, and analyze attributes of two-and three-dimensional geometric figures;
- Classify two-and three-dimensional shapes according to their attributes and develop definitions of classes of shapes (e.g., triangle, pyramid);
- Investigate describe, and reason about the results of subdividing, combining, and transforming shapes using models and representations;
- Investigate and reason about properties of geometric figures (e.g., the number of diagonals of a regular polygon);
- Build and use geometric vocabulary to describe two-and three-dimensional shapes;

Activity 5.6

Mathematical Reasoning

Lesson: Individual

Provide students with reproductions of 8 to 10 traditional quilt patterns, such as Log Cabin, Spools, Churn Dash, or Ohio Star (sources are provided in the chapter bibliography). Challenge the students to think about what patterns belong together. Invite a student to come to the front of the room and sort the patterns, without revealing the basis for the sorting. Encourage the rest of the students to try to identify the reasoning behind the sorting. The student who successfully identifies the reasons for the sorting is invited to sort the quilt patterns in another way.

Journal Reflection

Write down a list of anticipated bases on which the quilts will be sorted. The longer you allow students to sort, the more creative they will become. Similarly, the longer you work on your list, the more inventive you will become.

Activity 5.7

Operations on Number

Lesson: Small Groups

Have available a generous quantity of colored squares, 14 cm on each side. Working in groups of 4 to 5 students, have each group find the answers to these questions and then obtain the appropriate number of colored squares for distribution in their group.

- How many people are in your group?
- If each person needs two squares of different colors, how many will your group need in all?
- If each 14-cm square will be cut into 4 triangles, how many triangles will each person have?
- If each 14-cm square will be cut into 4 triangles, how many triangles will your group have in all?

- Explain how you solved the last problem.

Journal Reflection

A problem for one person is not necessarily a problem for another. While the questions in this Activity don't pose a problem for you, they will pose a problem for many students. Reflect on a situation in your own life where you were less adept in a situation than others around you. How did you feel? How could those around you enable you to improve in that situation?

- Understand and demonstrate congruence;
- Make conjectures about properties and relationships of shapes and use spatial reasoning and geometric tools to test them. (p. 170)

As adults, we tend to limit our discussions of shapes and their characteristics to two-dimensional plane figures. However, the objects that make up a child's world are more often three-dimensional than they are two-dimensional.

Activity 5.8

Geometry

Lesson: Individual

Using the 14-cm squares from Activity 5.7, have the children fold each square along its diagonal, and then cut along that diagonal. You may wish to take this opportunity to define the resultant triangles as congruent isosceles right triangles. They are congruent because they are the same size and the same shape, and when placed one on top of the other, they match perfectly. They are isosceles because they have two sides of equal measure, and they are right triangles because they contain a right angle. Challenge the students to answer these questions:

- Is it possible to have an isosceles triangle that is not also a right triangle? How do you know?

- Is it possible to have a triangle that has two right angles? How do you know?

Instruct the children to fold each of the congruent isosceles right triangles in half, and then cut along the fold line. This is a good opportunity to define the smaller isosceles right triangles as similar to the original triangles, since the angles are of equal measure and the lengths of the sides are in proportion.

At this point, each child should have eight congruent isosceles right triangles, four of one color and four of another. Invite the children to use these eight triangles to create quilt designs, such as those shown in Figure 5.22.

Journal Reflection

Do you think that this lesson, based on American quilt designs, is appropriate for children who were born in another country? Why or why not? If not, what activity would you substitute?

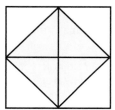 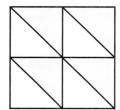 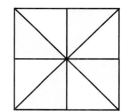

Figure 5.22

Activity 5.9

Number and Numeration

Lesson: Individual

Using the quilt designs created above in Activity 5.8, challenge the students to numerically represent their quilt design in as many ways as they can. Some possible examples are:

4 blue triangles + 4 yellow triangles = 8 triangles in all

$\frac{1}{2}$ blue triangles + $\frac{1}{2}$ yellow triangles = 1 design of triangles

$\frac{4}{8}$ blue triangles + $\frac{4}{8}$ yellow triangles = $\frac{8}{8}$ triangles

Journal Reflection

How would you deal with a child who was at a loss as to where to begin to answer this question?

Activity 5.10

Measurement

Lesson: Individual

Distribute paper clips, Unifix cubes, red Cuisenaire rods or some other small object and challenge the students to predict the length of one of the sides of the quilt square in terms of their non-standard measuring device. After students have predicted the length of the side, have them actually measure the side and compare their measurements with their predictions.

Repeat the above procedure with the diagonal of the square. Ask the students to predict if the diagonal of any square will *always* be longer than the sides, and to defend their claim.

Journal Reflection

Do you think that this Activity would be improved by having students use rulers to measure the sides and diagonals of the squares? Why or why not?

Activity 5.11

Probability

Lesson: Individual

Using the quilt designs created by the students in Activity 5.8 (let's assume the design in question is blue and yellow), ask the students to make the following predictions:

- If you were to drop a coin onto your quilt design 30 times, how many times would the coin land on yellow?

- How many times would it land on blue?

- How many times would it land off the quilt?

Distribute coins and the tops of gift boxes to the children. Having them place their quilt design in the boxtop will prevent the coins from rolling onto the floor. Instruct the children to keep their elbows on the desk, to hold the coin over the center of the design, and then to drop it. Have them record the outcome of each coin drop. Have the students compare the actual outcomes of dropping the coin thirty times with their predictions. Challenge them to explain why their outcomes either did or did not match their predictions. Encourage the students to write a generalization based on the outcome of this experiment, with an understanding that one half of the design was blue and one half of the design was yellow.

Journal Reflection

Children sometimes have beliefs about outcomes that have no evidential basis. How would you respond to a child who predicted in this activity that all of his coins would land on blue because blue was his favorite color?

Activity 5.13 (on page 166) involves children in creating many different arrangements of toothpicks. Try to solve this problem yourself before you examine the possible solutions.

Another important concept for elementary school children is the concept of *symmetry*. An intuitive appreciation of line symmetry often appears in

Activity 5.12

Patterns and Functions

Lesson: Whole Class

Read *Tar Beach* by Faith Ringgold, or *The Mountains of Quilt* by Nancy Willard, to the children. Both of these books have illustrations that include borders of quilt designs. Distribute pattern blocks to the students, and invite them to use the pattern blocks to create borders for their quilt design. Have the students record their borders in one of several ways: (1) by tracing around the pattern blocks to reproduce the pattern, (2) by describing the border in words, or (3) by symbolizing the border with letters to represent the colors, such as R R G R R G R R G . . . . Additionally, children can be challenged to predict how many of each block they will need for the entire border, after completing one side of the square.

Journal Reflection

Explain how this lesson could be used to introduce the concept of perimeter.

children's art work or block creations. Young children often build tabletop block structures with both hands simultaneously. As they place a cylinder on the right with their right hand, they place a cylinder on the left with their left hand. The study of symmetry readily allows integration with art, social studies, and science. For example, you can give children a butterfly cutout and some paint, asking them to splatter paint on one side of the cutout and then fold the two halves together. When the halves are unfolded, a design with line symmetry is created (Figure 5.28). Children find pattern blocks very appealing, and many of the designs they create with them are symmetrical (Figure 5.29, on page 168). Notice that design (a) illustrates both rotational and line symmetry, design (c) exhibits only rotational symmetry, and (b) is asymmetrical. If you give the children a piece of ribbon or yarn, they can lay it on top of their designs to try to find the line or lines of symmetry.

If you distribute triangle grid paper to students, they can reproduce their designs with crayons or markers, and then test to see if they have identified the lines of symmetry by folding the design along the purported line. If the two superimposed halves match exactly, the fold line is a line of symmetry. To test for rotational symmetry, encourage the children to rotate the paper on their desk to see if the design looks the same after partial rotations. While any design will look the same after a full 360-degree rotation, the description of rotational symmetry is appropriate only for designs that look exactly the same after a quarter turn, a half turn, or any other partial rotation.

Many science topics can include the study of symmetry. For instance, the human skeleton is essentially symmetrical. When children create a human-sized skeleton using paper-towel and wrapping-paper rolls they can see that the vertical line of symmetry is apparent. In another example, the study of leaves and plants provides an opportunity for illustrations and discussions of line symmetry. The following performance-based assessment activity allows children to demonstrate their understanding of, and ability to create, symmetrical designs.

Activity 5.13

Congruency

Lesson: Individual

Distribute to each child a piece of paper measuring $8\frac{1}{2} \times$ 14 and a pair of scissors. Ask the children to accordion-fold the paper into five sections, as shown in Figure 5.23.

Invite the children to draw a figure whose hands extend completely to the edges on the first fold of the paper, and then cut around the figure to make paper dolls. As the paper dolls are unfolded, invite the children to describe the figures. Introduce the word *congruent* to describe things that are exactly the same size and exactly the same shape. Explain that a simple test for congruency is to lay one object over the other to see if all parts match. Encourage the children to fold up their paper dolls once again to illustrate the congruency of each doll figure.

Then, distribute six toothpicks to each child (for this problem, the flat ones work better than the round ones). Ask the children to use their six toothpicks to form a figure that contains four congruent triangles. Various solutions are possible. Many children begin by forming a square with four of the toothpicks, and crossing the remaining two to form diagonals, as shown in Figure 5.24.

A weakness of this solution is that, since the toothpicks are used to form the sides of the square, the same toothpicks cannot be long enough to form the diagonals. This is an appropriate time to examine the relationship between the lengths of the sides of a square and the lengths of the diagonals of that square.

Another possible solution is to construct two parallel toothpicks and four transversal toothpicks, as shown in Figure 5.25. This solution can result in four congruent triangles, if the transversal toothpicks are placed in exactly the right positions. This solutions also results in the creation of one additional shape. A rhombus is formed in between the two pairs of transversal toothpicks.

Some children also form the shape of Figure 5.26. This solution can actually result in the creation of six congruent triangles, plus an enclosed hexagon.

All of these solutions consist of figures that lie in the two-dimensional plane. How about a three-dimensional solution? If three toothpicks are used to form a triangular base, and the remaining three toothpicks are used to form a pyramid above that base, the result is the regular tetrahedron shown in Figure 5.27. This solution has no extraneous shapes, and the four triangles formed are necessarily congruent, since all of the edges are congruent.

Journal Reflection

Due to weaknesses with coordination, some children have trouble manipulating toothpicks. An alternative is to use unsharpened pencils or flat wooden coffee stirrers, and follow the same procedure as outlined above. Think of other alternatives. What are some ways to use this problem that do not involve the manipulation of any objects? What are the disadvantages and advantages of these approaches?

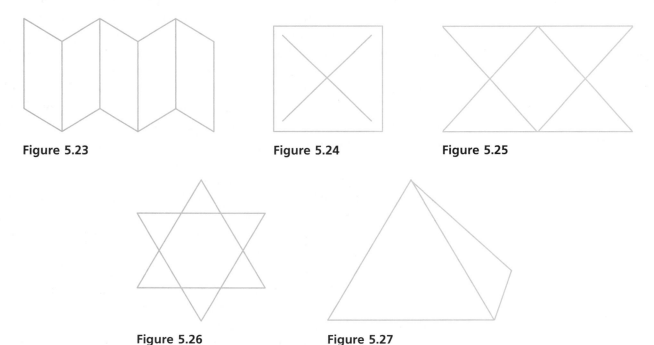

Figure 5.23   **Figure 5.24**   **Figure 5.25**

Figure 5.26   **Figure 5.27**

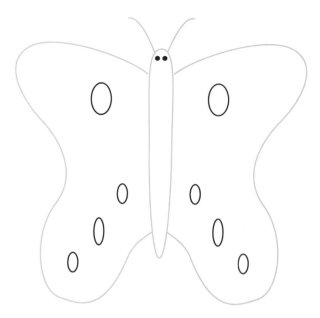

Figure 5.28

Performance-Based Assessment: Line and Rotational Symmetry

Provide each child with a supply of construction-paper cutouts of the six pattern block shapes. (Templates of these six shapes are commercially available to allow for ease of tracing.) Ask the children to create three designs by gluing the shapes onto a sheet of paper: one with line symmetry, one with rotational symmetry, and one with both line and rotational symmetry. Encourage the children to use at least eight shapes in each design. The designs can be assessed according to the following rubric:

3   Child accurately creates a non-simplistic design with line (or rotational, or both) symmetry.

2   Child creates a non-simplistic symmetrical design with only one error.

1   Child creates a non-simplistic design with two or more errors.

0   Child is unable to create a symmetric design, or creates one so simplistic (ie, two squares next to each other) that it is impossible to assess the child's understanding of symmetry.

Another important concept for children to explore is the concept of *similarity*. Children have had experience with this concept. They have played with matchbox cars, toy tea sets, child-sized footballs, and dolls. They have ridden on small bicycles and sat in child-sized furniture. Activity 5.14 will illustrate similarity to children.

Computer Software

A big advantage of using computer software to explore geometric concepts with children is that the technology allows them to create accurate images and manipulate them, regardless of their level of fine or gross

(a)

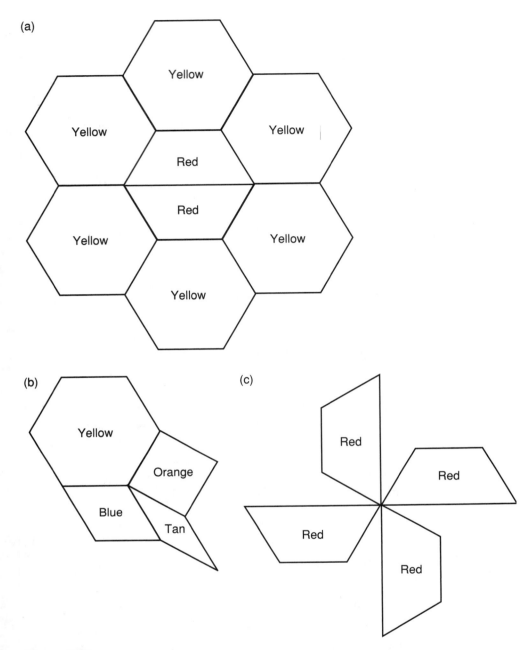

(b)

(c)

Figure 5.29

motor coordination. Young children who lack the coordination necessary to create a large tessellating pattern with pattern blocks can benefit from a computer program that allows them to drag and click pattern blocks and then "locks" them into place.

Many types of interactive software are available on the market today. One example is *Tenth Planet,* a supplementary curriculum program that integrates computer software with classroom activities and Internet resources for elementary classrooms. The geometric investigations available integrate the study of geometry with other topics (Latin America folk art, Japanese fish prints, Native American baskets). The classroom activities

Activity 5.14
Similarity

Lesson: Whole Class

Begin by reading a version of *The Three Bears* to the class. After the class has enjoyed the story, invite the children to draw a picture of either the Mama Bear's chair, her bowl of porridge, or her bed. Collect the drawings, and have them reproduced twice on a copier, one reproduction being set at 120% and the other at 80% of the original. Redistribute the three versions of each drawing, and have the children label each one as belonging to Papa Bear, Mama Bear, or Baby Bear (Figure 5.30).

Point out to the children that each of these drawings is similar to each other. *Similar* refers to figures that differ only in size, not in shape. This would also be an appropriate time to reinforce such comparative terms as wider, narrower, taller, shorter, and so on.

Journal Reflection

Would you encourage first-graders to use the terms *congruent* and *similar*? Why or why not?

Figure 5.30

involve children in the study of quilts and origami. An unusual aspect of this software is the links it provides to related websites and other teacher resources.

Summary

The chapter began by discussing the important clinical research on children's geometric thinking done by Piaget and Inhelder and the van Heiles. It stressed the importance of giving children the opportunity to create their own understandings and the need to offer children hands-on experiences with two- and three-dimensional objects.

Once again, emphasis was placed on the primacy of engaging children in the processes of observation, description, and classification. Specific examples were offered as to how this might be accomplished.

Several geometric concepts—area, perimeter, congruency, similarity, and line and rotational symmetry—were introduced in the context of child-centered activities. In addition, such classic geometric materials as tangrams, geoboards, and pattern blocks were addressed.

Seven integrated activities, built around the theme of patchwork quilt designs, illustrated how several areas of mathematics could be connected within a single topic of study. These key ideas were offered as a structure to create an integrated unit of study.

Extending Your Learning

1. Describe in detail classroom activities that would be appropriate for children functioning at each of the first three van Heile levels of geometric development.

2. Develop a list of at least ten children's books that could be used to investigate geometric concepts. For each book, include a description of an appropriate activity that could accompany the book.

3. Obtain a copy of *The Tangram Magician* by Ernst & Ernst (1990), ISBN 0-8109-3851-0. Write a lesson plan that uses that book to teach some geometric concept.

4. Describe in detail three art activities that can be used to illustrate the concept of congruency to children.

5. How might you connect the operation of multiplication with the concept of similarity? Write a lesson plan, appropriate for the third or fourth grade, that makes such a connection.

6. Write a geometrical autobiography. Discuss your memories of learning geometry as an elementary and secondary school student. Explain your geometrical understandings. Did they result from courses you took or from life experiences? Based on your experiences, do you think that teaching and learning geometry is different from teaching and learning any other area of mathematics? If so, in what ways does it differ?

7. Obtain a copy of the 1987 NCTM Yearbook, *Learning and Teaching Geometry, K–12*. Read three of the articles and summarize their contents. Present these summaries to your classmates.

8. Cut out twelve commercial logos from newspapers or magazines. Sort them into four groups; those with only line symmetry, those with only rotational symmetry, those with both line and rotational symmetry, and asymmetrical logos. Is one of these four groups overrepresented? Why do you think that is so?

9. List five aspects of your favorite sport and indicate specifically how each aspect could be used to develop a geometry lesson. Then, choose one of the aspects and develop it into a formal lesson plan.

10. Refer to the list of seven key ideas that appeared in this chapter. Using the theme of Native American blanket patterns, develop connections with that theme for each of the key ideas.

Internet Resources

www.earthmeasure.com
This website, devoted to Native American geometry, offers a description and a rationale of the geometry of Native American culture, and a wealth of teacher resources to translate this topic into classroom activities.

www.FunBrain.com
This rich and visually appealing website contains an extensive database of assessment instruments, appropriate for grades K–8. In addition, the site offers a variety of interactive mathematical games.

www.hopepaul.com/kids/kids.htm
This website enables you to print out nets to construct twenty-five different three-dimensional shapes, including pla-tonic solids and a variety of other prisms and pyramids. Each net comes with directions.

www.teachingk-8.com
If you wish to become familiar with the monthly journal, *Teaching K–8,* this website presents articles appearing in the current issue. The website also allows the user to research back issues of the journal, and to access lesson plans and activities.

Bibliography

Andrews, Angela Giglio. (1999). Solving geometric problems by using unit blocks. *Teaching Children Mathematics 5*(6).

Austin, Richard A., and Patricia Biafore. (1995). Perimeter patterns. *Teaching Children Mathematics 2*(4).

Battista, Michael T. (1990). Spatial visualization and gender differences in high school geometry. *Journal for Research in Mathematics Education 21*(1):47–60.

Burns, Marilyn. (1992). *Math and literature.* Sausalito, CA: Math Solutions.

Clements, Douglas H., and Michael T. Battista. (1992). Geometry and spatial reasoning. In Douglas A. Grouws (ed.), *Handbook of research on mathematics teaching and learning.* New York: Macmillan.

Coerr, Eleanor. (1986). *The Josefina story quilt.* New York: HarperCollins.

Confer, Chris. (1994). *Math by all means: Geometry, grade 2.* Sausalito, CA: Math Solutions.

Crowley, Mary L. (1987). The van Heile model of the development of geometric thought. In Mary M. Lindquist and Albert P. Schulte (eds.), *Learning and teaching geometry, K-12: 1987 yearbook.* Reston, VA: National Council of Teachers of Mathematics.

Ernst, Lisa Campbell, and Lee Ernst. (1990). *The tangram magician.* New York: Harry Abrams.

Fennema, Elizabeth, and G. Leder. (1990). *Mathematics and gender.* New York: Teachers' College Press.

Flournoy, Valerie. (1985). *The patchwork quilt.* Illustrated by Jerry Pinkney. New York: Dial.

Hannibal, Mary Anne. (1999). Young children's developing understanding of geometric shapes. *Teaching Children Mathematics 5*(6).

Paul, Ann Whitford. (1991). *Eight hands round: A patchwork alphabet.* New York: HarperCollins.

Piaget, Jean, and Barbel Inhelder. (1967). *The child's conception of space.* New York: Norton.

Ringgold, Faith. (1991). *Tar Beach.* New York: Crown.

Seidel, Judith Day. (1998). Symmetry in season. *Teaching Children Mathematics 4*(5).

Tompert, Ann. (1990). *Grandfather Tang's story.* New York: Crown.

Usiskin, Zalman. (1987). Resolving the continuing dilemmas in school geometry. In Mary M. Lindquist and Albert P. Schulte (eds.), *Learning and teaching geometry, K-12: 1987 yearbook.* Reston, VA: National Council of Teachers of Mathematics.

van Heile, Pierre M. (1999). Developing geometric thinking through activities that begin with play. *Teaching Children Mathematics 5*(6).

Willard, Nancy. (1987). *The mountains of quilt.* Illustrated by Tomie dePaola. San Diego: Harcourt Brace Jovanovich.

6

Continuing the Study
of Geometry

In the last chapter, you learned of the need to involve children in first-hand investigations of geometric materials, and the desirability of encouraging them to make sense of problems in their own way. These two themes continue here. You will be invited to think about measurement from a geometric perspective, considering measurement of one-dimensional attributes (angle measurement), two-dimensional attributes (area), and three-dimensional attributes (volume). In addition, you will see how one mathematical concept can be built upon knowledge of others; the process of leading children through these steps is one of guided discovery. Through guided discovery, this chapter addresses the perimeter and area of rectangles, triangles, circles—and then the volume of cylinders.

This chapter also introduces two technological tools for geometric investigations, LOGO and geometric drawing utilities. Using technology for geometric investigations removes the tedium and effort from trying to prove conjectures by repeated constructions and attempts. Technology truly allows students to construct their own understandings.

Finally, we will turn to transformational geometry, where certain changes, such as slides, flips, rotations, and dilations, are visited upon figures. You will be asked to think about how these physical transformations connect to the world in which children find themselves.

Geometry as Measurement

The literal meaning of the word *geometry* is measurement of the earth. Of the many attributes of figures that geometry can measure are perimeter (linear), area (square), and volume (cubic). A linear measure answers the question "How many lengths cover the distance?" A square measure answers the question "How many squares cover the region?" A cubic measure answers the question "How many cubes fill the space?"

Geometry and Spatial Sense for Grades 6–8

The NCTM *Principles and Standards* recommend the following focus areas in geometry. In grades 6–8, all students should

- Precisely describe, classify and compare types of plane and solid figures (angles, triangles, quadrilaterals, cylinders, cones) according to their main features;

- Analyze and understand geometric relationships among two-dimensional and three-dimensional figures;

- Recognize and apply geometric ideas and relationships outside the mathematics classroom, in areas such as art, science, and everyday life. (p. 225)

An introduction to the concepts of perimeter and area can be achieved by asking students to use the geoboard to create as many different shapes as possible that have a perimeter of eight units with horizontal or vertical sides. (In early investigations of perimeter on the geoboard, it is important to limit explorations of perimeter to figures with horizontal or vertical sides, since horizontal or vertical distances between two pegs can be assigned a length of one unit. A diagonal distance between two pegs, however, would have a length of $\sqrt{2}$. Do you see why? Since this number, or its decimal approximation of 1.414, are awkward to use, it is advisable to use only horizontal and vertical lengths.) If the class you are working with does not have geoboards, dot paper can be substituted. Figure 6.1 shows three possible shapes, each with perimeters of eight units.

Ask the students to examine the area of each figure and note that, although the perimeter of each shape is the same, the area is not. Next, ask the students to create as many shapes as possible with an area of four square units. Figure 6.2 shows three possibilities. Repeat for the students that, although the area of each shape is the same, the perimeter is not.

It is important that students have ample experience in creating figures of varying area and perimeter. Many students erroneously believe that if the area of a figure increases (or decreases), the perimeter must also increase (or decrease), and vice versa. The area of a rectangle, which is easily found, can be used to find the area of a related triangle, parallelogram, or trapezoid, as shown in Activity 6.1. Then, in Activity 6.2, students can work with the length of the hypotenuse.

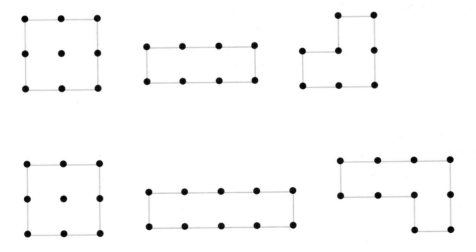

Figure 6.1

Figure 6.2

Activity 6.1

Finding Areas

Lesson: Individual

Invite the students to create a rectangle of any dimensions on their geoboard. After they have determined the area of the rectangle, ask them to create a diagonal (Figure 6.3). Encourage the students to articulate that the diagonal of a rectangle separates it into two triangles, each with an area ½ of the area of the original rectangle. In the rectangle pictured below, the area of each triangle is 2 ½ square units.

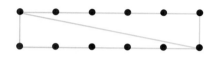

Figure 6.3

Next, have the students form a parallelogram of any dimensions. By partitioning the parallelogram into a rectangle and two triangles (Figure 6.4), the area can be easily deter-

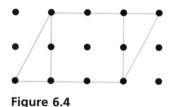

Figure 6.4

mined. You can see that the area of this parallelogram is 6 square units. The method of partitioning a trapezoid into a rectangle and two triangles is very similar. How might you create an isosceles trapezoid with an area of 10 units on the geoboard? How might you create a right trapezoid? How would you use the method of partitioning shapes into triangles and rectangles (Figure 6.5) to find the area of this shape?

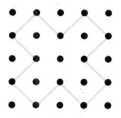

Figure 6.5

Journal Reflection

Some children have trouble visualizing how many squares fit into a given figure and thus have trouble determining its area. One solution is to have small paper squares and triangles available to lay on top of the figure on the geoboard. What other solutions can you imagine?

Activity 6.2

Length of the Hypotenuse

Lesson: Individual

Distribute to each child the following set of Cuisenaire rods: five yellow rods, four purple rods, and three light green rods. Challenge the students to create a square with the

five yellow rods. Then invite them to arrange the remaining four purple rods and three light green rods on top of the yellow rods in order to cover the yellow rods completely. Three different arrangements are possible (Figure 6.6).

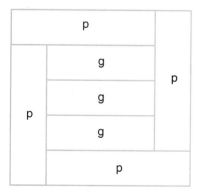
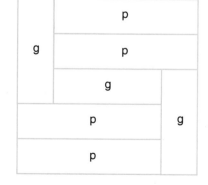
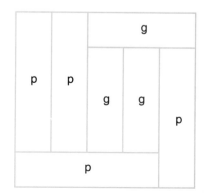

Figure 6.6

(continued)

Activity 6.2 (continued)

Length of the Hypotenuse

After the students have discovered the three arrangements, encourage them to articulate that three rods, each with a length of 3 cm and four rods, each with a length of 4 cm, completely cover five rods, each with a length of 5 cm. In other words, a 3 × 3 square and a 4 × 4 square cover the same area as a 5 × 5 square. Does Figure 6.7 help you to see what famous theorem has just been demonstrated?

Journal Reflection

Elaborate on the connection between this activity and the classic form of the Pythagorean Theorem, $a^2 + b^2 = c^2$.

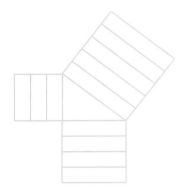

Figure 6.7

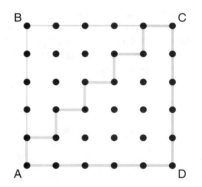

Figure 6.8

Performance-Based Assessment: Perimeter

Given that Square ABCD has a perimeter of 48 cm, what is the perimeter of the outlined, step-like Figure 6.8? There are at least four methods for solving this problem, and they are summarized here. But, before going any further, try to solve the problem yourself.

1. A visual solution relies on the insight that if the step-like portion of the figure were made of string, it could be straightened out and made to lie coincidentally on top of the perimeter of ABCD. Therefore, the perimeters of both figures are equal.

2. Another visual solution envisions the four horizontal segments of the steps being pushed up to lie on segment AB. Likewise, the four vertical segments of the steps would be pushed to the right to lie coincidentally on BC. Therefore, the perimeters of both figures are equal.

3. A numerical solution entails counting up the units in the perimeter of the step-like figure, and realizing that the perimeter is 20 units. Since the perimeter of Square ABCD is also 20 units, the perimeter of both figures is 48 cm.

4. Since the perimeter of ABCD is 48 cm, the length of each unit on the perimeter is 48 ÷ 20, or 2.4 cm. Since there are 20 units composing the perimeter of the step-like figure, the perimeter must be equal to 2.4 × 20, or 48 cm.

The following rubric can be used to assess student performance:

4   Student shows evidence of understanding the problem, uses an appropriate strategy, accurately carries out the strategy, and evaluates the reasonableness of the solution.

3 Student is successful in three of the four steps of problem solving, either understanding, planning, carrying out the plan, or evaluating the solution.

2 Student is successful in two of the steps of problem solving.

1 Student is successful in only one of the four steps of problem solving.

0 Student is unable to successfully perform any of the four steps of problem solving.

Performance-Based Assessment: Area

Given that the area of square QRST is 100 cm^2, what is the area of square WXYZ (Figure 6.9)? Estimate the area of WXYZ before you solve the problem, and then compare your estimate with your actual solution. There are at least four different solutions to this problem, and they are summarized for you in the following. However, before going any further, attempt to solve the problem on your own.

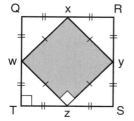

Figure 6.9

1. A visual solution requires imagining how the figure would look if the small triangles XRY, YSZ, ZTW, and WQX were folded over the inner square WXYZ. Since the four small triangles completely cover square WXYZ, the area of WXYZ and the sum of the areas of the four triangles must be the same. Half of 100 is 50; therefore, the area of WXYZ is 50 cm^2. (Most students originally estimate the area to be between 60 and 75 cm^2, and are surprised that the area of the inner square is half the area of the outer square.)

2. Another visual solution requires that line segments XZ and WY be drawn, dividing square QRST into four smaller congruent squares. Since half of each of the smaller squares lies inside WXYZ, half of the entire square QRST falls inside WXYZ, or 50 cm^2.

3. If the areas of the four small triangles XRY, YSZ, ZTW, and WQX can be found, the total of those four areas can be subtracted from 100 cm^2, and the area of WXYZ determined. Since $\sqrt{100}$ = 10, each side of QRST has a length of 10 cm, and each of the legs of the four isosceles right triangles has a length of 5 cm. Since the area of a triangle is half the area of its related rectangle, the area of each of the four small triangles is half of 25, or 12.5. As 4 × 12.5 = 50, the solution is that the area of WXYZ is 50 cm^2.

4. Since each of the four small triangles is a right triangle, the Pythagorean Theorem can be used to find the lengths of each of the hypotenuses XY, YZ, ZW, and WX. Finding these lengths would allow you to find the area of WXYZ by multiplying a side by a side.

The Pythagorean Theorem states that the square root of the sum of the squared lengths of each of the legs of the triangle equals the length of the hypotenuse, or, more elegantly, $a^2 + b^2 = c^2$.

$$5^2 + 5^2 = c^2$$

$$25 + 25 = c^2$$

$$50 = c^2$$

$$\sqrt{50} = c$$

Since the length of each hypotenuse is $\sqrt{50}$, the area of WXYZ can be found by squaring that length, which equals 50 cm.

The same rubric that was used to assess performance in the performance-based assessment on perimeter can be used in this case, or in any situation where students are asked to apply knowledge to solve a problem.

Angle Measurements

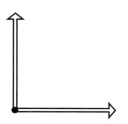

Figure 6.10

Before moving to formal instruction on angle measurement with a protractor, you will serve your students well by helping them learn to estimate the size of an angle. If students are given two cardboard arrows and a paper fastener, they can construct an angle maker like that of Figure 6.10.

Then, model for students the approximate size of a right angle, straight angle, acute angle, and obtuse angle, as shown in Figure 6.11. Provide students with the opportunity to construct their own versions of these angles, using their angle makers. After the children have had the opportunity to become comfortable with these angles and their approximate size, introduce the concept of degree measurement. Place your angle maker on an overhead, and slowly sweep one of the arrows around to illustrate a 10-degree, 20-degree, 30-degree angle, and so on all the way up to 360 degrees. Once again, model different-sized angles for the students, but this time include an approximate angle measurement. For example, show the angles of Figure 6.12 to students, including the angle type and approximate measurement. Provide students with the opportunity to construct angles with their angle maker, and have their partner estimate the measures of the angles.

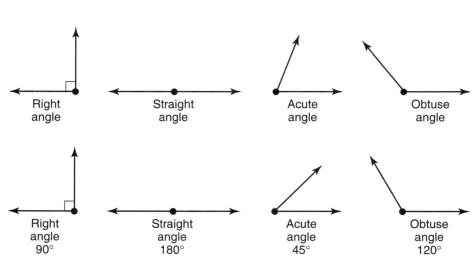

Figure 6.11

Figure 6.12

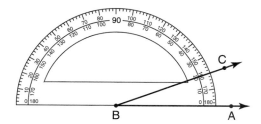

Figure 6.13

At this point, it is appropriate to introduce students to the use of a protractor. The protractor pictured in Figure 6.13 measures an angle of 20 degrees. The base of the protractor coincides with one of the rays forming the angle. The "center" of the protractor is placed on the vertex of the angle. Since ray BC intersects the protractor at the point that shows both 20 degrees and 160 degrees, it is necessary for students to recall the approximate size of an acute angle and realize that the angle pictured in Figure 6.6 could only measure 20 degrees.

Students often mistakenly think that there is a relationship between the length of the rays forming an angle and the measure of that angle. It can easily be shown that the measure of an angle is not dependent upon the length of its rays by extending the rays of any angle and re-measuring the angle with the protractor. The angle measure is invariant.

Activities 6.3 and 6.4 present interesting ways to demonstrate to students that the sum of the interior angles in a triangle equals 180 degrees, and the

Activity 6.3

The Sum of the Angles of a Triangle

Lesson: Individual

Ask students to follow this procedure:

- Draw a triangle on a sheet of paper and cut it out. The larger the triangle, the better.
- Draw arrows pointing to each of the vertices, as shown in Figure 6.14

Figure 6.14

- Tear off each of the three vertices. Arrange the three torn angles around a common point, as shown in Figure 6.15.

Figure 6.15

This exercise illustrates that the three interior angles of a triangle form a straight angle. Therefore, the sum of the measures of the interior angles of any triangle is equal to 180 degrees.

Journal Reflection

Predict what would happen if the above procedure was followed with any quadrilateral. Test your prediction by actually performing the steps. Write out the procedure to be followed by students that would illustrate the number of degrees in the interior angles of a quadrilateral.

Activity 6.4

Another Approach to Interior Angles

Lesson: Individual

Ask the students to follow this procedure:

- Draw any large triangle. Lay a pencil along any one of the sides. Note the direction of the pencil point (Figure 6.16).

Figure 6.16

- Holding the point on a vertex, sweep the pencil around so that it now lies on an adjacent side (Figure 6.17).

Figure 6.17

- Holding the eraser end on the nearest vertex, again sweep the pencil around so that it lies on the third side of the triangle (Figure 6.18).

Figure 6.18

- Holding the point on the nearest vertex, sweep the pencil around to the side you began with. Note that the pencil point is facing in exactly the opposite direction as when you began. In other words, the pencil has been rotated through a 180-degree angle, which is the sum of the three interior angles of the triangle.

Journal Reflection

Write a procedure that would allow the same illustration to be made for any quadrilateral. Which method do you prefer, the one described in Activity 6.3 or the one described here? Why?

sum of the interior angles in a quadrilateral equals 360 degrees. The first activity involves removing the vertices of a figure and joining them to form a new figure. The second involves rotating a pencil through the interior angles of a figure.

Guided Discovery

Because of the hierarchical nature of mathematical curricula, the sequence of activities you structure for students and the sequence of lessons you prepare reflect an implicit view of mathematical connections. In addition to illustrating an image of mathematical connections, a structured series of lessons also contains an implicit view of how students can build their mathematical understandings on prior knowledge. Many educators call this progression a *guided discovery* lesson. The following series of investigations has been delib-

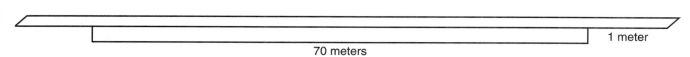

Figure 6.19

erately structured to lead students through a step-by-step process, where prior understandings lead to subsequent understandings.

A weakness in the way geometry has been taught is that topics used to be presented in isolation, with little attention paid to the way they connect. The following progression allows students to see that many different tools of geometry can be brought together to solve problems. These investigations are appropriate for grades 6 through 8.

Pose the following problem to students:

■ A gardener has 72 m of fencing to enclose a garden along three sides, with the fourth side of the garden being formed by a stone wall. (For the purposes of this problem, we will assume that the stone wall is perfectly straight.) What are the dimensions of a rectangular garden that will allow for the greatest area being enclosed?

Using Polya's steps for problem solving, encourage students to **restate the problem** in their own words:

■ "With a total length of fencing that is 72 m long, what are the lengths of three sides of a rectangle that will enclose the greatest area if one side of the enclosure is already provided?"

Help the students set up the parameters:

■ "Is it possible that the dimensions of the garden would be 1m by 70m, as shown in Figure 6.19? If so, what would the enclosed area be?"

■ "Is it possible that the dimensions of the garden would be 35m by 2m, as shown in Figure 6.20? If so, what would the enclosed area be?

Students find it helpful to set up parameters for the possible range of solutions. Knowing that the solution falls somewhere between the two extremes shown in the figures imparts a sense of confidence that, with diligence and care, they can find the correct solution.

While it is possible that the dimensions of the garden could be 1m by 70m or 35m by 2m, it is not at all likely, since these dimensions both result in an enclosed area of 70 m^2. Even a slight widening of the garden to, say, 10 m by 52m, results in a greatly increased area of 520 m^2.

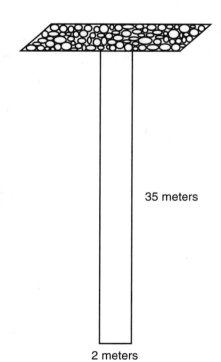

Figure 6.20

Encourage the students to **develop a strategy** of making a chart to determine what dimensions maximize the area. Their chart might look something like this:

Length	Width	Width	Area
70	1	1	70 m^2
52	10	10	520 m^2
42	15	15	630 m^2
32	20	20	640 m^2 . . .

Having students **carry out their strategy** in a group setting, with access to calculators, will help to make this experience valuable.

After a solution has been reached, encourage the students to **look back** at their solution and evaluate its reasonableness. You can require that the students prove, in any way that they want, that their dimensions maximize the area. Most students chose to prove that their solution is correct by showing that a garden slightly longer, and a garden slightly wider, both result in a smaller enclosed area. Since the dimensions of 18×36 m result in an area of 648 m^2, while the dimensions of 17×38 m (slightly longer) and 19×34 m (slightly wider) both result in an area of 646 m^2, it is reasonable to assume that 648 m^2 is the greatest possible area. You might want to challenge students to discover if sides not limited to whole-number lengths can result in an area greater than 648 m^2.

An interesting extension to this problem is to see what would happen if the shape of the garden were changed. For example, what if the stone wall formed the hypotenuse, and the 72m of fencing formed the two legs of an isosceles right triangle, as shown in Figure 6.21?

Since the students can determine the length of both the base and the height of the triangle, finding the area is easily done. Before they perform the calculations, encourage students to predict: Will the area of the triangular garden be greater than the area of the rectangular garden? Will it be less? Will it be the same?

Take a moment and solve this problem yourself. Does the answer surprise you? Here's a hint: Does it matter if your sandwich is sliced into two rectangular halves or two triangular halves?

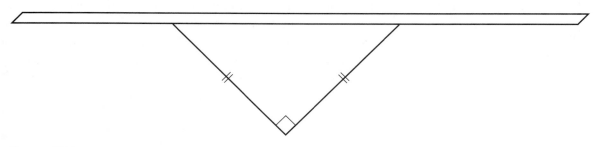

Figure 6.21

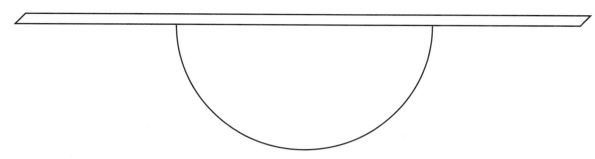

Figure 6.22

A further extension involves lifting the restriction that the garden have straight sides. What would happen if the 72 m of fencing were used to create a semi-circular garden, with the stone wall forming the diameter (Figure 6.22)?

Before the area of this semi-circular garden can be determined, a little background work needs to be done. Many teachers clearly see how the rule for the area of a rectangle can be developed by having children form many rectangles on a geoboard or dot paper, count up the squares inside, and eventually generalize that the area can be found by multiplying the length of the rectangle by the width. However, when it comes to generating the rule for the area of the circle, they are at a loss. Actually, it is easily done, and it can be based on the rule for the area of a rectangle. Begin by having students measure the distance around and the distance across the center of many different-sized circles. Organize this information into a chart, similar to the one shown here:

Distance around (circumference)	Distance across (diameter)
32 cm	10 cm
16 in	5 in
120 mm	38 mm
10 in	3 in

Challenge the students to identify a pattern. If they do not recognize that the length of the circumference is approximately three times the length of the diameter, have them use a calculator to add, subtract, multiply, and divide the two numbers to look for patterns. The only relationship that will yield a consistent answer is C ÷ d, which always turns out to be a little bit more than 3. Explain to the students that this consistent relationship was recognized by both ancient Egyptians and ancient Greeks, and is commonly called *pi,* or π. Numerically, π is commonly accepted to be approximately 3.14. However, many calculators have a π key, which allows greater accuracy than just carrying out to two decimal places.

Next, have the students cut up a paper plate into eight congruent sectors, and rearrange those sectors into parallelogram-like shape, as shown in Figure 6.23.

Figure 6.23

Ask the students to imagine what the shape would look like if there were 16 sectors, or 32 sectors, or 64 sectors. As the number of sectors increases, the curvature of the sectors decreases, and the figure looks more and more like a parallelogram. Since the area of a parallelogram can be found by multiplying the base times the height, label the vertical distance *h* for height and the horizontal distance *b* for base.

It will be helpful now to translate these distances into the vocabulary commonly used with circles. Since the distance labeled *h* is the distance from the circumference of the circle to the center of the circle, it can be called a radius (r). Since the distance labeled *b* is half the distance around the circle, it can be called ½ of the circumference (c).

Earlier in this investigation, the students discovered that the circumference of a circle equals π times the diameter (d). Since the distance labeled *b* is half the circumference, the students easily see that half the circumference should equal π times half the diameter, or times the radius. This can be shown algebraically in the following manner:

$$c = \pi \times d$$

$$\tfrac{1}{2}(c) = \tfrac{1}{2}(\pi \times d)$$

$$\tfrac{1}{2}c = \pi \times \tfrac{1}{2}d$$

$$\tfrac{1}{2}c = \pi \times r$$

At this point, substituting r for *h* and π × r for *b*, allows the following rule to be generalized for finding the area of the circle:

$$\text{Area} = r \times \pi \times r$$

or, more commonly written,

$$\text{Area} = \pi r^2$$

Now that they know how to find the area of a circle, the children can determine the area of the semi-circular garden. Before they actually perform the calculations, encourage them to predict (estimate) again whether the area of the semi-circular garden will be greater than, less than, or equal to the area of the rectangular and triangular gardens.

To find the area of the semi-circular garden, we will first find the area of the entire circle that would be formed with 144 m (72 + 72) of fencing, and then take half of that area:

$$c = 72 \text{ m} + 72 \text{ m}$$

$$c = 144 = \pi \times d$$

$$144 \div \pi = d$$

$$45.8366236105 = d$$

$$45.8366236105 \div 2 = r$$

$$22.9183118052 = r$$

$$525.249016002 = r^2$$

$$\pi \times 525.249016002 = \text{area of circle}$$

$$1650.11844998 = \text{area of circle}$$

$$1650.11844998 \div 2 = \text{area of semi-circle}$$

$$825.059224988 = \text{area of semi-circle}$$

As you can see, the area enclosed by a semi-circular garden is considerably greater (825 m^2 vs. 648 m^2) than the area enclosed by a rectangular or triangular garden.

This is an appropriate time to engage the students in a discussion about cultures where circular houses are, or were, common (Inuit, igloos; Plains Indians, tipis; East Africans, round houses; and Central Asians, yurts). It is impressive that these people, in areas where timber was not available, discovered that a circular living space would enclosed a greater area than a straight-sided one. Your students would enjoy reading *The Village of Round and Square Houses* by Ann Grifalconi (1986), set in an African village in the Cameroons, telling the legend about why the men of that culture live in straight-sided houses, and the women live in round houses.

Other examples of literature with mathematical connections are two amusing books by Cindy Neuschwander. The first, *Sir Cumference and the First Round Table* is an investigation of the attributes of various polygons and the contrasting characteristics of circles and polygons. The second, *Sir Cumference and the Dragon of Pi,* considers the relationship between the circumference and the diameter of a circle.

The final connection that will be made in this investigation is to explore the attribute of volume, and to see how it relates to the attributes of area and perimeter. Begin by using four wooden cubes to build the first story of the "building" shown in Figure 6.24a. Ask the students to determine the perimeter of the base (8 units), the area of the base (4 square units), and the volume of the structure (4 cubes). Add four more cubes to form the second story, as shown in Figure 6.24b. Again, determine the perimeter (8 units), the area of the base (4 square units), and the volume (8 cubes). Continue in this fashion for the third and fourth stories of the building, as shown in Figure 6.24c and d. Encourage the students to develop a rule for finding the volume of a rectangular prism (l $\times$ w $\times$ h)

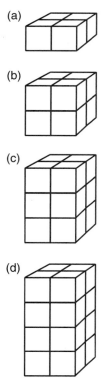

(a)

(b)

(c)

(d)

Figure 6.24

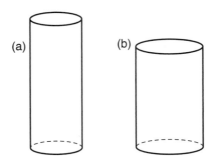

Figure 6.25

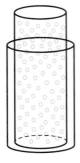

Figure 6.26

The Relationship Between Surface Area and Volume

and to generalize this to any solid prism or cylinder (volume = area of the base × height).

Next, form two cylinders from two standard overhead transparencies, each measuring 8.5 × 11 in. Create them so that the circumference of the base of one cylinder is 8.5 in, and the circumference of the base of the other cylinder is 11 in, as shown in Figure 6.25.

Ask the students to predict which of the following is true:

- The volume of cylinder A is greater than the volume of cylinder B.
- The volume of cylinder A is less than the volume of cylinder B.
- The volumes of both cylinders are the same.

Then, with cylinder A *inside* cylinder B, fill cylinder A to the top with crispy rice cereal, as shown in Figure 6.26.

If the volumes of both cylinders are the same, when cylinder A is carefully lifted up, the same amount of cereal will completely fill cylinder B, with some allowance made for settling. If the volume of cylinder A is greater, some cereal will spill over the top of cylinder B. If the volume of cylinder B is greater, the cereal will not fill it. To find out which of these outcomes will occur, perform the experiment! And then, offer an explanation of the outcome.

As you worked through the preceding section, you probably realized why many students think that if two cylinders are constructed from congruent sheets of paper the volume of the two cylinders should be equal. However, your work demonstrated that this is not always the case. The following series of Activities provides a more deliberate investigation of the relationship between the surface areas and volumes of rectangular prisms, and is designed to help you and your students understand the relationship between the surface area and the volume of three-dimensional solids. Work through these investigations yourself as preparation for doing them with students (Activity 6.5).

Activity 6.5

Constructing Rectangular Prisms

Lesson: Individual

Working with a generous supply of centimeter grid paper and centimeter cubes, have the students cut out a 15 × 20 cm rectangle from the grid paper. Ask the students to

predict what will happen if 1 centimeter from each corner is cut out and the resultant flaps are folded and taped, as shown in Figure 6.27.

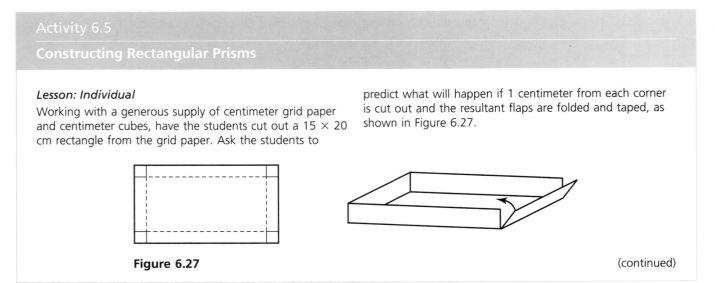

Figure 6.27

(continued)

Activity 6.5 (continued)

Constructing Rectangular Prisms

Define the new structure as an open-top rectangular prism, with dimensions of 1 × 13 × 18 cm. By filling the rectangular prism with centimeter cubes, have the students determine its volume. Use this opportunity to illustrate the reason volume is considered a **cubic** measurement. Just as area is a square measurement, since it measures how many squares cover a region, so is volume a cubic measurement, since it measures how many cubes fill a space. *Area* describes the covering of a two-dimensional region, while *volume* describes the filling of a three-dimensional space.

Invite the students to continue the process of cutting out larger and larger square corners from the grid paper, and determining the changing volumes. Students can record their results in a chart like this one:

Area of removed corner	Length	Width	Height	Volume
1 cm	13 cm	18 cm	1 cm	234 cu cm
4 cm	11 cm	16 cm	2 cm	352 cu cm

As the process of filling the rectangular prisms with cubes to determine the volume becomes more and more laborious, have students generalize the rule for determining the volume as L × W × H = Volume. While some students will need actually to place the centimeter cubes into the prisms to understand the concept of volume, others will be able to dispense with this step and simply multiply the dimensions.

Challenge the students to continue this process in order to determine the dimensions of the rectangular prism that result in the greatest volume.

Journal Entry

Explain the results. Do you think it would have been possible to obtain an even greater volume if you had cut away partial squares instead of only full ones? Explain. What do you think would have happened if you had begun this investigation with a square grid of dimensions 25 × 25, instead of a rectangular grid of dimensions 15 × 20?

To continue this investigation, it is necessary to introduce students to the concept of *surface area,* the measurement of the areas of all of the surfaces that compose a three-dimensional solid. Activity 6.6 helps students to investigate this concept and draw some conclusions about the relationship

Activity 6.6

Surface Area

Lesson: Individual or Small Group

Using one of the open-top rectangular prisms from Activity 6.5, cut a top out of centimeter grid paper to form a closed rectangular prism. Ask students to determine the total area of grid paper needed to form this solid. After students have had the opportunity to solve this problem on their own, help them organize their investigation by pointing out that rectangular prisms are formed by three pairs of congruent, parallel, rectangular faces. Therefore, the surface area can be determined by finding the area of the three distinct rectangles, and then doubling each measurement.

Distribute a sheet of 20 × 20 cm grid paper to each child or group of children. Challenge them to construct a closed rectangular prism with the greatest possible volume using no more than the provided piece of grid paper, or, in other words, with a maximum surface area of 400 cm².

Encourage the students to keep track of their investigations with a chart something like this:

Area of rect. 1	Area of rect. 2	Area of rect. 3	Total surface area	Volume
6 × 10 = 60	6 × 10 = 60	6 × 6 = 36	312 cm³	360 cm³

When the dimensions of the prism resulting in the greatest volume have been determined, challenge the students to explain their results.

Journal Entry

Do you think that a greater volume would have been obtained if a cylinder rather than a rectangular prism had been constructed out of the 20 × 20 sheet of grid paper? How could you find out?

Activity 6.7
Volume

Lesson: Individual

Obtain a bag of rice and a plastic prism-and-pyramid set, where the related prisms and the pyramids both have congruent bases and height. If a plastic set is not available, a set can be made from heavy paper. Display both the prisms and the pyramids to the class. Invite the students to predict how many pyramids full of rice would be needed to completely fill its related prism. After the students have written down their predictions, invite a student to come up and test the predictions by filling the pyramid with rice and repeatedly pouring it into the prism.

Encourage the students to develop a symbolic representation of the relationship between the volume of the pyramid and the volume of the prism. Have the students test their hypotheses on the various prisms and pyramids in the set, including triangular prisms, rectangular prisms, pentagonal prisms, and so on.

Journal Reflection

What relationship do you think would hold between the volumes of a cone and a cylinder that share congruent bases and height? How might you test your hypothesis?

between the surface area and the enclosed volume of solids. Once again, I recommend that you work through this activity yourself.

Finally, in our examination of volume, students are invited to investigate the relationship between the volume of prisms, both rectangular and triangular, and their related pyramids. You will recall from your own mathematics courses that prisms and pyramids differ in several ways. While both are considered three-dimensional solids, prisms have at least one pair of parallel faces, while pyramids do not. Rather, the triangular faces of a pyramid rise to form a vertex called the *apex*. The lateral faces of prisms are quadrilaterals, while the faces that rise from the polygonal base of a pyramid are triangles. A prism looks the same if it is turned upside down, while a pyramid does not. Activity 6.7 engages students in an investigation of the relative volumes of prisms and their related pyramids, where the two parallel bases of the prisms and the base of the pyramid are congruent and both solids have the same height.

Geometry is a topic of study that affords numerous opportunities to make connections with art, social studies, and science. The following Interdisciplinary Lesson Plan connects geography, cultural studies, history, art, and mathematics.

Interdisciplinary
Lesson Plan

Grade 6   **Concept** Geometry

Topic Tessellations

Student Objectives After completing this lesson, students should be able to

- Locate the Middle East on a world map.
- Create a tessellation.
- Identify which polygons will tessellate and which will not.
- Determine the interior-angle measurements of a regular polygon.

Materials Pattern blocks, markers, world map, examples of tessellations in Islamic art.

Motivation Display the examples of tessellations. Ask students to describe them (they are composed of repetitive patterns and shapes, there are no gaps or empty spaces, there are often floral designs embedded in them). Explain to the students that, during the seventh century, the Islam religion developed in the Middle East. Eventually, Islam spread into neighboring areas of Asia and northern Africa, as well as to Spain. Invite a student to find these areas on the world map. Islamic places of worship are called mosques. Mosques are often decorated with geometric patterns, called tessellations, that are sometimes embellished with flowers or leafy designs.

Procedure (1) Invite the students to use the pattern blocks to reproduce the tessellation shown in Figure 6.28, which is an example of a

Figure 6.28

tessellation that might be found in a mosque. (2) Invite the students to choose any two colors of pattern blocks, and create an original tessellation using only those two colors. Ask them to choose any point in their tessellation where several blocks meet, and list the pattern blocks that meet at that point. Possible answers are: 2 triangles and 2 hexagons, 3 rhombi, 3 trapezoids, 2 rhombi and 2 triangles. (3) Invite the students to determine the angle measurements of each vertex of each pattern block, in any way that makes sense to them. Possible methods are to use a protractor, or to see how many blocks of one color form a straight line or a circle, and divide 180 or 360 by that number of

(continued)

blocks. (4) Since the measurement of each angle is now known, encourage the students to look back at the combination of blocks identified in step 2, and to generalize that the sum of the angle measurements of the vertices that meet at any given point must equal 360 degrees. (5) Display a regular octagon on the overhead or board. Challenge the students to predict if the octagon will tessellate a plane by itself. If it will not tessellate by itself, what shape could be used with the octagon? Some students may chose to solve this problem by actually manipulating a paper octagon or other shapes.

This would be an appropriate time to introduce the following method for determining the angle measurements of a regular polygon. Draw diagonals inside the octagon to form as many triangles as possible, as shown in Figure 6.29.

Figure 6.29

Since it is possible to create six triangles inside the octagon, each containing 180 degrees, the total measure of the interior angles of the octagon is 6 × 180, or 1080 degrees. Since Figure 6.29 is a regular octagon, the measure of each individual interior angle is 1080 ÷ 8, or 135 degrees. Since 135 is not a factor of 360, this explains why regular octagons, by themselves, do not tessellate the plane. It is necessary to include another shape or shapes. One possible combination of shapes that will tessellate the plane is two octagons and a square, since 135 + 135 + 90 = 360.

Assessment Have the students write a summary of the lesson. The summary should include a description of Islamic art, a definition of a tessellation, and an explanation as to why certain shapes do tessellate the plane (with examples) and why certain shapes do not (with examples.)

References Norman, Jane, and Stef Stahl. *The mathematics of Islamic art.* New York: Metropolitan Museum of Art. (This is a kit of slides and teaching materials.)

Zaslavsky, Claudia. *Multicultural math.* New York: Scholastic, 1994.

Journal Entry An analysis of the lesson, to be filled in by the teacher at the end of the day.

Geometric Drawing Utilities

Within the last two decades, it is clear that technology has brought enormous changes in the way we live our lives. In the classroom, technology has made some areas of mathematics more accessible to elementary school children. Children need no longer be constrained by their inability to draw precise and accurate geometric figures, and they need not be discouraged by the great amount of time required to construct dozens of shapes manually. Because computer programs allow students to construct specific geometric shapes easily and rapidly, technology makes it possible for children to make and test conjectures. A *conjecture* is a hypothesis that students develop as a result of interacting with their environment.

While children certainly benefit from physically manipulating blocks and tiles and toothpicks and rubber bands, the process of conjecturing requires that ideas be tested many, many times in various situations. The results of the tests must be collected as evidence to support generalizations and explanations. Multiple investigations of ideas and the accumulation of evidence is much more easily done with technology. Many exciting geometric tools are now available that enable students to do just these things. Drawing and graphing utilities are available in the form of computer software, CD-ROMs, laser discs, and graphics calculators. These tools make it possible for children to create and test ideas. In this section we will first discuss the computer language LOGO, and then offer some activities made possible by geometric drawing tools, of which the *Geometers' Sketchpad* and the *Geometric superSupposer* are examples.

In the 1970s, under the direction of Seymour Papert, a group of researchers at the Massachusetts Institute of Technology developed a computer programming language called LOGO. This language grew out of their work with artificial intelligence. The researchers wanted to create a language that would make it easier for children to interact with computers. The language that allowed for this interaction is very simple and allows children to formulate and test ideas. Although easy to learn, LOGO is also powerful enough to allow some sophisticated programming. Papert refers to LOGO as *turtle geometry*. Graphics are drawn on the screen by a cursor called the turtle. Different types of LOGO display different turtles, ranging from an icon that resembles an actual turtle to a simple triangle. The student directs the movement of the turtle on the screen through a series of commands, some of which we will outline in this section.

It is not the purpose of this text to introduce any one particular type of LOGO. The various languages available are basically the same, with few exceptions. We encourage you to read through a LOGO manual and adapt this section to the program that is available to you.

Turtle geometry is based on position and heading (the direction in which the turtle is facing). The position of the turtle can be likened to a location on the coordinate axes. In some versions of LOGO there is even a command that allows the user to locate the turtle at a particular point on the screen that is defined by x-and y-coordinates.

All basic LOGO commands are referred to as *primitives*. The primitives used to change position and heading are shown in the following:

Command	Abbreviation	Result
FORWARD #	FD #	Maintains the current heading and moves the turtle a certain number of spaces in a forward direction.
BACKWARD #	BK #	Maintains the current heading and moves the turtle a certain number of spaces in a backward direction.
RIGHT #	RT #	Maintains the current position and rotates the turtle a certain number of degrees to the right.
LEFT #	LT #	Maintains the current position and rotates the turtle a certain number of degrees to the left.
HOME	HOME	Returns the turtle to the center of the screen with a heading of 0 degrees.

Any movement forward or backward will leave a trail on the screen in the form of a line segment. This is how turtle graphics are created. If you wish to move the turtle from one position on the screen to another without displaying a line segment, the command PENUP (PU) should be entered. Once the turtle is located at the desired position, the command PENDOWN (PD) is used. The screen can be cleared at any time using the CLEARSCREEN (CS) command. The cursor can be located at any point on the screen and can be oriented in any direction. The direction is measured using 360 degrees, as shown in Figure 6.30.

The heading labels are fixed. However, commanding the turtle to rotate 90 degrees right or left (RT 90 or LT 90) will not always result in the turtle facing 90 or 270 degrees. The turtle will interpret a rotation command based on its present heading. For example, suppose the turtle is facing down, as shown in Figure 6.31a. The turtle's heading is 180 degrees. The command RT 90 will cause the turtle to rotate 90 degrees in a clockwise direction, resulting in a new heading of 270 degrees, as shown in Figure 6.31b. An additional command, RT 90 will cause the turtle to rotate

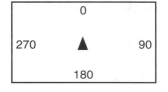

Figure 6.30

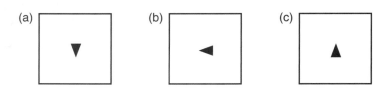

Figure 6.31

90 degrees to the right once again, resulting in a new heading of 0 degrees, as shown in Figure 6.31c.

In some versions of LOGO, the command PR HEADING (print heading) can be entered to display the heading of the turtle at any given time. If a particular heading is desired, some versions allow the command SETH # (set heading at number), which will set the heading to the desired fixed-degree location.

Notice that, in Activity 6.8, the sequence of commands FD 30 RT 90 FD 50 RT 90 was repeated. In LOGO, it is possible to have the turtle duplicate actions a certain number of times by using the REPEAT command. This command takes the following form:

REPEAT # [commands]

REPEAT # refers to the number of times the commands listed in the brackets are to be executed. The command for constructing a 50 × 30 rectangle could be written as:

REPEAT 2 [FD 30 RT 90 FD 50 RT 90]

In Activity 6.9, a program is written that will result in the construction of a square, a triangle, and a hexagon. This procedure can be saved to a disk and loaded at any time. By typing SHAPES, LOGO will execute the series of commands that display a square, triangle, and hexagon.

LOGO has the ability to set up and store variables. A variable in LOGO is the same concept as a variable in algebra. A variable represents a number or a set of numbers. In algebra, we restrict variable names to single letters, whereas in LOGO the name TOM could be a variable. In LOGO programming, it is preferable to use descriptive variable names. The variable LENGTH might be

Activity 6.8

Using LOGO to Draw a Rectangle

Lesson: Computer
Invite the students to construct a set of commands that will result in the creation of a 50-unit by 30-unit rectangle. Figure 6.32 shows one possible solution.

Journal Reflection
How can you use LOGO to illustrate that the sum of the interior angles of a quadrilateral is 360 degrees?

Command	Interpretation	Display
FD 30	Moves forward 30 units.	
RT 90	Turns right through 90°.	
FD 50	Moves forward 50 units.	
RT 90	Turns right through 90°.	
FD 30	Moves forward 30 units.	
RT 90	Turns right through 90°.	
FD 50	Moves forward 50 units.	
RT 90	Turns right through 90°.	

Figure 6.32

Strength in Numbers

LOGO

Cooperative Group Model: JIGSAW

Working in groups of three, each person will write a set of commands utilizing REPEAT that will construct one of the following regular polygons—triangle, pentagon, hexagon—each of whose sides measure 60 units.

When trying to solve this problem, it is a good idea to sketch the desired outcome on a sheet of paper. Also, this will allow those without access to LOGO to solve the problem. The segments and turns required to draw the triangle, the square, and the pentagon are shown in Figure 6.33.

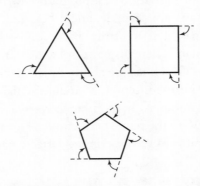

Figure 6.33

Notice that, in each case, the turtle turns through an exterior angle that is formed when a side is extended. This exterior angle is the supplement of the interior angle. Recall that in regular polygons of side n, the number of degrees in each interior angle can be determined by $[180(n - 2)] \div n$.

One of the advantages of LOGO is that its vocabulary of commands is limitless. Once the basic commands are learned, they can be joined together to form a procedure. A *procedure* is a set of commands that are executed by a user-defined command name. The method for setting up a procedure differs according to the particular version of LOGO you are using. In general, the user defines a procedure in the edit mode by first giving it a descriptive name, listing the commands that will result in a desired display, and closing the definition with the command END. The name of a procedure cannot be a LOGO primitive.

Examine Figure 6.34, which is formed by a square, a triangle, and a hexagon. Suppose that you wish to

Figure 6.34

use it a number of times as you draw another figure. The set of commands that draw the square/triangle/hexagon can be stored in the procedure SHAPES as follows:

```
TO SHAPES
REPEAT 4 [FD 50 RT 90]
RT 180
REPEAT 3 [RT 120 FD 50]
BK 50 RT 90
REPEAT 6 [RT 60 FD 50]
END
```

used to represent the length of a rectangle, or ANGLE could be used to represent the measure of an angle. Examine the following LOGO procedure, which employs the variables LENGTH and WIDTH to draw rectangles of varying sizes.

```
TO RECTANGLE :LENGTH :WIDTH
REPEAT 2 [FD :WIDTH RT 90 FD :LENGTH RT 90]
END
```

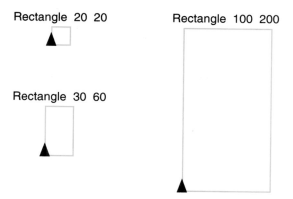

Figure 6.35

The first line defines a procedure called RECTANGLE that contains the variables LENGTH and WIDTH. When variables are used in commands, the variable name is preceded by a colon. The second line of this procedure is a basic REPEAT command. Notice that the variables :WIDTH and :LENGTH take the place of any specific numerical value. Once out of the edit mode, this procedure can be executed as shown in Figure 6.35.

LOGO can be used to help students develop their visualization and estimation skills. In Activity 6.9, students are asked to determine the effect on

Activity 6.9
Triangles

Lesson: Computer

Invite the students to write a LOGO procedure that could be used visually to estimate the effect on the area of an equilateral triangle when the sides are doubled, and when the sides are tripled. A single procedure that uses a variable to draw equilateral triangles of various sizes can be used to solve this problem. One possible procedure is this:

```
TO TRIANGLE :SIDE
RT 30
REPEAT 3 [FD :SIDE RT 120]
HOME
END
```

Notice that the first command in the procedure rotates the turtle 30 degrees to the right from the 0-degrees heading. This command is included in the procedure so that the triangle will have a horizontal base. The third command reorients the heading of the turtle back to 0 degrees so that subsequent triangles will be drawn with the same orientation. This will make

the visual comparison of the triangles easier for the students.

Exiting from the edit mode and executing the following commands will result in a display like that of Figure 6.36.

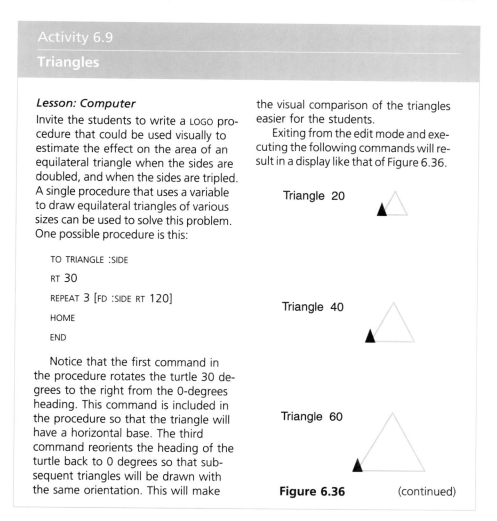

Figure 6.36   (continued)

Activity 6.9 (continued)
Triangles

Students may wish to cut out the smallest of the triangles, and either trace or lay it on top of the other two triangles to help them estimate the relative differences in area. After the students have estimated the effect on the area of multiplying the length of the sides, they write a description and an explanation of what they discovered.

Journal Reflection
What would be the effect on the area of a square of doubling and then tripling the length of the sides? Describe how you might tie this investigation into the activity.

the area of an equilateral triangle when the measure of each side is doubled, and then tripled.

Finally, we will examine the effect of a procedure that calls upon itself during execution. This is called a *recursive procedure*. Examine the following two procedures:

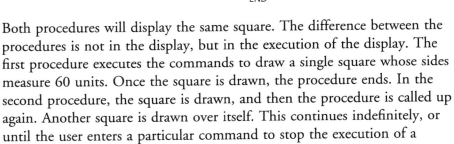

Both procedures will display the same square. The difference between the procedures is not in the display, but in the execution of the display. The first procedure executes the commands to draw a single square whose sides measure 60 units. Once the square is drawn, the procedure ends. In the second procedure, the square is drawn, and then the procedure is called up again. Another square is drawn over itself. This continues indefinitely, or until the user enters a particular command to stop the execution of a procedure.

Obviously, using recursion in this way makes no sense. Recursion can, however, be used to construct interesting figures. Examine the following procedure and the resulting display (Figure 6.37).

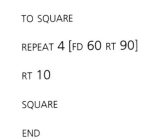

Figure 6.37

Challenge students to determine how many squares are printed before overwriting occurs. To answer this question, they will need to determine what causes the squares to "turn." Notice that an RT 10 is included in the procedure. After a square has been drawn, the turtle returns to its original heading. Had the RT 10 command not been included, overwriting would have occurred with the second square. The RT 10 command causes the turtle to change its heading by rotating 10 degrees to the right, and then begin drawing the next square. This causes a succession of squares to be drawn. Since the rotation is 10 degrees, there are 360 ÷ 10, or 36 such squares drawn before the design overwrites.

Recursion can be used to construct shapes within shapes. Activity 6.10 challenges students to construct a star within a regular pentagon. Activities 6.11 and 6.12 are designed to be done with a geometric drawing software

Activity 6.10

Pentagrams

Lesson: Computer

A pentagram is a five-pointed star. It can be formed by drawing the diagonals of a regular pentagon (Figure 6.38). Invite the students to write a LOGO procedure that uses recursion to construct a pentagram inside a pentagon, as shown.

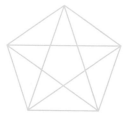

Figure 6.38

It will first be necessary for the students to determine angle measurements. Some students prefer to do this through a process of trial and error, by experimenting with different commands until they succeed in drawing a pentagon. Recall, however, that it is possible to determine the measure of the interior angles of a regular polygon by drawing triangles inside the pentagon, multiplying that number by 180 degrees, and then dividing that product by 5, since there are 5 interior angles. More simply,

$$3 (180) = 540 ÷ 5 = 108$$

Knowing that each interior angle measures 108 degrees allows us to determine that the measure of each of the three vertex angles that partition each interior angle is 36 degrees, since 108 ÷ 3 = 36. The pentagram within the regular pentagon can thus be formed by five congruent isosceles triangles. Since the triangles are congruent, recursion can be used. The following recursive procedure will draw the pentagram within the pentagon:

TO PENTAGRAM

RT 18

FD 95

RT 144

FD 95

RT 108

FD 60

RT 72

FD 60

RT 90

PENTAGRAM

END

Journal Reflection

Notice that the first command orients the turtle 18 degrees to the right before drawing the first triangle. Why do you think this is so? What do you predict would happen if that command were deleted?

Activity 6.11

The Medians of Equilateral Triangles

Lesson: Computer
Either with the help of a geometric drawing utility or by hand, have the students draw an equilateral triangle. Then invite them to construct the median to each side of the triangle. (A *median* of a triangle is the line drawn from a vertex to the midpoint of the opposite side.) The students should repeat this procedure at least ten times with ten different equilateral triangles.

Encourage the students to develop a conjecture about the medians of equilateral triangles and their relationship to the angles from which they are drawn. Ask the children to consider if their conjectures hold true for all triangles. Invite them to try to find a triangle in which their conjectures do not hold true. When the students have had sufficient opportunity to test their conjectures, have them present their conjectures and the evidence to support them to the rest of the class.

Journal Reflection
Discuss the advantages and disadvantages of having students construct their own explanations as opposed to having definitions and theorems presented to them.

program such as the *Geometric superSupposer* or *Geometer's Sketchpad*. If programs such as this are unavailable, the activities can still be done manually. They will simply require more time and persistence.

Other Computer Software

In addition to geometric drawing utilities, other software programs are available to help children experience and understand geometry. One such

Activity 6.12

The Medians of Triangles

Lesson: Computer
Either by hand, or with the help of a geometric drawing utility, invite students to draw any triangle (not necessarily an equilateral triangle) and to construct the medians. Ask them to measure the lengths of the medians, the distances from the vertices to the point of concurrence, and the distances from the point of concurrence to the midpoint of the opposite side. Encourage them to develop a conjecture about the relationships among these lengths. Challenge them to provide evidence to support their conjectures—and to search for a counterexample that would refute their conjectures.

Journal Reflection
In an activity like this, students are learning both mathematical content and the nature of inquiry, investigations, justifications, and arguments. While mathematical content is discipline-specific, inquiry is not. Discuss the role of inquiry across the curriculum. How can a focus on inquiry help to connect mathematics to other areas of the curriculum? What are some advantages and disadvantages of doing this?

program is *Geometry World: Middle Grades Interactive Explorer* (Cognitive Technologies, 1999). This interactive software, suitable for students from grades 5 to 9, illustrates the advantage of using technology in a geometry classroom. While it is possible to engage children with materials such as pattern blocks to create laterally symmetric designs in the plane, it is more difficult to provide materials that can demonstrate rotational symmetry. *Geometry World* contains computer animations that allow students to rotate designs they have created to test for rotational symmetry. In addition to being exciting, this software also allows for the visual manipulations of figures that would otherwise be impossible.

Another software program that allows the construction and manipulation of geometric figures is *Geometry Inventor* (Wings for Learning, 1992). A strength of this software is that it allows students to perform a sequence of constructions repeatedly. This repetition encourages them to form generalizations based upon the specific instance of, for example, the medians of one triangle, to the general instance of the medians of all triangles.

Spatial Sense (Sunburst) provides three different contexts in which students of grades 4 and up can investigate geometric concepts: The Factory, Building Perspective, and The Super Factory. All of these choices are designed to help students develop their spatial perception and spatial reasoning by predicting top views of buildings they create, by predicting the outcome of combining certain shapes, and by solving problems.

Transformational Geometry

Children are fascinated with the idea of transformations. Many fictional characters that appeal to children undergo transformations. Think of Cinderella, Superman, or Sylvester from *Sylvester and the Magic Pebble.* Part of the attraction that children feel for wearing costumes or playing dress-up stems from the pleasure of transforming into a different identity.

Geometry and Spatial Sense for Grades 6–8

The NCTM *Principles and Standards* "recognize the usefulness of transformations and symmetry in analyzing mathematical situations" (p. 228). The following focus areas are recommended. In grades 6–8, all students should

- Describe size, position, and orientation of figures under informal transformations such as flips, turns, slides, and magnification;

- Use line and rotational symmetry to describe and classify polygons and polyhedra;

- Understand the concepts of congruence and similarity using transformations. (p. 228)

Transformational geometry is a branch of mathematics that focuses on the different ways that figures can be transformed. Some transformations, such as translations, reflections, and rotations, change only the position of the figure. Others, such as dilation (or magnification), also change the size of the figure. Activities 6.13 through 6.16 address ways of incorporating transformational concepts into the classroom.

Activity 6.13

Translations

Lesson: Individual

Supply each student with the plastic top from a coffee can or food storage container. Ask the students to create a template by cutting a figure of their own design from the plastic lid. Also, ask them to draw a chord in the circle of the lid to define the horizontal edge (Figure 6.39).

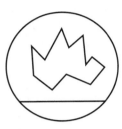

Figure 6.39

Invite the students to use their template to trace their design at various locations on the paper, always remembering to keep the horizontal edge parallel to the edge of the paper. By coloring in different parts of the creation, an attractive visual effect can be obtained.

A transformation such as this, which is obtained simply by sliding a figure in a plane, is called a *translation.* Ask the students to write their own descriptions of a translation, including examples of translations such as wallpaper designs, fabric designs, or advertising logos.

Journal Reflection

How might you connect this activity to locating points on the coordinate axes?

Activity 6.14

Reflections

Lesson: Pairs

Engage students in a game of "Mirror." With students working in pairs and facing each other, one student initiates simple motions. The partner, who acts as the mirror, attempts to copy exactly what the other person is doing. After a period of time, have the students switch roles.

Begin a discussion of the relationship between the initiator and the mirror. Focus on the fact that when the initiator raised the right hand, the person acting as the mirror had to raise the left hand. Invite the students to draw a design or a word on one side of a folded piece of grid paper, and then to draw its *reflection* on the

other side (Figure 6.40). Encourage students to locate and sketch the line of symmetry in their work.

Figure 6.40

Journal Reflection

How would you use small, pocket-sized mirrors to help students who have difficulty with this activity?

Activity 6.15

Rotations

Lesson: Individual

Have the students use the angle makers that were described at the beginning of the chapter. Invite them to cut a shape out of an index card and tape it to the end of one of the arrows of the angle maker. Working on a large sheet of unlined paper, the students then point that arrow straight up and trace their design. Keeping the vertex of the angle maker in the same spot, the students rotate the arrow and trace their cutout in various positions (Figure 6.41).

A *rotation* is a turn around some fixed point. In the above activity, the fixed point is the vertex of the angle maker.

Journal Reflection

List as many examples of a rotation as you are able (certain dance steps, a pinwheel, the blade of a food processor). How might you connect some of these examples to the above activity?

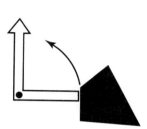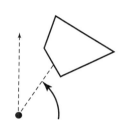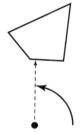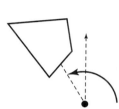

Figure 6.41

Activity 6.16

Dilations

Lesson: Individual

Distribute two sheets of graph paper to each student, one with centimeter squares and one with inch squares. Have the students draw axes to construct the first quadrant of the coordinate plane, and then plot the following points on each sheet of graph paper:

(3,0), (2,2), (0,3), (2,4), (3,6), (4,4), (6,3), (4,2)

Then, ask the students to connect the points in order. Figure 6.42 shows the two outcomes.

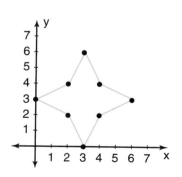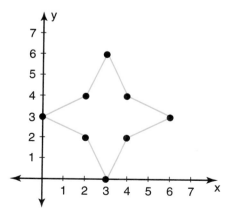

Figure 6.42

(continued)

Engage the children in a discussion about the differences between the two figures. An enlargement or reduction of a figure is known as a *dilation*. Notice that the only characteristic that differs in the parts of Figure 6.42 is the size. How can you connect the transformation of dilation to the concepts of similarity and congruence?

Journal Reflection
Think back to classic stories like *Through the Looking Glass* by Lewis Carroll, or *Gulliver's Travels* by Jonathan Swift. Write a lesson plan that explores the concept of dilation in the context of such a piece of literature.

p w b

Figure 6.43

Figure 6.44

Performance-Based Assessment: Transformations
Present the students with the letters shown in Figure 6.43. In each case, ask them to sketch a letter of the alphabet that demonstrates a reflection, a rotation, a dilation, or some combination of the three. Some possible solutions are shown in Figure 6.44.

Rotation: **p d**   Dilation: **w W**   Reflection: **b d**

The students' work can be scored according to the following rubric:

4 Student supplies a letter that accurately reflects a transformation in each of the four cases.
3 Student supplies a letter that accurately reflects a transformation in three out of four cases.
2 Student supplies a letter that accurately reflects a transformation in two out of four cases.
1 Student supplies a letter that accurately reflects a transformation in only one case.
0 Student is unable to supply any letters that accurately reflect a transformation.

As you can see from these activities, transformational geometry offers students an opportunity to explore certain ways to change visual designs. These changes are apparent in many media with which students are already familiar; thus, transformational geometry provides another means to connect mathematics with other areas of interest to children.

Strength in Numbers

Conjectures

Lesson: Partners—Think, Pair, Share

By hand, or using a geometric drawing utility, each student constructs a triangle, connecting the midpoints of each side of the triangle. The process is repeated with several triangles. Individually at first, each person describes what has been observed, and develops a conjecture about the observed evidence. Then, forming pairs, each person compares his or her conjecture with a partner. Together, the partners attempt to answer the following questions:

- What is being observed? How can it be described?

- Does it occur consistently? Can a counterexample be found?

- How can this phenomenon be explained and justified? Can you offer an informal "proof" of your initial conjecture?

Finally, the partners prepare a presentation for the class that contains their answers to the questions. During the presentations, classmates are encouraged to question and challenge the conjectures and explanations of their peers.

Summary

This chapter, the second devoted to geometry, began by addressing the concepts of perimeter and area in a more formal fashion than the previous chapter. It expanded the concepts of perimeter and area into that of surface area and then developed the concept of volume. It explored which polygons and which polyhedra maximized area and volume, respectively.

The chapter investigated classes of polygons, and used angle measurements to learn more about polygons. Prisms and pyramids were introduced as three-dimensional versions of polygons. *Geometric Supposer* and LOGO are software tools that allow students to construct their own understandings by drawing shapes easily and quickly using the computer.

In conclusion, the chapter dealt with the concept of transformations of figures—slides, rotations, reflections, and shrinking and enlarging—and the results of those transformations.

Extending Your Learning

1. Investigate the regular or platonic solids. See, for instance, *An Introduction to the History of Mathematics* by Howard Eves (1990). Use this information to write a lesson plan for seventh or eighth grade.

2. Describe two additional ways (beyond those contained in this chapter) to explain why the area of a circle can be obtained by multiplying *pi* times the radius squared.

3. Choose three different cans from your food cabinet. For each can, determine its surface area and its volume. Do each of these cans contain the maximum volume for the given surface area? How do you know? If not, why not?

4. Some above-ground swimming pools are circular and others are oval. Use your knowledge of geometry to argue that one shape is preferable over the other. What arguments, other than geometrical, could be made?

5. Visit a nursery school, daycare center, or kindergarten. Observe children building with blocks. Take notes about what you observe, and compare these notes to the suggested geometric experiences for children listed in the NCTM's *Principles and Standards*. How can an early-childhood teacher develop geometric experiences for children through block building?

6. How might you connect the concepts of area and perimeter with the activity of planting a garden? Write one, or a series, of lesson plans appropriate for sixth or seventh grade that makes such a connection.

7. Write a recursive LOGO procedure that will display each of the following figures:

   ■ Eighteen equilateral triangles drawn about a fixed vertex.
   ■ Twelve regular pentagons drawn about a fixed vertex.

8. Begin to create a file of examples of transformational images and/or tessellations. Find several examples of advertisements, corporate logos, or pieces of art that contain one or more transformations or tessellations. Annotate each piece according to source, artist (if known), and potential uses.

9. In this chapter, Activity 6.16 illustrated the concept of dilation by plotting a figure on two different-sized sheets of graph paper. How might you connect the operations of multiplication and division to the concept of dilation? Describe a classroom activity that makes the connection.

10. Obtain copies of two articles about tessellations from journals such as *Teaching Children Mathematics* or *Mathematics Teaching in the Middle School*. Use these articles to develop a set of classroom activities based on tessellations. At least one of the activities should connect geometric and numerical concepts.

Internet Resources

www.eduplace.com/math/brain/ index.html
This is a website maintained by Houghton-Mifflin, the textbook publishing company. Problems are posted each week for grades 3 to 7, and a week later their solutions appear. The site also offers an archive of previous problems.

http://www.keypress.com/sketchpad
This is the website of Key Curriculum Press, publishers of the *Goemeter's Sketchpad,* a geometric drawing software program. It contains a demonstration of the Sketchpad, along with teacher resources, links to the web, and a bibliography.

www.kyes-world.com
On this website, the Event Inventor engages students in simple math and science discoveries, many involving geometric concepts and their relationship to astronomy.

http://pegasus.cc.ucf.edu/~mathed/ 2801site.htm
This website contains an introduction and five activities for the *Geometer's Sketchpad*. A strength of this website is that it involves users in investigating geometrical phenomena and then drawing their own conclusions.

Bibliography

Carroll, Lewis. (1993). *Through the looking glass and what Alice found there.* New York: Morrow, Williams.

Charischak, Igor, and Robert Berkman. (1995). Looking at random events with LOGO software. *Mathematics Teaching in the Middle School 1*(4).

Duke, Charlotte. (1998). Tangrams and area. *Mathematics Teaching in the Middle School 3*(7).

Eves, Howard. (1990). *An introduction to the history of mathematics.* Orlando: Saunders College Publishing.

Geometer's Sketchpad. Software. Emeryville, CA: Key Curriculum Press.

Geometry Inventor. Software. Scotts Valley, CA: Wings for Learning.

Geometry World: Middle Grades Interactive Explorer. Software. Rockville, MD: Cognitive Technologies.

Grifalconi, Ann. (1986). *The village of round and square houses.* Boston: Little, Brown.

Harrell, Marvin E., and Linda S. Fosnaugh. (1997). Allium to zircon: Mathematics and nature. *Mathematics Teaching in the Middle School 2*(6).

Kajander, Ann E. (1999). Creating opportunities for children to think mathematically. *Teaching Children Mathematics 5*(8).

La Saracina, Barbara A., and Sharon K. White. (1999). The restless rectangle and the transforming trapezoid. *Teaching Children Mathematics 5*(6).

Leeson, Neville J. (1994). Improving students' sense of three-dimensional shapes. *Teaching Children Mathematics 1*(1).

Maupin, Sue. (1996). Middle grades geometry activities. *Mathematics Teaching in the Middle School 1*(10).

Nitabach, Elizabeth, and Richard Lehrer. (1996). Developing spatial sense through area measurement. *Teaching Children Mathematics 2*(8).

Neuschwander, Cindy. (1990). *Sir Cumference and the first Round Table.* Watertown, MA: Charlesbridge Publishing.

Neuschwander, Cindy. (1999). *Sir Cumference and the dragon of pi.* Watertown, MA: Charlesbridge Publishing.

Oberdorf, Christine D., and Jennifer Taylor-Cox. (1999). Shape up! *Teaching Children Mathematics 5*(6).

Papert, Seymour. (1980). *Mindstorms: Children, computers and powerful ideas.* New York: Basic Books.

Robertson, Stuart P. (1999). Getting students actively involved in geometry. *Teaching Children Mathematics 5*(9).

Schwartz, Judah L., and Michal Yerushalmy. *The Geometric superSupposer.* Software. Pleasantville, NY: Sunburst.

Schwartz, Judah L., Michal Yerushalmy, and Beth Wilson (Eds). (1993). *The Geometric Supposer: What is it a case of?* Hillsdale, NJ: Lawrence Erlbaum.

Schifter, Deborah. (1999). Learning geometry: Some insights drawn from teacher writing. *Teaching Children Mathematics 5*(6).

Selke, Donald H. (1999). Geometric flips via the arts. *Teaching Children Mathematics 5*(6).

Shaw, Jean M., et al. (1995). Using concept diagrams to promote understanding in geometry. *Teaching Children Mathematics 2*(3).

Slavit, David. (1998). Above and beyond AAA: The similarity and congruence of polygons. *Mathematics Teaching in the Middle School 3*(4).

Spatial Sense. Software. Pleasantville, NY: Sunburst.

Steig, William. (1973). *Sylvester and the magic pebble.* New York: Simon & Schuster.

Swift, Jonathan. (1950). *Gulliver's Travels.* New York: McGraw-Hill.

Tepper, Anita Benna. (1999). A journey through geometry: Designing a city park. *Teaching Children Mathematics 5*(6).

Trafton, Patricia A., and Christina Hartman. (1997). Exploring area with geoboards. *Teaching Children Mathematics 4*(2).

Wallace, John, and Jennifer Pearson. (1995). What makes a corner a corner? *Teaching Children Mathematics 2*(4).

Wheatley, Grayson, and Anne M. Reynolds. (1999). Image maker: Developing spatial sense. *Teaching Children Mathematics 5*(6).

Zilliox, Joseph T., and Shannon G. Lowery. (1997). Many faces have I. *Mathematics Teaching in the Middle School 3*(3).

Standards for Extending
the Number Line

Early on, children have the need to describe quantities that cannot be named by using only whole numbers. For example, young children are generous creatures (to which anyone who has been offered a bite of a drool-ly cookie can attest), and they often break food items into pieces to share. In the beginning, children refer to every partial quantity as "half," whether or not the two pieces are even remotely equal in size. "Half" seems to be, for many children, a synonym for "partial." According to researchers, when dealing with fractional concepts children often lack the number sense they exhibit in dealing with whole numbers (Van de Walle and Watkins, 1993). Young children, who can look at three items and easily identify the quantity as "three," cannot look at a pie cut into three equal pieces and easily identify each piece as one-third.

Decimal concepts and decimal language are even less familiar to children, since the United States has not yet embraced the metric system of measurement. Therefore, children rarely hear such phrases as 2.1 liters or 5.6 kilometers. While there are three contexts in which children do regularly hear decimal notation (sports, when reporting batting or earned-run averages; the weather, when reporting barometric pressure or rainfall amounts; radio stations, when identifying their band location), none of these contexts clearly connect numerical labels with visible quantities, and thus do not contribute to the development of number sense. Knowing that your favorite radio station can be found at 104.7 on the dial does not help you develop an image of what 104.7 looks like.

Thus it is important to give children a variety of experiences with quantities that are not limited to whole numbers. This can be done in several different contexts. For example, a group of four children can be given a strip of red licorice, 1 meter in length, that needs to be shared. This is the sharing of a *continuous* quantity, and most children would solve this problem by folding the licorice in half and then in half again to obtain four equal pieces, each one-quarter the length of the original piece.

Recall from Chapter 2 that a continuous quantity is one that can be *measured,* as opposed to a *discrete* quantity, which refers to items that can be *counted.* Giving children experience in sharing discrete quantities could involve handing each group of five children a box of fifteen plastic farm animals to be equally shared. It will be interesting for you to see which children share the animals by doling them out one at a time until they are gone, and which children use their prior knowledge that $3 \times 5 = 15$ to give each group member three animals, or one-fifth of the original group.

It is recommended (Langford and Sarullo, 1993) that children in grades K–4 have many experiences with manipulating fractional parts of continuous quantities *and* fractional parts of discrete quantities before receiving formal instruction in fractions. Since decimal quantities are often used in a measurement context, they often refer to continuous quantities (the level of mercury in a thermometer, the depth of water in a graduated cylinder). Powers-of-ten blocks, which were used in earlier chapters to represent whole-number quantities, can also be used to represent decimal quantities. Specific strategies for doing so will be spelled out later in the chapter.

In addition, some calculators (for example, the TI Math Explorer Plus) have the capability of performing all fraction computations in fractional form. These calculators can find the sum of ⅔ and 1⅛ at the push of a button, representing the sum in simplest form. This technological tool allows teachers to take the emphasis off the purely symbolic computation with fractions and devote more time to developing an understanding of fractional, decimal, and proportional concepts.

Typically, instruction in fractional and decimal concepts should follow this progression:

1. *Nonverbal experiences* with fractional or decimal parts, where an individual child might work with a set of materials designed to illustrate parts of a whole.

2. The beginning of *manipulative language,* where children working together with red circles cut into halves and blue circles cut into fourths might comment that "The red pieces are bigger than the blue pieces" or "One red piece is as big as two blue pieces." If children were working with *powers-of-ten* blocks and the large cube was identified as being equal to 1 whole, then the flats would each equal ¹⁄₁₀ (since 10 of them equal 1 whole), the longs would each equal ¹⁄₁₀₀ (since 100 of them equal 1 whole), and the units would each equal ¹⁄₁₀₀₀ (since 1000 of them equal 1 whole), as shown in Figure 7.1. Children working with these materials might comment that "Ten flats are the same size as one cube" or "It takes ten longs to make one flat."

3. An introduction to *mathematical language,* where children working with the circles described earlier would use the terms *one-half* and *one-fourth,* and such comparison phrases as "One-half is greater than

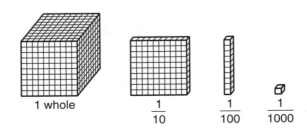

Figure 7.1

one-fourth" and "One-fourth is less than one-half." Children working with powers-of-ten blocks would use the appropriate decimal language, and would make such comparisons as "One-tenth is much greater than one-hundredth. That's surprising, since ten is much less than one hundred."

4. An introduction to *symbolic language,* where children working with the circles would be able to represent symbolically that

$$\frac{1}{2} > \frac{1}{4}$$

$$\frac{1}{2} + \frac{1}{2} = 1 \text{ whole}$$

$$\frac{1}{2} = \frac{1}{4} + \frac{1}{4}$$

or

$$.1 = .01 + .01 + .01 + .01 + .01 + .01 + .01 + .01 + .01 + .01$$

$$.01 > .001$$

$$.05 + .05 = .1$$

Number and Operation for Grades Pre-K–2 and 3–5

In agreement with the researchers just cited, the NCTM *Principles and Standards* recommend the following focus areas in number and operation. In grades Pre-K–2, all students should

- Understand and represent familiar fractions, such as ½ and ¾. (p. 109)

In grades 3–5, all students should

- Develop meaning for fractions as part of a unit whole, as part of a collection, as numbers, and as a division of whole numbers;
- Read and write fractions and decimals and relate the notation to the meaning of these numbers;
- Develop strategies for judging the size of fractions and decimals and for comparing them using a variety of models and of benchmarks (such as ½ or 0.5);
- Recognize and use common fraction, decimal, and percent equivalents. (pp. 156–57)

In this chapter and the next, you will read about two commercially available manipulatives that clearly illustrate fraction and decimal concepts—Cuisenaire rods and powers-of-ten blocks—and connections will be made among fractions and decimals and two important measurement systems, the English standard system of measurement (sometimes referred to as the "customary system" of measurement) and the metric system.

Figure 7.2

Models and Concepts of Fractions and Decimals

Figure 7.3

As mentioned earlier, fractions can be represented using both discrete and continuous models, while decimals are more commonly represented using a continuous model. Figure 7.2 shows a discrete model of ⅘. Figure 7.3 presents a continuous (area) model of ⅘. Figure 7.4 shows a continuous (linear) model of 0.8.

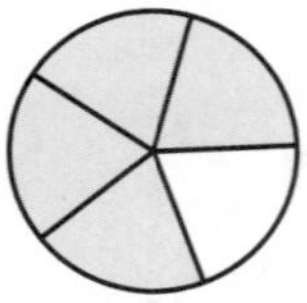

If you have the opportunity, show the area model of ⅘ (Figure 7.3) to children in first or second grade. Ask them to tell you what fraction it illustrates. Many of the children will say that it illustrates ¼. This is because they see *one* section unshaded and *four* sections shaded. To avoid this confusion, structure students' early introductions to fractions in such a way that each of the fractional parts of the whole are simply identified, as in Figure 7.5. You will notice here that there is no shading; that each fractional piece is labeled. This method is used in the book *Eating Fractions* by Bruce McMillan, which is composed of lovely photographs of various foods cut up into equal pieces. The fractions introduced in the book are ½, ⅓, and ¼, and recipes are included for many of the foods pictured in the book. Activity 7.1 suggests a way that *Eating Fractions* could be used to introduce the continuous model of fractions.

The activity of dividing a rectangular region into congruent, fractional parts can easily be adapted for older children. If you ask students to use rubber bands to divide a geoboard into sixths, for example, you encourage precision of thought, since there are many strategies that students can use to "prove" that they have actually created sixths. They may chose to compare the sixths based on the area the pieces cover, based on the number of interior and boundary pegs of each piece, or based on the symmetry of the divisions of the geoboard. The geoboard allows students to see that sixths can cover an equal area, while not necessarily being congruent. Working on a geoboard or on paper "bread" reinforces for children the idea of fractional pieces as *equal parts of a whole*.

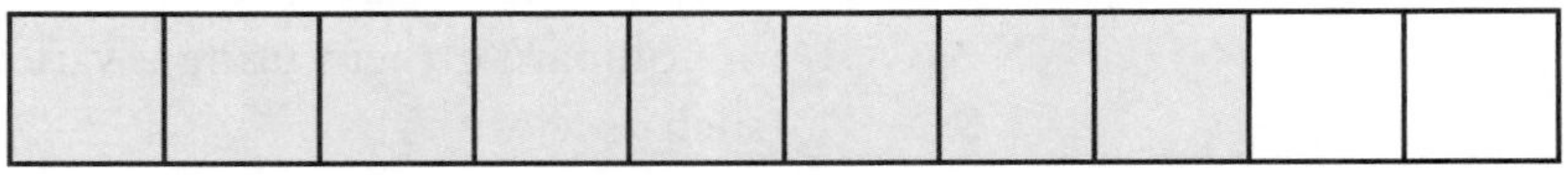

Figure 7.4

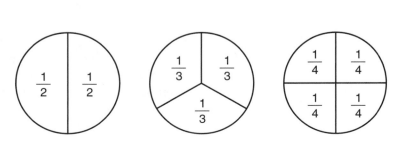

Figure 7.5

Activity 7.1

Introducing Fractions, Continuous Model

Lesson: Whole Class

Read *Eating Fractions* by Bruce McMillan (Scholastic, 1991) to the class. Encourage the children to articulate that fractions are numbers that name parts of things. When there are two equal parts, each part is called *one-half;* when there are three equal parts, each part is called *one-third;* when there are four equal parts, each part is called *one-fourth.* Ask the children to predict what the parts would be called when there are five equal parts and when there are six equal parts.

Distribute "pieces of bread" cut from construction paper to each child. Ask the children to draw a line on the "bread" to separate it into two halves. Some possible solutions are shown in Figure 7.6.

Although children of this age lack the precision required to divide the "bread" exactly in half, make sure they understand that halves are equal pieces. For children who do not

easily see that Figure 7.3c is divided in half, actually cut the "bread" along the line drawn, and then rotate one half and place it over the other to demonstrate congruency.

After students have had the opportunity to create many different halves, ask them to draw lines to separate the bread into thirds, and then fourths.

Journal Reflection

For children who have difficulty drawing an accurate line, you can provide them with yarn to place on the "bread" to mark the line of separation, or they can fold the "bread" into equal parts. What other alternatives can you think of? Would you have the children label their pieces with the symbols ½, or ⅓, or ¼? Why or why not?

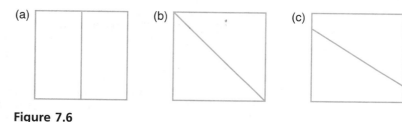

Figure 7.6

Activity 7.2 is focused on a problem that involves the concepts of congruency, area, and fractions, and provides an opportunity for connecting geometric concepts and fractional concepts. The problem posed in Activity 7.2 illustrates fractions as equal parts of a whole. However, interpreting ¼ as one of four equal parts is not the only possible interpretation. In addition to the *part-whole* meaning of fractions, students should also investigate fractions in contexts where the numbers represent a *quotient,* such as when three sandwiches shared among four children is represented as ¾. A third interpretation of fractions is as a *ratio,* where three out of four chocolate cookies is represented as ¾, or 3:4 (Curcio and Bezuk, 1994). Each of these interpretations is addressed in this chapter. Activity 7.3 illustrates fractions as equal parts of a whole using discrete items.

Another introduction to fractions can be provided by Cuisenaire rods, which are continuous, linear models of fractions. Cuisenaire rods were invented about fifty years ago by George Cuisenaire, a Belgian schoolteacher. Obtain a set of Cuisenaire rods and explore with them. Use these questions to help structure your explorations:

- How many different colors are there?

- How many different sizes are there?

Activity 7.2

Fractions as Equal Parts of a Continuous Whole

Lesson: Whole Class

Pose the following problem to the students:

- Five friends bought a plot of land. One person contributed ¼ of the money, and the other four friends contributed equally to cover the remaining ¾ of the cost. How could the square plot of land be fairly divided among the five friends? The four friends who contributed ¾ of the cost want each of their plots to look exactly the same.

Ask a few students to restate the problem in their own words to ensure that the problem has been understood. Provide the students with graph paper and sufficient time to try to solve the problem. (Try it yourself before reading any further!) Here are some possible solutions, and sample explanations of the strategies used.

Solution 1 (Figure 7.7)

"We constructed a 12 × 12 square, because we knew it would make it easier to show ¼. First, we marked off ¼ for the first investor. That was easy. Then we looked at the remaining ¾ and knew we had to divide that rectangle into four equal pieces that look the same. Since there were 9 squares across the top, it wouldn't be easy to divide that side into 4 congruent pieces, so we looked at the other side. That vertical side was 12 boxes long, so we counted off 3 boxes, drew a line, counted off 3 boxes, drew a line, and so on. We were able to divide the rectangle into 4 congruent, smaller rectangles."

Solution 2 (Figure 7.8)

"We wanted to put a square, ¼ the size of the whole square, right in the middle, and then divide the border up

into four equal pieces. We started with a 10 × 10 square, but that made it too hard to put the smaller square exactly in the middle. We tried 11 × 11, but that didn't work either, so we used a 12 × 12 square. The 6 × 6 square in the middle is ¼ the size of the whole square, and the trapezoids that go around the outside are all congruent. We checked by adding up all of the boxes inside the shapes. There are 36 boxes in the middle square, and 27 boxes in each of the trapezoids."

Solution 3 (Figure 7.9)

"We didn't work on the graph paper because those little boxes were too small. Instead, we marked off ¼ of the square, and then we had to figure out a way to share the rest of the square into four equal pieces. That was the hard part. But then Juan said that the shape that was left could easily be be divided into three squares. And then Nadia said that if they were three sandwiches, we could share them with four people by giving each person ¾ of a sandwich. That's when we figured out how to divide up the rest of the square."

Journal Reflection

Which solution appeals to you most? Why? Which solution shown here is closest to the way you solved the problem? Is this the solution you like best? How does a teacher keep an open mind and quickly evaluate alternate methods of solving problems, especially when the teacher may not have thought of some of the solutions until someone in the class suggests them?

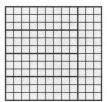

Figure 7.7

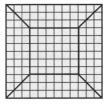

Figure 7.8

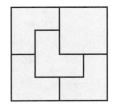

Figure 7.9

Activity 7.3

Introducing Fractions, Discrete Model

Lesson: Whole Class

Begin by playing a recording of "The Teddy Bears' Picnic" (Kennedy and Bratton, 1947) for the children, and then engaging them in a simplified version of the game "I'm Going on a Picnic." The first child says "I'm going on a picnic, and I'm going to bring 1 banana." The second child says "I'm going on a picnic and I'm going to bring 2 pretzels." The third child says "I'm going on a picnic, and I'm going to bring 3 apples." Play continues until each child has a chance to make a contribution. For children who have trouble keeping track of the number, display a hundreds chart or a number line on which progress can be tracked. The game can be made more challenging by linking the number of items to the letters of the alphabet. So, for example, 1 apple and 2 bananas and 3 coconuts can be brought to the picnic. In addition, the repetitive aspect of the game can be introduced, where the children have to repeat what has already been said before they can make their own contribution.

After this introductory game is over, distribute twelve teddy bear counters (or some other appropriate material) to each child, along with a paper plate having a line down the center that marks off two halves. Explain to the children that the teddy bears are having a picnic, and they want to play a game that requires two teams. Invite the children to use the paper plate to separate the teddy bears into two equal teams. Encourage the children to articulate that *half* of the teddy bears are on one side of the plate and *half* of the teddy bears are on the other. Repeat the procedure with paper plates divided into thirds, and then fourths.

Journal Reflection

One common means of introducing a concept to children is to define and illustrate the concept, and then offer a *counterexample* of that concept. What counterexamples might you use in this activity to help children develop an understanding of ½, ⅓, and ¼?

■ Are they of uniform width? How do you know?

■ What is the length of each color?

Activity 7.4 uses Cuisenaire rods to introduce children to the concepts of one-half, one-third, one-fourth, and so on.

Activity 7.5 introduces a new rod, "orange-red," which is used for many fractional investigations. This activity engages students in identifying fractional parts of the orange-red whole.

Performance-Based Assessment: Naming Fractions

Pattern blocks can be used to name and define fractions. For example, if the yellow hexagon is defined as one whole, the other pattern blocks acquire related fractional identities. Invite the children to use the pattern blocks to determine the fractional name for each shape of Figure 7.13, on page 216, and ask them to explain their answers.

Activity 7.4

Defining Fractions

Lesson: Individual

After the children have had an opportunity to explore with the Cuisenaire rods, ask them to show you two rods where one is half the other. Several possible answers follow as part of Figure 7.10.

White is half of red:

Red is half of purple:

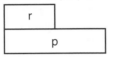

Light green is half of dark green:

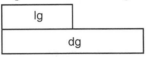

Purple is half of brown:

Yellow is half of orange:

Figure 7.10

(It is not possible to show half of white, light green, yellow, black, or blue with only one rod. Challenge the students to discover that this is because rods come in whole-centimeter lengths, and thus it is not possible to find halves of rods of lengths 1, 3, 5, 7, and 9 cm).

Next, ask the students to explain why they believe, for instance, that yellow is half of orange. Most children will say something like "Two yellows make an orange, so one is called one-half." Since most children are familiar with sandwiches being cut in half, this is not a difficult concept. Encourage children to articulate that when two equal parts make one whole, each part is called one-half. Follow the same procedure to help children use the rods to define one-third, one-fourth, and so on, up to one-tenth. Again, encourage them to articulate that when three (or four or five) equal parts make one whole, each part is called one-third (or one-fourth, or one-fifth.)

Journal Reflection

Another linear model of fractions, fraction bars, have the ½, ⅓, ¼ . . . demarcations right on the bars, unlike Cuisenaire rods, which have no markings at all. What do you see as advantages and disadvantages of each?

The students' responses can be scored according to the following rubric:

4 Student correctly identifies all three fractions, and is able to justify each answer.

3 Student correctly identifies two fractions, and is able to justify both answers.

2 Student correctly identifies one fraction, and is able to justify the answer.

1 Student is able to give one or more fractional names, but is unable to justify any answers.

0 Student is unable to name any fractions.

Activity 7.5

Comparing Fractions

Lesson: Individual

This activity asks the students to create one-color trains that are equal in length to the orange-red rod (a train made up of one orange and one red rod, end to end). Recall from earlier chapters that a one-color train is composed of rods that are all the same color. This activity, and many that follow, will treat the orange-red rod as if it were a single rod.

Figure 7.11 shows the one-color trains that are as long as the orange-red rod. Having children create this arrangement of trains inside the plastic top that comes on an individual set of Cuisenaire rods will help to keep the rods organized on the children's desks.

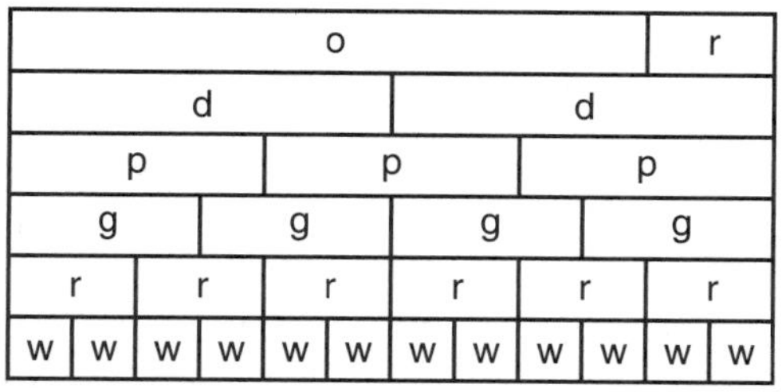

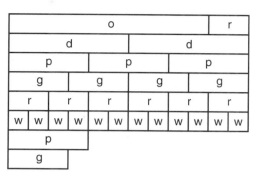

Figure 7.12

This is the same as asking them to determine which fraction is greater, ⅓ or ¼. Continue with several other examples. After the students appear to be comfortable with the comparison of the rods, encourage them to symbolize these comparisons in the following manner:

$$\frac{1}{3} > \frac{1}{4} \qquad \frac{1}{2} > \frac{1}{6}$$

$$\frac{1}{12} < \frac{1}{6} \qquad \frac{1}{3} < \frac{1}{2}$$

Explicitly address the apparent (to children) contradiction that although 3 < 4, ⅓ > ¼. Most children respond to this issue by saying that the ¼ rods are shorter than the ⅓ rods because four of the light-green rods have to fit in the same space as three of the purple rods, and they have to be smaller. Therefore, ¼ < ⅓.

Journal Reflection

Why was the orange-red rod used to define one whole? What are the advantages and disadvantages of using some other rod to define one whole?

Figure 7.11

Encourage the children to name the fractions that are represented by the one-color trains. For example, the two dark-green rods each represent ½, since two dark-green rods are as long as orange-red, which represents one whole. Following this reasoning, purple represents ⅓, light green represents ¼, red represents ⅙, and white represents ¹⁄₁₂. (What significance do the numbers 2, 3, 4, 6, and 12 have in relation to the length of the orange-red rod?)

Invite the children to place a purple rod and a light-green rod under the set of rods (Figure 7.12).

Ask the children to determine which rod is longer, the purple or the light green, and to explain their reasoning.

When engaging children in performance-based assessments, it is important that you circulate throughout the room and observe the children as they work. Some children may need assistance in articulating the justification for the fractional names, others may need encouragement, and still others may need clarification of the task. Remember that an important goal of assessment is to determine how children think and what they understand, so that future instruction can be planned.

After children have had an introduction to the concept of fractions and to comparing fractions, the next concept that is usually addressed is that of equivalent fractions. Activity 7.6 develops a visual basis for understanding equivalent fractions.

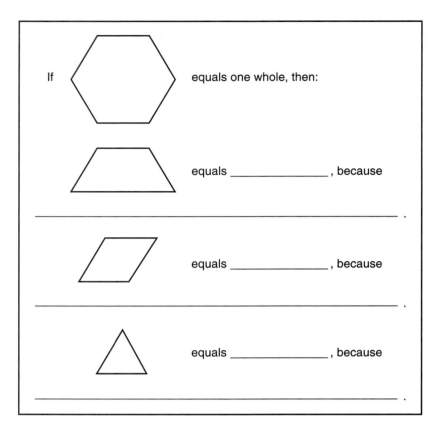

Figure 7.13

Performance-Based Assessment:
Equivalent Fractions

With access to a set of pattern blocks, invite the students to determine the indicated equivalent fractions.

- If the yellow hexagon has a value if 1 whole, then think of two ways to show ½, ⅓, and ⅔. Show the blocks and the symbols.

$\frac{1}{2}$

Blocks	Blocks
Symbol: _____	Symbol: _____

$\frac{1}{3}$

Blocks	Blocks
Symbol: _____	Symbol: _____

$\frac{2}{3}$

Blocks	Blocks
Symbol: _____	Symbol: _____

Activity 7.6

Equivalent Fractions

Lesson: Individual

Invite the students to create all of the one-color trains that are as long as the orange-red rod. These trains are pictured in Figure 7.11. Review the fractional names for each rod, then distribute a coffee stirrer to each child. Have the children hold the coffee stirrers vertically above the set of rods, at the break in the dark-green train that shows ½ (Figure 7.14).

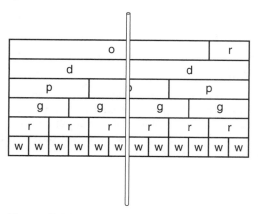

Figure 7.14

Have the students follow down the coffee stirrer to identify other fractions that are equivalent to ½. The students can see that the other breaks that occur along the same vertical line as ½ are ¾, ⅜, and ⁶⁄₁₂.

To help students apply this concept to other fractions, invite them to use the rods and the coffee stirrer to find all of the other fractions that are equivalent to ⅓, to ¼, to ⅙, to ⅔, and to ¾. Display all of these equivalent fractions:

$$\frac{1}{2} = \frac{2}{4} = \frac{3}{6} = \frac{6}{12}$$

$$\frac{1}{3} = \frac{2}{6} = \frac{4}{12}$$

$$\frac{1}{4} = \frac{3}{12}$$

$$\frac{1}{6} = \frac{2}{12}$$

$$\frac{2}{3} = \frac{4}{6} = \frac{8}{12}$$

$$\frac{3}{4} = \frac{9}{12}$$

Encourage the students to generalize about the relationships within each of these sets of equivalent fractions and to develop a procedure that could be used to generate equivalent fractions, even if the rods were not available. For example, students might say that in each case above, the numerators and denominators of the original fractions were multiplied by 2, or 3, or 4, or 6 to generate the sets of equivalent fractions.

Respond by asking them into which set they would place the fraction ⁵⁄₁₀, and why. Help the students to recognize that when both numerator and denominator of a fraction are multiplied by the same factor the resulting fraction is equivalent to the original fraction. You can see here that the students are developing their own "rule" for generating equivalent fractions, based on their observation of a pattern.

Journal Reflection

In this activity, what other materials might be substituted if Cuisenaire rods are not available? What do you see as advantages and disadvantages to each?

The development of the rubric for scoring this assessment is left to you, to give you practice in this skill. After you are finished, compare your rubric with those of other students. Try to improve your rubric based on this sharing of ideas.

Activity 7.7 is similar to some of the preceding activities, and offers a means to introduce children to decimal concepts.

It is valuable for children to have experience with a variety of materials that illustrate fractional and decimal concepts; this is how they develop number sense with the concepts. By offering several models, you enable students to perceive the pertinent characteristics and develop mental images of fractional and decimal quantities.

Activity 7.7

Comparing Decimals Using a Physical Model

Lesson: Small Groups

Equip each group of four or five children with a set of powers-of-ten blocks. Ask them to name the fraction and the decimal that each block represents if the large cube has a value of one whole, and to offer a justification for each answer. (These values were shown in Figure 7.1.) Then, invite the students to make comparisons of decimal quantities, using the blocks as a basis for the comparisons and offering a justification for each answer. Here is a sample student response to the request to compare 12 hundredths with 4 tenths:

0.12   ?   0.4

- "We think that 0.4 is greater than 0.12, even though we know that 12 is greater than 4. We think this because 0.4 can be shown with four flats, like [Figure 7.15]."

- "And 0.12 can be shown with one flat and two longs like [Figure 7.16]."

- Since four flats is more than one flat and two longs, we think that 0.12 < 0.4."

It is possible to use the powers-of-ten blocks to explain why annexing a zero to 0.4 results in a clearer symbolic comparison of

0.12 < 0.40

In this case, each decimal will be represented using *only* the smallest block needed by either number, which in this case is the long. Thus, 0.4 would need 40 longs instead of 4 flats, which makes its representation as 0.40 understandable. Comparing it with 12 longs instead of one flat and 2 longs, makes the comparison obvious (Figure 7.17):

0.40 is greater than 0.12

Journal Reflection

How could an analogy to money help children understand these decimal comparisons? How do the two models (powers-of-ten blocks and money) compare to each other? What do you see as advantages and disadvantages of each?

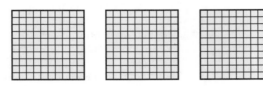

Figure 7.15

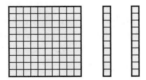

Figure 7.16

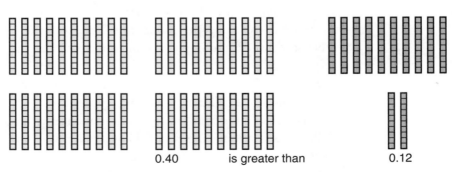

0.40   is greater than   0.12

Figure 7.17

Adding and Subtracting with Fractions and Decimals

There are many advantages to using physical models to introduce fractional and decimal concepts. They allow students to develop number sense, explore relationships between and among quantities, and arrive at solutions to computational examples *before* they have learned the "rules" for adding and subtracting fractions and decimals. Recall from Chapter 3 that giving children tangible experiences with combining and separating quantities provides a strong basis for the eventual introduction of symbolic notation. Jumping to the symbolic notation without first giving children hands-on experiences usually results in the children's memorizing computational steps but with no understanding of their underlying meaning. When children start to believe that math is meaningless, they stop trying to make sense of things and wait passively for the teacher to tell them the "rule." Rather than thinking of math as a collection of ways for figuring things out, they begin to think of it as a set of prescribed steps to be followed. Figuring things out is fun and interesting, but memorizing rules is dull and boring. The role you play in defining mathematics for children is of tremendous significance in their present learning and their later lives.

Number and Operations for Grades 3–5

The NCTM *Principles and Standards* recognize the need to relate the symbolic processes of computing with fractions and decimals to tangible or mental models. They offer the following recommendations in the focus areas for number and operation. In grades 3–5, all students should

- Estimate sums and differences of common fractions and decimals using benchmarks (for example, $\frac{3}{8} + \frac{1}{3}$ must be less than 1 since both fractions are less than $\frac{1}{2}$);

- Develop and use visual models, benchmarks, and equivalents to add and subtract with common fractions ($\frac{1}{2} + \frac{1}{4}$ is the same as $\frac{1}{4} + \frac{1}{4} + \frac{1}{4}$ or $\frac{3}{4}$; $1 - \frac{1}{5}$ leaves four-fifths of the "pie" remaining);

- Develop and use visual models, benchmarks, and equivalents to develop computational procedures for the addition and subtraction of decimals (determining $0.10 + 0.15$ by shading in a 10×10 grid, calculating $0.75 - 0.25$ by relating these numbers to fraction equivalents);

- Choose appropriate computational procedures and tools e.g., (calculators, pencil and paper, mental computation, estimation) to solve problems. (p. 157)

Activities 7.8 and 7.9 will help children construct an understanding of the addition and subtraction of fractions. Students need to be provided with ample hands-on opportunities to compare, add, and subtract fractions *before* receiving instruction in the standard paper-and-pencil methods, and the connection between these two approaches needs to be made explicit. Otherwise, the value of using manipulatives is severely compromised.

One of the prerequisite steps that allows for the paper-and-pencil comparison and computation of fractions is that of rewriting fractions with like denominators. This step was unnecessary when working with Cuisenaire

Activity 7.8

Adding Fractions

Lesson: Individual

Ask the children to create all of the one-color trains that are as long as the orange-red rod. (These trains were pictured in Figure 7.11.) Review the fractional names of each rod. Invite the students to use the rods to find the solution to this problem:

- On Monday, Kate swam $\frac{1}{3}$ of a mile. On Tuesday, she swam $\frac{1}{4}$ of a mile. How far did she swim on both days?

Most students solve this problem by making a train of the purple rod ($\frac{1}{3}$) and the light-green rod ($\frac{1}{4}$) under the entire set of rods, as shown in Figure 7.18.

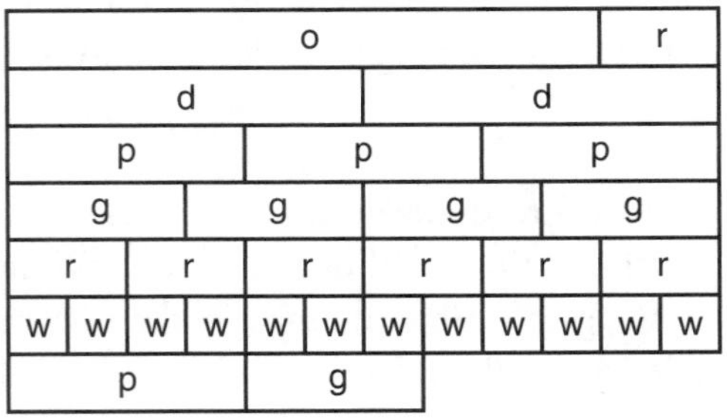

Figure 7.18

They then count up the number of white rods that are as long as this train and name the sum as $\frac{7}{12}$. Therefore, Kate swam $\frac{7}{12}$ of a mile on both days.

After all of the students have had the opportunity to arrive at a solution and to share their method of solution with the class, invite the students to find the sums for each of the following:

$$\frac{1}{2}+\frac{1}{3}= \qquad \frac{1}{2}+\frac{1}{4}= \qquad \frac{1}{3}+\frac{1}{3}=$$

$$\frac{1}{3}+\frac{1}{6}= \qquad \frac{1}{6}+\frac{1}{2}= \qquad \frac{1}{12}+\frac{2}{3}=$$

Notice that one of the big advantages of using Cuisenaire rods to introduce students to the addition of fractions is that they can add fractions with unlike denominators without having to rewrite them with the same denominator. Another advantage is that the answer can easily be given in simplest form. The students can determine the simplest form of a fraction by following the breaks in the one-color trains upward until they locate the break closest to the orange-red rod. Figure 7.19 shows this process with the sum of $\frac{1}{3}$ and $\frac{1}{6}$, where the sum can be written as $\frac{6}{12}$, $\frac{2}{4}$, or in its simplest form as $\frac{1}{2}$.

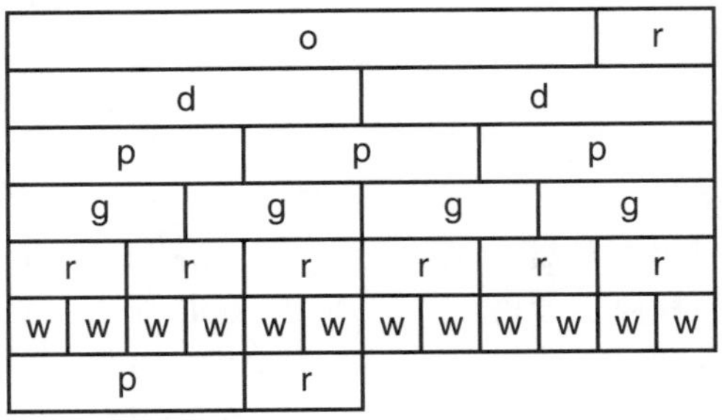

Figure 7.19

Journal Reflection

What specific strategies might you use to encourage students to estimate the sum of two or more fractions before working out the solution with materials or paper-and-pencil?

rods, because the conversion to equivalent fractions with like denominators was implicit in the solution. For example, as shown in Figure 7.9, when the sum of $\frac{1}{3}$ and $\frac{1}{4}$ was found to be $\frac{7}{12}$, the conversion of $\frac{1}{3}$ to $\frac{4}{12}$ and the conversion of $\frac{1}{4}$ to $\frac{3}{12}$ was implicit in the trains that were used to identify the solution as $\frac{7}{12}$. Directly above the purple rod were four white rods ($\frac{4}{12}$) and directly above the green rod were three white rods ($\frac{3}{12}$). Therefore, the sum was easily identified as $\frac{7}{12}$. When comparing, adding, or subtracting fractions in symbolic form, this implicit conversion to like fractions needs to be made explicit, since there is no visual means for identifying the solution.

Not every fraction can be easily represented with Cuisenaire rods or other materials, so some attention should be paid to the symbolic algo-

Activity 7.9

Subtracting Fractions

Lesson: Individual

Again working with the set of one-color trains equal in length to the orange-red rod, pose the following problem to the students:

■ Kate swam ½ of a mile. Geoffrey swam ⅓ of a mile. How much further did Kate swim?

Most students place a dark-green rod (½) under the set of one-color trains, and the purple rod (⅓) under that for comparison purposes, as shown in Figure 7.20.

Finding the solution to the problem now becomes a question of determining which rod represents the difference between ½ and ⅓, or the difference between the distance swum by each child. Since the red rod (⅙) fits in the indicated space, Kate swam ⅙ mile more than Geoffrey.

Journal Reflection

Recall the models of whole-number subtraction discussed in Chapter 3. Do those models have any significance for the subtraction of fractions? If so, what? If not, why not?

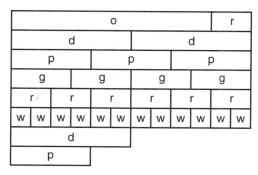

Figure 7.20

rithm. Encourage the students to recall the procedure they identified for generating equivalent fractions and use that information to solve the following problem:

■ Liz bought ½ pound of peanuts, ¾ pound of walnuts, and ⅛ pound of cashews to make a nut mixture. What would be the weight of the mixture of these three varieties of nuts?

Encourage the students to estimate the sum before solving the problem. Symbolically, the problem looks like this:

$$\frac{1}{2} + \frac{3}{4} + \frac{1}{8} =$$

Since 8 is the least multiple shared by all of the denominators, rewrite the first two fractions as equivalent fractions with like denominators:

$$\frac{1}{2} \times \frac{4}{4} = \frac{4}{8} \qquad \frac{3}{4} \times \frac{2}{2} = \frac{6}{8}$$

This results in the problem being rewritten as:

$$\frac{4}{8} + \frac{6}{8} + \frac{1}{8} = \frac{11}{8} = 1\frac{3}{8}$$

Therefore, the weight of the nut mixture is 1⅜ pounds. Students should be encouraged to compare this answer with their estimates of the sum. After some practice with problems of this sort, encourage your students to write their own problems involving the subtraction of fractions, and to follow the same method of rewriting the fractions with like denominators to solve them.

Writing subtraction word problems for fractions is not as simple as you might think. There is a very fine line between problems requiring the subtraction of fractions and those requiring multiplication. For example, which operation would you perform to solve each of these problems?

- Ana bought ¾ pound of pretzels. She ate ½ pound. How much did she have left?

- Ana bought ¾ pound of pretzels. She ate ½ of that amount. How much did she eat?

Activity 7.10

Adding with Decimals

Lesson: Small Groups

Distribute a set of powers-of-ten blocks to each group of students. Then pose the following problem:

- Elizabeth's height measured 1.35 m at the end of fourth grade. Over the next year, she grew .09 m. How tall was she at the end of fifth grade?

Invite the students to use the powers-of-ten blocks to solve this problem. One possible solution is shown in Figure 7.21.

Notice the exchanging that takes place when 14 hundredths are traded for 1 tenth and 4 hundredths. This exchanging is mirrored in the trading that takes place in

the symbolic algorithm when the 14 hundredths are recorded as 4 hundredths and the 1 tenth is recorded in the tenths column, as shown here:

$$\begin{array}{r} \overset{1}{1.35} \\ +\ 0.09 \\ \hline 1.44 \end{array}$$

Journal Reflection

What other materials could be used to model the addition of decimals? What do you see as the advantages and disadvantages of each?

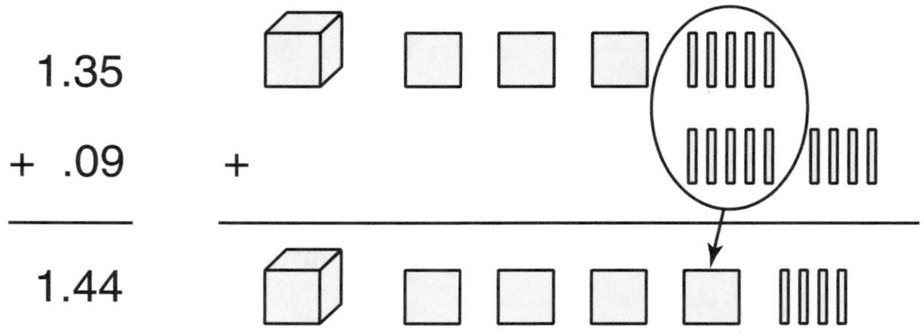

Figure 7.21

Activity 7.11

Subtracting with Decimals

Lesson: Small Groups

Distribute a set of play money consisting of dollar bills, dimes, and pennies to each group of children. Then pose the following problem:

- Juan had $1.25. He spent $0.59 on a pack of gum. How much did he have left?

Invite the students to use the coins to solve the problem. One possible solution is shown in Figure 7.22.

Notice the subsequent steps of exchanging that are necessary before the coins spent can be "taken away." These steps are mirrored in the symbolic algorithm when regrouping occurs:

$$\begin{array}{r} \overset{0}{\cancel{1}}.\overset{11}{\cancel{2}}5 \\ -\ 0.59 \\ \hline 0.66 \end{array}$$

When working with manipulatives such as powers-of-ten blocks or coins, it is absolutely essential that the students see a clear connection between the physical manipulation of objects and the symbolic manipulation of numbers. Point out to the students, for example, that the exchanging of a dime into pennies is mirrored by the regrouping of 1 tenth (1 dime) into 10 one-hundredths (10 pennies). Likewise, the exchanging of a dollar bill into dimes is mirrored by the regrouping of 1 unit (1 dollar) into 10 tenths (10 dimes).

Journal Reflection

Could this lesson have been taught using powers-of-ten blocks? Which material do you think is preferably? Why?

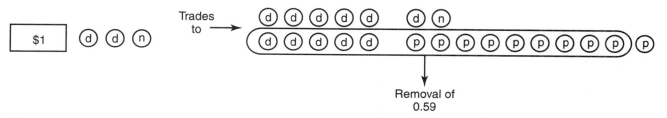

Figure 7.22

Do you see that the first problem is symbolized as

$$\frac{3}{4} - \frac{1}{2} =$$

while the second is symbolized as

$$\frac{1}{2} \times \frac{3}{4} = ?$$

Multiplication of fractions will be addressed in the next chapter, where the meaning of the operation will be discussed more fully. At this point, I want to caution you that word problems for the subtraction and multiplication of fractions are very similar, and it requires care on your part to distinguish the two. *Subtraction of fractions* is the operation that removes some part of the whole, or compares two parts of the whole, while *multiplication of fractions* is the operation that examines a part of a part to determine how much of the whole it is.

Activities 7.10 and 7.11 help children construct an understanding of the addition and subtraction of decimals. They demonstrate that the

Activity 7.12

Rounding Rational Numbers

Lesson: Individual

Before introducing this activity, ask the children to create their own rational number line. Distribute a number line showing only whole numbers, and invite the students to fill in the inches with the correct quarter inch, as shown in Figure 7.23.

Then, distribute to each student a blank 4 × 4 grid having cells of approximately one square inch. Ask the students to fill in the cells randomly with the following numbers (Figure 7.24).

1   1½   2   2½   3   3½   4   4½
5   5½   6   6½   7   2   4   6

Toss three number cubes, each labeled with the digits 1 through 6, to generate a mixed number. For example, if the digits 4, 5, and 6 are tossed, the mixed number 4⅚ can be formed. Record the mixed number on the overhead or blackboard, and invite the students to cover the number closest to the number tossed on their playing card. In this case, that would be 5. Play continues until someone covers a complete row, column, or diagonal. Encouraging students to refer to their rational number line will help them to develop rational number sense.

This game can be adapted in many ways. When students become adept at rounding to the nearest ½, challenge them to round to the nearest ¼. This version requires a 5 × 5 grid, randomly covered with the following 25 numbers:

1   1¼   1½   1¾
2   2¼   2½   2¾

3	3¼	3½	3¾
4	4¼	4½	4¾
5	5¼	5½	5¾
6	6¼	6½	6¾	7

In addition, the game can be used to provide practice in rounding decimals to the nearest whole number. For this version of the game, students need to construct a number line like that of Figure 7.25.

The cells in the 4 × 4 grid should be randomly filled with the following rational numbers:

1   1.5   2   2.5   3   3.5   4   4.5
5   5.5   6   6.5   7   2   4   6

In this decimal version of the game, continue to play with three dice, even though the third die is irrelevant. For example, both 2.3 and 2.36 will round to 2.5. Regardless of what digit is in the hundredths place, the number will still round to 2.5. However, giving students practice rounding numbers containing a hundredths place is a valuable experience and helps to demystify decimals.

Journal Reflection

This activity is only valuable if it helps students become better able to estimate sums and differences of fractions and decimals before performing the computation. How, specifically, would you help students to make that connection?

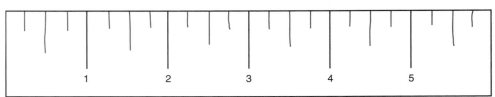

Figure 7.23

6	$4\frac{1}{2}$	2	1
5	$6\frac{1}{2}$	$1\frac{1}{2}$	2
3	4	7	$5\frac{1}{2}$
4	$2\frac{1}{2}$	$3\frac{1}{2}$	6

Figure 7.24

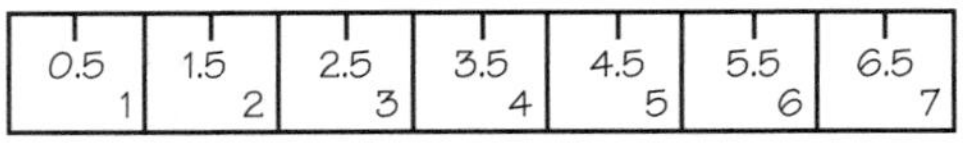

| 0.5 | 1.5 | 2.5 | 3.5 | 4.5 | 5.5 | 6.5 |
| 1 | 2 | 3 | 4 | 5 | 6 | 7 |

Figure 7.25

operations of addition and subtraction with decimals are very similar to those operations with fractions.

Estimating Sums and Differences of Rational Numbers

One of the reasons that students often have trouble with fraction and decimal computations is that they lack any real-world referent for many of the rational numbers they are dealing with, and are therefore unable to estimate the outcome of computations. The lack of a visual/mental image of rational numbers makes rounding the numbers difficult, and one of the first steps in estimating a sum or a difference is to round the addends or the minuend and subtrahend. Activity 7.12 provides students with practice in rounding fractions and decimals. The Strength in Numbers activity below utilizes tangrams to present problem-solving strategies for fractions.

The following interdisciplinary lesson plan teaches children a folding pattern through the Japanese art of origami. Some children initially have difficulty with the steps of paper folding; however, with practice they become quite adept. Recycled wrapping paper has a good texture and thickness for origami. Keep a supply in the classroom so that children can practice when they have a moment.

Strength in Numbers

Tangrams and Fractions

Cooperative Group Model:
Tangrams—Think, Pair, Share

Think: If the value of the tangram shown in Figure 7.26 is equal to 1, what is the fractional value of each individual piece in the tangram? If the value of the tangram is equal to 2, what is the fractional value of each individual piece? If the value of the tangram is equal to 3, what is the fractional value of each individual piece?

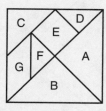

Figure 7.26

Pair: Discuss with a partner your strategies for solving these problems. Pay special attention to any connections you may have made among the questions. For example, did you solve each situation separately, or did you develop subsequent solutions from the initial solution? Come to an agreement with your partner about the best strategies for solving these problems.

Share: Share these strategies with the rest of the class. When sharing, incorporate appropriate pedagogy. For instance, you may choose to involve the class with actual tangram puzzles, or to distribute calculators, or to create a chart that highlights certain patterns in the data that are generated.

**Interdisciplinary
Lesson Plan**

Grade 4   **Concept** Fractions

Topic Various Partitions of the Whole

Student Objectives After completing this lesson, students should be able to

■ Identify various fractional parts of a whole

■ Create an origami pinwheel.

Materials square origami paper, thumbtacks, unsharpened pencils

Motivation Invite a child to locate Japan on a globe or world map. Display some samples of origami to the children. Share with the children the information that, in Japanese, *ori* means fold and *gami* means paper. Although origami is usually associated with the Japanese culture, it originated in China during the seventh century when paper was invented there. Today in Japan parents teach origami patterns to their children.

Procedure Model the following steps and pose the following questions as you teach the children to make an origami pinwheel. The easiest way to model the paper folding steps to children is to tape four small origami paper squares together to form a large square. Use this large square to demonstrate the folds, one by one, to the class.

(1) Holding the paper diagonally, with the unshaded side of the paper facing you, bring the top vertex of the paper down to meet the bottom vertex (Figure 7.27). Make a sharp crease. Into how many equal parts have you folded the paper? [2] What is the fractional name for each part? [Each isosceles right triangle is ½ the original square.]

(2) Fold the half in half again by bringing the left vertex over to meet the right vertex (Figure 7.28). Make a sharp crease. Into how many equal parts is the paper now folded? [4] What is the fractional name for each part? [Each isosceles right triangle is ¼ of the original square.]

(3) Open the previous folds and bring the four vertices into the center point (Figure 7. 29). Make sharp creases. What can you say about the

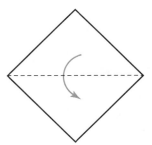

Figure 7.27

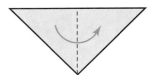

Figure 7.28

Figure 7.29

(continued)

area covered by the four isosceles right triangles on the front and the area covered by the square on the back? [The areas are equal.]

(4) Unfold the top and the bottom triangle, and fold them back over the crease line, so that the top and bottom vertices meet on the back of the square (Figure 7.30). What fractional part of the front square is shaded? [¾ or ½] What fractional part of the back square is shaded? [¾ or ½]

(5) Bring the top left and bottom right vertices into the center to meet, and crease sharply (Figure 7.31). Fold the top right and bottom left vertices back so they meet on the back. How many different ways can you represent the amount of shaded area on the front of the paper? On the back of the paper? [⅝, ¾, ½, .5, 50%, etc.] (6) Unfold the shaded triangles on the front, and the unshaded triangles on the back (Figure 7.32). How many triangles are now visible? [12] What fractional part of them form the inner square of the pinwheel face? [⁴⁄₁₂ or ⅓] What fractional part of them extend out from the inner square? [⁸⁄₁₂ r ⅔] (7) Use the thumbtacks to attach the center of each pinwheel to the eraser of an unsharpened pencil. Allow the children to bring the pinwheels outside so that the wind can make them spin. Do all of the pinwheels spin in the same direction? Why?

Assessment Observe the children as they work, and note which children appear able to answer the fractional questions. Distribute the sketch of Figure 7.33. Invite the children to color ⁴⁄₁₂ of the pinwheel red, to color

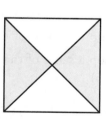

Figure 7.30

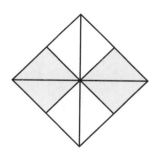

Figure 7.31

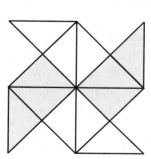

Figure 7.32

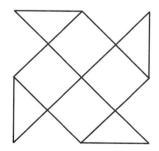

Figure 7.33

(continued)

**Interdisciplinary
Lesson Plan**

$\frac{3}{12}$ of the pinwheel blue, and to color $\frac{1}{6}$ of the pinwheel green. Evaluate the accuracy of their work.

References Franco, Betsy, and Jeanne Shimizu-Yost. *Using Tomoko Fuse's Unit Origami in the Classroom.* Berkeley: Key Curriculum Press, 1991.

Journal Entry This might contain practical suggestions about helping children master origami, suggestions as to how this activity might, in the future, be connected to a science lesson on wind, or a reflection on the students' understanding of fractional parts of a whole.

**Linear
Measurement**

Measurement is the context in which children often use fractions and decimals. Measuring actual distances, volumes, and masses frequently requires representing amounts that are not whole numbers. Combining the study of fractions with the study of the English standard system of measurement, and combining the study of decimals with the study of the metric system of measurement, helps children make connections and see the practical uses of fractions and decimals. This section deals with linear measurement, while measuring volume and mass will be addressed in Chapter 8.

**Measurement for
Grades Pre-K–2**

The NCTM *Principles and Standards* recommend the following focus areas in measurement. In grades Pre-K–2, all students should

- Recognize the attributes of length, capacity, weight, area, and time;
- Compare and order objects qualitatively by these attributes;
- Make and use measurements in natural situations;
- Develop referents for estimation:
- Develop a sense of the unit (e.g., length, area) through estimation. (p. 125)

One of the earliest ways children begin to measure is by directly comparing two things. Children stand back to back to see who is taller; they run races to see who is faster; they arrange their baseball cards in vertical stacks to see who has more. Children also engage in indirect comparisons. A child might hold up her arm to the height of a box and then walk over to a shelf without moving her arm to determine if the box will fit on the shelf. When describing the size of a toy, a child might say to his friend that it is "this big," while holding his hands a certain distance apart. But children eventually become dissatisfied with these measurement processes, since they are neither efficient nor accurate. At this point, the measurement process begins to formalize into the following three steps:

1. *Attribute identification.* What characteristic is to be measured?
2. *Unit quantification.* What is the unit of measurement?

Activity 7.13

Direct Comparison

Lesson: Pairs

With the children working in pairs, distribute to each pair two sheets of construction paper, one bearing the word *longer* and the other bearing the word *shorter*. Give each pair of students a box of items whose length is to be compared. For example, the box might contain the following pairs of items, all of different lengths: two crayons, two ribbons, two strips of paper, two feathers, two lengths of plastic links, and two drinking straws. The children are to compare the pairs of items, then place them on the paper designated either longer or shorter. The boxes can be rotated among the pairs of children to allow each pair to work with several different boxes.

Journal Reflection

How could this activity be adapted to having children compare masses and volumes? What words would you put on the papers? What objects would you place in the boxes? Lengths can be visually compared. Can volumes? Can masses?

3. *Comparison.* How many units of measurement are equivalent to the amount of the attribute to be measured?

Activities 7.13 and 7.14 offer ways to engage children in the preliminary measurement activities of direct and indirect comparison.

When children first begin to engage in indirect comparisons they often employ nonstandard units of measurement. For example, a child might

Activity 7.14

Indirect Comparison

Lesson: Whole Class

Invite two students of very different heights to stand approximately 10 feet apart. Ask the class to think of different methods they could use to determine which student is taller without having the students stand back to back. Some comments from the students might be:

- "I can tell that Michael is taller because his head is higher than the number line on the wall. Zach's head is below the number line."

- "I think that Michael is taller because he is about as tall as six of the cinderblocks in the wall, but Zach is only about $5\frac{1}{2}$ cinderblocks tall."

- "I know that Zach is shorter because I can touch the top of Zach's head, but I can't reach Michael's head."

Point out to the students that, in each of these cases, the heights of the boys were *compared* to something, either the number line, the cinderblocks, or to a child's reach. Measurement is the process of comparing an attribute (in this case, height) to some standard or nonstandard unit of measurement. Repeat the activity with another pair of students whose difference in height is less pronounced.

Journal Reflection

How can you structure comparison activities in such a way that children who are shorter, or slower, or younger, or heavier will not feel uncomfortable?

Activity 7.15

Nonstandard Units of Measurement

Lesson: Whole Class

This activity will go more smoothly if parents are invited into the room to assist, if there is an aide available, or if there are some sixth-grade volunteers to help with the cutting.

Invite the children to place one foot on approximately 20 sheets of newspaper. Trace around each child's foot. Cut through as many thicknesses of the paper as you can to create "footsteps" of each child. These footsteps can be used to measure distances within the classroom, or between the classroom and the library, or between the classroom and the lunchroom.

Eventually, children question why it takes 28 of the teacher's footsteps to get to the library but 35 of Kate's footsteps. A question such as this can be an opportunity to introduce the need for standard units of measurement.

Journal Reflection

Many children mistakenly think that it should take *fewer* of the smaller footsteps and *more* of the larger footsteps to measure the same distance. How can you help children clarify this misunderstanding?

know that dinner will be served after one more cartoon show, that the ride to Grandma's house will be over when two cassette tapes have been played, that it takes seventeen steps to get from the play area to the block area, or that it takes two boxes of animal crackers to fill the cookie jar. Activity 7.15 engages children in the creation of a nonstandard unit of measurement.

The history of standard systems of measurement is interesting to children, and it provides an opportunity to compare and contrast the two systems of measurement currently in use in the United States: the English standard system and the metric system. Since the rest of the world uses the metric system almost exclusively, and since the United States is still reliant upon the English standard system, it is important for children to become fluent in both measurement systems.

Measurement for Grades 3–5

The NCTM *Principles and Standards* recommends the following focus areas in measurement. In grades 3–5, all students should

- Develop awareness of measurements as approximations and understand how the tools used to measure affect the level of precision;

- Understand the need for uniform units of measurement and develop facility in using the common units of the English and metric systems of measurement. (p. 176)

The English standard system of measurement evolved over many hundreds of years, and the units of measurement were created from commonly available items. Some say that an inch was determined to be as long as three barleycorn kernels laid end to end. Others say that an inch was the width of a man's thumb, a foot was the length of a man's foot, and a yard was the

Unit	Equivalence
Inch	12 inches = 1 foot
	36 inches = 1 yard
Foot	3 feet = 1 yard
	5280 feet = 1 mile
Yard	1760 yards = 1 mile

Figure 7.34

distance from a man's nose to his outstretched thumb; further, a pint was the capacity of a beer stein. Although they have been standardized, all of these units of measurement were arbitrary and variable in their origin. Their origination is identified with the reigns of English royalty: Edgar, King of England from A.D. 957 to 975, standardized the yard, while King Henry III standardized the foot (Mein, et al., 1989). Figure 7.34 summarizes the units that comprise the English standard system of linear measurement.

In contrast, the metric system of measurement was developed in its entirety over a very short period of time. At the end of the eighteenth century, the people of France were in rebellion against their royal rulers. The French Revolution led to a rejection of all things associated with royalty, including the English standard system of measurement. The French Academy of Arts and Sciences decided to create an entirely new system of measurement, one based not on odd and arbitrary units but perfectly predictable and consistently structured. They chose as the basis of their system of measurement the meter, which was defined as $\frac{1}{10,000,000}$ of the distance from the North Pole to the Equator. In this metric system of measurement (*meter* means "measure" in French) every unit, whether it be a unit of length, capacity, or mass, would be connected to the meter. While in the English system, asking "How many inches are in a quart?" is a meaningless question, its equivalent in the metric system is not meaningless. The relationship among the units of linear (meter), volume (liter), and mass (gram) will be addressed elsewhere. At this point, it is appropriate to introduce the prefixes that are used throughout the metric system.

These prefixes are used with the three root words of meter, liter or gram, depending on whether you are measuring length, volume, or mass. Each unit is related to the adjacent units by a power of ten, which allows easy conversion between the units. (For example, while it can be easily determined that there are 2500 centimeters in 25 meters, the answer to how many inches are in 25 yards is not as easily achieved.) Figure 7.35 lists the prefixes of the metric system. Moving up, each unit is ten times larger than the adjacent unit. Moving down, each unit is $\frac{1}{10}$ the size of the adjacent unit.

	Unit	Symbol	Relationship to Root Unit
kilo-	**kilo**meter	km	1000 meters
hecto-	**hecto**meter	hm	100 meters
deka-	**deka**meter	dam	10 meters
meter		m	**root unit**
deci-	**deci**meter	dm	0.1 meter
centi-	**centi**meter	cm	0.01 meter
milli-	**milli**meter	mm	0.001 meter

Figure 7.35

For people who are not very familiar with the metric system of measurement, it is important to develop mental images of the sizes of the various units of measurements. Here are some suggestions to help you do that.

- *Kilometer.* A kilometer is 1000 meters, or approximately 0.6 mile. (Remember that a 10K race is slightly more than 6 miles.) The next time you are driving, pick out a landmark, and then clock 0.6 mile on your odometer. Use this distance as your definition of a kilometer.

- *Hectometer.* A hectometer is 0.1 the distance of a kilometer, or 100 meters. This distance is slightly longer than a football field.

- *Dekameter.* A dekameter is 0.01 the distance of a kilometer, or 10 meters. This distance is approximately the length of a classroom.

- *Meter.* A meter is 0.001 the length of a kilometer. It is slightly longer than a yard, and can be visually defined for children as the approximate distance from the floor to a doorknob.

- *Decimeter.* A decimeter is 0.1 the length of a meter, or the length of an orange Cuisenaire rod. It is slightly longer than a crayon.

- *Centimeter.* A centimeter is 0.01 the length of a meter, or the length of a white Cuisenaire rod. It is approximately the width of your pinkie finger.

- *Millimeter.* A millimeter is 0.001 the length of a meter, or the *thickness* (not the diameter) of a dime. If you draw nine horizontal lines between two adjacent blue lines on a sheet of lined paper, the distance between any of the lines is approximately 1 millimeter.

As you can see, there are many opportunities to connect the study of fractions with the English standard system of measurement, and to connect the study of decimals with the metric system. Activities 7.16 and 7.17 are designed to do just that.

Performance-Based Assessment:
Linear Measurement

Have unlined paper, markers, rulers, and pencils available for the students. Invite them to create a bar graph with five bars of the following dimensions:

1 inch by 5¼ inches		2 cm by 6.6 cm
1 inch by 2½ inches		2 cm by 7.5 cm
1 inch by 3¾ inches	*or*	2 cm by 8 cm
1 inch by 4 inches		2 cm by 9.9 cm
1 inch by 3⅞ inches		2 cm by 5.2 cm

After creating bars of these dimensions, the students are to use them to create a bar graph. They should use their imagination to title the graph and

Activity 7.16

Creating an Inch Ruler

Lesson: Individual

To each child, distribute a six-inch ruler that is marked only with inches (Figure 7.36). Invite each child to determine a way to mark the ruler with half-inch and quarter-inch marks.

Some children may choose visually to approximate the half- and quarter-way marks. Others may fold each inch in half, and then half again to mark those spots. Other children may use the ruler to cut an inch-long strip of paper from scrap paper, fold that in half twice, and use this pattern to mark of each half- and quarter-inch on the ruler.

After students have completed this task, invite them to locate the following lengths on their ruler:

$4\frac{1}{3}$ $2\frac{1}{3}$ $5\frac{1}{8}$

$3\frac{2}{3}$ $4\frac{5}{8}$ $1\frac{7}{8}$

Journal Reflection

What strategies would you offer to children who were unable to locate thirds or eighths on the ruler, since these were unmarked and required estimation?

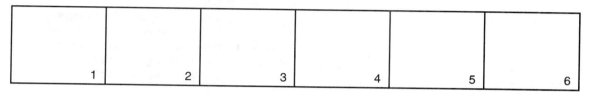

Figure 7.36

Activity 7.17

Creating a Centimeter Ruler

Lesson: Individual

To each child, distribute a 15-cm ruler that is marked only with 5-cm and 10-cm marks (Figure 7.37).

Invite the children to label the ruler with marks at each centimeter. Their strategies will be similar to those described in Activity 5.16. Ask the students to locate the following lengths on their rulers:

4.7 cm   10.9 cm   1.01 cm

0.25 dm   0.5 dm   1.00 dm

Journal Reflection

How might you make the connection of this Activity to the process of tuning in a radio station?

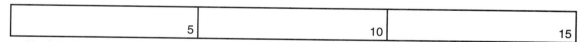

Figure 7.37

title and number each axis in a way that has meaning, and then write three sentences interpreting the graph.

The following rubric can be used to assess the students' performances.

4   Student's measurements are accurate, graph is meaningful, and interpretation is cogent.

3   Student's measurements are accurate, graph is meaningful, but written interpretation is weak.

Activity 7.18

Making a Meter

Lesson: Small Groups

Distribute a meter stick, three to four different-colored toothpicks, a blank plastic spinner face, and a copy of the spinners of Figure 7.38 to each small group of children.

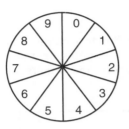 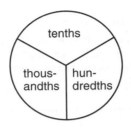

Figure 7.38

The object of the activity is to move your toothpick from one end of the meter stick to the other, with moves dictated by the number and unit spun on the spinners. For ex-

ample, if Player 1 spins a "2" followed by a "tenth," he or she is allowed to move the toothpick 0.2 meter, or 2 dm. If, on the next turn, Player 1 spins a "7" followed by a "thousandth," that player moves his or her toothpick a distance of 0.007 meter, or 7 mm. The game is over when one player reaches the end of the meter stick. You may wish to have students record each move in their notebook. For example, Player 1 might write:

Turn 1 $0 + 0.2 = 0.2$

Turn 2 $0.2 + 0.007 = 0.207$

Journal Reflection

What strategies would you offer to students who experienced difficulties in accurately recording their moves? In many European countries, notebooks that are used for math have grids printed on them instead of lines. What do you think of that?

2   Student's measurements are accurate, but graph is illogical, and written interpretation is weak.

1   Only one aspect (measurement, graph or interpretation) is adequate.

It is difficult for students to believe that 1000 millimeters are needed to make a meter. To children, 1000 seems like an enormous quantity. It is equally difficult for them to imagine what $\frac{1}{1000}$ of something looks like. Activity 7.18 is designed to give children practice in relating landmark decimals—0.1, 0.01, and 0.001—to distances on a meter stick, in order to provide a tangible model for these decimal quantities.

Strength in Numbers

Linear Measurement

Cooperative Group Model: Jigsaw

Each three-person group is to measure the length of a dollar bill to varying degrees of accuracy. Student 1 is to measure the bill to the nearest ¼ of an inch. Student 2 is to measure the bill to the nearest ⅛ of an inch. Student 3 is to measure the bill to the nearest ¹⁄₁₆ of an inch. The U.S. Bureau of Printing and Engraving reports that the length of a bill is approximately 6.14 inches. Whose measurement was the most accurate? How can you find out? In what contexts are each of these measurements appropriate and adequate?

In ending this chapter, I invite you to think about degrees of accuracy. Since all measurement is an approximation, how do you know how much precision you need? The preceding Strength in Numbers: Linear Measurement activity encourages you to think about this.

Summary

This chapter expanded the study of whole numbers to include the study of quantities that are parts of wholes. Fractions and decimals can be parts of continuous quantities (How much of a mile have we run?) or parts of discrete quantities (What part of the dozen cookies have we eaten?). Fractions are defined in three categories: fractions as parts of a whole, fractions as quotients, and fractions as ratios.

Following an examination of the nature of fractional quantities, the chapter addressed the comparison of fractions and decimals, equivalent fractions, and the addition and subtraction of fractions and decimals. While the two primary models of Cuisenaire rods and powers-of-ten materials were used for these purposes, connections were also made to pattern blocks in several performance-based assessment tasks.

The chapter then turned to linear measurement to offer a context in which children often use fraction and decimal concepts. Both the English standard system and the metric system of measurement were introduced, and students need to become equally comfortable with both systems.

Extending Your Learning

1. Describe the difference between a discrete and a continuous model of fractions. Offer realistic contexts in which each are used by children.

2. How is the teaching of addition and subtraction with fractions similar to teaching addition and subtraction with whole numbers? How is it different?

3. Discuss the similarities and differences between teaching fractional and decimal concepts to children. Write a lesson plan, suitable for fourth or fifth grade, building on the connections between these two topics.

4. Write a realistic word problem to correspond to the following examples:

$$\frac{1}{2} + \frac{3}{4} =$$

$$\frac{3}{4} - \frac{1}{2} =$$

$$0.5 + 0.7 =$$

$$2.5 - 1.9 =$$

5. Write a children's book that is designed to introduce fractional concepts to children. Include "Notes to Parents and Other Interested Adults" similar to those found in many books by Mitsumasa Anno.

6. Write a lesson plan to connect fractional concepts to linear measurement in the English standard system. Include a performance-based assessment in your lesson plan.

7. Write a lesson plan to connect decimal concepts to linear measurement in the metric system. Include a performance-based assessment in your lesson plan.

8. Develop a list of ten connections that could be made among the Olympics, decimal concepts, and linear measurement. Choose one of these connections, and develop it into a formal lesson plan.

9. Think back to the two previous chapters on geometry. What connections do you see among these three chapters? Describe, in detail, the ways in which knowledge of geometry can inform children's understanding of fractional and decimal concepts, and ways in which knowledge of fraction and decimal concepts can inform children's understanding of geometry.

10. Offer examples of objects that are approximately:

- 10 cm long
- 2 meters long
- a distance of 25 km from you
- 3 mm long
- 150 cm tall

Internet Resources

http://www.csun.edu/~vceed009/index.html/
This website offers nine categories of links to sites that provide classroom resources. Under the mathematics category, almost three hundred links connect you to puzzles, problems, games, organizations, and lesson plans.

http://school.discovery.com/schrockguide/
This Discovery Channel website serves as a guide other Internet sites that specialize in curricular and teacher resources. It contains many categories organized under the heading of Kathy Schrock's *Guide to Educators.* For the mathematics category, more than thirty links are provided.

http://unite.ukans.edu/
Under the title of *The Explorer,* this website serves as a resource for math and science teachers from grades K to 12. Lesson plans, software information, and lab activities can be found under hundreds of subject and topic headings.

Bibliography

Caldwell, Janet H. (1995). Communicating about fractions with pattern blocks. *Teaching Children Mathematics 2*(3).

Curcio, Frances R., and Nadine S. Bezuk. (1994). *Understanding rational numbers and proportions. Addenda series, grades 5–8.* Reston, VA: National Council of Teachers of Mathematics.

Franco, Betsy, and Jeanne Shimizu-Yost. (1991). *Using Tomoko Fuse's unit origami in the classroom.* Berkeley: Key Curriculum Press.

Kamii, Constance, and Mary Ann Warrington. (1999). Teaching fractions: Fostering children's own reasoning. In

Lee V. Stiff (ed.), *Developing mathematical reasoning in grades K–12.* Reston, VA: National Council of Teachers of Mathematics.

Langford, Karen, and Angela Sarullo. (1993). Introductory common and decimal fraction concepts. In Robert J. Jensen (ed.), *Research ideas for the classroom: Early childhood mathematics.* New York: Macmillan.

Mack, Nancy. (1990). Learning fractions with understanding: Building on informal knowledge. *Journal for Research in Mathematics Education 21*(1):16–32.

McMillan, Bruce. (1991). *Eating Fractions.* New York: Scholastic.

Reynolds, Anne, and Grayson H. Wheatley. (1990). Third-grade students engage in a playground measuring activity. *Teaching Children Mathematics 4*(3).

Ruggles, JoLean, and Barbara Sweeney Slenger. (1998). The "Measure Me " doll. *Teaching Children Mathematics 5*(1).

Van de Walle, John, and Karen Bowman Watkins. (1993). Early development of

number sense. In Robert J. Jensen (ed.), *Research ideas for the classroom: Early childhood mathematics.* New York: Macmillan.

Wantanabe, Ted. (1996). Ben's understanding of one-half. *Teaching Children Mathematics 2*(8).

Zulie, Mathew. (1975). *Fractions with pattern blocks.* Palo Alto California: Creative Publications.

8

Standards For Multiplication and Division of Fractions and Decimals

While the addition and subtraction of fractions and decimals are rather easily understood by students because they are connected to familiar experiences, the same is not always true for multiplication and division. These operations are more difficult to relate to realistic situations, and the results of these operations on fractions and decimals are often counter-intuitive for students.

This chapter connects operations on fractions to those on decimals. Cuisenaire rods and powers-of-ten materials again illustrate these operations. In addition, this chapter points up the connections among fractions, decimals, and percents, and offers an introduction to measuring both capacity and mass.

Multiplying and Dividing with Fractions and Decimals

The operations of multiplication and division of fractions are algorithmically quite simple since they do not require finding common denominators. However, they are conceptually complex, and students often find it difficult to relate these operations to their reality. In addition, the result when multiplying fractions is opposite to that obtained when multiplying whole numbers, and the result when dividing fractions is opposite to that obtained when dividing whole numbers.

Number and Operation for Grades 6–8

The NTCM *Principles and Standards* recommends the following focus areas for grades 6–8. In grades 6–8, all students should

- Extend understanding of operations to include operations on fractions, decimals, percents, . . .;

- Understand the effects of operating among fractions, decimals, percents . . .;

- Develop analyze, and compare algorithms for computing with fractions, decimals, percents . . . and become efficient and accurate in computing with them;

- Develop, analyze, and explain methods for solving problems involving proportions (scaling, finding equivalent ratios). (pp. 216–17)

The language you choose to introduce the operations of multiplication and division of fractions is critical to students' understanding. It is helpful to connect these operations on fractions to what students already know about the operations on whole numbers. For example, 2 × 6 can be thought of as 2 groups *of* 6. Likewise, ½ × ⅙ can be thought of as ½ *of* ⅙. Activity 8.1 offers a model for introducing multiplication of fractions to students.

The language used to introduce division of fractions is equally critical to students' understanding of that operation. Refer again to the division of whole numbers. One way in which 12 ÷ 3 can be interpreted is to ask "How

Activity 8.1

Multiplying Fractions

Lesson: Individual

Ask the students to construct all of the one-color trains that are equal in length to the orange-red rod (Figure 8.1). Then, pose the following problem.

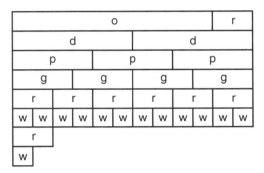

Figure 8.1

■ Kate had to swim ⅙ of a mile during swim team practice. After she swam ½ of that distance, she had to stop and rest. How far had she gone?

Encourage the students to restate the problem in their own words. Point out that this problem asks "What is ½ of ⅙ ?" This problem can be solved using the Cuisenaire rods by placing a red rod (⅙) under the set of one-color trains and then determining what rod is ½ of that red rod. Since the white rod (1/12) is ½ of red, the answer to the problem is that Kate swam 1/12 of a mile before she had to rest.

Now, pose the following problem to students.

■ Miguel had ⅔ of a quart of juice in the refrigerator. He drank ¼ of that amount. How much juice did Miguel drink?

Again, encourage the students to restate the problem, and to articulate that the problem asks "What is ¼ of ⅔?" Cuisenaire rods can be used to solve this problem by placing two purple rods under the set of one-color trains, and then determining what rod is ¼ of that train of two purple

rods. Since 4 red rods are equal in length to the two purple rods, ¼ of ⅔ is one red rod, or ⅙. The answer to the problem is that Miguel drank ⅙ of a quart of juice.

Invite the students to write word problems for the following examples, and then use the Cuisenaire rods to solve each problem. (Try this yourself.)

Writing word problems is not as easy as you might think. Remember that multiplying fractions involves determining a part of a part.

$$\frac{2}{3} \times \frac{3}{4} = \qquad \frac{1}{2} \times \frac{2}{3} = \qquad \frac{1}{6} \times \frac{1}{2} =$$

$$\frac{1}{3} \times \frac{1}{2} = \qquad \frac{3}{4} \times \frac{2}{3} = \qquad \frac{1}{4} \times \frac{1}{3} =$$

After students have had the opportunity to write word problems and then solve them (this will likely take more than one day), display the following set $\frac{1}{12}$ of examples that the class has just worked out:

$$\frac{1}{2} \times \frac{1}{6} = \frac{1}{12} \qquad \frac{1}{4} \times \frac{2}{3} = \frac{2}{12} = \frac{1}{6}$$

$$\frac{2}{3} \times \frac{3}{4} = \frac{6}{12} = \frac{1}{2} \qquad \frac{1}{2} \times \frac{2}{3} = \frac{2}{6} = \frac{1}{3} \qquad \frac{1}{6} \times \frac{1}{2} = \frac{2}{12}$$

$$\frac{1}{3} \times \frac{1}{2} = \frac{1}{6} \qquad \frac{3}{4} \times \frac{2}{3} = \frac{6}{12} = \frac{1}{2} \qquad \frac{1}{4} \times \frac{1}{3} = \frac{2}{12}$$

Invite the students to generalize a procedure that will allow them to find the product of any fractions, whether they have access to a set of Cuisenaire rods or not. Students usually see that multiplying the numerators together and multiplying the denominators together results in the product of the two fractions.

Journal Reflection

How would you help students understand that when 2 is multiplied by 6, the product is greater than either of the two factors, but when ½ is multiplied by ⅙, the product is less than either of the two factors?

many threes are in 12?" This language is the most useful when dealing with fractions. Interpreting $\frac{1}{2} \div \frac{1}{6}$ as "How many sixths are in $\frac{1}{2}$?" helps students make sense of division of fractions. Activity 8.2 offers a way to introduce this operation to students.

Many people know that the "rule" for dividing fractions is to invert the second fraction and then multiply, but most people do not know *why* that is the rule or what the rule actually means. In addition, most people are unable to estimate the quotient of two fractions before carrying out the algorithm, because they have no understanding of the process of dividing fractions. Perhaps the following explanation will help you to understand the "rule." If

Activity 8.2

Dividing Fractions

Lesson: Individual

Invite the students to create the one-color trains that are as long as the orange-red rod, as they did earlier in Activity 7.5. Pose the following problem to students:

- A carton containing $\frac{1}{2}$ quart of cream is to be used to fill creamers that hold $\frac{1}{6}$ quart each. How many creamers can be filled?

Encourage the students to restate the problem in their own words. Articulate that this problem asks "How many one-sixths are in $\frac{1}{2}$?" Ask the children to estimate the quotient before proceeding.

This problem can be solved using Cuisenaire rods by placing a dark green rod ($\frac{1}{2}$) under the set of one-color trains, and determining how many red rods ($\frac{1}{6}$) are as long as that rod. Since three red rods are as long as the dark-green rod, the answer to the question "How many one-sixths are in $\frac{1}{2}$?" is "three." Within the context of the problem, it means that three creamers can be filled from $\frac{1}{2}$ quart of cream. Symbolically, $\frac{1}{2} \div \frac{1}{6} = 3$.

Now, pose another problem to students:

- A cookie recipe calls for $\frac{1}{3}$ cup of sugar. If you have $\frac{1}{2}$ cup of sugar, how many batches of cookies can you make?

Encourage students to articulate that this problem asks "How many one-thirds are in $\frac{1}{2}$?" Ask the students to estimate if the answer will be more than one or less than one, based on their mental images of fractions. This problem can be solved using Cuisenaire rods by placing a dark green rod ($\frac{1}{2}$) under the set of one-color trains, and determining how many purple rods ($\frac{1}{3}$) are as long as that rod (Figure 8.2.)

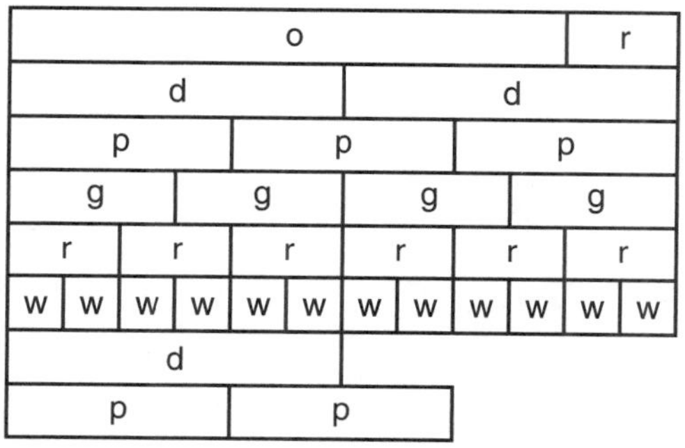

Figure 8.2

As you can see, $1\frac{1}{2}$ purple rods are as long as a dark-green rod. Within the context of this problem, that means that $\frac{1}{2}$ cup of sugar is enough to make $1\frac{1}{2}$ batches of cookies. Symbolically, $\frac{1}{2} \div \frac{1}{3} = 1\frac{1}{2}$.

Invite the students to write word problems for the following examples, and then solve them. Try to do this yourself!

$$\frac{1}{2} \div \frac{1}{6} = \qquad \frac{3}{4} \div \frac{1}{12} = \qquad \frac{2}{3} \div \frac{1}{6} =$$

$$\frac{3}{4} \div \frac{1}{6} = \qquad \frac{2}{3} \div \frac{1}{4} = \qquad \frac{1}{2} \div \frac{2}{3} =$$

Journal Reflection

How can you help students understand that, when 4 is divided by 2, the quotient is less than the dividend, but when $\frac{1}{4}$ is divided by $\frac{1}{8}$, the quotient is greater than the dividend?

the product of two fractions can be found by multiplying the numerators and then multiplying the denominators, doesn't it make sense that the quotient of two fractions should be found by dividing the two numerators and dividing the two denominators? First try the following examples using the "invert-and-multiply" rule that you are familiar with:

$$\frac{6}{8} \div \frac{2}{4} =$$

$$\frac{4}{10} \div \frac{1}{2} =$$

$$\frac{6}{15} \div \frac{3}{5} =$$

Now, try using the algorithm that was described above:

$$\frac{6 \div 2}{8 \div 4} = \frac{3}{2}$$

$$\frac{4 \div 1}{10 \div 2} = \frac{4}{5}$$

$$\frac{6 \div 3}{15 \div 5} = \frac{2}{3}$$

As you can see, in each case the same quotient is obtained. If so, why weren't you taught this algorithm in the first place? It certainly seems easier. Stop for a minute and consider this. Does the algorithm shown above *always* work? Well, you may have noticed that the numbers given were carefully chosen so that each pair of numerators and denominators divided without remainder. What would happen if this were not the case? Let's examine the following:

$$\frac{3}{7} \div \frac{2}{4} \rightarrow \frac{\frac{3}{2}}{\frac{7}{4}} \times \frac{\frac{4}{7}}{\frac{4}{7}} \rightarrow \frac{\frac{3}{2} \times \frac{4}{7}}{1} \rightarrow \frac{3 \times 4}{2 \times 7} \rightarrow \frac{3 \times 4}{7 \times 2} \rightarrow \frac{3}{7} \times \frac{4}{2}$$

To simplify this complex fraction, multiply numerator and denominator by 4/7 so that the denominator will equal 1.

Since multiplication is commutative, the order of the factors is irrelevant.

Compare the final arrangement of the fractions with the original example. What is the difference between them? Notice that the second fraction has been rewritten as its reciprocal and that the operation of division has been changed to the operation of multiplication. Since this will always be the outcome when dividing fractions, most people have been taught simply to take the shortcut and invert and multiply from the beginning. But this is not some mysterious procedure; it is simply a shortened version of the process just demonstrated.

While *generating* the above progression is beyond the abilities of most fifth- and sixth-graders, *observing* the process being modeled by the teacher is not. Moreover, it allows children to see that mathematical procedures resulted from people trying to make sense of things. Different people make sense in different ways, and all operations on numbers can be performed in a variety of ways.

Here is another algorithm that can be used for finding the quotient of two fractions. As you read through this section, mentally justify to yourself each step of the algorithm. Consider the following situation:

$$\frac{3}{7} \div \frac{2}{5} \rightarrow \frac{\frac{3}{7}}{\frac{2}{5}}$$

Choose a multiple common to both 7 and 5 (in this case 35), and multiply each fraction by this multiple, as shown here:

$$\frac{\frac{3}{7}}{\frac{2}{5}} \times \frac{35}{35}$$

$$\left(\frac{3}{7} \times \frac{35}{1}\right) \div \left(\frac{2}{5} \times \frac{35}{1}\right)$$

Simplify before multiplying:

$$\left(\frac{3}{7} \times \frac{\overset{5}{\cancel{35}}}{1}\right) \div \left(\frac{2}{\cancel{5}} \times \frac{\overset{7}{\cancel{35}}}{1}\right)$$

Multiply the expressions within each set of parentheses:

$$(3 \times 5) \div (2 \times 7)$$

$$15 \div 14 = \frac{15}{14}$$

What do you see as advantages and disadvantages of this algorithm over the standard invert-and-multiply algorithm?

Many of the suggestions that have guided our study of multiplication and division of fractions also pertain to those operations on decimals. For example, it is important to have students estimate the product or quotient before performing the algorithm and it is important to give students a tangible experience with the operation before introducing the standard algorithm. Students can often generalize from several examples and discover the rules themselves, and thus it is important to connect the operations with realistic contexts. Activity 8.3 offers a visual way to illustrate the process of multiplying decimals. Activity 8.4 offers a method for estimating products and quotients of decimals.

When introducing the algorithms for decimal multiplication and division, it is necessary to help students understand the reasons behind the movement and placement of the decimal points. One strategy that can be

Activity 8.3

A Visual Model for Multiplying Decimals

Lesson: Pairs

Distribute powers-of-ten blocks and graph paper to pairs of students. Pose the following problem:

- Decorative molding costs $3.70 per meter. How much would 0.8 of a meter cost?

Invite the students to share with their partner their estimate and the way they arrived at it. Most children should estimate a cost of approximately $3.00, since 0.8 meter is slightly less than a meter.

Illustrate $3.70 with the powers-of-ten blocks, as shown in Figure 8.3.

Since this represents the cost of one full meter of molding, we need a way to determine what part of this would represent the cost of only 0.8 meter. Provide students with the opportunity to think about how 0.8 of this amount could be represented. After sufficient time has elapsed, suggest that students trace the 3 flats and 7 longs onto graph paper, and shade in 0.8 of the boxes (Figure 8.4).

The students can now see that 0.80 + 0.80 + 0.80 + 0.56 = 2.96, and that this figure compares favorably with the original estimate of $3.00. Pose several other problems, and invite students to solve them with the blocks and graph paper.

Journal Reflection

Try to use this same visualization technique to illustrate the following fraction examples:

$$\frac{2}{3} \times \frac{5}{6} = \qquad \frac{3}{7} \times \frac{4}{9} = \qquad \frac{2}{5} \times \frac{2}{6} =$$

In your mind, how does this visual representation compare with that supplied by Cuisenaire rods? What do you see as advantages and disadvantages of each model?

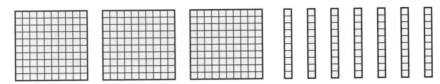

Figure 8.3

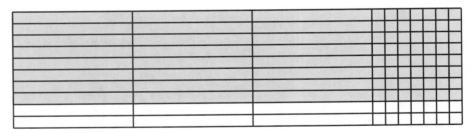

Figure 8.4

used to explain decimal multiplication is to obtain upper and lower limits for the product. Activity 8.5 shows how this might be done.

Performance-Based Assessment: Multiplying Decimals

It is useful to invite students to write an explanation of the major concepts they have been studying. Writing an explanation of a concept requires that students organize their thoughts and articulate them clearly. Often, while writing an explanation, students "see" connections they had not previously

Activity 8.4

Estimating Products and Quotients

Lesson: Whole Class

This activity will require the use of an overhead calculator. Two children each call out one number containing a whole number and a decimal, for example, 5.8 and 12.9. The members of the class then write down an estimate of their product. The overhead calculator is used to determine the actual answer, and the students compare their accuracy and share their strategies with each other. The activity continues for several minutes, before switching the operation to division.

Journal Reflection

Would you eventually expand the activity to include numbers carried out to the hundredths or thousandths place? Would you include whole numbers? Why or why not? Would it change the activity at all?

Activity 8.5

Multiplying Decimals

Lesson: Individual

Pose the following problem to students:

- Ribbon sells for $0.70 a meter. What is the cost of 2.5 meters of ribbon? After giving the students the opportunity to estimate the product (in this case, $1.50 would be a good estimate), invite the students to "sandwich" the example between the upper and lower whole-number bounds, as shown here:

$$
\begin{array}{ccc}
2 & 2.5 & 3 \\
\times\,0 & \times\,0.70 & \times\,1 \\
\hline
0 & & 3
\end{array}
$$

Therefore, the product of 2.5 and 0.70 must fall in between 0 and 3. When the actual multiplication is carried out, it results in a product of 1750, as shown here:

$$
\begin{array}{r}
2.5 \\
\times\,0.70 \\
\hline
1750
\end{array}
$$

There are only two places that the decimal could be placed to have a product that falls within the bounds of 0 and 3—either before the 1 or after the 1. Since the estimate of the product was $1.50, an answer of $1.75 is more reasonable than an answer of $0.175.

After doing several examples like this, display all of the examples to the students, and invite them to generalize about what happens with the decimal point in each product. It should be clear to them that the number of decimal places in the product can be predicted by finding the sum of the decimal places in each factor.

Journal Reflection

How could an understanding of fraction multiplication—specifically, an understanding that $\frac{1}{10} \times \frac{1}{10} = \frac{1}{100}$ and $\frac{1}{10} \times \frac{1}{100} = \frac{1}{1000}$—help students to understand decimal multiplication? Describe an activity that would help the children see this connection.

seen, and that they realize what they do and do not understand. Here is an example of a written task that requires students to explain the process of multiplying decimals. The task is followed by three sample student responses: one poor, one adequate, and one outstanding.

■ Imagine that your cousin is visiting from Iowa. She is in the same grade as you, but she has not yet learned anything about multiplying decimals. Use language to explain to her what it means to multiply decimals.

Inadequate response: When you multiply decimals you put one number on top of the other and you multiply regular. You have to do something with the dot.

Adequate response: Multiplying decimals is when you're finding some part of some part, or some part of a number and a part. It is important to estimate the answer before you multiply. This will help you put the decimal point in the right spot. If the top number has two decimal places and the bottom number has one, you need to have three (2 + 1) decimal places in the answer.

Outstanding response: Multiplying decimals is like multiplying fractions. You're not finding whole groups of whole groups. You're finding partial groups. Sometimes you're finding partial groups of partial groups, like when you know the cost of something and you want just a piece of it. You can find upper bounds and lower bounds for the answer by rounding both factors down to the nearest whole number and finding the product and then rounding both factors up to the nearest whole number and finding that product. The answer you're looking for has to be between those two bounds. If one factor is carried out to the tenths place and the other factor is carried out to the hundredths place, the answer will be carried out to the thousandths place. This is because a tenth of a hundredth is a thousandth.

When you ask students to write about a mathematical concept, it is helpful to sort their responses into three groups representing the different levels of understanding. If you list the characteristics and content of "adequate" and "outstanding" responses to share with the class, they can understand the assessment, and they can compare outstanding papers with their own. For example, the "adequate response" given above could be evaluated in the following way:

■ Response is understandable and clear

■ Response accurately indicates placement of decimal point

■ Response describes the process of multiplying fractions reasonably well

The "outstanding response" given above could be described in the following way:

- Response is comprehensive, clear, and complete
- Response connects multiplying decimals with other similar operations, and indicates context in which it could be used
- Response addresses strategies for obtaining an accurate answer
- Response explains *why* decimal is placed in a particular position

Students become more comfortable with mathematical writing assignments as they get more practice. Ideally, these tasks will help them become better able to articulate their solutions to problems, their questions, and their conceptions of mathematical ideas. This is one of the reasons that every Activity in this text is followed by a Journal Reflection. It gives you the opportunity to develop your own mathematical writing abilities, and to recognize the importance of writing in learning and teaching mathematics.

Division of decimals is similar to division of fractions in that the standard algorithm is not the only way the quotient can be obtained, but it is a fairly simple way, and it helps students correctly locate the decimal point in the quotient. Activity 8.6 models a way students can be introduced to the standard algorithm.

Activity 8.6

Division of Decimals

Lesson: Individual

Pose the following problem to students:

- A class treasury contains $57.75. Each student in the class contributed $1.75. How many students are in the class?

An estimate of the quotient can be found by rounding 57.75 to 60 and rounding 1.75 to 2, and then dividing to arrive at an estimate of 30 students in the class. Finding the precise answer will be simpler if the divisor were to be a whole number, since it is difficult to determine how many 1.75s are in 57.

  Invite students to examine the following progression, and to generalize about what is happening:

$$8 \div 4 = 2$$
$$80 \div 40 = 2$$
$$800 \div 400 = 2$$
$$8000 \div 4000 = 2$$

The students can see that multiplying both dividend and divisor by the same multiple of 10 does not affect the quotient. Multiplying both 57.75 and 1.75 by 100 will cause the divisor to be rewritten as a whole number, and the algorithm will become simpler, as shown here:

$$1.75 \times 100 = 175 \qquad 57.75 \times 100 = 5775$$

$$
\begin{array}{r}
3\ 3 \\
1\,7\,5\,\overline{)5\,7\,7\,5} \\
-\,5\,2\,5 \\
\hline
5\,2\,5 \\
-\,5\,2\,5 \\
\hline
0
\end{array}
$$

Therefore, there are 33 students in the class.

Journal Reflection

How might you incorporate calculators into this activity?

Computer Software

Software programs are available to help students practice their computational skills on fractions and decimals. *Mighty Math Number Heroes* (Edmark) has a character, Fraction Man, who invites students to create fireworks composed of, say, $\frac{7}{12}$ purple and $\frac{5}{12}$ yellow. This software engages children in the addition, subtraction, and multiplication of fractions, and the conversion of decimals to fractions.

In *Reader Rabbit's Math* (The Learning Corporation), part of the Reading and Math Series, a visually appealing program invites children to practice their skills in fractions, time, money, and symmetry. As with many software programs, the students receive a certain reward for correct answers (in this case, they are able to save Reader Rabbit).

Some programs, such as *Teasers by Tobbs: Numbers and Operations* (O'Brien, Sunburst), offer opportunities to practice mathematical skills in several areas. In this program students can work on computation in such areas as whole numbers, decimals, integers, and fractions. Through the use of a grid for recording answers, this software allows for multiple answers. As with any opportunity to practice skills, students benefit most from sessions that are brief, frequent, and use a variety of modalities.

Percents

It is a logical progression to move from a study of decimals to a study of percents. Percent, which literally means "per one hundred," is a useful way

---

Activity 8.7

Percent Designs

Lesson: Individual

Distribute a sheet of grid paper, 10 units by 10 units, to each student, along with markers, crayons, or colored pencils. Discuss the meaning of the root "cent." Most children are familiar with the words *century, Centigrade, centipede, centimeter,* and *cent.* Help the children to articulate that percent means "how many out of 100." Invite the students to color a design in the squares in the grid paper, then write a few sentences about the percents of different colors and the strategies used to create the design. Figure 8.5 offers an example.

Journal Reflection

An alternative to inviting students to create a visual design and then determine the percent of each color contained in their design is to assign those values first and then ask the students to create a design that is, for example, 55% red, 15% blue, and 30% yellow. Which approach do you think is more appropriate? Do you think it matters? Why?

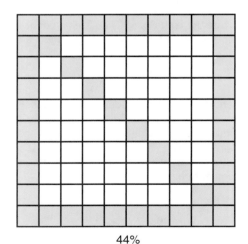

44%

I colored in 44% of my square. First, I colored the outside edges. That was 36 squares because 10 × 4 is 40, but I had to subtract 4 because the 4 corners got counted twice. I also colored 8 squares along the diagonal. 36 + 8 = 44

Figure 8.5

to compare a partial quantity to the whole quantity. Like fractions and decimals, percents are parts of a whole. If we think of decimals as fractions all of whose denominators are powers of ten, then we can think of percents as fractions whose denominators are all one hundred. You can see the close elationship between decimals to the hundredths place and percents. Activities 8.7 and 8.8 are examples of the ways in which percents can be introduced to students.

Activity 8.8

Eating Percents

Lesson: Individual

Distribute a clean sheet of 11 × 14 paper and a Fun Pack of candy-coated chocolate candies to each student. Invite them to record their estimate of the number of chocolate pieces in their pack, and to predict if everyone's pack contains the same number of candies. After the estimates have been made, invite the children to open their packs and pour the candies onto the clean sheet of paper. (Caution the students that the candies cannot be eaten until the end of the lesson.) Have the students count the candies, and compare that number to their estimate.

Have the students arrange the candies into groups by color. Discuss which color is usually the scarcest in the packs, and which color is usually the most common. Invite the students to create a chart that compares the number of candies of each color in fractional, decimal, and percent form. A sample is shown in Figure 8.6.

The process of converting a fraction to a decimal can be explained by pointing out that $\frac{12}{27}$ is another way to represent 12 ÷ 27. Since this division will clearly result in a quotient less than 1, the division will be symbolized in decimal form, as shown here. If each decimal quotient is carried out to the hundredths place, the conversion to a percent will be simplified.

$$27 \overline{)\begin{array}{r} .44 \\ 12.00 \end{array}}$$

Students can verify that their fraction and decimal values are correct by making sure that their TOTAL column adds to one whole, whether that whole is represented as $\frac{27}{27}$, 1.00, or 100%.

Journal Reflection

Converting a fraction with a denominator other than 100 to a percent is often confusing for children. Would you alter this activity so that each child gets a baggie with exactly 100 candies in it? Why or why not?

	Number	Fraction	Decimal	Percent
brown				
orange				
yellow				
green				
red				
blue				
TOTAL				

Figure 8.6

Activity 8.9

Mental Percents

Lesson: Small Groups

Supply a calculator to each group of three or four students. Present the following scenarios and invite the students to estimate the answer mentally. They then discuss the different strategies used by members of the group, and use the calculator to determine the accuracy of their estimates.

■ A skateboard, originally priced at $49.99, is on sale for 10% off. What is the sale price? One possible strategy is: "I know that 10% means 10 out of 100. So if the skateboard cost $100.00, it would mean $10.00 off. Since the skateboard only costs about $50.00, the amount off should be $5.00. That would make the new price about $45.00."

■ What is the tax on a television set that costs $199.99?

One possible strategy is: "The tax in this county is 7%, which means 7 cents for every dollar. That means the tax is 700 cents for every hundred dollars, or $7.00 for every hundred dollars. Since the TV costs almost $200.00, the tax should be about $14.00."

■ The bill in a restaurant is $41.20. What is an appropriate tip?

One possible strategy is: "I think a tip should be 15%, and 15% can be found by figuring out 10% and adding on half of that amount (5%). I know that 10% of $40.00 is $4.00, so half of that is $2.00. Four dollars plus two dollars is six dollars. That is the tip I would leave, if the service was good."

Journal Reflection

What suggestions would you make to students who have difficulty doing mental math? Do you think everyone can become skilled at mental math if they are given enough practice? What ramifications does this belief have for your teaching?

Percents are used most frequently in day-to-day life to determine mentally a sale price, sales tax, or a gratuity in a restaurant. Activity 8.9 gives an example of how students can develop their mental math powers. Demonstrating how the different topics of mathematics can relate to and inform each other, Activity 8.10 offers a way to connect the concept of percents with number concepts.

Measurement of Mass and Volume

In the elementary classroom, measuring mass and volume are not always given the same amount of attention as linear measurement. This is unfortunate, since measuring these attributes is fundamental to many science activities.

Activity 8.10

Percents on a Grid

Lesson: Pairs

Distribute two copies of a hundreds chart, two different-colored pencils, and a blank spinner face to each pair of children. Engage them in the following activity (Figure 8.7).

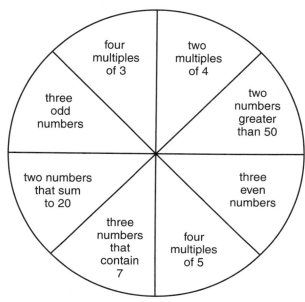

Figure 8.7

■ Take turns spinning the spinner. When it is your turn, use your colored pencil to color in the numbers that are described on the spinner. The game is over when one of you cannot make a move. When you have finished playing the game, fill in this information:

Player 1: Number of colored squares represented as a

Fraction _____ Decimal _____
Percent _____

Player 2: Number of colored squares represented as a

Fraction _____ Decimal _____
Percent _____

Number of blank squares represented as

Fraction _____ Decimal _____
Percent _____

If you added up each column, what would you predict about each of your totals?

Journal Reflection

What memory aid would you offer to students who had trouble remembering the place-value names for decimals?

Measurement for Students in Grades 6–8

The NCTM *Principles and Standards* offer the following suggestions for helping students in grades 6–8 to understand measurement. In grades 6–8, students should

■ Understand both metric and customary systems of measurement, including relationships among units of the same system.

■ Use ratios and proportions to solve problems. . . . (pp. 232–33)

Although many people use the terms *weight* and *mass* interchangeably, the words are not synonymous. **Weight** is the measure of the pull of gravity on a given **mass.** Since the force of gravity varies according to the proximity of an object to the center of gravity, the same mass would have a slightly greater weight at the bottom of Death Valley than it would have at the top of Mt. McKinley. This is because the gravitational pull of the earth is greater as you get closer to the center of the earth.

The basic measure of weight and mass in the English standard system of measurement is the pound. A **pound** is defined as the gravitational force at sea level on an object that has a mass of 1 pound. Since the numerical difference between weight and mass on the surface of the earth is virtually indistinguishable, and since elementary school students are more familiar with the term *weight,* in this book we will use "weight" to refer to both weight and mass.

There are only two units of measurement for weight in the English Standard system. They are listed here:

$$16 \text{ ounces (oz)} = 1 \text{ pound (lb)}$$
$$2000 \text{ pounds} = 1 \text{ ton}$$

In the metric system, the basic root unit of measure for weight is the gram. A raisin weighs approximately 1 gram. In the metric system, the units of weight conform to the pattern that was established for its units of linear measurement. The relationships among the metric units of weight measurement, along with realistic examples to help you develop a mental image of the units, are illustrated here.

Unit	Symbol	Relationship to root unit	Real-world example
Kilogram	kg	1000 grams	Textbook
Hectogram	hg	100 grams	Box of gelatin dessert mix
Dekagram	dag	10 grams	Stick of gum
Gram	g	root unit	Raisin
Decigram	dg	0.1 gram	(These small units are
Centigram	cg	0.01 gram	commonly used within
Milligram	mg	0.001 gram	a pharmaceutical context.)

In addition, 1000 kilograms is equal to a metric ton. Since a kilogram weighs approximately 2.2 pounds, 1 metric ton is approximately equal to 2200 pounds. Activities 8.11 and 8.12 will help children develop an understanding of measuring weight.

Activity 8.11

Comparing Weights

Lesson: Pairs

Distribute to each pair of children a box of "stuff" (rocks, jar lids, crayons, coins, shells, buttons, rubber bands) and a sheet of paper with HEAVIER written on one side and LIGHTER written on the other. The children take turns choosing two objects from the box, holding them in each hand, and placing them on the appropriate side of the paper. The other partner can take the opportunity to hold the objects and agree or disagree with the partner's placement.

Journal Reflection

How would you settle any disagreements that might arise between partners?

Activity 8.12

Finding a Particular Weight

Lesson: Small Groups

Equip each group of four children with a balance scale and a set of metric weights. Ask them to answer the following questions:

- How many objects can you find that weigh approximately 1 kg? What are they?

- How many objects can you find that weigh more than 1 kg? What are they?

- How many objects can you find that weigh approximately 1 hg? What are they?

- How many objects can you find that weigh approximately 1 dag? What are they?

- How many objects can you find that weigh approximately 1 g? What are they?

Provide an opportunity for the students to share their lists with the class and to discuss any strategies they used to locate the objects.

Journal Reflection

What strategies would you use to help children remember the various prefixes of the metric system and their relative dimensions?

The volume of a three-dimensional object is a measure of the amount of space it occupies. When we speak of the volume of a container, we typically refer to the amount of matter it can contain. Children often confuse the concepts of weight and volume. They think that if one object is bigger than another, it must also be heavier. You can help then to distinguish between weight and volume by displaying a brick and a sponge of approximately the same size. If they occupy the same space, they have equal volumes, but they certainly do not weigh the same.

When area was introduced, it was described as a measure of the number of squares that *cover* a region. Volume is the measure of the number of cubes that *fill* an object. The following table contains the units of volume measurement for the English standard system of measurement:

$$1 \text{ tablespoon (tbsp)} = \tfrac{1}{2} \text{ fluid ounce}$$

$$1 \text{ cup (C)} = 8 \text{ fluid ounces}$$

$$1 \text{ pint (pt)} = 2 \text{ cups}$$

$$1 \text{ quart} = 2 \text{ pints}$$

$$1 \text{ gallon} = 4 \text{ quarts}$$

Offering student a visual representation of the way in which these units connect with each other can help them remember the equivalences. Figure 8.8 is an example of a display you might make for the classroom. The students can copy their own version into their math notebooks for future reference.

Figure 8.8

The metric system units of volume conform to the pattern already introduced for measuring length and mass. The relationships among the metric units of volume measurement, along with real-life examples to help you develop mental images of these units, are illustrated here.

Unit	Symbol	Relationship to root unit	Real-world example
Kiloliter	Kl	1000 liters	Two-person hot tub
Hectoliter	hL	100 liters	Small bathtub
Dekaliter	daL	10 liters	Water-cooler container
Liter	L	root unit	Bottle of seltzer
Deciliter	dL	0.1 liter	Juice glass
Centiliter	cL	0.01 liter	Serving spoon full
Milliliter	Ml	0.001 liter	Eyedropper full

Activities 8.13 and 8.14 are designed to introduce children to volume measurement. However, recall from Chapter 2 that most children in kindergarten and many children in first grade are unable to conserve number,

Activity 8.13

Comparing Volumes

Lesson: Pairs or Small Groups

This activity will be most easily done at a water table or in a sandbox. If not available, have pairs of children work in the top or bottom of a gift box to limit the mess. Distribute to each group of children a variety of clear, plastic containers such as food storage containers, empty juice bottles, empty medicine bottles, or empty liquid soap containers. Invite the children to arrange the containers in order, from least to greatest volume. Encourage the children to test their hypotheses by pouring sand, water, or rice into the containers. After ample time has been devoted to this activity, invite the students to try to identify the container with the least volume in the whole classroom, and the container with the greatest volume in the whole classroom. Engage the children in a discussion about the various strategies that were used to determine relative volume.

Journal Reflection

This activity engages children in an exploration of liquid volume. Describe an activity that would help children explore the volume of solid objects, or objects that are not filled with pourable contents.

Activity 8.14

Making Lemonade

Lesson: Small Groups

Distribute to each group of students a plastic pitcher, a measuring cup with metric measures (most commercially available measuring cups have both English standard and metric measurements), a spoon, lemon juice, and superfine sugar. Invite each group to follow this recipe for lemonade:

> 1 liter of water
>
> 50 Ml of superfine sugar
>
> 50 Ml of lemon juice

Measure the water into the pitcher, Stir in the sugar until dissolved. Add the lemon juice, and lemon slices, if you wish. Enjoy!

After each group has made their lemonade, pose the following problem to the class.

- Each of the paper cups can hold approximately 200 Ml. How many cups will we get from each recipe? How can we tell if we have made enough lemonade for everyone?

Journal Reflection

How would you respond to a parent who questions your classroom emphasis on measuring with the metric system?

length, weight, or volume. This means that, for these children, the appearance of an object defines the reality of the object. They do not yet understand that certain properties of an object or a set of objects (number, weight, volume, length) are *invariant* despite any changes made to their appearance.

A child who does not yet conserve volume will think that a tall glass of milk poured into two cups is "more" milk when it is in the two cups. Likewise, a tall, narrow glass will be judged to contain more liquid than a short, squat glass, even if equal amounts of liquid are poured into each glass in the child's presence. If a child is shown two identical balls of clay, and one is flattened in the child's presence, the child who does not yet conserve volume will no longer think that the amounts of clay are the same.

Piaget's findings indicate that children's early experiences with measuring length, volume, and weight should be informal, comparative, and experiential. Be cautious about judging children's responses to be wrong. For the child's level of development, the response may be perfectly reasonable.

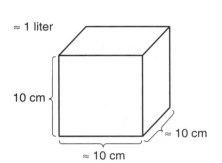

Figure 8.9

If someone were to ask you "How many ounces are in a yard?" you would likely think them crazy. In the English standard system or customary system of measurement this question has no meaning, since there are no connections among the units for measuring length, weight, or volume. However, this is not the case for the metric system. You will recall that the entire metric system was created out of the basic unit of the meter. If you were to cut off the top of a milk container so that a height of 10 cm was left (Figure 8.9), the resulting container would hold approximately 1 liter of water. In addition, the container filled with cool water would weigh approximately 1 kg.

Notice the connection that has been made here. A cube of approximately 1 dm on each side holds approximately 1 liter of water, and weighs approximately 1 kg. If the original cube were exactly 1 dm^3, then it would hold exactly 1 liter and, if filled with water, weigh exactly 1 kg. A connection has been made among a measurement of length (a cube that measures 1 dm on each side), a measurement of volume (holds 1 liter) and a measurement of weight (weighs 1 kg). Two versions of this relationship are pictured in Figure 8.10.

The accompanying interdisciplinary lesson plan incorporates science and involves students in measuring a given volume of water, placing the water in a freezer, and comparing the volumes of the liquid and the ice.

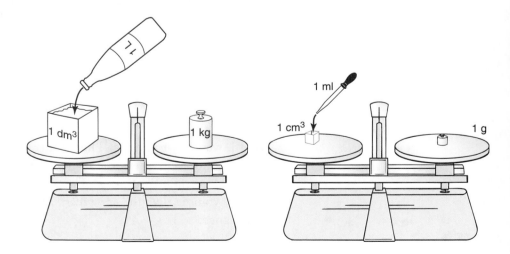

Figure 8.10

Interdisciplinary Lesson Plan

Grade 4 or 5   **Concept** Expansion of Liquids

Topic Measuring Volumes and Making Predictions

Student Objectives After completing this lesson, students should be able to. . .

- Measure liquid volumes
- Make and explain predictions
- Generalize about the behavior of water when its temperature changes.

Materials Plastic containers, graduated cylinders, waterproof markers.

Motivation Explain to the students that you have an above-the-ground pool in your backyard. Every fall, to get the pool ready for the winter, you have to drain about ⅛ of the water out of the pool. Ask the children to explain why they think this must be done. Possible responses are:

- "So the water doesn't get too dirty."
- "To leave room for the snow."
- "So you can take the filter out of the pool."

Tell the students the experiment they are going to perform will help them understand why some water is drained from the pool before the beginning of winter.

Procedure (1) Using the graduated cylinders, have the students measure precisely 100 Ml of water. Pour this water into plastic containers, in preparation for freezing. As accurately as possible, use a marker to mark the water level in the container. Pose the following question to students: You have measured out exactly 100 Ml of water. After the water is frozen, do you think there will still be exactly 100 Ml? Do you think there will be more? Do you think there will be less? Discuss

(continued)

An important aspect of learning about measurement is knowing when to use what unit of measurement to obtain needed information. The following performance-based assessment helps you determine which students have an understanding of the uses of the different units of measurement.

Performance-Based Assessment: Identifying Appropriate Measures

Ask the students to respond to the following questions. What unit of measurement might you use if you wanted to know

- Your height
- Your weight
- The amount of juice in a pitcher
- The weight of your baseball bat

Lesson Plan (continued)

with your partners what you think is going to happen, and why you think that. (2) Place the containers in a freezer overnight. (3) Remove the containers and ask the students to compare the level of the ice in the containers with the levels marked on each container. Ask them to explain the difference in the levels. (4) Ask the students to predict what would happen to the level if the ice melts. (5) Place the containers in a warm spot to hasten the melting of the ice. When the ice has melted, pour the water back into the graduated cylinders for a more accurate measurement. Ask the students to explain why the water measurement is once again at the original level. (6) Invite the students to write a paragraph summarizing the experiment, their predictions, and their findings. As water approaches its freezing temperature, at about 39°F (4°C), the water molecules take on a crystalline form. "The latticelike arrangement of these crystals takes up more space, about 4% more, than an equal amount of free-moving water molecules." (Gega, 1986). Since the crystals take up more space, the volume of the water expands as it changes to ice. When the ice melts, the molecules lose their crystalline structure, and the volume of the water reverts back to its original measure.

Assessment Read carefully the paragraphs written by the students. Look for the following characteristics: a well-sequenced account of the steps taken, an attempt to make sense of the activity that takes all of the data into account, inclusion of the students' predictions, and whether the outcomes of the activity supported those predictions.

References Hazen, Robert, and James Trefil. *Science Matters: Achieving Scientific Literacy*. New York, Doubleday, 1991.

Zeman, Anne, and Kate Kelly. *Everything You Need to Know About Science Homework*. New York, Scholastic, 1994.

Journal Entry An analysis of the lesson, to be filled in by the teacher at the end of the day.

- The distance to Hawaii
- How much water was in your bathtub
- The size of your bedroom
- How far you could throw a baseball
- The amount of medicine in a medicine bottle
- The weight of a chocolate chip

It is possible to respond to these questions with either metric or English standard system units. The students' responses can be characterized as either accurate, close, or inaccurate. Depending on students' responses, you might decide to spend more time on the measurement of length, volume, or mass.

Proportional Thinking

Proportional reasoning is an important concept, not only because of the real-life applications of proportions in such fields as art, architecture, and science but also because it is an example of a concept that depends upon the ability to generalize about a relationship and then apply it to a new situation. In this way, it is not dissimilar to an analogy, where a relationship between two things is suggested as a basis for a relationship between two other things. The ability to identify and create analogies is an important thinking skill.

Despite the importance of proportional reasoning, it is a concept with which many people struggle. Cramer, Post, and Currier (1993) write:

> Consider this problem. Sue and Julie were running equally fast around a track. Sue started first. When she had run 9 laps, Julie had run 3 laps. When Julie completed 15 laps, how many laps had Sue run? Thirty-two out of 33 preservice elementary education teachers in a mathematics methods class solved this problem by setting up and solving a proportion: $\frac{9}{3} = \frac{x}{15}$; $3x = 135$; $x = 45$. While these students knew a procedure for solving a proportion, they did not realize that this particular problem did not represent a proportional situation. Therefore, the traditional proportion algorithm was not an appropriate strategy to use. (p. 159)

Distinguishing between a nonproportional situation such as the one above, where the relationship between the two quantities is defined by addition or subtraction (Sue was 6 laps ahead of Julie, but was running at the same rate of speed), and a proportional situation, where the relationship is defined by multiplication, is critical. Take a moment to think how the problem about Sue and Julie could be rewritten to make it a problem involving proportional reasoning. Here is an example:

- For every 9 laps that Sue runs, Julie runs 3. When Julie has completed 15 laps, how many laps has Sue run?

The correct answer to this problem is 45, because the relationship between Sue's pace and Julie's pace is a multiplicative one. It could be expressed as: Sue's pace = Julie's pace times 3.

Young children can be given an informal introduction to proportional relationships by involving them in a one-to-many correspondence, as described in Activity 8.15. Activity 8.16 offers an informal introduction to proportions by involving children in a cooking activity. The two important concepts to be demonstrated by a cooking activity with children are *combination* and *transformation*. Ingredients are combined in such a way that they form a new substance that does not resemble the individual ingredients, and then they are transformed, typically through exposure to heat or cold. In this activity, water and gelatin dessert powder are combined to form a sweet, colored liquid, and then the mixture is chilled to form a gelatin dessert.

Activity 8.15

Gingerbread People

Lesson: Individual

Begin by reading a version of the classic story "The Gingerbread Man" to the class. Then distribute construction-paper cutouts of a gingerbread person to each child. Invite the children to draw a face and to glue three buttons on each one of their gingerbread people. Involve the class in a discussion about how many buttons are needed for one gingerbread person, for two, for three, and so on. Display the cutouts so that the children can count the actual buttons to arrive at the answers. Record the data in a chart something like this:

Number of gingerbread people	Number of buttons
1	3
2	6
3	9
4	12
5	15

Challenge the children to predict how many buttons six gingerbread people will require. Encourage the children to explain how they arrived at their answers.

Journal Reflection

This activity was introduced as being an example of a one-to-many correspondence. What do you see as the connection between a one-to-many correspondence and a proportion? What do you see as the connection, if any, between a many-to-one correspondence and a proportion?

Activity 8.16

Making a Gelatin Dessert

Lesson: Pairs

Pose the following problem to students:

- To make this box of gelatin dessert, I need to add 2 cups of water. If I want to make 6 boxes, how many cups of water will I need?

Allow time for the children, working in pairs, to solve the problem. Encourage them to share their strategies. Some possible responses are:

- "We drew six squares and wrote '2' inside each square. Then we counted up all the twos."
- "We made a chart, like this:

  1–2
  2–4
  3–6
  4–8
  5–10
  6–12

  so we knew that we needed 12 cups of water."
- "We put up 6 fingers, and then we counted by twos, like this: 2, 4, 6, 8, 10, 12."

To culminate the activity, of course, make the gelatin! This provides other opportunities for mathematical problem solving as the students try to determine how many servings are needed for the class, how many servings are contained in each box, how many servings can be obtained from the six boxes, how many ounces are in a half-cup serving, and so on.

Journal Reflection

Would you use this lesson as an opportunity to introduce the words *combination* and *transformation*? Why or why not? If you would, at what point in the lesson and in what manner would you do so?

There is a clear connection between the concept of a proportion and certain measurement concepts, such as using the key of a map to determine actual distances. Since a proportion represents an equality between two ratios, the ratio of map scale to map distance can be used to predict the ratio between map distance and actual distance. Bringing this mathematical concept into social studies lessons involving maps and their interpretation will allow you to show students one practical application of proportional reasoning.

There are many other applications of proportional reasoning. For example, the concepts of a pattern or a scale model are based on proportions. Activity 8.17 offers an example of a way to engage students in proportional reasoning as they design a quilt pattern. It is not always the case that proportional relationships can be defined by a whole-number factor. Activity 8.18 uses a function machine to illustrate to students how numbers can be proportionally related by other than whole numbers.

Performance-Based Assessment: Proportions

Invite the students to think of a situation that could be accurately described by the following proportion, and to explain why this proportion is reasonable in the described context:

$$\frac{1}{4} = \frac{4}{16}$$

Activity 8.17

Designing a Quilt

Lesson: Individual

To each student, distribute a sheet of cm-squared graph paper, a straight edge, and a pencil. Invite the students to design a quilt pattern in a 4 × 4 square on the graph paper. Figure 8.11 presents some possible student designs.

Explain to the students that the designs must be enlarged so that a pattern can be created to make the actual quilt squares. Invite the students to recreate their design on a 20 × 20 cm square, and to be prepared to share their strategies with the class. Here are some strategies that might be offered by the creators of the above designs:

- "With a pencil, I drew lines to divide the large square into four smaller squares. Then I sketched ¼ of the original design in each of the smaller squares."

- "Since the length of the sides of the larger square were five times the length of the sides of the original square, I knew that the coordinates of any point on the original square should be multiplied by 5 to get the coordinates of the larger square. The center of my original design was at point (2, 2). This means that the center of the enlarged design should be at (10, 10). This helped me find the location of each of the parts of the design on the larger square."

- I realized that the base of each of the triangles in the original design was 2 lengths long. This meant that the base of each of the triangles in the larger version should be 10 lengths long. This helped me draw the triangles the right size."

Journal Reflection

In this activity, the lengths of the sides of the original square were increased by a factor of 5. Was this also the case with the area of the original square? How can you explain the change in area from the original square to the larger square?

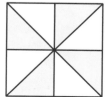 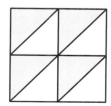 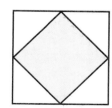

Figure 8.11

Activity 8.18

Function Machines

Lesson: Whole Class

For the first few examples, you should probably be the "machine" to illustrate how the game is played. Make up a set of index cards with instructions similar to the following:

Multiply by $\frac{1}{2}$

Divide by 3

Multiply by $2\frac{1}{2}$

Multiply by 5

Invite the students to call out a number. As they call out their number, you write it down as the INPUT, and also write down the OUTPUT (defined by the instructions on the index card) on the following chart. If the card that reads "Multiply by ½" is used, the chart would look something like this:

INPUT	OUTPUT
2	1
5	$2\frac{1}{2}$
10	5
7	$3\frac{1}{2}$

When students think they have identified the function, they are encouraged to write it down and sit quietly. When the game has been played for an adequate amount of time, invite a student to define the function both verbally and symbolically. In this case, a student might say:

- "Every number that went in was divided in half. I symbolized this by

$$O = \frac{1}{2} I$$

since the Output was ½ the Input."

When students have had some practice with this activity, encourage students to make up their own rules, and to challenge the rest of the class to identify the operation.

Journal Reflection

Specifically describe three extensions of this activity.

Strength in Numbers

Fractions and Decimals

Cooperative Group Model: Jigsaw

Working in groups of three, each member chooses one of these three continents: Europe, Africa, or South America. Each group member conducts research to obtain copies of the flags of six countries from their assigned continent. After sketching the flags on graph paper, members identify the three or four predominant colors of each flag, and determine the portion of the flag covered by each of these colors. Members represent these regions covered by the predominant colors as fractions, decimals, and percents.

After filling out the following information on each flag:

Predominant colors: _____

Portion of each color in fractional form:

_____

Portion of each color in decimal form:

_____

Portion of each color in percent form:

_____

each group member displays copies of the six flags along with the above numerical description. The other two group members are challenged to connect each flag with its appropriate numerical description.

As an extension, discuss these questions in your groups, and again with the whole class:

- Is it possible to generalize about flags from a particular continent?
- Do certain colors predominate in certain regions?
- Are certain designs popular on certain continents?
- If a new country were to be created on your continent, predict what its flag might look like.

For example, students could describe a box of 16 cookies, ¼ of which are chocolate; they could describe a paper folded into 16ths, where each fourth of the paper contained 4 of the 16ths; they could describe a group of 16 people, 4 of whom wear glasses. Think about a rubric you would use to evaluate students' responses. Would you have the students write down their descriptions? Why or why not?

Fractions, decimals, percents, measurement, and proportions are challenging topics for students and for teachers. Keep in mind that connecting these topics to real-world applications and focusing on the understanding of concepts as opposed to memorization of computational rules will help students see the value of studying these topics.

Summary

The content of this chapter moved from addition and subtraction to multiplication and division of fractions and decimals. Apparent in the progression of activities recommended for students is the continuing belief in the importance of having students understand the concept of an operation before asking them to learn and apply an algorithm. The chapter introduced percents as an example of one of the ways in which parts of a whole can be imagined, and made connections among fractional representations, decimal representations, and percents.

Introductory work on linear measurement that appeared in the previous chapter was expanded here to include the measurement of capacity and mass. The chapter underscored the pattern-like nature of the metric system, and made connections among units for measuring length, capacity, and mass.

The final section of this chapter addressed the concept of proportional thinking, and you were asked to consider the connections between the concept of proportional reasoning and the geometric concept of similarity. Do you see how ease in understanding and computing with fractions and decimals can help students solve proportional problems?

Extending Your Learning

1. In your own words, describe the nature of the relationship among fractions, decimals, and percents. How are they the same? How are they different?

2. How is the teaching of multiplication and division with fractions similar to teaching multiplication and division with whole numbers? How is it different?

3. Write a realistic word problem to correspond to the following examples:

$$\frac{1}{2} \times \frac{3}{4} =$$

$$\frac{3}{4} \times \frac{1}{2} =$$

$$5 \times 3.5 =$$

4. Research a manipulative called *fraction circles.* (See, for example, *Start with Manipulatives* by Rosamond Welshman-Tischler, published by Cuisenaire Corporation of America, or *Fraction Circle Activities: A Sourcebook for Grades 4–8* by Barbara Berman and Fredda Friederwitzer, Dale Seymour Publications.) Compare fraction circles with pattern blocks and Cuisenaire rods, the two manipulatives discussed in this chapter. What advantages and disadvantages do you see in each material? How would you justify to an administrator a request to purchase any or all of these materials?

5. What do you think about creating a classroom store to help students connect the study of decimals with their understanding of money? Describe in detail how the store might operate and the activities in which students might engage.

6. Write a clear, succinct explanation, appropriate for students in grades 5 or 6, as to why any number over itself equals one.

7. Examine an elementary mathematics textbook currently in use. Do a count of the pages devoted to the development of fractional *concepts* compared with the number of pages devoted to *computation* with fractions. Discuss your findings with classmates who examined different textbooks. Do you see any difference among the books?

8. Write an interdisciplinary lesson plan on a measurement concept for grade 8.

9. Many people use the cross-multiply rule to test for the equivalence of two fractions. Discuss this method, and explain why it works. Would you teach it to students? Why or why not?

10. Discuss the connection between the concepts of similarity and proportions. How, specifically, might you use one to illustrate the other?

Internet Resources

http://www.ed.gov/pubs/parents/Math/index.html
This website, titled Helping Your Child Learn Math, is sponsored by the U.S. Department of Education. It contains simple but worthwhile activities that parents and children can do together at home to help develop mathematical confidence and competence. The site contains several measurement, estimation, consumer, and fractional activities.

http://www.mathcounts.org
This website is devoted to students in the seventh and eighth grades. It offers problems of the week, interactive challenges, and information about the annual national competition for "mathletes" known as MATHCOUNTS. Winners of local competitions are sent to Washington, D.C. in the spring for the annual national competition.

http://www.tenet.edu/teks/math
This website has been developed by the Texas Statewide Systemic Initiative. It contains information on curriculum by grade level and content strand, professional development resources, and suggestions on implementing and evaluating programs. It also addresses such issues as equity, technology, and instruction and assessment.

Bibliography

Artzt, Alice. (1991) The secondary mathematics curriculum in action: Using the copy machine to explore ideas of congruence and similarity. *New York State Mathematics Teachers' Journal 41*(1): 22–24.

Baroody, Arthur J. (1989). One point of view: Manipulatives don't come with guarantees. *Arithmetic Teacher 37: 4–5.*

Berman, Barbara, and Fredda Friederwitzer. (1988). Fraction circle activities: A sourcebook for grades 4–8. Palo Alto, CA: Dale Seymour.

Copeland, Richard W. (1970). *How children learn mathematics: Teaching implications of Piaget's research.* New York: Macmillan.

Cramer, Kathleen, Thomas Post, and Sarah Currier. (1993). Learning and teaching ratio and proportion: Research implications. In Douglas T. Owens (ed.), *Research ideas for the classroom: Middle grades mathematics.* New York: Macmillan.

Edelman, Leslie. (1997). The fractions of a day. *Mathematics Teaching in the Middle School 3*(3).

Geddes, Dorothy. (1994). *Measurement in the middle grades.* Reston, VA: NCTM.

Gega, Peter C. (1986). *Science in elementary education,* 5th ed. New York: Macmillan.

Hazen, Robert, and James Trefil. (1991). *Science matters: Achieving scientific literacy.* New York: Doubleday.

Kamii, Constance, and Mary Ann Warrington. (1999). Teaching fractions: Fostering children's own reasoning. In Lee V. Stiff (ed.), *Developing mathematical reasoning in grades K–12. National Council of Teachers of Mathematics 1999 yearbook.* Reston, VA: NCTM.

Kieren, Tom, Brent Davis, and Ralph Mason. (1996). Fraction flags: Learning from children to help children learn. *Mathematics Teaching in the Middle School 2*(1).

Mack, Nancy. (1998). Building a foundation for understanding the multiplication of fractions. *Teaching Children Mathematics 5*(1).

Mack, Nancy. (1990). Learning fractions with understanding: Building on informal knowledge. *Journal for Research in Mathematics Education 21*:16–32.

Mein, Anne, W., Christine Rauscher, and Ellen Taylor. (1989). *Content area reading: Math measurement,* p. 28. New York: Random House.

Middleton, James A., and Marja van de Heuvel-Panhuizen. (1995). The ratio table. *Mathematics Teaching in the Middle School 1*(4).

Mighty math number heroes. Software. Redmond, WA: Edmark.

O'Brien, Thomas C. *Teasers by Tobbs: Numbers and operations.* Pleasantville, NY: Sunburst.

Oppenheimer, Lauren, and Robert P. Hunting. (1999). Relating fractions and decimals: Listening to students talk. *Mathematics Teaching in the Middle School 4*(5).

Reading and math series: Reader Rabbit's math. Cambridge, MA: Learning Company.

Reys, Barbara J., Ok-Kyeong Kim, and Jennifer M. Bay. (1999). Establishing fraction benchmarks. *Mathematics Teaching in the Middle School 4*(8).

Rocke, Judy. (1995). A common cents approach to fractions. *Teaching Children Mathematics 2*(4).

Roper, Ann, and Linda Holden Charles. (1990). *Fraction circles plus.* Palo Alto, CA: Creative Publications.

Warrinton, Mary Ann. (1997). How children think about division with fractions. *Mathematics Teaching in the Middle School 2*(6).

Welchman-Tischler, Rosamond. (1992). *Start with manipulatives.* New York: Cuisenaire Company of America.

Zeman, Anne, and Kate Kelly. (1994). *Everything you need to know about science homework.* New York: Scholastic.

Zulie, Mathew. (1975). *Fractions with pattern blocks.* Palo Alto, CA: Creative Publications.

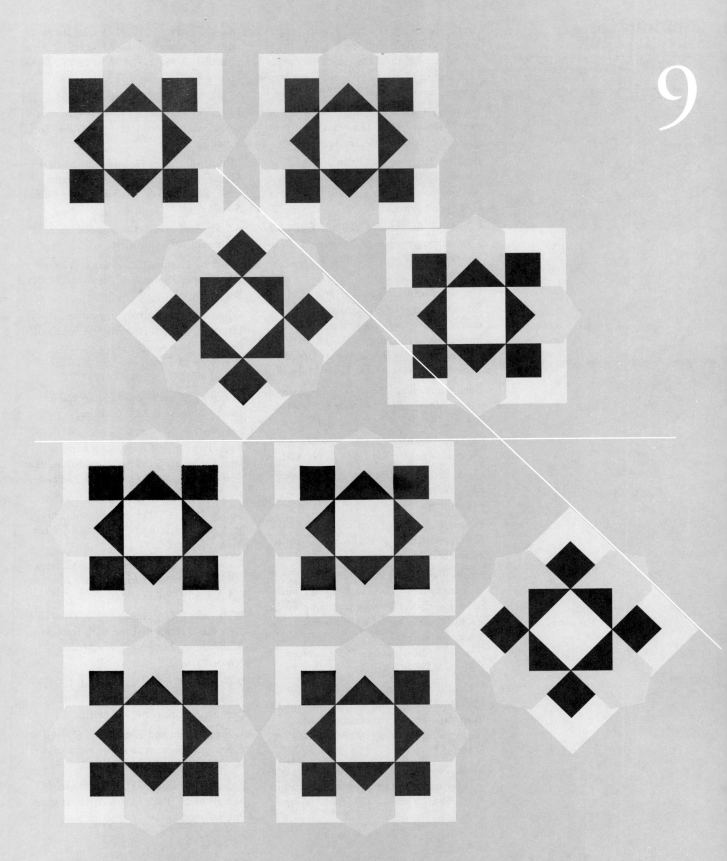

9

Standards for Patterns and Relationships

Children do not arrive in school as mathematical *tabula rasa* (blank slates). They bring with them several years of experience with mathematics. They have already combined and separated things; they have already compared and shared things; they have already created and constructed things. The mathematics children subsequently learn in school needs to be assimilated into the mathematical concepts they already possess (Ginsburg and Baron, 1993). This is why you are being encouraged continually to ask children to explain what they think and why they think it. Not only does this practice give recognition and respect to the understandings of children but it also gives you valuable information about what they know and understand. You can then use this information as the basis on which you make curricular and instructional decisions.

One of the most important constructs that young children develop early on is the ability to recognize patterns and regularities. For example, children enjoy predictable books where a certain phrase is continually repeated, and they are charmed by songs or nursery rhymes with obvious rhyming schemes. Children's attention to and recognition of patterns is important for the development of their skills of literacy and numeracy. Recognizing a pattern is the first step toward developing the ability to describe and continue a pattern. For example, recognizing the pattern of 1, 2, 3, 4, 5, . . . allows for the continuation of 21, 22, 23, 24, 25, . . . and 31, 32, 33, 34, 35, ...

Simple Patterns, Functions, and Algebra

The NCTM *Principles and Standards* recommend that all students in grades Pre-K–2 should

- Identify analyze, and extend patterns and recognize the same pattern in different manifestations,

- Describe how both repeating and growing patterns are generated. (p. 117)

Although not all of the discipline of mathematics is predictable and consistent, a good part of school mathematics is. Stressing the regularity of mathematics is one way to help students develop confidence in their ability to understand

Activity 9.1

Geometric Patterns

Lesson: Individual or Small Group

Using rolls of adding-machine paper, trace pattern blocks in an ABABABAB . . . pattern as shown in Figure 9.1.

Trace the pattern in the center of the strip to allow children to continue the pattern in either direction. Make the rolls of paper and a supply of pattern blocks available in a math center to allow children the opportunity to continue the pattern by placing pattern blocks on the blank parts of the roll. Encourage the students to verbalize a description of the pattern to their neighbors.

When children are comfortable with recognizing, describing, and continuing ABABABAB patterns, provide ABC ABCABC or ABCBABCBABCB patterns. Also, supply a blank roll of adding-machine paper and markers to allow children to create their own patterns. Don't be surprised if children have difficulty producing their own patterns. Many young children are unable to create consistent patterns, and simply string items together. When asked to "tell about your pattern," children frequently cannot offer any rationale, saying that the yellow hexagon comes after the red trapezoid because "It comes next."

Creating a pattern is more difficult than recognizing and continuing one. Regardless of children's abilities, however, it is important to provide all children with the opportunity to experience pattern recognition, description, extension, and creation.

Journal Reflection

In what other areas of the curriculum is pattern recognition important? Describe three contexts in which you (or the children you teach) identify and continue patterns. What do each of these contexts have in common?

Figure 9.1

and create mathematics. Young children are reassured by regularity and predictability, and they delight in supplying the next number or word or picture or structure in a sequence. Activity 9.1 offers a means to help children develop their skills of pattern recognition, pattern description, and pattern continuance.

Even as adults, your ability to recognize and continue patterns is important. This skill allows you to make sense of the world. It allows you to perceive regularity instead of chaos, and it can often help you solve problems. The Strength in Numbers activity on page 269 is more easily solved if you recognize the underlying pattern.

After the groups have worked on this problem singly, in pairs, and as a foursome, each group presents their solution to the entire class. As part of these presentations, you try to identify any patterns you found helpful in the solution of the problem. Try to present these patterns verbally, visually, and symbolically.

Activity 9.2 uses a classic piece of literature to introduce the odd/even/odd/even pattern of the counting numbers.

Engaging children in one-on-one or one-on-two performance assessment tasks allows you to monitor what they know and can do. Observing children as they work, asking probing questions, and taking notes based on their performance allows you to evaluate a particular child's progress and helps you

Strength in Numbers

Problem Solving

Cooperative Group Model: Think-Pair-Share

Working in groups of four, each group member begins by working on this problem individually. After sufficient time, two groups of two are formed, with each pair sharing strategies and successes. Again, after enough time, both groups join to allow all four members to contribute to a final solution to the problem.

■ In a particular school library, there are 100 books for 100 students. The books are numbered and arranged in order on shelves. On the first day of school, a prank was played. The first student opened every book. The second student closed every second book. The third student changed every third book; if the book was opened, she closed it and if the book was closed, she opened it. The fourth student changed every fourth book, the fifth student changed every fifth book, and so on. After the 100th student did his mischief, which books remained open?

Activity 9.2

Odd and Even Numbers

Read *Madeline,* by Ludwig Bemelmans, to the students. After the students have enjoyed the first reading of the book, read it again. When you read the line about " . . . twelve little girls in two straight lines . . . " ask the children to draw twelve little girls in two straight lines. For younger children, you can simplify this task by supplying paper that has already been divided into twelfths, as shown in Figure 9.2.

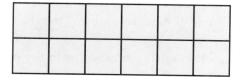

Figure 9.2

Ask the children to describe number sentences suggested by their pictures. Some possible responses are:

■ "My picture looks like 2 + 2 + 2 + 2 + 2 + 2 = 12 because there are six sets of partners holding hands."

■ "When I look at my picture it makes me think of 6 + 6 = 12, because there's one line of 6 girls, and another line of 6 girls right next to it."

When you get up to the part in the story when Madeline is taken to the hospital, ask the children to describe what will happen to the "twelve little girls in two straight lines." Invite the children to cover up one of the little girls in their picture, and describe what they see. Take this opportunity to define an even number as a number that allows everyone to have a partner, and an odd number as a number that leaves one person without a partner.

Invite the children to think about ways to determine if there is an even number of children in the class or an odd number of children. As an extension, invite the children to draw a picture of the people in their family or extended family, and to explain how they know if there is an even number or an odd number of people in their family.

Journal Reflection

Examine several other children's books. Explain how you might use each one to identify patterns or regularities. How might you symbolize these patterns? How might you encourage children to verbalize the regularities they observe?

make curricular decisions about areas in need of greater attention. The following performance-based assessment will inform you about children's rational counting abilities, their ability to use grouping strategies when counting a group of objects, and their understanding of odd and even numbers.

Performance-Based Assessment: Even and Odd Numbers

This requires a basket of counters, such as bingo chips, beans, or buttons. Choose a material that would allow a child to hold approximately 15 items in one hand. Invite the child to take a big handful of the counters and lay them on the table. Ask the child to count the items. Then, ask the child to count the items "in a different way." Notice if the child counts by twos or uses some other grouping strategy. Ask the child to tell you if there are an even number of items or an odd number of items, and to explain how she knows. Children's responses can be assessed according to this rubric:

4 Child accurately counts the items in more than one way, correctly identifies the number as an even or an odd number, and offers some justification for this claim.

3 Child accurately counts the items in more than one way and identifies the number as even or odd, but is unable to explain or justify this claim.

2 Child accurately counts the items, but can only do so in one way, and accurately identifies the number as even or odd, but without any explanation or justification.

1 Child has difficulty with one or more aspect of the task, but shows some understanding of cardinal numbers and even vs. odd.

0 Child is unable to count items accurately, and shows no evidence of understanding even or odd numbers.

Recognizing patterns and regularities is an important problem-solving skill, one that children can use to understand and remember basic number facts. Recall from Chapter 4 that, when children recognize that the multiples of 5 end in 5 or 0, and when they recognize that the sum of the digits of the multiples of 9 equals 9 or a multiple of nine, committing the basic facts to memory becomes an easier task.

Activity 9.3 combines a problem-solving situation with the opportunity for children to practice their basic facts. It also illustrates a recommendation from the NCTM *Principles and Standards* for grades 3–5, which says that all students should

■ Identify and use relationships between operations to solve problems (e.g. multiplication as the inverse of division) (p. 164)

Relationships

In addition to engaging children in tasks that encourage them to identify patterns and regularities, it is appropriate to help them identify relationships

Activity 9.3

Get to 24

Lesson: Individual

Present the following problem to students:

- On each card below there are four digits. Use any of the four basic operations of addition, subtraction, multiplication or division with *all* of the numbers so that the result is 24. The first one is done for you. See how many different ways you can get to 24 on each card (Figure 9.3).

Take this opportunity to remind children of the four steps of problem solving: read, plan, carry out, and look back.

1. To help the students understand what the problem is asking, ask one of them to **read** the problem out loud, and to then restate the problem in their own words. In this case, a child might say "I need to use all of the numbers on the card and get them to equal 24. I can add them, subtract them, multiply or divide them. There may be more than one way to get 24 on each card."

2. To encourage students to **plan** a strategy, encourage them to give some thought to numbers that are factors of 24. Working toward these numbers can help the students see a solution. Random attempts quickly become frustrating.

3. To help children **carry out** the plan, distribute small squares of paper for writing down the individual digits on a particular card. Moving these squares around can help students see connections among numbers.

4. Model how to **look back** at the problem by inviting several children to share the different strategies they used. Encourage the students to analyze the different strategies and identify the strengths and weaknesses of each one.

Journal Reflection

Discuss how problems like this might be used to help children gain ease in recalling basic facts. How could the game be modified for students who find it too difficult? Too easy? Do you think it is advisable to combine work on problem solving with work on basic facts? Why or why not?

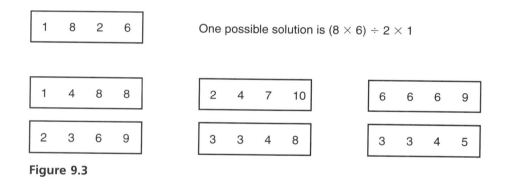

One possible solution is $(8 \times 6) \div 2 \times 1$

Figure 9.3

that exist among objects or numbers. For example, students can be engaged in a series of activities where the goal is to identify and verbalize the relationship that exists between two things. Imagine that you show children, one at a time, pairs of Cuisenaire rods like those of Figure 9.4.

Then invite the children to describe the relationship that exists between the first rod and the second rod (in this case, the second rod is twice as long as the first) and ask the children to predict what rod should follow the light green rod in order to represent the same relationship. As another example, you could show the children the pairs of Unifix cubes shown in Figure 9.5.

After displaying the pairs, ask the children to discuss with their neighbor what they think should be paired with a stack of 7 white cubes, and why. In order to solve this problem, students need to recognize that the relationship

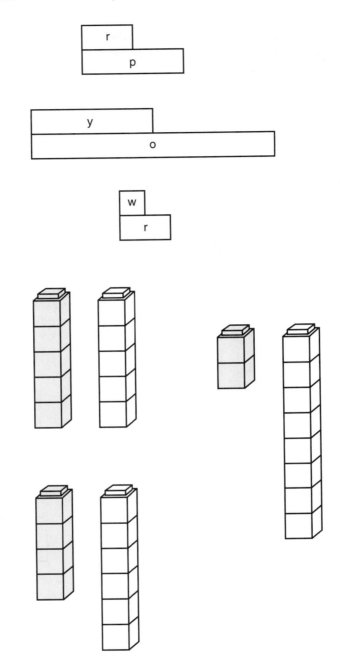

Figure 9.4

Figure 9.5

that exists between the two stacks of cubes is $x + y = 10$. After some practice with identifying relationships in this way, invite the children to create their own relationships among objects and to challenge their neighbor to describe the relationship verbally. Creating their own relationships is much more difficult for children than identifying another's relationship.

In addition to visual relationships, helping children to identify numerical relationships is a valuable activity. Introducing children to the concept of a "function machine" helps them to construct relationships mentally to explain different outcomes. For example, young children can be encouraged to say a number, which you respond to by saying the next greater number.

This back-and-forth exchange continues until the children are able to articulate the "rule" that governs your response. You can then change the rule, responding with a number that is one less, or two greater, and so on. As children become older and more adept at identifying relationships, the "input" and the "output" can be recorded on the board, and the rules can become more complex, such as $(x \times 2) - 1$. The following performance-based assessment offers an example of a function machine.

Performance-Based Assessment: Identifying Relationships

Distribute the following sheet to students.

IN	OUT
2	10
1	5
10	50
3	15
5	25
4	?
7	?
?	?

What is the relationship between the number that goes in and the number that comes out? Use this information to fill in the missing numbers. The following rubric can be used to evaluate student responses:

4 Student correctly completes the columns and correctly describes the relationship that exists.

3 Student correctly describes the relationship that exists, but makes some arithmetic errors in completing the columns.

2 Student correctly completes the columns, but is unable to describe the relationship that exists, or describes it incorrectly.

1 Student makes both arithmetical and descriptive errors, but shows some evidence of understanding the relationship between the two columns of numbers.

0 Student's work is incorrect, and shows no evidence of understanding.

The Hindu-Arabic system of numeration is based on repetitions and regularities. Encouraging students to examine a hundreds chart and identify inherent patterns is a way to help them develop their own number sense, and to provide them the opportunity to internalize the structure of our number system.

Providing students with opportunities to "make sense" of numbers encourages them to take an active role in their own mathematical learning, and to construct their own understandings.

■ What patterns do you see? What regularities do you notice?

0	1	2	3	4	5	6	7	8	9
10	11	12	13	14	15	16	17	18	19
20	21	22	23	24	25	26	27	28	29
30	31	32	33	34	35	36	37	38	39
40	41	42	43	44	45	46	47	48	49
50	51	52	53	54	55	56	57	58	59
60	61	62	63	64	65	66	67	68	69
70	71	72	73	74	75	76	77	78	79
80	81	82	83	84	85	86	87	88	89
90	91	92	93	94	95	96	97	98	99

Comments that children are likely to make include:

■ "All the numbers in the column that starts with 3 have a 3 in the ones place."

■ "All the rows have the same number in the tens place except the first row. "

■ "Every number is ten more than the number directly above it."

■ "If you start with the one and move down along the diagonal, the numbers are 1, 12, 23, 34, 45, 56, 67, 78, 89. These digits follow the pattern of 1, 1, 2, 2, 3, 3, 4, 4, 5, 5, . . . and each two-digit number is 11 greater than the number before it."

■ "If you start with the zero and move down along the diagonal, the numbers are 0, 11, 22, 33, 44, 55, 66, 77, 88, and 99. These are all multiples of 11."

After children have had the opportunity to study the hundreds chart and comment on patterns, introduce them to "arrow arithmetic." Arrow arithmetic requires students to follow a series of directions and predict the outcome at the end of the series. Activity 9.4 is an example of arrow arithmetic. It introduces the directions of Arrow Up (AU) Arrow Down (AD), Left Arrow (LA) and Right Arrow (RA)

The Relationship Between Variables and Problem Solving

Introducing children to the use of variables and open sentences can help them develop their problem-solving abilities by providing them with a "language" to represent complex situations. The NCTM *Principles and Standards* recommends that, in grades 3–5, all students should

■ Develop the concept of a variable as a useful tool for representing unknown quantities; . . . (p. 164)

Suppose you displayed a brown paper bag to second-graders, telling them that the bag contained ten cubes, only red and blue. Pose the following problem:

Activity 9.4

Arrow Arithmetic

Lesson: Whole Class

Provide each student with a hundreds chart. Display symbols like those of Figure 9.6 and invite comments.

Most students will recognize that, if you begin at 26 and move up two boxes, the destination will be 6. This, in fact, is how the symbols are to be interpreted. Provide the students with several more opportunities to practice interpreting the symbols by inviting them to fill in the destination at the end of the strings of symbols shown in Figure 9.7.

Once students have become comfortable with interpreting the symbols, challenge them to write strings of symbols that will connect the following pairs of numbers:

36	89
14	71
6	8 (Can you do this with 6 arrows?)
52	52 (Can you do this with 6 arrows?)
27	48 (Do this in three different ways.)
Any number	That number plus 10
Any number	That number minus 5
Any number	That number plus 22

Journal Reflection

Discuss how this activity can be viewed as an introduction to algebraic thinking and computing. What do you see as the advantages and difficulties of moving from specific cases to general cases in mathematical investigations?

35   $\overrightarrow{RA}$ AD$\downarrow$ AD$\downarrow$ _____

9   AD$\downarrow$ $\overleftarrow{LA}$ AD$\downarrow$ $\overleftarrow{LA}$ _____

55   $\overleftarrow{LA}$ $\overleftarrow{LA}$ $\uparrow$AU $\uparrow$AU $\overrightarrow{RA}$ _____

Figure 9.7

26   $\uparrow$AU $\uparrow$AU   6

Figure 9.6

■ If some of the 10 cubes are red and some of the 10 cubes are blue, how many different pairs of numbers are there to describe how many red and blue cubes might be in the bag?

Children typically begin to solve a problem like this by calling out random pairs of numbers, some of which might not even sum to 10. Asking the rest of the class "What do you think about that?" after each pair of numbers is offered provides the opportunity for the children to analyze each other's responses.

When you are convinced that the children understand the problem, invite them to work in groups to list as many pairs of numbers that sum to 10 as they can. So that the children can record their pairs of numbers, post a large sheet of chart paper with the following heading:

RED CUBES (R) + BLUE CUBES (B) = 10

After the children have had an opportunity to list all of the possible pairs of numbers and to discuss their strategies for obtaining them, ask them to suggest different numbers that could be used to fill in the columns for a chart with this heading:

G + Y = 12

In this way, students have the opportunity to move from a concrete situation (ten red and blue cubes in a bag) to a more abstract situation that bears some similarity to the original. Make use of this type of symbolism whenever appropriate in the daily functioning of the classroom. For example, the heading for attendance can be listed on the board as Girls + Boys = Total, and then later abbreviated to G + B = Total. The lunch count can be written on the board as Hot Lunch + Pizza + Salad = Total, and later shortened to A + B + C = Total. Students can then be invited to list possible numbers that the letters can represent. If they know the total number of students present in the class and they also know the number of girls present that day, they can solve for the missing variable, in this case the number of boys present. If the students know that twenty-three children buy lunch and twelve have chosen the hot lunch, they can offer possible pairs of number that can represent the number of children choosing Pizza or Salad.

Activity 9.5 suggests the kinds of problems that can be presented to students to encourage them to think about patterns and relationships. Recall

---

Activity 9.5

Patterns and Relationships

Lesson: Individual

Present the following problem to the children:

- I have seven coins that total 55 cents. What are some combinations of coins that I could have?

It may be helpful to provide play or actual coins that can be manipulated to help children solve this problem.

When children first begin to solve problems of this type, it is difficult for them to keep in mind simultaneously both of the limitations (value and number of coins) of the problem. Children may well arrive at solutions that meet the limitation of seven coins, but do not equal 55 cents, or they may offer solutions that sum to 55 cents, but do so with more or fewer than seven coins. Class discussion about how to proceed may be helpful before they begin the actual work of solving the problem. Although you need to be careful not to impose your own solution method on the students, when they first begin to solve problems of this type you may want to offer a structure. A chart with a heading such as the following can

help students organize their attempts while keeping in mind both the number of coins and their value.

Encourage the children to write down combinations of coins even if they are incorrect, since incorrect answers often lead to correct ones. For instance, a solution of

DIME + DIME + DIME + DIME + DIME + NICKEL + NICKEL

is a set of seven coins that sums to 60 cents. Students may see that simply by changing one dime to a nickel, they have decreased the value of the coins by 5 cents, but have kept the total number of coins constant, and thus have arrived at a correct solution.

Journal Reflection

Practice writing three more problems just like this, and invite some of your classmates to try to solve them. Are some of your problems better than others? Why? Would you invite students to write their own problems of this type? Why or why not?

Coin 1	Coin 2	Coin 3	Coin 4	Coin 5	Coin 6	Coin 7	Total Value

Activity 9.6

Algebraic Reasoning

Lesson: Individual, Whole Group

Pose the following problem to the students:

- A bicycle shop has several cycles in for repairs. Some are bicycles and some are tricycles. If there are 48 wheels in all, how many could be bicycles and how many could be tricycles?

Since students have had experience solving similar problems, invite them to discuss with their neighbors how they are going to organize their attempts. It is likely that they will develop a chart that resembles this:

No. of Bicycles	No. of Tricycles	Total No. of Wheels

A more sophisticated version of this chart might look something like this:

$$(\text{Bicycles} \times 2) + (\text{Tricycles} \times 3) = 48$$

Provide students with the opportunity to solve the problem. When they report their solutions to the class, either individually or in groups, encourage them to address the following questions:

- How did you go about solving the problem?
- Would you solve a similar problem in the same way? Why?
- How do you know that your solution is correct?
- Do you think that there are any other solutions? Why?

Journal Reflection

A useful extension for students who quickly solve problems like this is to challenge them to find all of the possible solutions to the problem and to justify why they believe that they have done so. What alteration to the problem might be appropriate for students who struggle?

the introduction to spreadsheets that appeared in Chapter 3. Both Activities 9.5 and 9.6 contain problems that lend themselves to solution on a spreadsheet. Try solving the problems manually and then using technology. What do you see as advantages and disadvantages of each method?

One of the ways you can help students become successful problem solvers is to offer them a series of problems that bear some similarity to each other. This provides students with a sense of comfort and familiarity with the problem, and gives them some idea of how to begin. After giving students several similar "*x* coins worth *y* cents" problems, introduce them to a related type of problem, as outlined in Activity 9.6. The following interdisciplinary lesson plan provides additional practice with symbolic representation.

More Complex Patterns, Functions, and Algebra

The study of patterns, relationships, and functions continues to be important as students move into the upper elementary grades, particularly for the role that an understanding of these concepts can play in an introduction to

Interdisciplinary
Lesson Plan

Grade 2 to 4   **Concept** Symbolic Representation

Topic Interpreting a Pattern

Student Objectives After the completion of this lesson, students should be able to

- Interpret a symbolic representation of a pattern
- String beads according to a symbolic representation of a pattern
- Write their own symbolic representation for a bead pattern of their own creation.

Materials A roll of gift wrapping paper with an obvious pattern, string-able beads of at least three colors, string.

Motivation Invite the class to develop a semantic web for the concept of patterns. Figure 9.8 shows an example of a possible web.

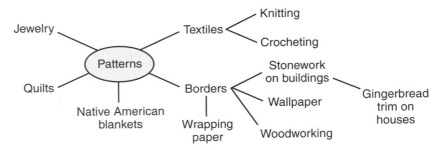

Figure 9.8

Procedure (1) Expose a short length of gift wrapping paper. Ask the children to predict how the rest of the roll would look. Ask the children to explain *how they can tell* what the rest of the roll looks like without unrolling it. Discuss the regularity and predictability of patterns. (2) Invite the children to create a pattern with the beads and string, and then to describe their pattern to their neighbors. (3) Mentally note one child's pattern—perhaps a red, red, blue, red, red, blue pattern—and write a symbolic representation of it on the board. Challenge the children to identify whose pattern is represented by R R B R R B . . . and to justify their claim. (4) Invite the children to write a symbolic representation of their own bead pattern. Have the children close their eyes while one child writes a symbolic representation on the board. Challenge the children to identify the string of beads that corresponds to the pattern written on the board. (5) Write on the board the following representation of a string pattern and invite the children to create the pattern with their beads.

R R G G R R B B R R G G R R B B R R . . .

(continued)

Lesson Plan (continued)

Have them compare their bead strings with others around them and discuss any differences. Point out that, since the letters represent specific colors (R stands for red, G stands for green, and B stands for blue), every child should have created the same pattern. Pose the following question: What bead pattern would correspond to this symbolic representation?

A A B B A A C C A A B B A A C C A A . . .

Since these letters or variables can represent any color—any bead pattern that has two of one color followed by two of a second color—then two of the first color followed by two of a third color would correspond to the symbolic pattern. Define the word *variable* as a symbol that can stand for *various* things.

Assessment Direct the children's attention to the semantic web for patterns that was developed previously. Invite the children to choose an example of a pattern from the web and to look for evidence of this pattern in books or magazines or through electronic research. Have the students print or copy or duplicate the pattern they find, and develop a symbolic representation of the pattern. Have the children share their work with the class.

References Irons, Calvin, James Burnett, and Stanley Wong Hoo Foon. *Mathematics from Many Cultures.* San Francisco, CA, Mimosa Publications, 1993.

Journal Entry In this section you will comment on the lesson after it has been taught, and include suggestions for the future.

algebra. The NCTM *Principles and Standards* recommend that in grades 6–8, all students should

- Use patterns to solve mathematical and applied problems;
- Represent a variety of relations and functions with tables, graphs, verbal rules, and, when possible, symbolic rules. (p. 221)

Students in grades 6 through 8 are often interested in codes and in breaking codes. This interest provides an opportunity to introduce problems requiring the recognition of patterns, regularities, or functional relationships. *Cryptarithms* are problems where letters are substituted for numbers in mathematical operations. These problems involve functional relationships, because each different letter stands for a different number, and the same letters stand for the same numbers. A *function,* of course, is a relation between two sets where each element in the first set (in this case, a letter) is paired with only one element in the second set (in this case, a number.)

Activity 9.7 introduces students to the concept of cryptarithms. Take some time to solve its cryptarithm problems. They involve breaking a code and require some perseverance. The problems are taken from *Creative Problem Solving in School Mathematics* by George Lenchner (1983, pp. 155–58).

Computer Software

In addition to having students investigate patterns with manipulatives and paper and pencil, there are some software programs that involve students in the study of patterns, functions, and algebraic thinking. The *Mighty Math Astro Algebra* program (Edmark) engages students in graphing equations and inequalities on a number line or the coordinate plane. It encourages students to use various modalities (concrete models, words, graphs, variables) for expressing mathematical ideas. A function machine allows students to practice substituting different values for variables in an expression or function.

Students are engaged in problem solving when they try to crack the codes in *Divide and Conquer* (Carraher). Symbols are used to stand for the numbers from 0 to 9. Through forming hypotheses and then testing them, students develop their reasoning abilities and strengthen their understanding of place value.

A program that helps students practice their skills in listening, map reading, measurement, rounding, multiplication, division, and set theory is *Awesome Animated Monster Maker Math* (Houghton Mifflin Interactive). This software provides a structured experience for students, allowing them to progress through increasingly difficult levels of activities.

Number Theory in Context

As students move into the upper elementary grades, they begin to perceive many more patterns and relationships in our number system. The concepts that come under the heading of number theory are interesting for students to consider. Understanding prime and composite numbers, factors, multiples, and divisibility can have many pragmatic uses; students can more easily work with fractions and predict whether numbers will divide without remainders. But studying the concepts of number theory can also provide students with the opportunity to develop their number sense and solve challenging problems.

Activity 9.8 engages students in a study of prime and composite numbers and factors. You can yourself investigated a similar, although more limited, version of this concept as part of the Strength in Numbers activity in Chapter 2 on page 43.

Activity 9.8 related arithmetic concepts to geometrical concepts by connecting rectangular arrangements of numbers of squares with the factors of those numbers. Activity 9.9 provides an alternative means of discovering the factors of numbers, and of identifying the prime numbers from 1 to 100.

Activity 9.7

Cryptarithms

Lesson: Individual, Pairs

Introduce the following cryptarithm to the students:

```
     A
     A
   + A
  ─────
   H A
```

Explain to the students that in a cryptarithm, different letters stand for different numbers and the same letters stand for the same numbers. To solve the cryptarithm, they are to use what they know about numbers and the sums of numbers to figure out which numbers are represented by the letters "A" and "H." After the students have had an opportunity to work on the problem for some time and to discuss their ideas with a partner, invite students to share their solutions. Some possible solutions and explanations are:

- I think that "A" stands for the number 5 and "H" stands for the number 1. I think this because I started with 1 and tried all of the numbers for "A." I realized that "A" couldn't equal 1 because 1 + 1 + 1 = 3, and "A" can't equal both 1 and 3. It couldn't equal 2 because 2 + 2 + 2 = 6, and "A" can't equal both 2 and 6. I tried 3, then 4, then 5. When I got to 5, I realized that 5 + 5 + 5 = 15. This means that "A" can equal 5 throughout the whole problem.

- When I looked at this problem, I realized that three times "A" would have to equal a 2-digit number with the same digit as "A" in the ones place. The only number that would work here is 5, because:

$3 \times 1 = 3$

$3 \times 2 = 6$

$3 \times 3 = 9$

$3 \times 4 = 12$

$3 \times 5 = 15$

$3 \times 6 = 18$

$3 \times 7 = 21$

$3 \times 8 = 24$

$3 \times 9 = 27$

This means that "A" equals 5 and "H" equals 1.

Once the students have had the opportunity to understand this simple cryptarithm, challenge them to crack the code for the following more difficult problems. (There is no connection among the problems. A letter that stands for a particular number in one problem may or may not stand for that same number in a different problem.)

```
  SEND        SONG        ABCD
+ MORE      + BIRD        × 4
───────     ───────      ──────
 MONEY       SINGS        DCBA
```

Encourage the students who have been successful with the cryptarithms to share their strategies with the class. Some students may have worked backwards, or accounted for all possibilities, or set up equations.

Journal Reflection

What hint would you offer to a student who simply didn't know how to begin to solve this problem? How would you attempt to keep the student's frustration level low so that he or she could make a real effort to solve the problem?

Performance-Based Assessment: Prime Factors

Distribute a supply of three different-color counters (red, white, and blue chips, for example) to the students and use them to introduce the following

Activity 9.8

Arranging Photographs

Lesson: Pairs

Distribute thirty colored tiles or squares of construction paper, all of the same color, to each pair of students, and present the following scenario:

- If you owned a photography studio, and you wanted to display the graduation photographs of the local graduates, how could you arrange between 1 and 30 photographs if you limited yourself to rectangular arrangements of photos?

Encourage the students to use the squares to model the different possible arrangements, and to record the information they discover about the factors of the numbers from 1 to 30. A chart of the recorded information might look like this:

Number of Photos	Arrangements
1	1×1
2	1×2
3	1×3
4	$1 \times 4, 2 \times 2$
5	1×5
6	$1 \times 6, 2 \times 3$
7	1×7
8	$1 \times 8, 2 \times 4$
9	$1 \times 9, 3 \times 3$
10	$1 \times 10, 2 \times 5$
11	1×11
12	$1 \times 12, 2 \times 6, 3 \times 4$
13	1×13
14	$1 \times 14, 2 \times 7$
15	$1 \times 15, 3 \times 5$
16	$1 \times 16, 2 \times 8, 4 \times 4$
17	1×17
18	$1 \times 18, 2 \times 9, 3 \times 6$
19	1×19
20	$1 \times 20, 2 \times 10, 4 \times 5$
21	$1 \times 21, 3 \times 7$
22	$1 \times 22, 2 \times 11$
23	1×23
24	$1 \times 24, 2 \times 12, 3 \times 8, 4 \times 6$
25	$1 \times 25, 5 \times 5$
26	$1 \times 26, 2 \times 13$
27	$1 \times 27, 3 \times 9$
28	$1 \times 28, 2 \times 14, 4 \times 7$
29	1×29
30	$1 \times 30, 2 \times 15, 3 \times 10$

Pose the following questions to help the students discover some regularities:

- How many numbers of photographs can be arranged in only one way? What numbers are they? How many unique factors do these numbers have?

Use this discussion as an opportunity to define prime numbers as numbers that have only two unique factors, the number itself and 1. Since the number 1 does not have two unique factors, it is not considered to be prime.

- Which numbers of photographs can be arranged in squares? What do you notice about the factors of these numbers? Why do you think these numbers are called the perfect squares?

- Which numbers of photographs can be arranged in a $2 \times x$ rectangle? Use this information to develop a definition of even numbers.

- The *aliquot parts* of a number are those factors other than the number itself. The aliquot parts of the number 12 are 1, 2, 3, 4, and 6. In *abundant numbers,* the sum of the aliquot parts is greater than the number itself. In *deficient numbers,* the sum of the aliquot parts is less than the number itself. In *perfect numbers,* the sum of the aliquot parts is equal to the number itself. Identify each of the numbers from 1 to 30 as abundant, deficient, or perfect.

Journal Reflection

Compare the definition of a perfect square developed in this activity with the way most people think about a square number ($5^2 = 5 \times 5$). Are these definitions similar? Compatible? Which, if either, do you prefer? Why?

game. Assign the values of 2, 3, and 5 to each of the different-color counters. For instance, you could let red chips be worth 2, white chips be worth 3, and blue chips be worth 5. Invite a student to chose any number of red, white, and blue chips, and to multiply their values together. Ask the student to tell you that product, without telling you either the *amount* or the *colors* of the chips chosen. Surprise the students by announcing how many chips were chosen, and their colors.

Activity 9.9

The Sieve of Eratosthenes

Lesson: Individual

Provide each student with a hundreds chart and several different-colored markers. First, invite the students to cross off the number 1. They are then to choose one color to circle the number 2, and place a dot in the box that contains each subsequent multiple of two. Encourage the students to discuss the pattern that appears on the hundreds chart. Choosing a second color, this time invite the students to circle the number 3 and place a dot in the box that contains each subsequent multiple of 3. Repeat this process with the numbers 5, 7, and 11, each time choosing a different color, and each time discussing the pattern that appears.

Many discoveries can now be made about the factors of the numbers from 1 to 100. Here are some observations that students typically make:

- "Numbers that are marked with the 2 color appear in every other column. These are also the even numbers."
- "Numbers that are marked with both the 2 and 3 color are the multiples of 6."

- "Numbers that are circled or are not marked at all have "fallen through the sieve" and are prime numbers. These numbers have only two unique factors, themselves and 1."
- "Two is the smallest prime number, and it is the only even prime number."
- Numbers that are not circled but are marked with at least one color are composite numbers, and the color(s) indicate the factor(s) of that number.

At this time you may wish to ask the students to choose additional colors and place a dot in each box of the multiples of 4, 6, 8, 10, and 12. This will allow them to discover, for example, that the multiples of 10 are also multiples of 2 and 5, that the multiples of 8 are also multiples of 4 and 2, and so on.

Journal Reflection

Many students have difficulty distinguishing between the multiples of a number and the factors of a number. How might you help students to make this distinction?

For example, if you were given a product of 2700, you could announce that the student had picked 2 red chips, 3 white chips, and 2 blue chips. How could you arrive at this determination? Stop for a minute and think about it: Two, three, and five are all prime numbers. Since every number has a unique prime factorization, every number obtained by multiplying sets of 2, 3, and 5 can be broken down into its prime factors. This set of prime factors predicts how many red, white, and blue chips were chosen by the student. By factoring 2700, you can find out how many 2s, 3s, and 5s were multiplied together to obtain that product. The factor tree of Figure 9.9 illustrates this process.

Once the students have understood how the game is played, invite them to play in pairs. Give them a worksheet like the one on the next page to record their work. You can allow students to play

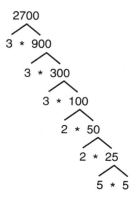

Figure 9.9

Worksheet

My name:_____ My partner's name:_____

My partner gave me this product:_____

I think that my partner used _____ red, _____ white, and _____ blue chips to obtain that product. I think this because

_____

_____

_____

_____

I gave my partner this product: _____

_____

I used _____ red, _____ white, and _____ blue chips to obtain this product. This is how I obtained the product:

_____

_____

_____

_____

I think that this is a game that other sixth-graders would (would not) like to play because: _____

_____

this game for a period of time, filling out the worksheet for each round played. Student's work can be assessed according to the following rubric:

3 Student can correctly multiply several factors together to obtain a product, and can correctly factor a number into its prime factors.

2 Student can correctly factor a number into its prime factors, but is unable to multiply several factors correctly.

1 Student can correctly multiply factors, but is unable to factor a number into its prime factors correctly.

0 Student can neither multiply factors nor factor a number.

Students' responses to the last question can provide you with information about their disposition toward this game.

Studying the rules for divisibility provides students with an opportunity to increase their number sense and to enhance their ability to make predictions about numbers. In addition, challenging students to justify *why* the rules for divisibility are as they are engages them in problem solving.

As you read through the following section, stop as each *why* question is asked and try to answer that question before you read on.

Divisibility

Divisibility by 2

A number is said to be divisible by 2 if the digit in the ones place is 0, 2, 4, 6, or 8. Why?

Any multidigit number, ABC, can be written in the form of

$$100A + 10B + C$$

Since 2 divides 10 and any multiple of 10, and since two divides 100 and any multiple of 100, and so on, it only remains to be seen if 2 divides the digit in the ones place. If C can be expressed as 2N, where N is a whole number, then it is divisible by two, and the entire number is divisible by two. Single digits that can be expressed in the form of 2N, where N is a whole number, are:

0	(2×0)	6	(2×3)
2	(2×1)	8	(2×4)
4	(2×2)		

Therefore, if any whole number has an even number in the ones place, it is divisible by 2.

Divisibility by 4

A whole number is said to be divisible by 4 if the last two digits are divisible by 4. Why?

Any multidigit number, ABCD, can be written in the form of

$$1000A + 100B + 10C + D$$

Since 4 divides 100 and any multiple of 100, and since 4 divides 1000 and any multiple of 1000, and so on, it only remains to be seen if 4 divides the last two digits. If these two digits are not an easily recognizable multiple of 4, (for instance, 72) simply determine if the number is divisible by 2 twice.

Divisibility by 8

A whole number is divisible by 8 if the last three digits are divisible by 8. Why?

Any multidigit number, ABCDE, can be written in the form of

$$10,000A + 1000B + 100C + 10D + E$$

Since 8 divides 1000, and any multiple of 1000, and since 8 divides 10,000, and any multiple of 10,000, and so on, it only remains to be seen if 8 divides the last three digits of the number. If 8 divides the last three digits, 8 divides the entire number.

Divisibility by 3 or 9

A whole number is divisible by 3 or 9 respectively if the sum of the digits is divisible by 3 or 9 respectively. Why?

Any multidigit number, ABCD, can be written in the form of

$$1000A + 100B + 10C + D$$

Neither 3 nor 9 divide 10, 100, or 1000 or any multiple of 10, 100, or 1000. However, they both divide 9, 99, 999, and so on. If ABCD is written in the form of

$$(999 + 1)A + (99 + 1)B + (9 + 1)C + D$$

and then the distributive property is used to rewrite the expression as

$$(999A) + A + (99B) + B + (9C) + C + D$$

you can see that the only parts of the expression that are not clearly divisible by 3 or 9 are A + B + C + D. If this sum is divisible by 3, the entire number is divisible by 3. If this sum is divisible by 9, the entire number is divisible by 9.

Remember that this chapter is devoted to the concept of patterns. Also recall that, at several points in this text, it was recommended that students be given several similar problems in a row, so that they might use insights and understandings from one problem to help them solve subsequent problems. The Strength in Numbers activity on the next page follows the pattern of the above investigations into divisibility. Having already read and worked through those sections, the next divisibility investigation should be accessible to you.

Integers

Recall Activity 9.4, where children were introduced to arrow arithmetic. When exploring arrow arithmetic, children often create symbol strings that take them off the number chart. What would happen, for example, if a child started at the number 17, and executed the following symbol string:

17   AU ↑   AU ↑

Use the following number chart to determine the answer.

−20	−19	−18	−17	−16	−15	−14	−13	−12	−11
−10	−9	−8	−7	−6	−5	−4	−3	−2	−1
0	1	2	3	4	5	6	7	8	9
10	11	12	13	14	15	16	17	18	19
20	21	22	23	24	25	26	27	28	29
30	31	32	33	34	35	36	37	38	39
40	41	42	43	44	45	46	47	48	49
50	51	52	53	54	55	56	57	58	59
60	61	62	63	64	65	66	67	68	69
70	71	72	73	74	75	76	77	78	79
80	81	82	83	84	85	86	87	88	89
90	91	92	93	94	95	96	97	98	99
100	101	102	103	104	105	106	107	108	109
110	111	112	113	114	115	116	117	118	119

Strength in Numbers

Divisibility by 11

Cooperative Group Model: Think-Pair-Share

The rule for divisibility by 11 is as follows:

- Beginning with the first digit and alternating to every other digit, find the sum.
- Beginning with the second digit and alternating to every other digit, find that sum.
- Find the difference between the two sums.

If this difference is divisible by 11, the original number is divisible by 11. So, for example, is 62,678 divisible by 11?

$$6 + 6 + 8 = 20$$
$$2 + 7 = 9$$
$$20 - 9 = 11$$

Since 11 is divisible by 11, then 62,678 is divisible by 11.

Think: Why does this rule for divisibility work? *Hint:* Another way to test if 62,678 is divisible by 11 looks like this:

$$6 - 2 + 6 - 7 + 8 = 11$$

Think about this rule for divisibility, and compare it to the rule for divisibility for 3 and 9. In what ways are the rules similar? In what ways are they different?

Pair: Working with a partner, share your thoughts about this problem. *Hint:* When testing for divisibility by 3 and 9, the numbers were first written in expanded form, and then rewritten to separate out that part of each place value that was clearly divisible by 3 and 9. A similar strategy is used in the rule for divisibility by 11.

Share: Present to the rest of the class the explanation developed by you and your partner as to why the rule for divisibility by 11 works.

Hint: 10,000 is not divisible by 11, but 9,999 is. In similar fashion, 1,000 is not divisible by 11, but 1,001 is. What about the rest of the place values?

Providing students with opportunities like this to perform arrow arithmetic on an expanded number chart illustrates addition and subtraction of integers as movement along a number line. Although the number chart is actually rectangular as opposed to linear, arrow arithmetic interprets addition as movements down and to the right, and interprets subtraction as movements up and to the left. This is a slight variation on the interpretation of addition as movement to the right on a number line, and subtraction as movement to the left.

Arrow arithmetic on an expanded number chart can be used to introduce students to integers as an extension of the set of whole numbers. However, viewing addition and subtraction of integers as movement on a number line or number chart is not the only way to illustrate these operations. An alternative model of operations on integers is the set model.

A strong theme of this book is that students learn mathematics by interacting with materials and constructing their own meanings, or "rules." If you had to explain operations on integers to sixth-graders, would you know how to structure an activity that would allow them to create their own understandings? Or would you simply have to resort to stating the rules? The following investigations are designed to provide students with the opportunity to discover on their own the "rules" for operations on integers.

Operations on Integers

As an introduction, invite students to offer a general statement to describe the following situations:

- You earn $5, then you spend $5.
- You lose 3 pounds, and then you gain 3 pounds.
- A river drops 1 meter below its normal level, and then rises 1 meter.
- The temperature rises 10 degrees during the day, and then drops 10 degrees at night.

Students should recognize that each situation can be described as one where a gain is offset by an equivalent loss, or vice versa. Challenge students to determine how two-color counters might be used to illustrate each of these situations.

Students might alternately represent the first situation by a set of five yellow chips followed by a set of five red chips, or they might set out five yellow chips to represent the acquisition of $5, and then flip the chips over to the red side to represent the loss of $5. In either case, the goal is to represent a situation where the outcome is neither a gain nor a loss. This experience will help the students to think of a red-yellow pair as having a value of zero.

Have the students take a handful of chips, lay them out on the desk, and then determine the value of the set of chips if yellow has a value of +1, and red has a value of −1. Then invite the students to represent their set of chips symbolically, and describe a realistic context. See Figure 9.10 for an example of a possible set of chips.

Addition

In Figure 9.10a, the student has placed 5 yellow and 7 red chips on the desk. In Figure 9.10b, the chips have been arranged in yellow-red pairs so that the value of the set of chips can be determined. Since the five yellow-red pairs have a combined value of zero, the total value of the set of chips is −2, as represented by the two red chips that are not paired with a yellow

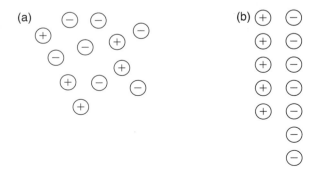

Figure 9.10

chip. This situation can be symbolized as $(+5) + (-7) = (-2)$. A context in which this operation on integers might occur would be a situation where you earned $5, but then spent $7, resulting in a net loss of $2.

Subtraction

The set model of integer subtraction can be interpreted as removing chips from a single set and examining what remains. The chips that are removed can have either a positive value or a negative value. Invite students to represent the following situations with chips, and then with symbols.

$$(-4) - (-2) = \qquad (-5) - (+4) =$$

$$(+4) - (-2) = \qquad (+5) - (+4) =$$

In the first instance, a set with a value of (-2) is removed from a set with a value of (-4), leaving a set with a value of (-2), as shown in Figure 9.11. Therefore, $(-4) - (-2) = (-2)$.

    In the second instance, $(+4) - (-2)$, a set with a value of (-2) needs to be removed from a set with a value of $(+4)$. In this case, two zero pairs need to be introduced into the set to allow for the removal of -2, as shown in Figure 9.12a. Any number of zero pairs can be introduced into any situation, since zero pairs do not change the value of any situation. The introduction of 2 zero pairs will now allow for the removal of a set of (-2), as shown in Figure 9.12b. Therefore, $(+4) - (-2) = (+6)$.

    In the third instance, $(-5) - (+4)$, a set with a value of $+4$ needs to be removed from a set with a value of -5 (Figure 9.13a). This will become possible with the addition of four zero pairs, as shown in Figure 9.13b. In Figure 9.13c four positive chips are removed, as required by the original example. Figure 9.13d shows what remains after the subtraction or removal process, which is nine negative chips. Therefore, $(-5) - (+4) = (-9)$.

Figure 9.11

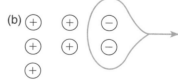

Figure 9.12

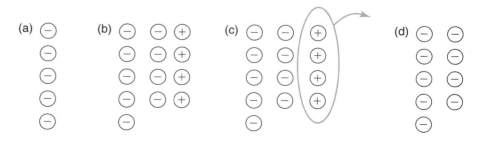

Figure 9.13

Figure 9.14

In the fourth instance, $(+5) - (+4)$, a set with a value of $+4$ needs to be removed from a set with a value of $+5$. The illustration of this process with two-color counters is left to the reader.

Multiplication and Division

In integer multiplication, four possibilities exist:

positive × positive   negative × negative

positive × negative   negative × positive

Two-color counters can be used to illustrate each of these possibilities. When the multiplier is positive, it will represent the *introduction* of that many groups of the multiplicand. When the multiplier is negative, it will represent the *removal* of that many groups of the multiplicand. For example: $(+3) \times (+2)$ means "introduce three groups of positive two," as shown in Figure 9.14. As you can see, $(+3) \times (+2) = (+6)$.

In another example, $(+3) \times (-2)$ means "introduce three groups of negative two, " as shown in Figure 9.15. As you can see, $(+3) \times (-2) = (-6)$.

Again, $(-3) \times (-2)$ means "remove three groups of negative two." Since there is not yet anything that can be removed, this requires introducing enough zero pairs to allow for the removal of three groups of negative two. Do you see that 6 zero pairs will allow for this, as shown in Figure 9.16? This process illustrates why:

$$(-3) \times (-2) = (+6)$$

We see that $(-3) \times (+2)$ means "remove three groups of positive two." Since this case is very similar to the one immediately preceding it, the illustration of this process is left to the reader.

Figure 9.15

Figure 9.16

The above investigations can be summarized as follows:

$$(+3) \times (+2) = (+6) \qquad (-3) \times (-2) = (+6)$$

$$(+3) \times (-2) = (-6) \qquad (-3) \times (+2) = (-6)$$

The related division facts can be summarized as follows:

$$(+6) \div (+3) = (+2) \qquad (+6) \div (-3) = (-2)$$

$$(-6) \div (+3) = (-2) \qquad (-6) \div (-3) = (+2)$$

Following this investigation, students can be invited to describe any patterns that they see. Most students quickly recognize that factors with like signs result in a positive product, while factors with unlike signs result in a negative product. Similarly, the quotient of two integers with like signs is a positive integer, while the quotient of two integers with unlike signs is a negative integer.

One of the reasons students have difficulty with integers and integer operations is that they assume operations on integers to be far removed from their "real" life. The following performance-based assessment is an opportunity for students to use integers in realistic contexts, and for you as the teacher to assess students' strengths and weaknesses. Armed with this information, you would be able to structure the curriculum for your class.

Performance-Based Assessment: Integers

Provide students with two-color counters and paper and pencil. Individually administering these items will allow you to observe students as they solve the problems, and to ask probing questions about their understandings.

- A stock price rose 7 points at the start of trading. By the end of the day, it had fallen 11 points. What was the outcome of the day's trading?

- The temperature fell 6 degrees overnight, and fell another 3 degrees the following day. What was the total change in temperature?

- After writing a $5 check, the balance in your checking account is $7. You wrote the $5 check for a catalog purchase. When you find out the item is out of stock, you tear up the check. What is the balance in your account now?

- Your credit card statement indicates that you owe $100. However, since you received that statement, you have returned a $20 item that had been charged to your account. If you wish to pay your balance in full, for how much should you write the check?

The electoral college table that follows will be utilized in the accompanying interdisciplinary lesson plan.

State	Electoral College Votes	Population
Alabama	9	4,040,000
Alaska	3	550,000
Arizona	8	3,670,000
Arkansas	6	2,350,000
California	54	29,760,000
Colorado	8	3,290,000
Connecticut	8	3,290,000
Delaware	3	670,000
District of Columbia	3	610,000
Florida	25	12,940,000
Georgia	13	6,480,000
Hawaii	4	1,110,000
Idaho	4	1,010,000
Illinois	22	11,430,000
Indiana	12	5,540,000
Iowa	7	2,780,000
Kansas	6	2,480,000
Kentucky	8	3,690,000
Louisiana	9	4,220,000
Maine	4	1,230,000
Maryland	10	4,780,000
Massachusetts	12	6,020,000
Michigan	18	9,300,000
Minnesota	10	4,380,000
Mississippi	7	2,570,000
Missouri	11	5,120,000
Montana	3	800,000
Nebraska	5	1,580,000
Nevada	4	1,200,000
New Hampshire	4	1,110,000
New Jersey	15	7,730,000
New Mexico	5	1,520,000
New York	33	18,000,000
North Carolina	14	6,630,000
North Dakota	3	640,000
Ohio	21	10,850,000
Oklahoma	8	3,150,000
Oregon	7	2,840,000
Pennsylvania	23	11,880,000
Rhode Island	4	1,000,000
South Carolina	8	3,490,000
South Dakota	3	700,000
Tennessee	11	4,880,000
Texas	32	17,000,000
Utah	5	1,720,000
Vermont	3	560,000
Virginia	13	6,190,000
Washington	11	4,870,000
West Virginia	5	1,800,000
Wisconsin	11	4,890,000
Wyoming	3	450,000

Grade 6 to 8   **Concept** Relationships

Topic Writing an Algebraic Expression to Represent a Relationship

Student Objectives After completing this lesson, students should be able to

▪ Write an algebraic expression to represent the relationship between the population of a state and its number of electoral college votes.

Materials Current resource materials (almanacs, for example).

Motivation Over the years, many people who live in New York City have spoken about "seceding" from New York State and forming their own state. If that were to happen, how many electoral college votes would the new city-state be entitled to?

Procedure (1) Invite the students to research the number of electoral college votes each state is currently entitled to, and how that number was determined. Students should discover that each state has as many electoral college votes as it has senators and representatives to Congress. This information, along with the population of each state rounded to the nearest ten thousand (as of the 1990 census), is summarized in the text that precedes this lesson plan. (2) Invite the students to look for a relationship between the population of a state and the number of electoral college votes it has. Encourage the students to generalize about this relationship, and write an algebraic expression to represent the number of electoral college votes each state is entitled to. Their expressions should look something like this:

$$ECV = (P \div 570{,}000) + 2$$

where ECV represents electoral college votes and P represents population. The number of representatives each state sends to Congress is a function of the population of that state, while each state sends two senators, regardless of population. While $P/570{,}000$ is not a perfect predictor of the number of representatives each state sends to Congress, it is a reasonable approximation based on the data. This expression changes every ten years as new census data is published, since the total number of representatives to the United States Congress is fixed at 435 members. (3) Encourage the students to answer the motivational question posed at the beginning of the lesson: How many electoral college votes would the new New York city-state be entitled to? Based on a 1990 population of approximately 8,550,000, the New York city-state would be entitled to 17 electoral college votes, as determined by the following expression:

$$ECV = (8{,}550{,}000 \div 570{,}000) + 2$$
$$ECV = 15 + 2$$
$$ECV = 17$$

(continued)

Lesson Plan (continued)

Assessment Assessment of the lesson will be accomplished by an examination of the algebraic expressions determined by each student, to see if the expressions can predict with reasonable accuracy the number of electoral college votes for each state.

References *The Universal Almanac,* John W. Wright, general editor, Andrews and McMeel Publishers, Kansas City, 1994.

Journal Entry This part of the lesson plan will be completed after the lesson has been taught. It will contain general comments, as well as suggestions for any changes that are warranted for the future.

Computer Software

Students can be assisted in recognizing number patterns by working with such software programs as *The King's Rule* (Sunburst, grades 4–8). This program presents students with sets of numbers and challenges them to identify the rules that structure the sets. Students who have had experiences since kindergarten with such informal games as "Guess My Rule" or tasks such as those described in the performance based assessment on page 291 would be familiar with the task of searching for relationships and would benefit from working with software of this type.

Geometric Patterns

One of the advantages of introducing students to such graphics programs as *Geo-Draw,* LOGO, or the *Geometric Supposer* is that they allow students to construct figures repeatedly with little effort. This repetition provides them with the opportunity to look for patterns and regularities and to observe the effect of certain changes on the outcomes. Activity 9.10 is designed to engage students in the repeated construction of geometric figures so they can arrive at some symbolic generalizations.

In previous investigations, we have made the connection between a numerical interpretation of the perfect squares and a geometric interpretation of the perfect squares. Numerically, the square of 5, for instance, can be thought of as 5 groups of 5, or 5×5. Geometrically, it can be thought of as a square built on 5. Figure 9.17 illustrates this square.

In addition, the perfect squares can be built by consecutively adding a "shell" to the original square. The addition of this shell results in progressively larger, similar shapes. The nature of this shell can also offer some insight into the numerical pattern that is being examined. Figure 9.18 depicts the inverted L-shaped shell that is progressively added to generate the perfect squares. In addition, it shows why 25, for instance, can be obtained by finding the sum shown.

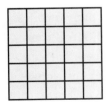

Figure 9.17

Activity 9.10

Chords and Regions

Lesson: Individual

Using a geometric draw program or pencil and paper, invite students to solve the following problem:

■ Into how many regions is it possible to partition a circle with one line? With two lines? Three lines? Four? Five? With 10 lines?

Students may begin to simply draw lines and try to get as many regions as possible. Students who develop a chart such as the one shown here will begin to see a pattern, and will be able to predict the number of possible regions without drawing the lines.

Number of Lines	Number of Regions
1	2
2	4
3	7
4	11
5	16
10	?

Journal Reflection

Drawing the lines in a circle becomes more difficult as the number of lines increases. Try to draw five lines that partition the circle into 16 regions. Do you see a familiar shape hidden in the lines? What shape do you think it might be, keeping in mind that five lines are being drawn?

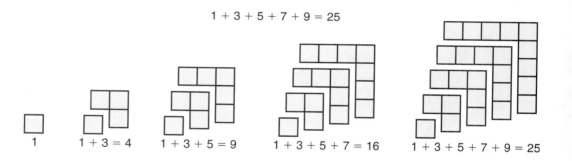

$$1 + 3 + 5 + 7 + 9 = 25$$

Figure 9.18

1   1 + 3 = 4   1 + 3 + 5 = 9   1 + 3 + 5 + 7 = 16   1 + 3 + 5 + 7 + 9 = 25

Polygons, like the squares in the figure, can be used to create successively larger, similar shapes with 1, 4, 9, 16, 25, . . . other polygons, and so on. Polygons that have this characteristic are called *reptiles*. Examine a set of pattern blocks. Which do you think will create a set of progressively larger, similar polygons by following the addition of a shell, and will use 1, 4, 9, 16, 25 . . . blocks to accomplish this? In other words, which of the pattern blocks do you think are reptiles? Activity 9.11 shows how this investigation might be introduced to students.

Activity 9.11

Reptiles

Lesson: Small Groups

Distribute a set of pattern blocks to groups of four students. Instruct the students to work only with the orange squares to construct as many squares of varying dimensions as they are able. As students successfully create squares, invite them to the front of the room to sketch on chart paper the squares they have created. Initiate a discussion about the number of smaller squares that can be used to create larger squares and define this sequence of numbers as the *perfect squares,* or square numbers.

Challenge the students to create successively larger, similar rhombi by using first 1, then 4, then 9, then 16 blue rhombi. This progression and its shell are shown in Figure 9.19.

After students have successfully determined the reptile progression for the orange squares and the blue rhombi, challenge them to see which of the remaining polygons in the pattern block set can also be called reptiles. Encourage the students to write a paragraph explaining why they think certain polygons are reptiles and why certain others are not. As an extension, ask students to consider a concave hexagon, as shown in Figure 9.20. Ask them to predict if this hexagon is a reptile or not, and to prove their claim.

Journal Reflection

Is the concave hexagon a reptile? Why do you think that? Try to develop a definition of polygons that are reptiles and polygons that are not.

Figure 9.19

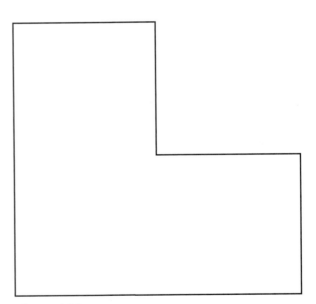

Figure 9.20

Multiplication of Whole Numbers and Binomials

One of the models of multiplication discussed in this text has been that of an array. When introducing 3×4 to children, one recommended model was a 3-square by 4-square quilt, or a 3-tile by 4-tile floor (Figure 9.21).

Figure 9.21

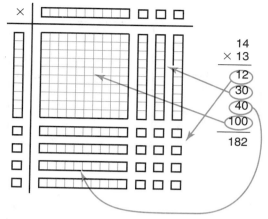

Figure 9.22

This array model was also used with powers-of-ten materials when we moved into double-digit multiplication. Examine the illustration of 13×14 (Figure 9.22) that has been connected to the symbolic partial products algorithm.

This same array model is useful to illustrate and help explain the multiplication of binomials. However, instead of powers-of-ten materials, the multiplication of binomials requires a manipulative called Algeblocks. The blocks that compose a set of powers-of-ten materials consist of one size block for each place value: a small cube to represent units, a long to represent a ten, a flat to represent a hundred, and a large cube to represent a thousand. Powers-of-ten materials are proportional, since 10 units are as long as one ten, 10 tens cover a hundred flat, and so on.

The corresponding Algeblocks include small cubes to represent units, two different-length longs to represent two different variables, x and y, and two different-size flats that represent x^2 and y^2, as shown in Figure 9.23.

An important difference between powers-of-ten blocks and Algeblocks is that Algeblocks are not entirely proportional. While the x^2 flat has sides of length x, and while the y^2 flat has sides of length y, there is not a whole-number relationship between the unit blocks and the x or the y longs. This is because the x and y longs can represent any quantity (variables). Therefore, they are not as long as a specific whole number of unit blocks.

This section will be more understandable if you can obtain a set of Algeblocks. Otherwise, you can trace and cut out the shapes provided in the Algeblocks template of Figure 9.23. The following figures will give you some familiarity with physical representations of algebraic expressions. Figure 9.24 illustrates the trinomial $x^2 + 2x + 3$.

Figure 9.25 illustrates the trinomial $y^2 + 3y + 1$. Stop reading for a minute. Use a set of Algeblocks to answer this question. How do you think you would use the array model of multiplication and Algeblocks to illustrate the product of:

$$(x + 2) \times (x + 1) =$$

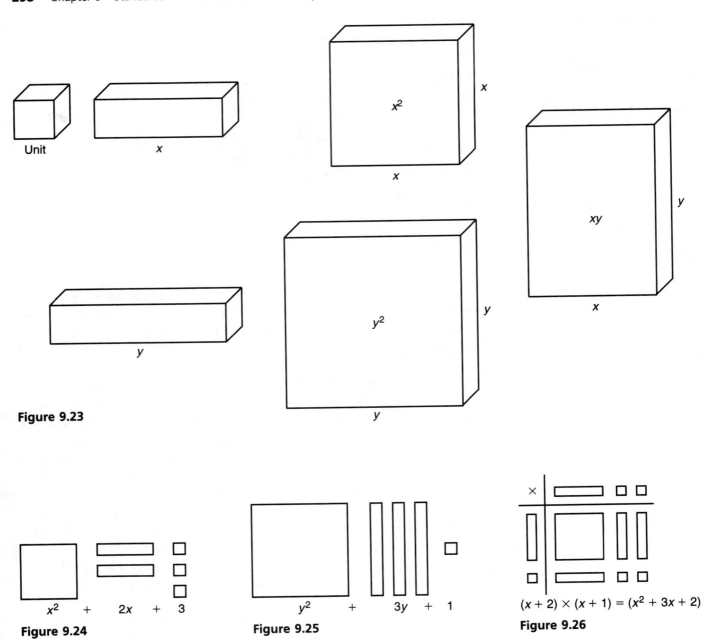

Figure 9.23

Unit x x^2 xy y^2 y

Figure 9.24

x^2 + $2x$ + 3

Figure 9.25

y^2 + $3y$ + 1

Figure 9.26

$(x + 2) \times (x + 1) = (x^2 + 3x + 2)$

Did you set up an array similar to that pictured in Figure 9.26? Do you see how the blocks correspond to the symbolic representation of the multiplication of these binomials? Do you see how Figure 9.26 and the algebraic terms associated with the blocks mirror what was done in Figure 9.22 with powers-of-ten blocks?

As practice, use Algeblocks (or some substitute) to illustrate the product of $(y + 3) \times (y + 2)$.

It is also possible to use Algeblocks to illustrate the multiplication of binomials involving two variables, such as:

$$(x + 3) \times (y + 2)$$

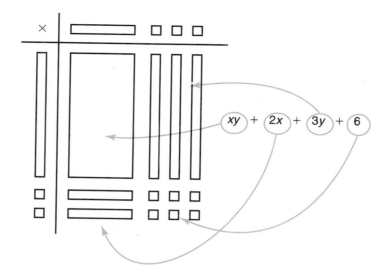

Figure 9.27

In this case, instead of representing the product of $x \times x$ as a square (or flat) of dimension x, we will need a way to represent the product of two variables, x and y. Since there are two distinct variables, their product cannot be represented by a square; it must be by a rectangle. Two opposite sides of the rectangle are of length x, and two opposite sides of the rectangle are of length y. The product of $(x + 3) \times (y + 2)$ is pictured in Figure 9.27.

If you are like many students I have taught, these physical representations of algebraic expressions are enlightening and valuable. Algeblocks provide another way to make sense of the symbolic manipulation of variables. Elementary school students often have the same reaction to manipulatives. They have an ah-ha! experience, and when they say "I see it!" they mean that as a literal statement. Providing a physical model helps students feel both satisfied and confident in their ability to understand mathematics.

Solving Equations with One Variable

Algeblocks can also be used to develop the concepts involved in solving an equation. The steps involved can be likened to keeping a pan scale in balance. Examine the equation $3x + 2 = 11$. Figure 9.28 depicts a balance model of this equation.

The scale is balanced because both sides of the equation are equivalent. To "solve" for the variable x, it is necessary to isolate that variable on one side of the scale while maintaining the balance (Figure 9.29).

- Remove 2 units from each side of the scale.
- Divide both sides by three.

Figure 9.28

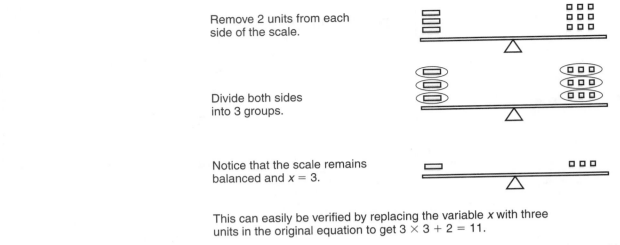

Remove 2 units from each side of the scale.

Divide both sides into 3 groups.

Notice that the scale remains balanced and $x = 3$.

This can easily be verified by replacing the variable x with three units in the original equation to get $3 \times 3 + 2 = 11$.

Figure 9.29

- Notice that the scale remains balanced and $x = 3$.

This can easily be verified by replacing the variable x with three units in the original equation to get $3 \times 3 + 2 = 11$.

Summary

This chapter addressed patterns in many guises: geometric patterns, visual patterns, numerical patterns, and patterns that can be represented geometrically, symbolically, and verbally. It made many connections between recognizing and identifying patterns and relationships, symbolizing patterns and relationships, and solving problems. As a teacher, your ability to recognize the underlying pattern of a problem offers the added advantage of allowing you to generate many other similar problems. When children try to solve a series of similar problems, they grow in confidence and ability, since experience with each previous problem informs subsequent problems and gives them a place to start.

This chapter dealt with operations on integers using the set model, which is designed to help students understand the reasons behind the often-confusing rules for adding, subtracting, multiplying, and dividing signed numbers. When mathematical operations make sense, they are easier to remember, reinforcing the image of mathematics as a sense-making discipline.

The chapter covered rules for divisibility, with special attention to the reasons they work. This provided an opportunity to work with algebraic symbolization since rules for divisibility, by their nature, are generalizable to any number.

Algeblocks, manipulatives that offer a physical representation of algebraic expressions, were introduced. These blocks are the algebraic version of powers-of-ten blocks, and in this chapter they were used to illustrate the array model of multiplying binomials with one and two variables.

Extending Your Learning

1. Write three different versions of the "bicycle and tricycle" type of problem found in Activity 9.6. In what contexts other than wheels on vehicles can these type of problems be placed? Can you write any problems that have more than one solution?

2. Describe how you might use a hundreds chart to introduce multiplication to second- or third-graders.

3. Explain how an understanding of patterns can help children to develop facility with basic addition/subtraction and multiplication/division facts. Describe three specific activities that can help children make that connection.

4. Describe three real-life situations in which knowledge of the rules for divisibility would be helpful. Use each of these situations to develop a mathematical activity appropriate for children in grades 6–8.

5. Write a realistic word problem for the following examples:

$$(+2) + (-5) = \qquad (-6) + (-6) =$$

$$(-7) - (+5) = \qquad (+4) - (-8) =$$

6. Research the role played by quilting in American history. Develop a lesson plan on patterning, using the theme of patchwork quilts.

7. Transfer three different patchwork quilt patterns onto graph paper. Represent each pattern symbolically in a way that makes sense to you. Invite your classmates to match each graph-paper pattern with its symbolic representation. Which types of symbol systems seem to be the most easily understood by your classmates? Why?

8. Describe three real-life contexts in which knowledge of prime and composite numbers are useful. Use each of these situations to develop a mathematical activity appropriate for children in grades 5–6.

9. Write a lesson plan, appropriate for grades K–1, to help children develop the skill of patterning. Use a piece of children's literature to motivate the lesson.

10. Obtain a copy of *One Grain of Rice* by Demi (1997). Use this book to develop a lesson plan, appropriate for grades 5–6, about exponential growth.

Internet Resources

www.edgate.com
This website, the Copernicus Education Gateway, contains such options as Teachers' Place, Parents' Place, School Notes, and a Collaboration Station that offers students access to bulletin boards, chat rooms, and e-mail discussion groups. Extensive links to math-related sites can be found here.

http://www.glenbrook.k12.il.us/gbsmat.population/pop.html
This website offers an activity of predicting how fast the population of Illinois is growing in comparison with the population of the United States. It suggests the user consult the U.S. census website

(*www.census.gov*) to obtain comparative data.

www.learner.org/teacherslab/math/patterns/index.html
This website, Patterns in Mathematics, is maintained by the Annenberg/CPB Math and Science Project. It provides classroom activities centered around number patterns, word patterns, and logic patterns.

http://www.xe.net/currency/
This website will be useful if you want to involve students in an algebraic activity about converting currency. It offers constantly updated information on currency conversions among more than seventy different currencies.

Bibliography

Awesome Animated Monster Maker Math. Software. Pleasantville, NY: Houghton Mifflin Interactive.

Bay, Jennifer M., Ann M. Bledsoe, and Robert E. Reys. (1998). Stating the facts: Exploring the United States. *Mathematics Teaching in the Middle School 4*(1).

Bemelmans, Ludwig. (1939). *Madeline.* New York: Scholastic.

Bradley, Elizabeth H. (1997). Is algebra in the cards? *Mathematics Teaching in the Middle School 2*(6).

Cantlon, Danise. (1998). Kids + conjecture = Mathematics power. *Mathematics Teaching in the Middle School 5*(2).

Carraher, David W. *Divide and conquer.* Software. Pleasantville, NY: Sunburst.

Clason, Robert G., Donna B. Ericksen, and Craig S. Ericksen. (1997). Cross-and-turn tile patterns. *Mathematics Teaching in the Middle School 2*(6).

D'Aboy, Diana A. (1997). Assessment through incredible equations. *Teaching Children Mathematics 4*(2).

Demi. (1997). *One grain of rice.* New York: Scholastic.

Ginsburg, Herbert P., and Joyce Baron. (1993). Cognition: Young children's construction of mathematics. In Robert J. Jensen (ed.), *Research ideas for the classroom: Early childhood mathematics.* New York: Macmillan.

Harrell, Marvin E., and Linda S. Fosnaugh. (1997). Allium to zircon: Mathematics and nature. *Mathematics Teaching in the Middle School 2*(6).

Irons, Calvin, James Burnett, and Stanley Wong Hoo Foon. (1993). *Mathematics from many cultures.* San Francisco: Mimosa Publications.

Johnston, Anita. (1994). *Algeblocks.* Cincinnati: South-Western.

Kenney, Patricia Ann, Judith S. Zawojewski, and Edward Silver. (1998). Marcy's dot pattern. *Mathematics Teaching in the Middle School 3*(7).

Lenchner, George. (1983). *Creative problem solving in school mathematics.* Boston: Houghton Mifflin.

Mighty Math Astro Algebra. Software. Redmond, WA: Edmark.

Quinn, Robert J. (1997). Developing conceptual understanding of relations and functions with attribute blocks. *Mathematics Teaching in the Middle School 3*(3).

Tracy, Dyanne M., and Mary S. Hague. (1997). Toys 'R' math. *Mathematics Teaching in the Middle School 2*(3).

Wickett, Maryann. (1997). Investigating problems and patterns with *The Thirteen Days of Halloween. Teaching Children Mathematics 4*(2).

Wright, John W. (Ed.). (1994). *The universal almanac.* Kansas City: Andrews and McMeel.

10

Standards for Data Analysis, Statistics, and Probability

Students in elementary school today are growing up in a world that is very different from the world in which you grew up. If you were to look at the front page of a leading newspaper from several decades ago, it would appear dense in comparison with newspapers of today. Years ago, newspapers contained columns and columns of text, few photographs, and almost no charts or graphs. In contrast, newspapers published today are filled with visual and graphical representations of data with relatively little text. This satisfies the desire for quick assimilation but may fail to present the complete picture necessary for citizens in a modern democracy. Sometimes the purpose of representing data visually is an unbiased attempt to inform the reader. Sometimes it is not. For example, the advertising industry presents information more to persuade than inform. Advertising today is both sophisticated and pervasive.

Students who are uncritical about interpreting and analyzing information presented in the media are at the mercy of those who wish to manipulate their beliefs and actions. In addition, there are currently many opportunities for people to engage in legalized gambling in the form of state-sponsored lottery games and casinos. People who choose to engage in legalized gambling need to understand that they are far more likely to lose than to win.

For these reasons, it is important that students have a strong background in the areas of statistics and probability. These topics are often fascinating to students. They are easily applied to real life situations, they lend themselves to classroom activities, and they provide an opportunity to connect many areas of mathematics, such as fractions, decimals, and percents, whole-number computation, measurement, geometry, and problem solving.

Graphing and Data Analysis

An underlying theme of this text is that mathematics is a discipline that helps people make sense of the world in which they live. Young children are delightfully curious about the world in which they live and are eager to communicate information they have uncovered. Graphing can serve the purpose of helping children think about how they might present information for others to examine, and how that information can then be interpreted.

Focus Areas for Grades Pre-K–2

According to NCTM *Principles and Standards*, in grades Pre-K–2 the mathematics curriculum should include experiences with data analysis, statistics, and probability so that students can

- Gather data about themselves and their surroundings to answer questions that involve multiple responses;

- Represent data to convey results at a glance using concrete objects, pictures, and numbers.

- Identify parts of the data with special characteristics, for example the category with the most frequent response.

- Understand notions such as certain, impossible, more likely, less likely. (pp. 130–31)

Just as early introduction to number should entail connecting a numerical symbol to some concrete reality, early introduction to graphs should entail connecting graphical symbols to concrete objects. Pictorial representations assist the young child in making numerical comparisons such as greater than, less than, equal to, as much as, and so on.

Physical Graphs

One of the first types of graphs that young children can create is a physical graph. A physical (iconic) graph employs actual physical objects in an organized display. Activity 10.1 involves creating and interpreting a physical graph of items that are important to children—their shoes!

Once children have had a variety of experiences with physical graphs, the teacher can progress to picture graphs. Here, pictures are used to represent items. In the very early grades, a one-to-one correspondence should be clearly made between the number of pictures and the number of items being graphed. Later on, a picture can be used to represent quantities of an item, which is an example of one-to-many correspondence. Figure 10.2 shows two stages of creating a picture graph about weather. Throughout the previous month, the class had been indicating the daily weather on a calendar using sun, rain, cloud, and snow symbols. The number of each type of symbol is determined and marked on a tally chart as shown in Figure 10.2a. The picture graph is then created to correspond to the tally chart as shown in Figure 10.2b.

Bar Graphs

A bar graph uses rectangles of varying lengths and uniform width to depict quantity. A bar graph is used for comparisons of categories. Generally, bar graphs are not used to depict continuous changes over a period of time. Representation of these kinds of data is more adequately provided by a line graph. As with all graphs, the numerical labels of the horizontal and vertical axes must be consistent; that is, the increments along a given axis must use a

Activity 10.1

Physical Graphs

Lesson: Whole Group

Invite each child to remove one shoe and place it in the center of the room. Invite some children to sort the shoes in any way they choose. Some possible bases for sorting the shoes would be color, style, number of lace holes, size, or materials. If no one has suggested it, invite the children to sort the shoes into two categories, sneakers and non-sneakers.

Using a large sheet of plastic on which lines have been drawn to create rows and columns as the background for the graph, invite the children to find their shoe and place it in the appropriate row on the graph. Index cards can be used to label the horizontal and vertical axes of the graph (Figure 10.1).

After the graph has been created, engage the children in a discussion about the information it communicates.

Some questions you might pose include:

- "How many children in our class are wearing sneakers? How do you know?"

- "How many more children are wearing sneakers than other types of shoes? How do you know?"

- "How many children are in class today? How do you know?"

- "If a child from the class next door walks by our room, what kind of shoes do you think he or she will be wearing? Why?"

Journal Reflection

What other contexts are appropriate for the creation of physical, or iconic, graphs?

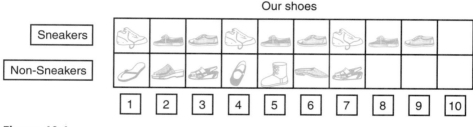

Figure 10.1

consistent scale throughout. Providing children with inch square graph paper can help them create a bar graph, as described in Activity 10.2.

Young children come to school with an enviable curiosity. Everything delights them and everything interests them. One of the ways you can

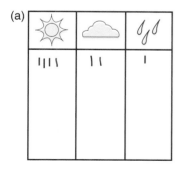

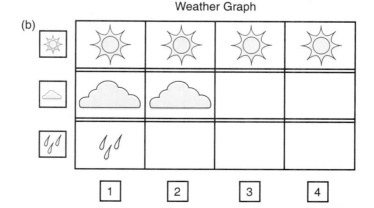

Figure 10.2

Activity 10.2
Bar Graphs

Lesson: Whole Class

Create on the board a tally chart of students' choices for lunch. With these data, invite the children to create a bar graph to represent the lunch choices (Figure 10.3).

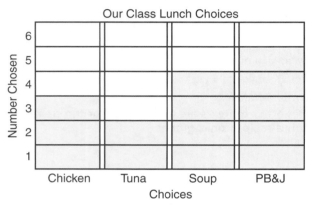

Our Class Lunch Choices

Figure 10.3

In addition to showing at a glance which lunch choice is most popular and which is least, this bar graph can also provide the opportunity for children to explore numbers. For example, after the graph pictured in Figure 10.3 is created, the children can be invited to write problems about the graph for their classmates. Some possible responses are:

■ "How many children wanted chicken? How many children wanted tuna fish? How many more children wanted chicken?"

■ "Can you tell how many children are in class today? How did you figure out your answer?"

Journal Reflection

Describe realistic contexts for early elementary grades in which a picture graph might be appropriate. Describe realistic contexts in which a bar graph is more appropriate.

encourage children to learn about the world around them is to help them to examine and organize their discoveries. Activity 10.3 involves young children in the creation of a concrete graph.

A Three Hat Day by Laura Geringer is a piece of children's literature that can be used to help students think about combinations and permutations. In this book, a character named R. R. Pottle collects hats. One day he puts on three of them and proceeds to go for a walk. A *combination* of three hats is simply a collection of three hats, and the order in which they are worn does not matter. A mathematical question about combinations can be asked:

■ If R. R. Pottle has 5 hats, how many different combinations of 3 hats are there?

A *permutation* of three hats is the set of different arrangements of the hats, and the order in which they are worn is what distinguishes one permutation from another. A mathematical question about permutations can be asked:

■ How many different arrangements or permutations of three hats are there?

Activity 10.4, which is adapted from an entry in *Math and Literature (K–3)* by Marilyn Burns, describes how children can be engaged in solving a problem about permutations.

Activity 10.3

The Very Hungry Caterpillar

Lesson: Whole Class

Begin by reading Eric Carle's book *The Very Hungry Caterpillar* to the children. Then ask them to recall what the caterpillar ate on Monday, on Tuesday, and so on. Challenge them to represent, in any way that makes sense to them, the number and the types of fruit the caterpillar ate on Monday, Tuesday, Wednesday, Thursday, and Friday. Encourage the children to refer to the book if necessary. Provide them with plain and construction paper, crayons, markers, and fruit stampers and a stamp pad. Invite the children to share with the rest of their class the method they used to represent the fruits eaten by the caterpillar.

On the floor spread a discarded white sheet or tablecloth, on which a nine-inch square grid has been drawn or marked off with colored tape. Provide the children with 6 pieces of each of the following: apples, oranges, strawberries, plums, and pears. Invite them to think of a way that the large grid and the fruit could be used to represent the number and types of fruit eaten by the caterpillar on the five weekdays. Probably the children will arrange the fruit to form a graph similar to the one pictured in Figure 10.4.

After the children have had a sufficient amount of time to think about and solve this problem, assess their understanding with questions such as:

- How many strawberries did the caterpillar eat on Thursday? How do you know?
- How can you tell what fruit the caterpillar ate on which day? (If the children have not yet thought of labeling each row or column of fruit with the days of the week, suggest that to them at this point.)
- How many more plums did the caterpillar eat than pears? How do you know?
- How many pieces of fruit did the caterpillar eat all together on the five days?
- How many pieces of fruit did you begin with? How do you know?
- How many pieces of fruit are left over after creating the graph? How do you know?

Journal Reflection

This type of graph is called a *concrete* graph, since actual objects are used to form the graph. What do you see as advantages or disadvantages of concrete graphs? In what other contexts would it be easy to form concrete graphs in the classroom?

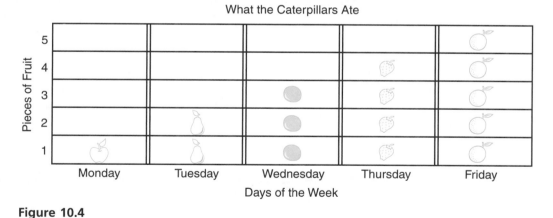

What the Caterpillars Ate

Figure 10.4

Data Collection and Representation

Involving children in the actual collection of data is preferable to handing them data already collected by you or someone else. Activity 10.5 describes a way to turn snack time into a data collection lesson.

When engaging young children in activities of data collection and analysis, it is important that the data gathered are meaningful to the children, reflecting their own personal interests and characteristics. To help children take responsibility for their own learning, they should be encouraged to

Activity 10.4

Permutations

Lesson: Whole Class

Read *A Three Hat Day* to the class. Pose the following question to the children:

- I wonder how many different ways R. R. Pottle could wear three different hats?

Have three hats available for the children to try on to model the problem. After the children have had an opportunity to think, draw, and write about the problem, engage the class in a discussion about the different ways to solve the problem.

Some children may have actually tried on the hats, others may have drawn pictures, and still others may have thought about it analytically. For instance, some children may have reasoned that each hat should have two chances to be first, since the second and third hats could switch places to create different permutations. If each hat has two chances to be first and there are three hats, then six permutations exist.

Journal Reflection

What strategies can you employ to help young children articulate their thoughts?

Strength in Numbers

Combinations

Cooperative Group Model: Jigsaw

Working in groups of three, each student is to solve this problem in a different way. Some possible strategies are to use: a visual approach, Pascal's Triangle, a calculator like the TI Explorer Plus, or the formula. After each member has had the opportunity to solve the problem, the group meets to share solutions and strategies. Discuss the advantages and disadvantages of each strategy. Share your group's solutions with the rest of the class, and examine the number of ways this problem might be solved.

- Ten people volunteered to test a new drug. Five of these volunteers will be administered a placebo and the remainder will get the actual drug. How many different placebo groups are possible?

---

identify a question they want answered and then attempt to answer it in ways that make sense to them. It is helpful for the teacher to have appropriate tools available—paper, pencils, crayons, rulers, scissors, newsprint, and so on. Curcio and Folkson (1996) claim that " . . . the success of child-generated data-collection tasks is based on two criteria: (1) the information to be collected must be *useful* to the children, and (2) the information must be naturally *interesting* to them."

Patricia Cartland introduced the concept of glyphs in the February 1996 issue of *Teaching Children Mathematics*. *Glyphs* are based on the historical symbol system of hieroglyphics and are used to communicate pieces of information visually. Each glyph has a key that is used to interpret the visually represented data. Glyphs can be used to represent three, four, or

Activity 10.5

Estimating the Number of Raisins in a Box

Lesson: Individual

Distribute a small box of raisins (14.1 g) to each child, along with a clean sheet of paper to act as a place mat. Encourage the children to describe the box (color, size, shape, weight) and to estimate the number of raisins they believe to be in the box. Record some of the estimates. Invite the children to empty the box and count and record the number of raisins inside (without eating any for now).

Invite the children to share the strategies they used to count the number of raisins, such as grouping them in fives or tens, counting them two-by-two, or arranging them in some visual pattern to assist in the counting. Challenge the children to compare the actual number of raisins in their box with their estimate and to determine how far their estimate was from the actual number of raisins.

While the children are eating the raisins, invite them to discuss with a partner how the information obtained from the activity could be displayed so it could be shared with others. Carry out any of their ideas that are feasible. It is likely that someone will suggest representing the information graphically. There are several ways that this might be done. Figure 10.5 shows one possible way.

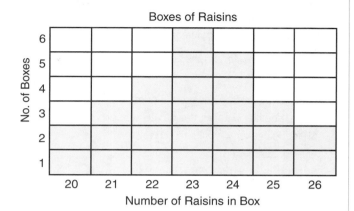

Figure 10.5

Journal Reflection

What other visual representations of the number of raisins in a box might first-or second-graders suggest? What would be the strengths or weaknesses of each?

even five pieces of data. For example, the following key could be used to interpret the Valentine glyphs pictured in Figure 10.6:

> White heart = likes chocolate hearts
>
> Shaded heart = likes candy hearts
>
> Rectangular background = male
>
> Oval background = female
>
> Number of small hearts = number of members in family
>
> Arrow on Valentine = has a pet
>
> No arrow on Valentine = does not have a pet

Do you see that the glyph on the left might have been made by a male child who likes chocolate hearts, has three members in his family, and has a pet? How would you describe the child who might have made the glyph on the right? Activity 10.6 indicates how glyphs can be used for data analysis in the classroom.

(a)    (b)

Figure 10.6

Activity 10.6

Glyphs

Lesson: Individual

At the start of the school year, glyphs can be used to help children get to know one another. Using the following key, invite the children to make a glyph that describes them.

Number of holes in sneakers = number of people in family

White sneaker = takes the bus to school

Shaded sneaker = walks to school

Curled laces = girl

Straight laces = boy

Letter "S" inside circle = eats school lunch

Letter "H" inside circle = brings lunch from home

Figure 10.7 shows a sample glyph for a girl with six people in her family who walks to school and eats the school lunch.

When the children have completed their glyphs, invite them to spread the glyphs out on the floor. Point to a particular glyph and ask if the children can identify its owner. Invite the children to explain how they made the identification.

Completed glyphs can be used for a variety of statistical investigations. Children can sort the glyphs into groups

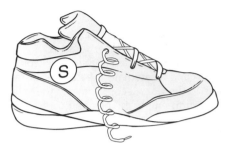

Figure 10.7

(male/female, takes the bus/ walks to school), they can form categorical graphs with the glyphs (different rows or columns of glyphs to identify those who walk to school or those who take the bus to school), and they can arrange the glyphs into Venn diagrams. Figure 10.8 shows how circles of string can be labeled to introduce children to Venn diagrams.

Journal Reflection

How might the sneaker glyphs be used to introduce the concepts of range, median, mode, and mean?

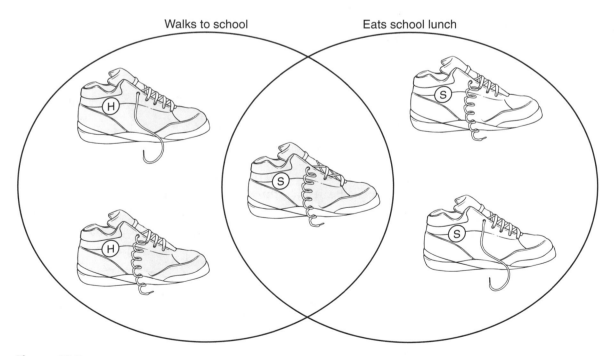

Walks to school   Eats school lunch

Figure 10.8

Using Graphs to Assess Children's Knowledge

A completed graph provides a valuable opportunity for the teacher to assess children's knowledge about the graph itself and what it represents, about number and numeration concepts, and about problem solving. After reading *Green Eggs and Ham* by Dr. Seuss, students might be asked how many eggs they could eat, and the information could be graphically displayed as in Figure 10.9. Assessment questions about interpreting the graph might be:

- What number of eggs did most children choose? How do you know?
- What number of eggs did the fewest children choose? How do you know?
- How many more children chose two eggs than five eggs? How do you know?

Assessment questions about number and numeration concepts might be:

- How many eggs would be eaten by all of the children who chose two eggs? Five eggs? Three eggs?"
- How many eggs were eaten by all of the children who chose five eggs *and* all of the children who chose one egg?

Assessment questions about problem solving might be:

- How many eggs would be eaten by all of the children in this class? How do you know?

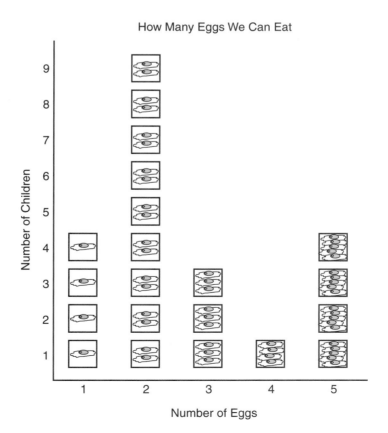

How Many Eggs We Can Eat

Number of Children

Number of Eggs

Figure 10.9

By paying attention to the way in which children arrive at these answers, teachers can learn a lot about what children know. For example, if asked how many eggs would be eaten by people who chose two eggs, a child might be observed to count by twos, while pointing to each pair of eggs on the graph, to arrive at the answer of 18. The teacher could then infer that the child was able to skip count and could use this skill appropriately. Alternately, in response to this same question, a child might quickly say "Eighteen." When asked to explain how he or she knew that, the child might answer that "Nine and nine make eighteen." The teacher could then infer that the child knew the double fact of $9 + 9$, and that the child also realized that if there were nine entries in the 2 column, that the total number of eggs represented by that column could be found by adding $9 + 9$.

When asked to combine the number of children who chose five eggs with the number of children who chose one egg, some children might find the total for five eggs and the total for one egg, and then add these numbers together. A more sophisticated response would be if a child skip-counted by five to find the total in the 5 column, and then counted by ones: "Five, ten, fifteen, twenty, twenty-one, twenty-two, twenty-three, twenty-four." This type of response would indicate to the teacher that the child was ready to engage in tasks involving counting money (especially with nickels and pennies) or time.

When presented with the problem of determining the total number of eggs represented by the graph, children might use a calculator, exhibiting an appropriate use of technology. They might find subtotals for each column, and then find the grand total, exhibiting knowledge of partial sums. They might use tally marks to enumerate each egg, exhibiting a relatively low-level problem-solving strategy. Alternatively, they might pick out compatible numbers and find the sum almost entirely mentally, exhibiting a high-level problem-solving strategy.

Good teachers continually assess children's knowledge and use this information to structure future learning experiences for the children in their classes. Having students spend a lot of classroom time creating graphs by hand is unwise, particularly since there are a number of graphing software packages available. *Graphers* (Sunburst, grades K–4), for example, enables students quickly and easily to create pictographs, bar graphs, circle graphs, loops, grid plots, and line graphs.

Another valuable aspect of developing competency in graphing is the ability to interpret graphs. The following performance-based assessment asks students to use their imaginations and their understanding of graphs to offer possible contexts for unlabeled graphs.

Performance-Based Assessment: Placing Graphs in Contexts

Duplicate the graphs shown in Figure 10.10 or have them copied onto overhead transparencies. Invite the students to offer possible contexts in which these graphs might be used. Ask them to include in their answers a title, the labels and scale for each axis, and a three- or four-sentence explanation for

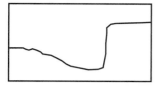
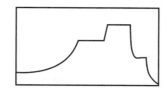
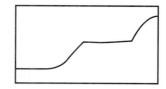

Figure 10.10

each graph. A sample response for the first graph that would have received five points on the rubric below might be:

- ◼ "This line graph might be a record of the height of snow on the ground over a week's time. The title would be 'Height of Snow in Centimeters.' The horizontal axis would be the seven days of the week and would represent the days on which the snow measurements were made. The scale along the vertical axis would be from 1 to 30 centimeters and would represent the height of the snow in a particular spot. According to this graph, the height of snow began to decrease a bit at first (I guess because it melted a little or because it became packed down). Then there was a real decrease; the temperature must have gone above freezing. Finally, the height of the snow increased, which must mean that there was a snowstorm."

The following rubric can be used for each graph to assess students' performance:

5 Student supplies reasonable title, labels and scales for both axes, and the explanation is both coherent and a good match with the graph.

4 Explanation of graph is both a good match and coherent, but one of the following is missing or inaccurate: title, scale and label of horizontal axis, scale and label of vertical axis.

3 Explanation of graph is both a good match and coherent, but two or more of the following are missing or inaccurate: title, scale and label of horizontal axis, scale and label of vertical axis.

2 Title, scales, and labels are all reasonable, but explanation is either lacking, incomplete, or a poor match to the visual graph.

1 While many errors or omissions exist, student shows some evidence of reasonable interpretation of graph.

0 No evidence of understanding.

Using Data to Solve Problems

Collecting data for the sake of collecting data is of dubious value. Rather, the purpose of collecting information and then organizing and representing it is to help people find out things they didn't already know, see patterns that were not previously apparent, and make decisions based on the data. The NCTM *Principles and Standards* recommend that, in grades 3–5, all students should

- ◼ Formulate questions they want to investigate;

- Design data investigations to address a question;

- Collect data using observations, measurement, surveys, or experiments;

- Organize data using tables and graphs (bar graph, line plot, stem-and-leaf plot, circle graph, line graph);

- Use graphs to analyze data and to present information to an audience;

- Compare data representations to determine which aspects of the data they highlight or obscure. (p.181)

Many problems that naturally occur during the course of the school day can be solved by collecting and analyzing data. Imagine that the fifth grade in a particular school has been asked to choose the movie that will be shown on the last day of school. The fifth-graders begin by asking their classmates to suggest movie titles. They soon realize, however, that dozens of movies have been suggested and that each has its staunch supporters. Activity 10.7 shows how this problem might be solved.

Activity 10.7
Conducting a Survey

Lesson: Whole Class

When faced with choosing a movie for the last day of school, students quickly realize that simply asking everyone what movie they would like to see does not result in a decision. This situation can be used as an opportunity to help children think about how they could collect a manageable amount of data.

Begin a discussion about how to present the entire school with a limited set of movies from which to choose. Suggest that your class members conduct a preliminary survey to narrow the field to four or five movies. Introduce the concept of random sampling by suggesting that fifth-grade students stand at the door of the cafeteria and ask every fourth student who enters the cafeteria to state their favorite movie. Students will easily see that this *random sampling* will produce a smaller number of suggested movies and that, after discarding unsuitable movies, they should be able to come up with a brief list to appear on a ballot that the entire school could vote upon.

When the ballots are collected, students can be invited to think of different strategies for tallying the votes. They may decide to keep running tallies for each movie on large sheets of chart paper, they may decide to record the votes on a spreadsheet or use a calculator to determine the number of votes for each choice, or they may physically sort the student responses into piles and bundle together groups of ten ballots for easy totalling. An appropriate culminating activity would be for the fifth-graders to write a summary statement for the rest of the school explaining how the winning movie was chosen. This will reassure their schoolmates that the choice was unbiased and reflected the wishes of the student body.

Journal Reflection

If the fifth-grade students decided to represent the results of the vote graphically, what form of visual representation do you think would be most appropriate? Why?

Line Graphs

Line graphs are used to represent change over time. One axis is typically used to represent time (hours, days, months, years) The other axis is used to represent the measure of a certain quantity (temperature in degrees, rainfall in centimeters, sales of cars in hundreds of cars, amount of oil imports in thousands of barrels). Line graphs are often used for recording weather data, since comparison of temperatures over time is useful in identifying trends. Activity 10.8 gives practice in constructing and interpreting line graphs.

Measures of Central Tendency

Measures of central tendency, like graphical representations, serve to organize data so that they can be quickly interpreted and analyzed. The three measures of central tendency most commonly used in elementary school are the mean, the median, and the mode. It is important that students have

---

Activity 10.8

Line Graphs

Lesson: Individual

Each day for one month, a student is given the task of determining the outdoor temperature at 10 A.M. and recording the temperature on a line graph (Figure 10.11). The information on the graph can then be used to answer these questions about that month's weather:

- On what day was the warmest temperature recorded?
- On what day was the coldest temperature recorded?
- What is the difference between the warmest temperature and the coldest temperature?
- Between what two days did the temperature drop the most?

- Between what two days did the temperature increase the most?
- During what week was the least change in temperature recorded? What does this look like on the line graph?

If another line graph is made several months later, students can compare temperature ranges for each month.

Journal Reflection

Why is a line graph more appropriately used to depict changes than a bar graph or picture graph?

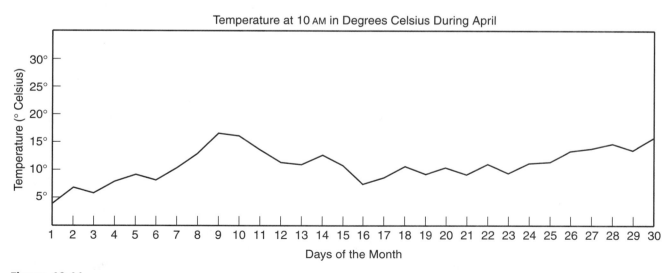

Figure 10.11

Activity 10.9

Measures of Central Tendency

Lesson: Small Groups

Arrange the class into groups of 4 to 6 and distribute a basket of Unifix cubes to each group. Introduce the activity by asking students to predict how many pencils are in their desk. Record some of the predictions on the board. Then ask the students to count all the pencils in their desk and make a tower of Unifix cubes where one cube stands for each pencil.

Ask the groups to decide what single number best describes the number of pencils in the desks of the people in their group, and to tell the class why they think that. Possible responses might be:

- "We think 6 is the best number to describe the number of pencils in a desk because two people in our group have 6 pencils. Everyone else has a different number."

- "We think that 5 is the best number because three people have fewer than 5 pencils and three people have more than 5 pencils. It's about in the middle."

Invite the students to stack the individual towers of Unifix cubes in the middle of the table, trying to make all the towers the same height by taking cubes from the taller towers to give to the shorter towers. The process might look something like Figure 10.12.

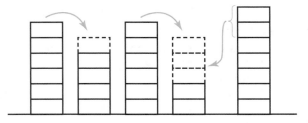

Figure 10.12

In this case, 5 is a good number to describe the number of pencils in each desk because the original towers can be rearranged into towers of five cubes. Use this opportunity to introduce the concept of *mean* as a number that represents the general tendency of a group of numbers. The mean of the number of pencils from the people in this group is 5.

Now, ask the students to put the Unifix cubes back into the original towers. Invite them to take their tower of cubes and arrange themselves around the room in order according to the number of cubes in their towers. Initiate a discussion of the number of students in class that day and how to determine the "middle" student if the students were arranged in some kind of order. For instance, if there were 25 students in class, the 13th student would mark the middle, since 12 students would be "below" and 12 students would be "above." Count off to find the 13th student. Use this opportunity to define the *median* as the middle value when the scores or objects or values are arranged in order.

Finally, ask the students, still holding their towers, to arrange themselves in columns along one wall according to the number of cubes in their tower. In essence, the students are forming a human bar graph. Identify the column that has the most students in it as representing the *mode,* or the most common value. If two columns of equal length both represent the mode, the set of data is said to be *bimodal.* Alternately, many sets of data have no mode.

Journal Reflection

In this instance, which measure of central tendency do you think is the most representative? Why? Describe three different situations in which each of the measures of central tendency would be the most representative.

many tangible experiences with these concepts so that their understanding of the concept of the mean, for example, is fuller than simply knowing to "add up the scores and divide by the number of scores." Activity 10.9 provides an opportunity to engage children in an analysis of data through measures of central tendency.

Introducing Concepts of Chance

Young children have an intuitive understanding of chance events, and these intuitive understandings become more refined as time goes on (Carpenter et al., 1981). When experiencing chance events, children sometimes impose a pattern where no pattern exists. For example, when tossing a fair coin and getting several heads in a row, many children believe that they are more likely to toss a tail next. They reason that it is "time" for a tail to come up or that the coin has "used up" all of its heads (Piaget and Inhelder, 1975.) To encourage the refinement of intuitive probability concepts, children of all ages will benefit from participating in activities that encourage them to think about chance events and attempt to make sense of them. Activity 10.10 provides experience with chance.

Representing Probability as a Fraction

Depending on the developmental level of the children with whom you are working, you may wish to use Activity 10.10 as an opportunity to introduce a numerical representation of the likelihood that a particular outcome will occur. For instance, after you share the contents of the brown paper bag with the students, you can define the probability of choosing a blue cube from the bag as 4 out of 5, or ⅘, since four of the five cubes are blue. Conversely, the probability of choosing a red cube out of the bag is 1 out of 5, or ⅕, since one of the five cubes is red.

These fractions can be posted on a number line that stretches from 0 to 1. You can encourage the students to generalize that the closer to 1 a probability fraction is, the more likely it is to occur, and the closer to 0 a probability fraction is, the less likely it is to occur.

This demonstration can be extended by asking students to represent as a fraction the probability of choosing a green cube out of the same bag of only 4 blue and 1 red cubes. The students should offer ⅘, or 0, as the appropriate fraction. Invite a student to post this fraction on the number line.

Finally, ask the students to represent as a fraction the probability of choosing either a red or a blue cube from the same bag of blue and red

---

Activity 10.10
Cubes in a Bag

Lesson: Whole Class

Display a brown paper bag into which you have previously placed 4 blue cubes and 1 red cube. Tell the children that there are 5 cubes inside the bag, and that some of the cubes are blue and some of the cubes are red. Explain that you will choose a cube from the bag without looking, show it to the class, and then replace it, and that you will repeat this many times. Challenge the children to figure out how many cubes of each color are inside the bag. Engage the children in a discussion of all of the possible combinations of red and blue cubes and record the different possibilities. (This is to avoid the situation where a child who sees that a blue cube has been chosen 15 times and a red cube has been chosen 4 times believes that there are, in fact, 15 blue and 4 red cubes in the bag.)

After choosing and recording the color of the cube approximately 25 to 30 times, invite the children to share with their classmates their beliefs about the cubes in the bag. If there are disagreements, encourage children to convince others of the validity of their belief. Repeat the activity with another combination of cubes.

Journal Reflection

How might this activity be used to reinforce an understanding of basic addition facts?

Figure 10.13

cubes. The students should represent the probability of this outcome as ⅘, or 1 whole, since all five cubes are either red or blue.

Associating the terms *impossible, unlikely, likely,* and *certain* to these fractional values (Figure 10.13) helps students connect their understanding of probabilistic outcomes to everyday language.

Probability for Grades 3–5

The NCTM *Principles and Standards* recommend that students understand and apply basic notions of chance and probability. They state that in grades 3–5, all students should

- Discuss events as likely or unlikely and give descriptions of the degree of likelihood in informal terms (unlikely, very unlikely, certain, impossible);

- Estimate, describe, and test probabilities of outcomes by associating the degree of certainty with a value ranging from 0 to 1 (in simple experiments involving spinners with different fractions shaded). (p. 182)

An important concept for children to investigate is the concept of events where the outcomes are *equally likely* and events where the outcomes are *not equally likely.* A chance device with equally likely outcomes is not necessarily fair when used in a game (imagine getting a point only if the coin lands on heads) and a chance device with not equally likely outcomes is not necessarily unfair when used in a game (imagine getting twice the points if the spinner landed on a section half the size of the others). However, children tend not to analyze probabilistic situations. Rather, their belief about the fairness or unfairness of situations is based on their limited personal experience with the chance device. This suggests that children need an informal introduction to the difference between *theoretical probability,* or probability based on a theoretical analysis of the chance device, and *experimental probability,* or probability based on the actual outcome of an event.

For example, consider tossing a fair coin. Since there are only two equally likely outcomes for this event, tossing a head or tossing a tail, the theoretical probability of each of these outcomes is 50%, or ½. However, if you actually performed the experiment of tossing a fair coin 10 times, you might get 3 heads and 7 tails. In this case, the theoretical probability of tossing a head (50%) does not equal the experimental probability of tossing a head (30%). But actually tossing a fair coin 1000 times would result in a much closer match between the theoretical probability of tossing a head and the experimental probability of the same outcome. Tossing a fair coin 1,000,000 times would result in a still closer match. In general, the more often a probability experiment is conducted, the closer the match between the theoretical probability and the experimental probability. Activity 10.11 gives the students practice with spinners and outcomes.

Probability is a concept that can be used to develop a greater understanding of fractions, decimals, and percents, and a greater understanding of basic facts. Despite the richness of this topic, the chapter on probability is relegated to the end of the book in many elementary school math textbooks.

Activity 10.11

Spinners

Lesson: Pairs

Distribute spinners similar to that of Figure 10.14 to each pair of children. Ask the children to predict what could happen when the spinner is spun. Probable responses are:

- "It could land on red, blue, or yellow."
- "It might land on the line."

"This is an unfair spinner. The outcomes for this spinner were not equally likely because
_____."

"Yellow was the most likely outcome because
_____."

Repeat the above activity twice more, using the two spinners pictured in Figure 10.15.

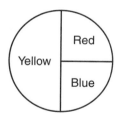

Figure 10.14

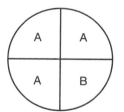 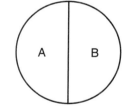

Figure 10.15

Define the word *outcome* as what could happen when the spinner is spun, and explain that if the spinner lands on a line, it should be spun again. Ask the students to predict the color they think will come up most often and discuss with their partner why they think that. Then, invite the children to spin the spinner 20 times, while their partner records the outcomes.

Record and summarize on chart paper the data from several pairs' outcomes, and ask the children what they think about the data. Encourage the children to recognize that, because the yellow sector was twice the size of either the red or the blue sector, it came up close to twice as often. Introduce the terms *equally likely* and *not equally likely*. Invite the students to complete the following sentences:

Finally, to assess the students' understandings, invite the children to make their own spinner that shows two different outcomes, where one outcome is more likely to occur than the other. Have the children present their spinners to the class. If there is any disagreement among the students about whether or not a particular spinner fits the description, invite the children to spin it many times and record the outcomes. Encourage them to use these data to support or refute the correctness of the spinner.

Journal Reflection

How would you respond to children who base their beliefs about the likelihood of certain outcomes on their own individual results and are not persuaded by the preponderance of evidence?

For this reason, teachers do not always get to it. However, addressing probability when basic facts are addressed, or when fractions are addressed, allows teachers and students to make connections among the various areas of mathematics and to explore one of the contexts in which fractions, decimals, and percents are used. Activity 10.12 describes a strategy that can be used to investigate the fractional representation of the probability of an event.

Activity 10.12

Probability Fractions

Lesson: Small Groups

Before this activity, prepare eleven unmarked brown paper bags. Into the first, place 10 black cubes. Into the second, place 1 white cube and 9 black cubes. Into the third, place 2 white cubes and 8 black cubes. Into the fourth, place 3 white ones and 7 black ones. Continue in this fashion until the eleventh bag contains 10 white cubes.

Distribute the bags randomly to groups of students. Invite them to choose a cube from the bag without looking, record its color, and then replace the cube in the bag. Ask them to repeat this action approximately 50 times. Since this activity requires students to perform an experiment, you can see that it investigates experimental probability. Tell the students that each bag contains 10 cubes, and challenge them to predict how many white cubes their bag contains.

Then ask the students to empty the bags and arrange the cubes into towers with the white cubes (if any) on the top. Since this activity requires the students to examine the chance device itself, you can see that it investigates theoretical probability. On an index card, have each group represent the number of white cubes in their bag as both a percent of the total number of cubes and as a fraction, where the number of white cubes in their bag is the numerator and the total number of cubes is the denominator. Then, display the towers in order along with their corresponding cards (Figure 10.16).

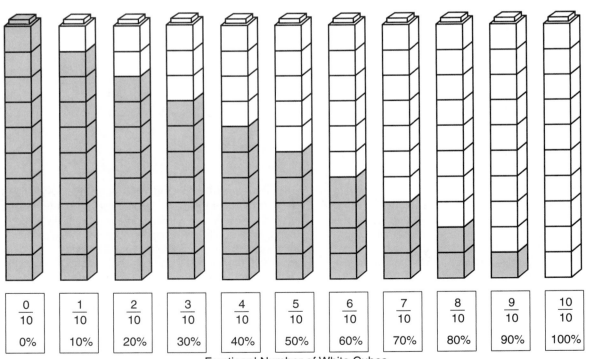

| $\frac{0}{10}$ | $\frac{1}{10}$ | $\frac{2}{10}$ | $\frac{3}{10}$ | $\frac{4}{10}$ | $\frac{5}{10}$ | $\frac{6}{10}$ | $\frac{7}{10}$ | $\frac{8}{10}$ | $\frac{9}{10}$ | $\frac{10}{10}$ |
| 0% | 10% | 20% | 30% | 40% | 50% | 60% | 70% | 80% | 90% | 100% |

Fractional Number of White Cubes

Figure 10.16

(continued)

Activity 10.12 (continued)

Probability Fractions

Invite the students to make some observations. Possible remarks are:

- "In each tower, the number of white cubes increases by one. The first tower has no white cubes, but the last tower has ten."

- "I knew there were no black cubes in our bag because we only picked out white ones."

Use this opportunity to introduce a theoretical probability fraction as one where the numerator is the number of favorable outcomes (in this case, white cubes) and the denominator is the total number of outcomes (in this case, 10). Encourage the students to generalize that the closer the value of the fraction gets to 0, the less likely it is for that outcome to occur, while the closer the value of the fraction gets to 1, the more likely it is for that outcome to occur. A probability value of 0 represents an impossible event (in this case, choosing a white cube from a bag containing only black cubes), while a probability value of 1 represents a certain event (in this case, choosing a white cube from a bag containing only white cubes.)

Encourage the students to write a fraction to describe various situations around them, such as the probability that a student chosen randomly from their class will be wearing glasses, the probability that a car chosen randomly from the parking lot that day will be green, or the probability that a crayon chosen randomly from a particular box will be blue.

Journal Reflection

How might you connect the concept of a fractional representation of the probability of an event to the area model of fractions?

As you teach lessons on probability, be aware that some children may not be permitted to use playing cards and/or dice at home. To guard against giving a child something at school that is not permitted at home, send a letter home prior to any lessons involving chance devices. If any concerns are expressed by parents or caregivers, inquire if plain wooden cubes with numerals on them are acceptable alternatives to dice, or if index cards with numerals written in different colors are acceptable alternatives to playing cards. If you decide to use standard dice, it is useful to have dice of two or three different colors. Using different-color dice will allow children to see more easily that 2 on the first die and 3 on the second die is a different outcome than 3 on the first die and 2 on the second. If you decide to use standard decks of playing cards, try to get decks with as many different designs as possible. This will help to identify any cards that become separated from the decks.

Having students toss dice and perform various operations to practice basic facts is an appealing alternative to worksheets or flashcards. Activity 10.13 shows how a probability investigation can be combined with practicing basic facts.

Performance Based Assessment:
Equally Likely Events

This assessment can be administered individually or in class, provided the students have sufficient skills to be able to explain their thinking in writing. Give each child a pair of dice and a sheet of lined paper. Ask the students to respond to the following problems:

1. How many numbers on the dice are even? What are they? How many numbers on the dice are odd? What are they?

2. Make a prediction. If you toss the dice 30 times and record each sum as being either even or odd, how many even sums will you get and how many odd sums will you get? Explain your reasoning.

3. Toss the dice 30 times and record the sum as either even or odd. Did the outcome of your experiment agree with your prediction? Explain.

Activity 10.13

Equally Likely Events?

Lesson: Pairs

Before distributing a pair of dice to each pair of students, engage the students in a discussion about what sums are possible when adding two dice together. Help the students to see that eleven sums are possible, and that these are the sums from 2 through 12, inclusive. Ask the students to predict if the eleven possible sums are equally likely or not equally likely to be tossed. (Stop and ask yourself the same question.)

Ask the students to list the numbers from 2 through 12 in their notebook, and to use this list to tally the sums they get when two dice are tossed and the numbers are added together. Each pair of students decides which one will toss the dice approximately 30 times and which will record the sums. Each pair of students should end up with a tally sheet similar to Figure 10.17.

Gather data from several pairs of students and display them on a large chart so that the trends suggested in Fig-

ure 10.17 are even more pronounced. Challenge the students to explain why the sums of 6, 7, and 8 are far more common than the sums of 2 and 12. Encourage the students to represent the theoretical probability of each sum in fractional form and to justify their representation. One possible response might be:

- "The probability of tossing a sum of 2 (or 12) is just ¹⁄₃₆, because there is only one way to get a 2, 1 + 1, and there is only one way to get a 12, 6 + 6. The probability of tossing a 7, however, is ⁶⁄₃₆, because there are six ways to get a sum of 7: 6 + 1, 1 + 6, 5 + 2, 2 + 5, 4 + 3, and 3 + 4."

Journal Reflection

How might you extend this activity to help students explore probability *and* practice their addition facts with greater numbers?

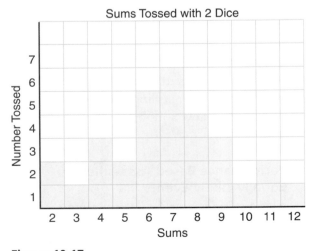

Figure 10.17

The students' responses to can be graded according to the following rubric.

Question 1

2   Student correctly identifies both the odd and even numbers.

1   Student correctly identifies only the odd or even numbers.

0   Student correctly identifies neither odd nor even numbers.

Question 2

3   Student makes a reasonable prediction and bases the prediction on an understanding of equally likely events.

2   Student makes an unreasonable prediction, but shows some understanding of equally likely events.

1   Student makes a reasonable prediction, but is unable to support the prediction with any references to equally likely or not equally likely events.

0   Student makes an unreasonable prediction, and justification is either lacking or unfounded.

Question 3

1   Student is able to compare prediction with actual outcome, and is able to make sense of the agreement or disagreement.

0   Student is unable to make sense of outcome of experiment.

Tree Diagrams

A useful tool for making sense of probabilistic events is a tree diagram. Figure 10.18 shows how a tree diagram could have been used in the task just described in the performance-based assessment.

Since there are three even numbers (2, 4, 6) and three odd numbers (1, 3, 5) on a standard die, these outcomes, even or odd, are equally likely events. Therefore, there are two branches in the first part of the tree diagram to represent that the probability of tossing an even number on the first die is ½, and the probability of tossing an odd number on the first die is also ½. The second part of the tree diagram shows that if the first die is even, the probability of the second die being even is ½, and the probability of the second die being odd is also ½. These probabilities are repeated in the branch of the tree diagram that shows the first die being odd.

The column to the right of the tree diagram shows how the information in the tree diagram is to be interpreted. The first line indicates that an even number plus an even number results in an even sum. The second line indicates that an even number plus an odd number results in an odd sum. The third and fourth lines continue in this fashion. Since ½ the possible sums are even and ½ the possible sums are odd, students can see that this event describes outcomes that are equally likely.

Students who are able to create a tree diagram to represent a probabilistic event can analyze a situation analytically instead of just intuitively.

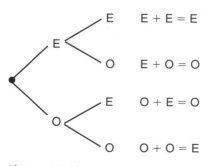

E   E + E = E

O   E + O = O

E   O + E = O

O   O + O = E

Figure 10.18

Activity 10.14

Not Equally Likely Events

Lesson: Pairs

Distribute a pair of dice to each pair of students. Discuss some possible outcomes for tossing the dice and recording the product of the two numbers. Ask the students to predict if even and odd products will be equally likely or not equally likely outcomes, and to justify their predictions. Invite the pairs of students to toss the dice, find the products, and record whether the products are even or odd. Engage the class in a discussion of whether the outcome of their experiment supported their prediction. Encourage the students to use a tree diagram to explain what happened. Students will recognize that, even though there are an equal number of even and odd numbers on a standard die, the products of even and odd numbers are sometimes surprising. For example, students will discover that:

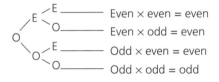

Even × even = even
Even × odd = even
Odd × even = even
Odd × odd = odd

Therefore, this event describes outcomes that are not equally likely.

Knowing that ¾ of the 100 basic multiplication facts are even can help students remember these facts. For example, a student who is unsure if 7 × 9 is 63 or 64 (a common confusion) can reason that since both factors are odd, the product must also be odd. In a situation where at least one of the factors is even, the product must also be even.

Journal Reflection

Maria Montessori represented an even number as a 2 × x rectangle, and an odd number as a 2 × x rectangle, plus one. Figure 10.19 shows what this might look like.

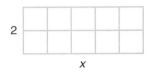 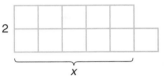

Figure 10.19

Activity 10.14 incorporates a tree diagram into a problem-solving activity. How can this visual model of even and odd numbers help students solve the problem presented in this activity?

Another connection between multiplication and probability is found in the *fundamental counting principle of probability.* Ask students to determine the number of possible combinations of two toppings and three flavors of ice cream, or four shirts and three pairs of shorts, or two beverages and four sandwiches. After listing all of the possible combinations for each of these situations, children see that two toppings and three flavors of ice cream result in 6 different combinations. They see that four shirts and three pairs of shorts result in 12 different outfits. They see that two beverages and four sandwiches result in 8 different meals. These probability situations can be illustrated as a *cartesian product* (Figure 10.20).

The fundamental counting principle can be used to determine the number of possible outcomes in any situation. If the first step of a two-step experiment has *m* outcomes, and the second step of a two-step experiment

		Flavors of Ice Cream		
		Vanilla	Chocolate	Strawberry
Toppings	cherry	cherry-Van	cherry-Choc	cherry-Straw
	sprinkles	sprink-Van	sprink-Choc	sprink-Straw

Figure 10.20

Grade 4   **Concept** Gathering and Analyzing Data

Topic Measurement, Line Graphs, Categorizing and Describing

Student Objectives After completing this lesson, students should be able to

- Measure water levels to the nearest millimeter
- Plot points on a double line graph
- Describe the weather on a "typical" day during a particular month

Materials Graduated cylinder, lined chart paper, weather displays from a variety of newspapers.

Motivation On the first day of a month, engage the class in a discussion of "typical" weather in your area for that particular month. Stress that, although it is possible to characterize weather in general for a given month, there can be great variability within that time frame. Explain that the class will be engaged in gathering weather data every day for a month for the purpose of describing "typical" weather.

Procedure (1) Show the newspaper weather displays to the class or pull up a local weather website. Engage students in a discussion of aspects of the weather that newspapers and websites typically report. Ask students the following question: "If we were to collect weather data for this month in order to describe a typical day, what aspects of the weather would you choose?" (2) Along with the students, decide what aspects of the weather will be studied, and the procedures to be followed in collecting the data. Some possibilities are: high and low

(continued)

has *n* outcomes, there are $m \times n$ outcomes in the experiment. The counting principle can be extended to experiments with any number of steps. The accompanying interdisciplinary lesson plan gives students practical experience in collecting, organizing, and anlyzing data.

Computer Software

Using computer software to help students create graphical representations of data has the advantage of being an efficient use of class time. Even young children can create graphs in two minutes using software, as opposed to twenty minutes by hand. This efficiency means that students can create several different kinds of graphs to represent the same data and then critically examine each one to determine its advantages and disadvantages. In addition to experimenting with different types of graphs, students can also vary the scale on line graphs and bar graphs to see the effect scale has on the appearance of the data. These experiences help students become thoughtful creators and interpreters of graphs.

temperatures; barometric pressure; description as sunny, cloudy, or precipitating; wind speed; and measurement of amount of precipitation. (3) Divide the students into groups and assign a specific information-gathering task to each group. Encourage the students to keep careful records of their data since the data will be graphically displayed at the end of the month. (4) When the data have been collected, charge each group with displaying their information clearly and accurately. High and low temperatures can be displayed on a double line graph, descriptions of sky conditions can be displayed in a bar graph, and precipitation amounts can be displayed in a histogram.

Assessment Ask the students to write a paragraph that could appear in a tourist brochure for your area. Ask them to use the data that have been collected by the class to describe the weather for a typical day during the preceding month. Require that the paragraph contain the temperature range, an average daily high and average daily low temperature, an average amount of precipitation, and the number of sunny days. Tell students that their paragraphs will be assessed on the accuracy and clarity of their data summaries.

References Zeman, Anne, and Kate Kelly. *Everything You Need to Know About Science Homework*, pp 70–78. New York, Scholastic Reference. 1994.

Journal Entry This section, to be filled in after the lesson has been taught, will contain reflections on the success of the lesson and suggestions for improvements.

Graph Power (ETA) has an integrated database and graphing tools that allow students to collect and analyze data and then choose which aspects of the data to graph. *Graphers* (Sunburst), designed for grades K–4, gives students the tools to create picture graphs, circle graphs, bar graphs, and line graphs. The software also enables students to collect, analyze, and sort data, which can then be graphed. A notebook feature allows students to write about the graphs they have created. *Data Explorer* (Sunburst), recommended for grades 4–8, allows students to create and manipulate a large variety of graphs, including stem-and-leaf plots, scatter plots, histograms, and box-and-whisker plots. This program also has a notebook feature.

In *The Logical Journey of the Zoombinis* (Broderbund), students solve problems that help them develop their skills of data organization and graphing. Two other software programs that help students make connections among various areas of mathematics are *Ice Cream Truck* (Sunburst) and *Hot Dog Stand: The Works* (Sunburst). These simulations invite students to act as owners of an ice cream truck or a hot dog stand, and to make business decisions informed by mathematics. The goal, as you might expect, is to maximize profits and minimize losses. In both simulations, the emphasis is on mathematical thinking and problem solving.

Summary

This chapter focused on three related areas of mathematics: data collection and analysis, statistics, and probability. The chapter began by examining the kinds of graphs most useful in primary and elementary grade classrooms, specifically, physical graphs, concrete graphs, bar graphs, line graphs, and picture graphs.

The chapter distinguished between combinations and permutations, and discussed real-life contexts in which one or the other would be appropriate. It cited some children's literature that is useful in teaching these concepts.

The chapter contained a section devoted to ways in which a lesson on graphing and graph interpretation could be used to assess students' understandings. Again it utilized children's literature to provide an opportunity for data collection and representation. Connecting data analysis with problem solving was also a focus of the chapter.

This chapter defined measures of central tendency and discussed briefly how these measures can be used to help students get a "feel" for a data set. An activity for introducing the mean as more than an add-and-then-divide algorithm was included.

The study of probability as a tool for interpreting data became the next focus of the chapter. Specific concepts, such as equally likely events, representing an outcome as a fractional value between 0 and 1, tree diagrams, and the fundamental counting principle concluded the chapter.

Extending Your Learning

1. Explain the difference between a bar graph and a histogram. Offer an example of data that would be appropriately represented by a bar graph, and an example of data that would be appropriately represented by a histogram.

2. Explain the difference between a combination and a permutation. Offer three real-life examples of situations involving a combination, and three real-life examples of situations involving a permutation.

3. Write a performance-based assessment, appropriate for grades 2 or 3, to assess students' knowledge and understandings of line graphs or circle graphs. Include a rubric that can be used to assess students' responses.

4. Certain measures of central tendency are better suited than others to represent certain types of data. For example, when ordering shoes, a shoe store cares more about the mode or modes of shoe sizes than about the median shoe size for a given population. Offer two examples of data that are best represented by each of the following: the mean, the median, and the mode.

5. Which aspects of board games or card games illustrate the concept of equally likely events? Which aspects of board games or card games illustrate the concept of not equally likely events?

6. Play *Candyland* with a youngster. Write a lesson plan that uses this game to teach either a data analysis or probability concept to young children.

7. Sketch a number line from 0 to 1. Place ten events at appropriate points on the number line to represent their probability of happening.

8. Write a lesson plan, suitable for grades 6–8, that uses a clothing catalog to teach students about the fundamental counting principle. Include a performance-based assessment activity in your lesson plan.

9. Write a lesson plan, suitable for grades 3–5, that uses a restaurant menu to teach one or more of the following concepts: combinations, permutations, tree diagrams.

10. List five ways in which concepts of data analysis and/or probability can be connected to the study of area and/or perimeter.

Internet Resources

www.MainXed.com
This website, entitled "Stock Market Education in the Classroom," allows students to participate in a stock market simulation game. Teacher resources, lesson plans, and links to CNN are included in this website.

www.nytimes.com/learning/teachers/ lessons/mathematics.html
Sponsored by *The New York Times,* this website offers math lesson plans connected to recent articles from *The New York Times.* The full text of the original article is available, along with detailed lesson plans.

www.21ct.org/
The 21st Century Teachers Network has a website to disseminate information about their nonprofit organization, whose goal is to help teachers integrate technology into their classrooms.

Bibliography

Botula, Mary Jean, and Margaret I. Ford. (1997). All about us: Connecting statistics with real life. *Teaching Children Mathematics 4*(1).

Bloom, Stephen J. (1994). Data buddies: Primary grade mathematicians explore data. *Teaching Children Mathematics 1*(2).

Logical Journey of the Zoombinis. Software by Broderbund. New York: Sunburst.

Burns, Marilyn. (1992). *Math and Literature (K–3).* Sausalito, CA: Math Solutions Publications.

Carle, Eric. (1987). *The Very Hungry Caterpillar.* New York: Philomel.

Carpenter, Thomas, M. Corbitt, H. Kepner, Mary Lindquist, and Robert Reys. (1981). What are the chances of your students knowing probability? *Mathematics Teacher 74*(4): 342–44.

Cartland, Patricia E. (1996). What's in a glyph? *Teaching Children Mathematics 2*(6):324–28.

Curcio, Frances, and Susan Folkson. (1996). Exploring data: Kindergarten children do it their way. *Teaching Children Mathematics 2*(6):382–85.

Data Explorer. Software by Lois Edwards Educational Design. New York: Sunburst.

Geringer, Laura. (1985). *A three hat day.* New York: Harper & Row.

Graph Power. Software. Vernon Hills, IL: ETA.

Graphers. Software by Lois Edwards Educational Design. New York: Sunburst.

Harbaugh, Kittylee. (1995). Glyphs? Don't let them scare you. *Teaching Children Mathematics.* April 1(8):506–511.

Hot Dog Stand: The Works. Software. New York: Sunburst.

Ice Cream Truck. Software. New York: Sunburst.

Peressini, Dominic, and Judy Bassett. (1996). Assessing students through data-exploration tasks. *Teaching Children Mathematics 2*(6).

Piaget, Jean, and B. Inhelder. (1975). *The origin of the idea of chance in children.* London: Routledge & Kegan Paul.

Pothier, Yvonne, and Christine M. Nickerson. (1997). Our heritage: Learning data-management skills meaningfully. *Teaching Children Mathematics 4*(2).

Russell, Susan Jo, and Jan Mokros. (1996). What do students understand about average? *Teaching Children Mathematics 2*(6).

Scavo, Thomas R., and Byron Petraroja. (1998). Adventures in statistics. *Teaching Children Mathematics 4*(7).

Seuss, Dr. (1987). *Green Eggs and Ham.* New York: Random House.

Sgroi, Laura A., et al. (1995). Assessing young children's mathematical understandings. *Teaching Children Mathematics 1*(5).

Zeman, Anne, and Kate Kelly. (1994). *Everything you need to know about science homework.* New York: Scholastic Reference.

11

Further Investigations into Data Analysis, Statistics, and Probability

As students progress into the upper elementary and intermediate grades, they become more and more interested in the world around them, and their definition of the world around them broadens rapidly. A continued emphasis on the topics of data collection and analysis and statistics can help students learn more about geography, economics, politics, history, science, and other high-interest fields of study. If these connections are made, students may become convinced of the value of studying mathematics and continue to do so as they enter high school, where math sometimes becomes an elective. The importance of *all* students continuing their study of rigorous mathematics is underscored by the NCTM *Principles and Standards*, which state:

> Consider our current culture, in which banks have become increasingly "self-service" with ATM machines and online banking. Widely available consumer reports offer information on product safety and effectiveness. Employment opportunities in fields such as health care, auto manufacturing, news reporting, and fashion design require a more sophisticated knowledge of mathematics. (p. 24)

If we wish to keep students in the mathematical pipeline, and if we want to connect the mathematics they study to the world in which they live, then we must continue to emphasize statistics and probability in the classroom.

Focus Areas for Grades 6–8

According to the NTCM *Principles and Standards*, in grades 6–8, all students should

- Design experiments and surveys, and consider potential sources of bias in design and data collection;

- Choose, create, and utilize various graphical representations of data (line plots, circle graphs, stem-and-leaf plots, histograms, scatter plots, circle graphs, and box-and-whisker plots) appropriately and effectively.

- Use data to answer the questions that were posed, understand the limitations of those answers, and pose new questions that arise from the data.

- Make judgements about the likelihood of uncertain events and be able to connect those judgements to percents or proportions;

- Understand what it means for events to be *equally likely* and for a game or process to be *fair;*

- Compute simple probabilities using appropriate methods, such as lists, tree diagrams, or area models;

- Identify . . independent and dependent events and understand how these relationships affect the determination of probabilities. (pp. 238–39)

Data Collection

Students are much more easily involved in data representation and analysis when they can participate in collecting the data. Some teaching materials provide and organize data for students; these data (for example, voting patterns) often are not very interesting to middle-grade students. You can provide many opportunities for students to collect, interpret, represent, and analyze their own data. The following series of classroom activities describe some statistical and probability investigations that can be done with empty cereal boxes brought in by the students themselves. Cereal boxes are an appropriate teaching material because obtaining them involves no cost, they are gender fair, they are colorful and attractive, and middle-grade students find them interesting and motivational. Activity 11.1 utilizes cereal boxes for practice in describing and organizing data.

Activity 11.1

Describing, Classifying, Ordering

Lesson: Individual

Describing

Ask each student to bring an empty cereal box to school. With the cereal boxes in front of them, ask the students to describe their box. Possible responses are:

- "It's in the shape of a rectangular prism. That means that it has three pairs of opposite, parallel, congruent, rectangular faces."

- "It's made of brightly colored cardboard with lots of writing on it and it's empty."

- "It has 12 edges, 6 faces, and 8 vertices."

Classifying

Invite a student to separate the boxes into two groups without telling the other students the basis for the classification, then challenge the other students to say what it was. The student who successfully figures it out is invited to do the next sorting. Some possible bases for sorting include: the brand of cereal, the shape of the cereal, the color of the box, whether the cereal is sweetened, whether the front of the box pictures the cereal with fruit, the number of words in the name of the cereal, or whether cartoon characters are pictured on the box.

Ordering

Invite a student to arrange the boxes in some kind of order, and challenge the other students to identify the characteristic on which the ordering was based. Some possible characteristics include: the height of the box, the price of the box, the weight of the box, the expiration date on the top of the box, a rainbow ordering of the colors of the boxes, an alphabetical ordering of the names of the cereals, and an ordering based on some nutritional aspect such as number of grams of fat or sugar.

Journal Reflection

Describing, classifying, and ordering are skills that are often developed in an early-childhood classroom. Do they have a place in an upper-elementary classroom? Why or why not?

After students have had an opportunity to observe and describe their cereal boxes, the examination can become more focused. In Activity 11.2, students explore the colors that cereal manufacturers use for cereal boxes.

The display of nutrition facts that appears on the side of every cereal box provides a rich source of data. The format is uniform, which makes comparisons of different cereals easy to accomplish. In Activity 11.3, students are deliberately given little direction for constructing bar graphs. The reason for this lack of direction will become clear to you.

Histograms, Line Graphs, and Circle Graphs

Elementary school students usually have a great deal of experience constructing and interpreting bar graphs, and they understand that bar graphs are used to represent categorical data. But they often have less experience with

---

Activity 11.2

Frequency Tally

Lesson: Whole Class

Prepare a chart with the names of colors written along the left side. Invite the students to identify the three colors that they think dominate the front of their cereal box. Gather the data in tally form (Figure 11.1).

Predominant Colors on Cereal Boxes

Red	‖‖‖ ‖‖‖ ‖‖‖
Orange	‖‖‖
Yellow	‖‖‖ ‖‖‖ ‖
Green	‖‖‖‖
Blue	‖‖‖ ‖‖‖ ‖‖‖
Purple	‖‖
Teal	‖‖‖‖
Brown	‖‖‖
Tan	‖‖
Black	‖‖
White	‖‖‖ ‖‖‖ ‖‖‖‖

Figure 11.1

The students will discover that red, white, yellow, and blue are the predominant colors on the fronts of cereal boxes. Engage the students in a discussion about why bright primary colors dominate the fronts of cereal boxes. Ask them to think of products that are marketed with similar colors (candy, cookies) and products that are marketed with very different colors (tissues, coffee), and to hypothesize why this might be so.

The data that were collected in the chart shown in Figure 11.1 were based on students' subjective responses

to a cereal box. The colors judged by the students to dominate the fronts of the cereal boxes may not necessarily be the colors that cover the greatest amount of area. Invite the students to think about how the colors on the front of their box could be measured more objectively. Suggestions might include cutting the front of the box into regions based on color and then rearranging these pieces into rectangles, which would allow for an approximate measure of the area covered by a particular color.

Other students might suggest cutting the front of the box into different regions based on color, but then weighing these regions, and using the measurement of weight of one color compared to total weight of the front of the box to arrive at a percentage of that particular color. Another suggestion involves superimposing a transparent centimeter grid on top of the front of the box, and identifying the color that appears under that square centimeter. Counting up all of the squares that lie on top of the color red, for example, would allow the student to estimate the amount of the front of the box that was red.

This more precise and objective measure of the amount of each color on the front of a cereal box can be used to compare the students' perception of dominant colors with their measurement of the actual dominant colors.

Journal Reflection

What would be your role in this activity if the students were unable to think of different ways to measure the amount of colors? How can you help students become creative and thoughtful without giving them answers?

Activity 11.3

Bar Graphs

Lesson: Whole Class

Invite the students to refer to the Nutrition Facts on the side of the cereal box in order to construct a bar graph that represents the Percent Daily Values of vitamin A, vitamin C, folic acid, and zinc in a single serving of their cereal without milk. Give no further directions about the actual form of the bar graph.

After the students have completed their graphs, choose several of them to display. Choose graphs that have different scales and different width bars. Ask the students to identify the graph of the cereal that *appears* to be the most nutritional. Figure 11.2 shows two possible graphs that students might construct.

Many students will identify the graph on the left without looking closely to see what scale was used, since it has the longest and widest bars. Use this opportunity to initiate a discussion of how data can be presented so as to encourage a certain interpretation. Invite the students to choose their own data and use them to construct two additional bar graphs for their cereal. One bar graph should emphasize the healthful aspects of the cereal, such

as might be used in an advertisement by the manufacturer of the cereal. The other graph should emphasize the non-healthful aspects of the cereal, such as might be used in an advertisement by a competitor. Have the students write a persuasive paragraph to accompany each graph.

There are many graphing utilities available, such as graphing calculators, statistical software, graphing software, and spreadsheet/database software. All of these tools can be used by the students to create their graphs. Advantages of these utilities include the ability to quickly change the scale, the appearance, and the type of graph. This ease in constructing a graph encourages students to experiment with different configurations and helps them to decide on the most appropriate representation of their data.

Journal Reflection

How could a computer graphics program be used to accomplish the same aim as this activity?

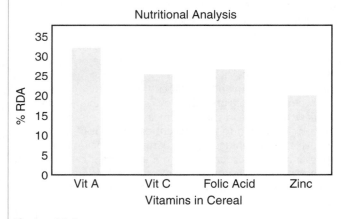
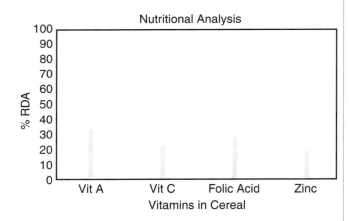

Figure 11.2

histograms, line graphs, and circle graphs, and less understanding of the purposes of these graphs.

Histograms are the most like bar graphs, since they employ horizontal or vertical rectangles (bars) to represent data. The difference between the two is that a bar graph has separate rectangles that do not touch, and a histogram has rectangles that do touch. This is because the data represented by a bar graph belong to separate categories, such as favorite brands of cereal. The data represented by a histogram lie along a continuum that captures all of

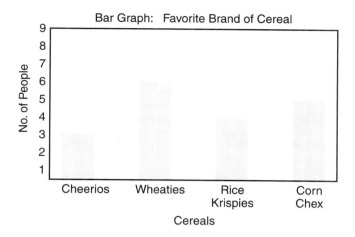

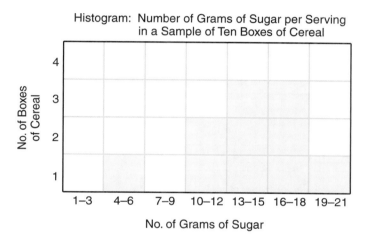

Figure 11.3

the data, such as the number of grams of sugar per serving in a sample of ten boxes of cereal. Figure 11.3 illustrates both of these graphs.

In an upper-elementary classroom, students can be invited to bring in samples of bar graphs, histograms, line graphs, and circle graphs that appear in the various print and electronic media. Display several examples of each to provide students with the opportunity to observe and generalize about the nature of each type of graph. In addition to the distinction between bar graphs and histograms illustrated in Figure 11.3, students will quickly see that line graphs are used to represent change over time, and that circle graphs are used to represent how subcategories relate to one another. Think about what data students might identify in the context of cereal boxes that would appropriately be represented by line graphs or circle graphs.

You might have thought that all the students in a class could record the number of bowls of cereal they ate during one month. Since these data represent change over time, a line graph would be the most appropriate means to represent these data. A line graph such as the one pictured in Figure 11.4 might result. This line graph was created using graphing software.

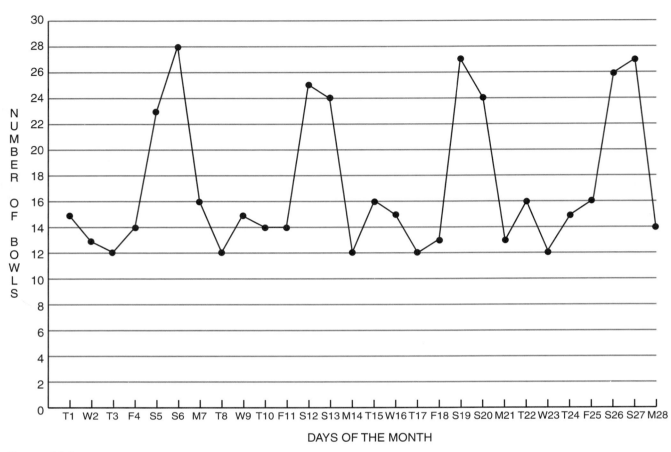

Figure 11.4

This graph would provide an opportunity for students to discuss the possible reasons for an increased consumption of cereal on the weekends. A valuable assignment would be to have the students write a letter to the CEO of General Mills or Kellogg's and include a copy of the graph. The students could be asked to interpret the graph and to offer a suggestion to the CEO for advertisement strategies that take into account the information represented by the line graph.

There are many ways to introduce students informally to circle graphs before they go through the lengthy process of using a protractor to create one. Data that are appropriately represented by a circle graph are data that represent parts of a whole. For example, cereal is composed primarily of carbohydrates, but these carbohydrates can be broken down into three subcategories; dietary fiber, sugars, and other carbohydrates. A typical cereal consumed by students in the upper elementary grades might contain 25

Figure 11.5

grams of carbohydrates, of which 1 gram is fiber, 11 grams are sugars, and 13 grams are other carbohydrates. To construct a quick circle graph with these data, distribute counters or chips or Unifix cubes to the students. Have them take 1 of one color, 11 of another color, and 13 of a third color, and arrange the items into a circle (Figure 11.5).

By estimating the center of the circle and drawing lines from the center to mark the boundaries between colors, an approximate circle graph has been formed. Based on their knowledge of fractions and percents, students might estimate that this cereal contains about 5% fiber, about 45% sugar, and about 50% other carbohydrates. Creating circle graphs to represent the breakdown of carbohydrates in different cereals allows for a true comparison among cereals, unlike the bar graphs described Activity 11.3, where there was no guarantee that the graphs were constructed with the same scale.

Another way to help students approximate a circle graph is to provide them with a template already divided into 10, 20, or 25 equal sectors (Figure 11.6). By estimating the percent of the circle that each subcategory of data covers, students can shade an appropriate number of sectors. For the carbohydrate data described above, since there were 25 grams of carbohydrates in all, students could choose the template that was already divided into 25 sectors.

When students are ready to construct a formal circle graph, they can use a computer graphics program or a pencil, a calculator, and a protractor. If students are constructing the graph manually, these are the steps that should be followed:

- Assume that a certain cereal contains 46 grams of total carbohydrate, of which 3 grams are dietary fiber, 16 grams are sugar, and 27 grams are other carbohydrates. The first step is to determine the percent of each category:

$$\text{Fiber } \frac{3}{46} = 6.5\%$$

$$\text{Sugar } \frac{16}{46} = 34.7\%$$

$$\text{Other carbohydrates } \frac{27}{46} = 58.7\%$$

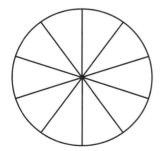
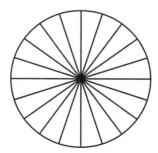
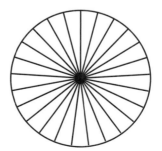

Figure 11.6

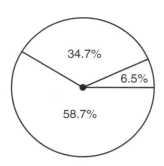

Figure 11.7

Some full-circle protractors are marked in percents, which allows the students to mark off sectors of 6.5%, 34.7%, and 58.7%. Other protractors only measure degrees, necessitating the conversion of percents into degrees:

$$6.5\% \text{ of } 360 = 24$$

$$34.7\% \text{ of } 360 = 125$$

$$58.7\% \text{ of } 360 = 211$$

Marking off central angles of 24, 125, and 211 degrees results in the circle graph shown in Figure 11.7, which represents the types of carbohydrates in a particular cereal.

Performance-Based Assessment: Graphs

This assessment is designed to be done over several weeks, since it requires the students to gather data from a variety of sources over an extended period of time. Pose the following problem situation to students:

■ Your task is to create a statistical portrait of yourself. This portrait is to include a circle graph, a histogram, a bar graph, a line graph, and a frequency tally. You may create the graphs by hand or use any graphing utility. The exact nature of the data that you choose to represent with each type of graph is up to you. In addition to the graphs themselves, you need to create a written summary of each graph, including an analysis and interpretation of the data represented, along with a justification of why that particular graph is appropriate to represent those particular data.

The students' work can be assessed according to the following rubric:

4 Student's portrait contains all five visual representations. Summary of each graph is concise, informative, and accurate. Data chosen for each graph are appropriate. Graphs are carefully constructed.

3 One graph and/or summary is missing, inaccurate, or inappropriate. Two or three errors may be apparent. Some carelessness is shown in graph constructions.

2 Two graphs and/or summaries are missing, inaccurate, or inappropriate. Work contains several errors, and graphs may be carelessly done.

1 The majority of the graphs are missing, inaccurate, or inappropriate. Errors in graph construction interfere with the accurate communication of information. Work is carelessly done.

0 Work shows evidence of little or no effort. Little or no information is communicated.

Graphing

Teaching students to read and interpret graphs accurately may be more important than teaching them to construct graphs. . . . Reading graphs is not a trivial task. Many graphs that are produced for commercial publications are in fact designed to magnify differences that may or may not be important. Students need to learn when information is accurately portrayed (Bright & Hoeffner, 1993, p. 91).

Graphing utilities such as graphics calculators and graphing software have decreased the need for students to labor over the creation of bar, line, and picture graphs. Rather, students need to know what information is needed to create a particular graph, what type of graph can appropriately be used to present the information, and how the data can be interpreted from the graph. Examine the graphs presented in Figure 11.8.

Both graphs depict the average age of entry for students in four kindergarten classes at an elementary school. In Figure 11.8a, the differences in the lengths of the rectangles are barely distinguishable. The same data are represented in Figure 11.8b, but here the vertical axis does not begin at zero, but with a number that allows the vertical axis to be divided into closer intervals. More specific information is communicated by the second graph. If the teacher of class 1 wanted to make the case that the children in his class were unusually young, he might choose Figure 11.8b, since this bar graph emphasizes the differences rather than the similarities in average ages.

The line graphs in Figure 11.9 illustrate the same information concerning the number of complaints lodged against a car dealership in a given year. Notice that the trend of an increase in complaints is barely discernible in Figure 11.9a, yet in Figure 11.9b, the rise in complaints as the year progresses is clear and dramatic. Both graphs are mathematically correct and yet they paint different pictures. As with the bar graphs, the manipulation of the scale on the vertical axis contributes to the appearance of the graph.

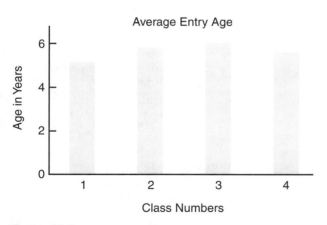
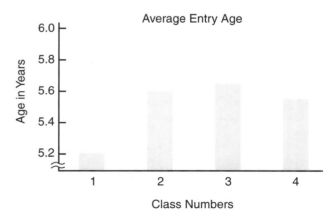

Figure 11.8

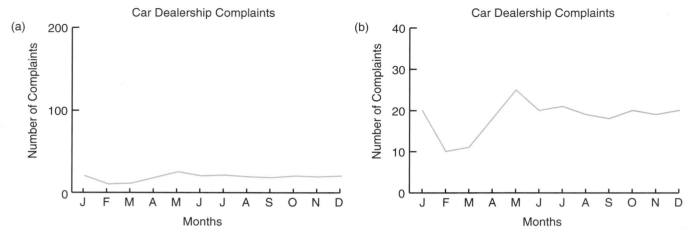

Figure 11.9

It is important that middle-level students have varied experiences in interpreting graphs of all kinds. Activities 11.4, 11.5, and 11.6 focus on line, bar, and circle graph explorations that are appropriate at this level.

Circle graphs represent data that are part of a whole. The creation of circle graphs is time consuming and requires an understanding of angle measurement, protractor use, and percents. These difficulties can be overcome in several ways. Several graphing software programs allow students to

Activity 11.4

Double Bar Graph

Lesson: Whole Class

The bar graph, shown in Figure 11.10 illustrates the high and low tempera-

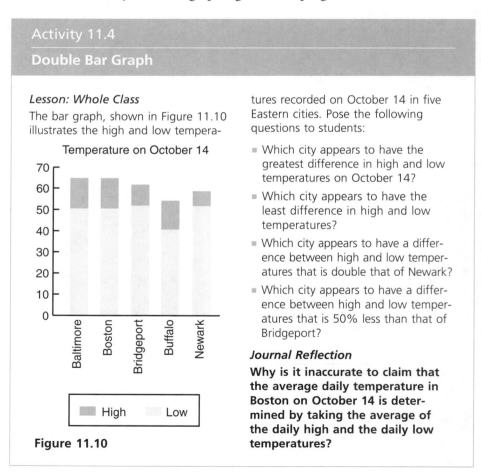

Figure 11.10

tures recorded on October 14 in five Eastern cities. Pose the following questions to students:

- Which city appears to have the greatest difference in high and low temperatures on October 14?
- Which city appears to have the least difference in high and low temperatures?
- Which city appears to have a difference between high and low temperatures that is double that of Newark?
- Which city appears to have a difference between high and low temperatures that is 50% less than that of Bridgeport?

Journal Reflection

Why is it inaccurate to claim that the average daily temperature in Boston on October 14 is determined by taking the average of the daily high and the daily low temperatures?

Activity 11.5

Double Line Graph

Lesson: Individual

Ask each student to use two graduated cylinders to perform the following experiment at home. They are to fill one cylinder with 50 ml of plain tap water and the other with 50 ml of rubbing alcohol. Then students are to plot on a graph like that of Figure 11.11 the volume of the water and the volume of the alcohol as measured by the cylinders over a period of time. Measurements of the level of the liquids should be taken at the same time each day. Class discussions can address the different rates of evaporation in each of the cylinders and differences in data recorded by different students. Students can attempt to identify environmental characteristics that lead to the fastest evaporation (water placed near a source of heat or near an open window) and those that discourage evaporation (water placed in a cool, moist basement).

Journal Reflection

What are the advantages of having each student record his or her own data? What are the disadvantages?

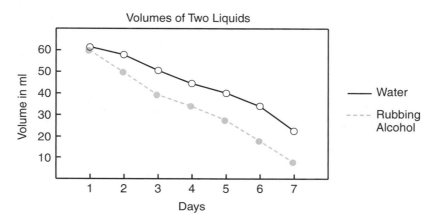

Figure 11.11

Activity 11.6

Circle Graph

Lesson: Individual

After reviewing some circle graphs with students, present them with the accompanying "blank" circle graph of Figure 11.12.

Ask students to define and describe five categories that might correspond to the five regions. Have the students write two or three questions that might be answered from the data presented in the circle graph.

Journal Reflection

Graphs are often used to display information about temperatures. Offer a situation in which a circle graph would appropriately be used to depict the temperature data. Offer another situation involving the representation of temperatures in which a circle graph would be inappropriate.

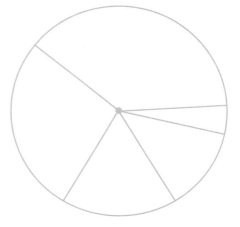

Figure 11.12

create circle graphs on the computer. Another alternative is to provide students with a circle already divided into a given number of sectors. For example, if students are asked to record the time spent in various ways over a 24-hour period, they can be provided with a circle already divided into 24 congruent sectors. It is also useful to know that many paper plates have 36 indentations around the edge. If lines are drawn from the center to each indentation, the central angle of each sector will contain (approximately) 10 degrees. If lines are drawn from the center to every third indentation, the central angle of each sector will contain (approximately) 30 degrees, and so on. Using a paper plate in this fashion allows for the creation of circle graphs by students who do not yet have mastery of percents and angle measurement. Activity 11.6 engages students in identifying a situation that can be represented by a given circle graph.

Simulations

An important benefit of understanding statistical and probabilistic concepts is that it helps students to make informed decisions. Activity 11.7 uses a

---

Strength in Numbers

Hanging Bar Graph

Use your knowledge of bar graphs to interpret the hanging bar graph of Figure 11.13.

- A certain airline considers 25 lost bags per day to be typical. The hanging bar graph below depicts the number of lost bags over an eight day period.

  (a) Interpret the data represented by the day 2 bar.

  (b) Interpret the data represented by the day 4 bar.

(c) How many more bags than average were lost on day 7?

(d) What is the median number of lost bags over the eight-day period, and what does this statistic tell you?

(e) Convert these data into a form that can be used to construct a regular bar graph. Explain how the bar graph would then be constructed.

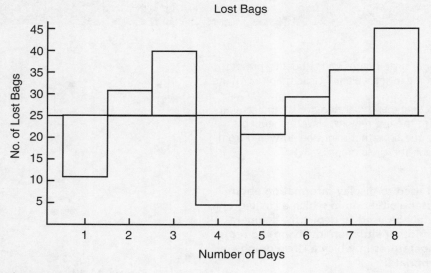

Figure 11.13

Activity 11.7

Monte Carlo Simulation

Lesson: Whole Class

Ask the class to assume that a certain cereal manufacturer is running a promotion in which each of four free prizes is equally and randomly distributed among all of the boxes of cereal to be sold. Imagine that some students wanted to buy enough boxes of cereal so that they could be reasonably sure that they got at least one of each of the four prizes. Ask the students to estimate how many boxes of cereal the students should buy.

Estimates will most likely range from 4 to 240 boxes of cereal. Help the students to understand that, while it is possible to get one of each of the four prizes in the first four boxes of cereal purchased, it is by no means assured. Introduce the concept of a simulation, where a probability situation that can be demonstrated in a classroom is used to represent a similar situation in the outside world. In this case, any chance situation where students can randomly choose 1 out of 4 possible outcomes can be used to represent the purchase of a box of cereal containing 1 out of 4 possible prizes. If students keep track of how many times it takes to get at least one of each of the four outcomes, they can infer that it would take that many boxes of cereal to get at least one of each of the four prizes.

Probability situations where students can randomly choose 1 out of 4 possible outcomes include a spinner divided into 4 equal sections, 4 different colored cubes in a bag, or a standard deck of cards. In each case, students keep track of the number on the spinner, the color of the cube, or the suit of the card chosen, and continue until at least one of each outcome occurs. By employing spinners, cubes, or cards, the following set of data might be generated in your classroom. Here are the numbers of cards chosen to obtain at least one of each suit:

4, 4, 4, 4, 5, 5, 5, 5, 6, 6, 6, 7, 7, 7, 7,
8, 8, 8, 9, 9, 9, 9, 10, 11, 14

Here, you can see that it took anywhere from 4 to 14 tries to get at least one of each suit. This experience simulates the purchase of anywhere from 4 to 14 boxes of cereal in order to obtain at least one of each prize.

The question for students to answer, however, is how many boxes they would purchase in order to be reasonably sure that they would get one of each prize. An analysis of the data indicates that 22 of the 25 students, or 88%, got all four "prizes" in 9 or fewer "boxes." Students should justify their decision about how many boxes of cereal they would purchase.

Journal Reflection

Engage in the simulation described above, using all three tools—the spinner, the cubes, and the cards. Did the data change as the tool changed? How would you respond to a student who asked if the same data would be obtained with two decks of cards shuffled together?

Monte Carlo simulation to help students estimate how many boxes of cereal they should purchase in order to be reasonably sure of getting one of each of the four prizes. A Monte Carlo simulation is used to model a probabilistic situation like this to allow for inferences about the likelihood of some occurrence.

Plots: Box-and-Whisker and Stem-and-Leaf

Two visual forms for representing data are box-and-whisker plots (Figure 11.14) and stem-and-leaf plots. They both clearly identify the shape of data as well as the range and the median of a set of data. A box-and-whisker plot, named

Box-and-Whisker Plot

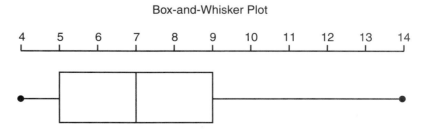

Figure 11.14

for its appearance, can be formed with the data of Activity 11.7 (about the number of cards chosen to get at least one of each suit). To construct a box-and-whisker plot, begin with a number line long enough to capture all of the data—in this case, the numbers from 4 to 14, inclusive (Figure 11.14). The difference between the lowest extreme value (4) and the highest extreme value (14) indicates the *range* of the set of data. Next, draw a vertical line at the median of the data. Recall that the *median* is that score above which half the data fall, and below which half the data fall. Since there are 25 scores, the median is the 13th score, in this case 7. The last step involves drawing vertical lines at the lower quartile (the median of the lower half of the data) and the upper quartile (the median of the upper half of the data) and drawing a box around these three vertical lines. In this set of data, the lower quartile is between the 6th and 7th score, in this case 5; the upper quartile is between the 19th and 20th score, in this case 9.

Figure 11.14 shows the completed box-and-whisker plot. This plot shows that 25% of the students got all four prizes in 5 or fewer boxes, that half the students got all four prizes in 7 or fewer boxes, and 75% of the students got all four prizes in 9 or fewer boxes.

Another visual representation of data is a stem-and-leaf plot, also named for its appearance. Stem-and-leaf plots partition the data into groupings according to place value. Since the data in this example will be grouped by tens, the tens places form the stem, while the ones places, written in order, form the leaves. A stem-and-leaf plot for the same set of data is shown in Figure 11.15. The second row of numbers in this stem-and-leaf plot contains the numbers 10, 11, and 14.

Stem-and-leaf plots are quickly formed and clearly indicate maximum and minimum values and any modes that might occur in the data. By counting to the middle score, the median can be found. Students can see from a glance at this stem-and-leaf plot that most of the scores in this set of data are less than 10, so the vast majority of students got all four prizes by buying fewer than 10 boxes of cereal.

In the classroom, you can use both box-and-whisker plots and stem-and-leaf plots to represent students' scores on an exam. If, for example, you wanted to compare anonymous grades on a pre-test and a post-test, you could encourage the students to construct a stem-and-leaf plot with leaves coming out from both sides of the stem. The leaves on the left hand side could represent the scores on the pre-test while the leaves on the right could represent the scores on the post-test. Figure 11.16 illustrates a possible distribution of grades.

When data are presented in this form, all of the individual pieces of data are present. The shape of the leaves makes clear, in this instance, that the

Stem-and-Leaf Plot

0	4 4 4 4 5 5 5 5 6 6 6 7 7 7 7 8 8 8 9 9 9 9
1	0 1 4

Figure 11.15

Pre-Test Grades		Post-Test Grades
5 2 1 1 0	6	8 8
8 8 6 2 2 1 1	7	1 3 5 7 9
9 9 8 7 6 5 5 5 0 0	8	0 0 1 1 2 3 5 5 6 6 8 9
3 2 1 0 0	9	1 2 2 3 4 7 9
	10	0

Figure 11.16

scores on the post-test are higher than the scores on the pre-test. By gathering data about the students themselves, such as grades, shoe size, height, number of movies they have seen in the past month, number of letters in their names, and representing these data, you can help students get to know one another and help them appreciate the value of visually representing data.

Performance-Based Assessment: Plotting

Distribute lined paper to the students and instruct them *not* to write their names on the paper. Ask them to write in 2 minutes the names of as many of the states as they can. Collect the papers, shuffle them, and randomly redistribute them to be scored by someone else. One point is given for each correctly named state.

Gather and display the data from the students. Ask each student to construct both a stem-and-leaf and a box-and-whisker plot for the data. Students' work can be assessed according to the following rubric:

3   Both plots are accurate and carefully done. Any errors are minor and do not alter the meaning of the data.

2   One or both of the plots contain two or three errors. The errors may have some effect on the meaning of the data.

1   One plot contains significant errors that interfere with the meaning of the data.

0   Both plots contain significant errors that interfere with the meaning of the data.

Using Data to Make Decisions

Consumerism is an important area in which the analysis and interpretation of data can help upper-elementary students make decisions. Students at this age are very concerned with fairness and honesty, and are quick to bristle at the thought of getting ripped off. Students at this age are also beginning to have some discretionary income from allowances and odd jobs. Schools provide a valuable service when they help students make informed decisions about spending their money.

Introducing students to periodicals like *Zillions* and *Consumer Reports* helps them see the kinds of information on which decisions can be made and suggests how those data might be obtained. The following interdisciplinary

Grade 7 or 8   **Concept** Statistics

Topic Surveys, Data Analysis

Student Objectives After completing this lesson, students should be able to

- Identify criteria important to them when considering a purchase
- Gather data using a survey, a taste test, or other analysis
- Present the data visually to the class
- Use the data to make an informed consumer decision

Materials Copies of *Zillions and Consumer Reports,* graph paper, markers, rulers, oak tag, paper cups of two different colors, box of Cheerios and box of store-brand equivalent of Cheerios.

Motivation Privately pour each box of cereal into a large bowl, placing cups of one color next to one bowl and the other color next to the other bowl. Invite the students to dip the appropriate paper cup into each bowl of cereal and taste it, taking a drink of water between tastes. Then, ask them to take the empty paper cup associated with the cereal they prefer and stack it on the chalk ledge with others of the same color. Have the class analyze the data and determine which cereal is preferred by more students. Reveal to the class whether the more popular cereal was the name brand or the store brand. Engage the class in a discussion about criteria that determine consumer choices (cost, taste, nutrition). Refer students to consumer magazines such as *Zillions and Consumer Reports,* which contain the results of numbers of studies of various items.

(continued)

lesson plan suggests a way that students might become involved in gathering data about items that are important to them.

Theoretical and Experimental Probability

Activity 11.8 helps students make predictions that are based on experimental or theoretical probabilities. As students undertake these and other probability activities, it is important for them to engage in discussions with their classmates and to justify their reasoning. This is another way of encouraging students to construct their own understandings and to consolidate their knowledge. "When dealing with content like probability, [which] is so process oriented, it is essential that students discuss their thought processes.

Lesson Plan (continued)

Procedure Arrange the students into groups of six. Charge each group with the following task: (1) Identify a product that the members of your group buy or consume regularly and that is available in several brands, such as paper, shampoo, toothpaste, cereal, maple syrup, gum, candy, potato chips, peanut butter. (2) Identify characteristics of that product that are important to the members of your group, such as taste, cost, durability, appearance. (3) Obtain at least two different brands of that item, and ask an adult, or a student not in your group, to disguise the name of the brand and distribute individual portions of the product to all of the members of the group. (4) Use or taste the product, and report back to the group your preference and your reasons. If possible, include other people in the class or at home to engage in the comparison. (5) Think of a way visually to present the data generated by the group to the rest of the class. Include a written summary of the process that was followed, the consensus of the group as to the preferred brand, and the justification for this preference.

Assessment The students are assessed based on the quality of their class presentations, the adequacy of the process followed to gather data, and the persuasiveness and completeness of their written summary.

References *Consumer Reports* and *Zillions,* published by Consumers' Union, Yonkers, NY.

Journal Entry To be filled in upon completion of the lesson, with suggestions for improvements for next year.

Processes are not likely to be changed unless they are explicitly examined and challenged by others" (Bright and Hoeffner, 1993).

Educating students about probability concepts helps prepare them for a world where legalized gambling is becoming ever more common. There *is* a form of gambling familiar to students—especially when they take a test for which they are unprepared! Activity 11.9 engages student in just such a situation.

Independent Events

Many people exhibit superstitious behavior in chance situations. For example, people who participate in sports often wear their "lucky socks" or go through a particular pre-game ritual. When a baseball team is losing in the bottom of

Activity 11.8

Making Predictions

Lesson: Individual

Distribute to each student six identical strings that are held together at the center by a stapled strip of paper, as shown in Figure 11.17a. The paper makes it impossible to match one end of a string with its other end. Invite the students to tie pairs of string together at the top and bottom, as shown in Figure 11.17b.

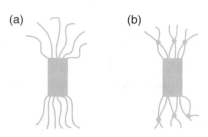

Figure 11.17

Without removing the stapled paper from the center of the set of strings, invite the students to predict all of the possible outcomes of this experiment. The set of all possible outcomes is called the *sample space* of an experiment. Students will discover that there are three possible outcomes in the sample space of this experiment: three separate loops that may or may not be linked, one small loop and one medium loop that may or may not be linked, and one large loop. These three possible outcomes are pictured in Figure 11.18.

Now ask the students to predict how many students in the class will get a large loop, and then remove the paper from the center of the strings to test their predictions. Most students are astonished to find that slightly more than half of the outcomes result in a single large loop. Challenge the students to compare their prediction with the experimental outcome, and to discuss and explain the theoretical outcome.

Students may choose to model the possible outcomes with an extra set of strings. The order in which the top strings are tied doesn't matter. Whether or not a large loop will be the outcome depends on how the bottom strings are tied. For the purposes of this explanation, let us assume that on the top, 1 is tied to 2, 3 is tied to 4, and 5 is tied to 6. Given this, on the bottom, if string 1 is chosen, tying it to 2 will result in a small loop, but tying it to 3, 4, 5, or 6 allows the possibility of a large loop. Therefore, the probability that the first tie on the bottom will eventually result in a large loop is ⅘. Assume that 1 is tied to 3. If so, then tying 2 to 4 will result in a medium loop, but tying 2 to 5 or 6 will allow the possibility of a large loop. Therefore, the probability that the second tie on the bottom will eventually result in a large loop is ⅔ Since there are only two strings on the bottom left to tie, the probability that the third tie on the bottom will result in a large loop is ¼.

The probability that randomly tying three pairs of string on the top and then three pairs of string on the bottom will result in a large loop can be determined by multiplying the probabilities of each step in the experiment:

$$\frac{4}{5} \times \frac{2}{3} \times \frac{1}{1} = \frac{8}{15} = 0.53 = 53\%$$

This explanation of the theoretical probability shows why more than half of the class got a large loop.

Journal Reflection

Many students who struggle in mathematics are helped when complex situations are simplified. If the students can understand a simpler version of a problem, it often gives them both the confidence and the mathematical basis for understanding the original, more complex, problem. Describe in detail how you might use the problem-solving strategy of Solve a Simpler Problem.

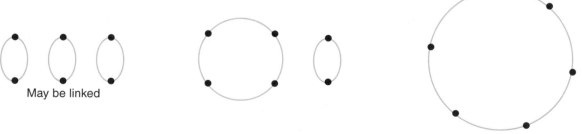

May be linked

Figure 11.18

Activity 11.9

Fundamental Counting Principle

Lesson: Whole Class

Engage the students in a discussion about what the outcome might be if a student simply tossed a coin to determine the answer to each question on a ten-question true/false test. Ask students to discuss with their neighbor what score they might expect. Then distribute lined paper to each student. Ask them to number the paper from 1 to 10, and then proceed to flip a coin 10 times. Tossing a head means they record their answer as true, tossing a tail means they record their answer as false. Call out the following answers to allow the students to "grade" their papers:

T F F T T F T F F T

What is the probability that a student will get all of the answers correct? If we treat each question as one step of a multi-step experiment, then each step has two possible outcomes. By the fundamental counting principle, there are

$$2 \times 2 \times 2 \times 2 \times 2 \times 2 \times 2 \times 2 \times 2 \times 2, \text{ or } 2^{10}$$

which equals 1024 different configurations of the 10 true/false answers possible on this exam. Since only the one set listed above is the correct response set, the probability that a student will toss this exact set of responses is $\frac{1}{1024}$, or approximately 0.00098. So, there is less than 0.1% ($\frac{1}{10}$ of a percent) chance that a student will get all of the answers correct.

Journal Reflection

Is the probability greater or less that a chance device will get all of the answers correct on a ten-question multiple-choice test (four choices for each question) than the probability on a true/false test? Explain.

the ninth, fans put on their rally caps. At a carnival, people often bet on their "lucky" numbers. All of these actions presume that people believe events that are independent are in fact dependent. People believe that the socks they are wearing will influence their ability to score a goal. People believe that the cap they are wearing will influence the course of the baseball game. People believe that a carnival wheel has a greater chance of landing on their lucky number than on another number. However, hoping or wishing that a particular event will occur is not the same thing as influencing the outcome of that event.

In dependent events, the probabilities of the outcomes are influenced by other events. In independent events, the probabilities of the outcomes are not influenced by other events. Distinguishing between these two concepts is often difficult for students because they confuse coincidence with causality. While it may be the case that the wearing of a particular pair of socks *coincided* with success in scoring a goal, that does not necessarily mean that the wearing of the socks *caused* the success in scoring a goal. Activity 11.10 illustrates for students the difference between independent and dependent events.

Activity 11.11 indicates how Pascal's Triangle can be used to understand certain probabilistic situations.

Permutations and Combinations

Mathematicians often ask "How many possibilities exist?" In probability, the answer to this question can be found by exploring permutations and combinations. Suppose a committee consists of five members. A chairperson and a recording secretary must be selected from the group. How many different sets of assignments to these positions are possible?

Activity 11.10

Independent and Dependent Events

Lesson: Whole Class

Engage the students in a discussion about the theoretical probability of choosing a face card (King, Queen, Jack) from a standard deck of cards. Since there are 52 cards in a deck and 12 of them are face cards, the probability of choosing a face card is $^{12}\!\!/_{52}$. If there are 26 students in the class, ask each to shuffle the deck, choose a card at random, replace the card, and repeat the process. In this way, 52 cards will have been randomly chosen, and approximately 12 of them should be face cards. Repeat the entire process at least five times, so there are five different outcomes representing the experimental probability of choosing a face card from a standard deck of cards.

Have the students go through the entire process a second time, but this time, instruct them not to replace the cards that were chosen. Compare the outcomes from the two different versions of the experiment, and invite the students to explain any discrepancies. The first time, since the cards were all replaced, the events were independent. The second time, since the cards were not replaced, the cards subsequently chosen were dependent upon the cards already chosen, since the chosen cards were missing from the deck.

Journal Reflection

Do you predict that fewer face cards will be chosen in the second version of this experiment? More? Approximately the same number? Explain your reasoning.

Strength in Numbers

Pascal's Triangle

Cooperative Group Model: Numbered Heads Together

Working in groups of three, examine the set of numbers illustrated in Figure 11.19. Record and discuss as many patterns as you can. Predict the next two rows in this pattern and be prepared to explain your reasoning. The students should all be able to explain their group's observations to the class, since the Numbered Heads Together model of cooperative learning requires that the student whose number is chosen by the teacher will act as the spokesperson for his or her group.

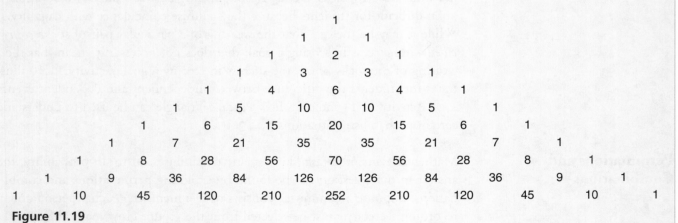

Figure 11.19

Activity 11.11

Applying Pascal's Triangle

Lesson: Whole Class

Distribute pennies and graph paper to students and pose the following questions:

- How many outcomes are possible when tossing one coin? What are they?

- How many outcomes are possible when tossing two coins? What are they?

- What about three coins? Four coins? Five coins?

- How does all of this relate to Pascal's Triangle?

When tossing one coin, there is **1** way to have one head and **1** way to have one tail. (**1 1**) When tossing two coins, there is **1** way to have two heads, **2** ways to have a head and a tail, and **1** way to have two tails. (**1 2 1**)

When tossing three coins, there is **1** way to have three heads, **3** ways to have two heads and one tail, **3** ways to have one head and two tails, and **1** way to have three tails. (**1 3 3 1**)

When tossing four coins, there is **1** way to have four heads, **4** ways to have three heads and one tail, **6** ways to have 2 heads and two tails, **4** ways to have one head and three tails, and **1** way to have four tails. (**1 4 6 4 1**)

How can the illustration of Pascal's Triangle in Figure 11.19 be used to predict the number of combinations of heads and tails for 5, 6, and 7 coins?

Journal Reflection

Sometimes, students have trouble distinguishing between a head/tail combination and a tail/head combination. They believe that these outcomes are the same, even though a head on the first coin and a tail on the second coin is clearly a different outcome than a tail on the first coin and a head on the second. How can you help students clarify this situation?

This situation can be modeled using the letters A, B, C, D, and E to represent the committee members. Here is a list of all 20 possible pairs:

AB AC AD AE

BA BC BD BE

CA CB CD CE

DA DB DC DE

EA EB EC ED

Notice that the pair AB is distinct from the pair BA, since Andy as chairperson and Barbara as recording secretary is different from Barbara as chairperson and Andy as recording secretary. When the order of two or more items is important, it is a *permutation*. This is in contrast to a *combination*, where order does not matter. An example of a combination in the above context would be the situation where two members of the committee were chosen to serve on a subcommittee. In this case, a combination, the pairs AB and BA would not be different.

Listing all of the possible permutations of groups of two out of a committee of five was simple, since the numbers were manageable. However, if the committee consisted of fifteen members, and if a chairperson, associate chairperson, secretary, and treasurer needed to be selected, the list of all possible "quartets" would have been much longer and much more difficult to generate. In complicated cases, the following formula (or the Permutation key on a calculator, such as the Texas Instruments Explorer Plus) can be used to determine the number of possible permutations.

You may recall from an earlier course that the number of possible permutations of n objects taken r at a time is

$$_nP_r = \frac{n!}{(n-r)!}$$

(Looking at this formula, do you see why 0! is defined as 1?) If we examine the original situation of a chairperson and a recording secretary being chosen from a committee of five people, the formula will offer the following result:

$$\frac{5!}{(5-2)!} = \frac{5!}{3!} = \frac{5 \times 4 \times 3 \times 2 \times 1}{3 \times 2 \times 1} = 20$$

You can see that this result from the formula matches the result obtained when the pairs were manually generated.

There is also a formula and a calculator key that can be used to predict the number of combinations for a given set of items. Recall that the original set of permutations for a chairperson and a recording secretary chosen from a committee of five. If, instead of a permutation, we are just concerned with finding two members to serve on a subcommittee, some of these permutations become redundant. The redundant pairs have been crossed out in this list, leaving only the combinations.

AB AC AD AE

B̶A̶ BC BD BE

C̶A̶ C̶B̶ CD CE

D̶A̶ D̶B̶ D̶C̶ DE

E̶A̶ E̶B̶ E̶C̶ E̶D̶

As you can see, half of the original permutations are redundant, since Andy and Barbara serving on the subcommittee is no different from Barbara and Andy serving on the subcommittee. You may recall the following formula for the number of possible combinations of n objects taken r at a time:

$$_nC_r = \frac{n!}{r!(n-r)!} = \frac{5 \times 4 \times 3 \times 2 \times 1}{2 \times 1\,(3 \times 2 \times 1)} = 10$$

This result could also have been obtained by using the Combination key on a calculator such as the Texas Instruments Explorer Plus.

Summary

This chapter revisited many topics that were introduced in the previous chapter, investigating them to greater depth. After an initial discussion of data collection and how data might be described, classified and ordered, it went on to cover frequency tallies, histograms, double bar graphs, double line graphs, and circle graphs. The data used for most of these graphs were obtained from the same source—cereal boxes—to illustrate how a statistical analysis might be centered around a certain theme. The chapter discussed the role of simulations in analyzing complex situations, and the concepts of combinations and permutations were re-examined in a more symbolic fashion. Box-and-whisker and stem-and-leaf plots provided the student with additional means of representing data.

This chapter's treatment of probability reinforced the difference between theoretical and experimental probability that was first introduced in the previous chapter. A new concept, that of independent events, rounded out the study of probability.

Extending Your Learning

1. Identify three areas of interest to middle-grade students that would provide opportunities to gather data, and then describe, classify, and order that data. Be conscious of choosing areas of interest that do not contain inherent biases, such as a sport that might appeal to some students but not others.

2. Obtain three examples of bar graphs and three examples of histograms from the print or electronic media. Identify the differences and similarities between them.

3. Obtain a copy of *Anno's Mysterious Multiplying Jar* by Masachiro and Mitsumasa Anno (1983). Develop a lesson about the concept of factorials, based on this book.

4. Write a lesson plan, appropriate for grades 6–8, to help students distinguish between permutations and combinations.

5. In your own words, write a description and explanation of simulations, and the role played by them in helping students understand probabilistic concepts.

6. Create a game or an activity, appropriate for students in grades 4 or 5, that is designed to help them understand the difference between dependent and independent events.

7. In the chapter, several activities were designed around the theme of cereal boxes. Keeping within the same theme, describe in detail an activity that can be used to help students understand the Fundamental Counting Principle.

8. Can you fill in the next line in this pattern?

```
1
1 1
2 1
1 2 1 1
1 1 1 2 2 1
3 1 2 2 1 1
1 3 1 1 2 2 2 1
1 1 1 3 2 1 3 2 1 1
3 1 1 3 1 2 1 1 1 1 3 1 2 2 1
?
```

9. Use the Random Number key on a calculator such as Texas Instruments Explorer Plus to generate 25 numbers between 1 and 10 inclusive. Find the mean, median, and mode of these 25 numbers. Was the result what you expected? Explain.

10. Begin with 500 ml of tap water at room temperature. Add five ice cubes. Immediately measure the temperature of the water, and continue to measure the temperature at ten-minute intervals for one hour. Using a graphing utility, represent the data you have gathered in more than one way.

Internet Resources

www.consumersunion.org
This is the website of Consumers Union, publishers of *Consumer Reports* and *Zillions*. Through this website, Consumers Union provides educational information and acts as a consumer advocate.

www.educast.com
This free, downloadable software provides links to lesson plans, Internet resources, and current educational news from *Education Week*, the U.S. Department of Education, PBS online, and *The New York Times*.

www.ni.au/mercury/mathguys/mercury.htm
Sponsored by the Australian Association of Math Teachers, the University of Tasmania, and the Hobart, Tasmania daily newspaper, the *Mercury*, this website offers samples of probabilistic concepts and language from articles in the *Mercury*. While

much of the discussion is too sophisticated for elementary and middle-school students, teachers will find it valuable to think about the use and misuse of probabilistic concepts in daily life.

www.nrich.maths.org.uk/primary/index.html
This primary mathematics enrichment website from the University of Cambridge, England, offers lesson plans and challenge problems to enrich the mathematics curriculum for grades 1–6.

www.wonderful.com
Wonderful Ideas for Teaching, Learning, and Enjoying Mathematics is a website connected with *Wonderful Ideas*, a monthly newsletter. This website offers classroom activities, a Kids' Corner, and games and problems appropriate for elementary and middle school students.

Bibliography

Anno, Masachiro, and Mitsumasa Anno. (1983). *Anno's Mysterious Multiplying Jar.* New York: Philomel.

Bright, George W., and Karl Hoeffner. (1993). Measurement, probability, statistics, and graphing. In Douglas T. Owens (ed.), *Research ideas for the classroom: Middle grades mathematics.* New York: Macmillan.

Friel, Susan, George Bright, and Frances R. Curcio. (1997). Understanding students' understanding of graphs. *Mathematics Teaching in the Middle School 3*(3).

Hofstetter, Elaine, and Laura Sgroi. (1996). Data with snap, crackle and pop. *Mathematics Teaching in the Middle School 1*(9).

Isaacs, Andrew C., and Catherine Randall Kelso. (1996). Pictures, tables, graphs and questions: Statistical processes. *Teaching Children Mathematics 2*(6).

Jones, Graham, et al. (1999). Understanding students' probabilistic reasoning. In Lee V. Stiff (ed.), *Developing mathematical reasoning in grades K–12.* 1999 NCTM yearbook. Reston, VA: NCTM.

Jones, Graham A, Cynthia W. Langrall, and Carol A. Thorton. (1996). Using data to make decisions about chance. *Teaching Children Mathematics 2*(6).

Jorgensen, Beth. (1996). Hamster math: Authentic experiences in data collection. *Teaching Children Mathematics 2*(6).

Kader, Gary, and Mike Perry. (1997). Pennies from heaven—nickels from where?" *Mathematics Teaching in the Middle School 3*(3).

Moore, Deborah A. (1999). Some like it hot. *Teaching Children Mathematics 5*(9).

O'Keefe, James. (1997). The human scatterplot. *Mathematics Teaching in the Middle School 3*(3).

Shaughnessy, J. Michael. (1992). Research in probability and statistics: Reflections and directions. In Douglas A. Grouws (ed.), *Handbook of research on mathematics teaching and learning.* New York: Macmillan.

Taylor, Judith V. (1997). Young children deal with data. *Teaching Children Mathematics 4*(3).

Appendix A   MASTERS

Appendix A is reproduced with permission from *Connections: Grade 6*. Paper Base-Ten Blocks. © 1989 Creative Publications.

Centimeter Grid Paper

Geoboard Dot Paper

Pattern Blocks Paper

Pattern Blocks Paper

Pattern Blocks Paper

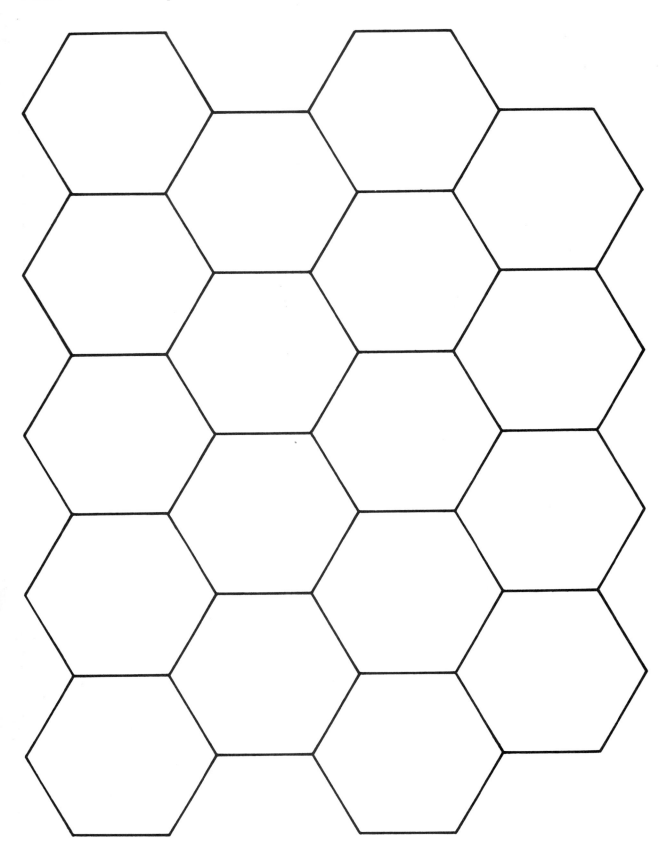

Pattern Blocks Paper

Appendix B   NCTM STANDARDS

Number and Operations Standard
for Grades Pre-K–2

Instructional programs from prekindergarten through grade 12 should enable students to—	*Expectations* In prekindergarten through grade 2 all students should—
Understand numbers, ways of representing numbers, relationships among numbers, and number systems	■ count with understanding and recognize "how many" in sets of objects; ■ use multiple models to develop initial understandings of place value and the base-ten number system; ■ develop understanding of the relative position and magnitude of whole numbers and of ordinal and cardinal numbers and their connections; ■ develop a sense of whole numbers and represent and use them in flexible ways, including relating, composing, and decomposing numbers; ■ connect number words and numerals to the quantities they represent, using various physical models and representations; ■ understand and represent commonly used fractions, such as $\frac{1}{4}$, $\frac{1}{3}$, and $\frac{1}{2}$.
Understand meanings of operations and how they relate to one another	■ understand various meanings of addition and subtraction of whole numbers and the relationship between the two operations; ■ understand the effects of adding and subtracting whole numbers; ■ understand situations that entail multiplication and division, such as equal groupings of objects and sharing equally.
Compute fluently and make reasonable estimates	■ develop and use strategies for whole-number computations, with a focus on addition and subtraction; ■ develop fluency with basic number combinations for addition and subtraction; ■ use a variety of methods and tools to compute, including objects, mental computation, estimation, paper and pencil, and calculators.

Algebra Standard
for Grades Pre-K–2

Instructional programs from prekindergarten through grade 12 should enable students to—	*Expectations* In prekindergarten through grade 2 all students should—
Understand patterns, relations, and functions	▪ sort, classify, and order objects by size, number, and other properties; ▪ recognize, describe, and extend patterns such as sequences of sounds and shapes or simple numeric patterns and translate from one representation to another; ▪ analyze how both repeating and growing patterns are generated.
Represent and analyze mathematical situations and structures using algebraic symbols	▪ illustrate general principles and properties of operations, such as commutativity, using specific numbers; ▪ use concrete, pictorial, and verbal representations to develop an understanding of invented and conventional symbolic notations.
Use mathematical models to represent and understand quantitative relationships	▪ model situations that involve the addition and subtraction of whole numbers, using objects, pictures, and symbols.
Analyze change in various contexts	▪ describe qualitative change, such as a student's growing taller; ▪ describe quantitative change, such as a student's growing two inches in one year.

Geometry Standard
for Grades Pre-K–2

Instructional programs from prekindergarten through grade 12 should enable students to—	**Expectations**
	In prekindergarten through grade 2 all students should—
Analyze characteristics and properties of two- and three-dimensional geometric shapes and develop mathematical arguments about geometric relationships	■ recognize, name, build, draw, compare, and sort two- and three-dimensional shapes;
	■ describe attributes and parts of two- and three-dimensional shapes;
	■ investigate and predict the results of putting together and taking apart two- and three-dimensional shapes.
Specify locations and describe spatial relationships using coordinate geometry and other representational systems	■ describe, name, and interpret relative positions in space and apply ideas about relative position;
	■ describe, name, and interpret direction and distance in navigating space and apply ideas about direction and distance;
	■ find and name locations with simple relationships such as "near to" and in coordinate systems such as maps.
Apply transformations and use symmetry to analyze mathematical situations	■ recognize and apply slides, flips, and turns;
	■ recognize and create shapes that have symmetry.
Use visualization, spatial reasoning, and geometric modeling to solve problems	■ create mental images of geometric shapes using spatial memory and spatial visualization;
	■ recognize and represent shapes from different perspectives;
	■ relate ideas in geometry to ideas in number and measurement;
	■ recognize geometric shapes and structures in the environment and specify their location.

Measurement Standard for Grades Pre-K–2

Instructional programs from prekindergarten through grade 12 should enable students to—

Expectations
In prekindergarten through grade 2 all students should—

Understand measurable attributes of objects and the units, systems, and processes of measurement

- recognize the attributes of length, volume, weight, area, and time;
- compare and order objects according to these attributes;
- understand how to measure using nonstandard and standard units;
- select an appropriate unit and tool for the attribute being measured.

Apply appropriate techniques, tools, and formulas to determine measurements

- measure with multiple copies of units of the same size, such as paper clips laid end to end;
- use repetition of a single unit to measure something larger than the unit, for instance, measuring the length of a room with a single meterstick;
- use tools to measure;
- develop common referents for measures to make comparisons and estimates.

Data Analysis and Probability Standard
for Grades Pre-K–2

Instructional programs from prekindergarten through grade 12 should enable students to—	*Expectations* In prekindergarten through grade 2 all students should—
Formulate questions that can be addressed with data and collect, organize, and display relevant data to answer them	▪ pose questions and gather data about themselves and their surroundings; ▪ sort and classify objects according to their attributes and organize data about the objects; ▪ represent data using concrete objects, pictures, and graphs.
Select and use appropriate statistical methods to analyze data	▪ describe parts of the data and the set of data as a whole to determine what the data show.
Develop and evaluate inferences and predictions that are based on data	▪ discuss events related to students' experiences as likely or unlikely.
Understand and apply basic concepts of probability	

Number and Operations Standard
for Grades 3–5

Instructional programs from prekindergarten through grade 12 should enable students to—	*Expectations* In grades 3–5 all students should—
Understand numbers, ways of representing numbers, relationships among numbers, and number systems	■ understand the place-value structure of the base-ten number system and be able to represent and compare whole numbers and decimals; ■ recognize equivalent representations for the same number and generate them by decomposing and composing numbers; ■ develop understanding of fractions as parts of unit wholes, as parts of a collection, as locations on number lines, and as divisions of whole numbers; ■ use models, benchmarks, and equivalent forms to judge the size of fractions; ■ recognize and generate equivalent forms of commonly used fractions, decimals, and percents; ■ explore numbers less than 0 by extending the number line and through familiar applications; ■ describe classes of numbers according to characteristics such as the nature of their factors.
Understand meanings of operations and how they relate to one another	■ understand various meanings of multiplication and division; ■ understand the effects of multiplying and dividing whole numbers; ■ identify and use relationships between operations, such as division as the inverse of multiplication, to solve problems; ■ understand and use properties of operations, such as the distributivity of multiplication over addition.
Compute fluently and make reasonable estimates	■ develop fluency with basic number combinations for multiplicaton and division and use these combinations to mentally compute related problems, such as 30×50; ■ develop fluency in adding, subtracting, multiplying, and dividing whole numbers; ■ develop and use strategies to estimate the results of whole-number computations and to judge the reasonableness of such results; ■ develop and use strategies to estimate computations involving fractions and decimals in situations relevant to students' experience; ■ use visual models, benchmarks, and equivalent forms to add and subtract commonly used fractions and decimals; ■ select appropriate methods and tools for computing with whole numbers from among mental computation, estimation, calculators, and paper and pencil according to the context and nature of the computation and use the selected method or tool.

Algebra Standard
for Grades 3–5

Instructional programs from prekindergarten through grade 12 should enable students to—	*Expectations* In grades 3–5 all students should—
Understand patterns, relations, and functions	■ describe, extend, and make generalizations about geometric and numeric patterns; ■ represent and analyze patterns and functions, using words, tables, and graphs.
Represent and analyze mathematical situations and structures using algebraic symbols	■ identify such properties as commutativity, associativity, and distributivity and use them to compute with whole numbers; ■ represent the idea of a variable as an unknown quantity using a letter or a symbol; ■ express mathematical relationships using equations.
Use mathematical models to represent and understand quantitative relationships	■ model problem situations with objects and use representations such as graphs, tables, and equations to draw conclusions.
Analyze change in various contexts	■ investigate how a change in one variable relates to a change in a second variable; ■ identify and describe situations with constant or varying rates of change and compare them.

Geometry Standard
for Grades 3–5

Instructional programs from prekindergarten through grade 12 should enable students to—	*Expectations*
	In grades 3–5 all students should—
Analyze characteristics and properties of two- and three-dimensional geometric shapes and develop mathematical arguments about geometric relationships	■ identify, compare, and analyze attributes of two- and three-dimensional shapes and develop vocabulary to describe the attributes; ■ classify two- and three-dimensional shapes according to their properties and develop definitions of classes of shapes such as triangles and pyramids; ■ investigate, describe, and reason about the results of subdividing, combining, and transforming shapes; ■ explore congruence and similarity; ■ make and test conjectures about geometric properties and relationships and develop logical arguments to justify conclusions.
Specify locations and describe spatial relationships using coordinate geometry and other representational systems	■ describe location and movement using common language and geometric vocabulary; ■ make and use coordinate systems to specify locations and to describe paths; ■ find the distance between points along horizontal and vertical lines of a coordinate system.
Apply transformations and use symmetry to analyze mathematical situations	■ predict and describe the results of sliding, flipping, and turning two-dimensional shapes; ■ describe a motion or a series of motions that will show that two shapes are congruent; ■ identify and describe line and rotational symmetry in two- and three-dimensional shapes and designs.
Use visualization, spatial reasoning, and geometric modeling to solve problems	■ build and draw geometric objects; ■ create and describe mental images of objects, patterns, and paths; ■ identify and build a three-dimensional object from two-dimensional representations of that object; ■ identify and build a two-dimensional representation of a three-dimensional object; ■ use geometric models to solve problems in other areas of mathematics, such as number and measurement; ■ recognize geometric ideas and relationships and apply them to other disciplines and to problems that arise in the classroom or in everyday life.

Measurement Standard for Grades 3–5

Instructional programs from prekindergarten through grade 12 should enable students to—

Expectations
In grades 3–5 all students should—

Understand measurable attributes of objects and the units, systems, and processes of measurement

- understand such attributes as length, area, weight, volume, and size of angle and select the appropriate type of unit for measuring each attribute;
- understand the need for measuring with standard units and become familiar with standard units in the customary and metric systems;
- carry out simple unit conversions, such as from centimeters to meters, within a system of measurement;
- understand that measurements are approximations and understand how differences in units affect precision;
- explore what happens to measurements of a two-dimensional shape such as its perimeter and area when the shape is changed in some way

Apply appropriate techniques, tools, and formulas to determine measurements

- develop strategies for estimating the perimeters, areas, and volumes of irregular shapes;
- select and apply appropriate standard units and tools to measure length, area, volume, weight, time, temperature, and the size of angles;
- select and use benchmarks to estimate measurements;
- develop, understand, and use formulas to find the area of rectangles and related triangles and parallelograms;
- develop strategies to determine the surface areas and volumes of rectangular solids.

Data Analysis and Probability Standard
for Grades 3–5

Instructional programs from prekindergarten through grade 12 should enable students to—	*Expectations* In grades 3–5 all students should—
Formulate questions that can be addressed with data and collect, organize, and display relevant data to answer them	■ design investigations to address a question and consider how data-collection methods affect the nature of the data set; ■ collect data using observations, surveys, and experiments; ■ represent data using tables and graphs such as line plots, bar graphs, and line graphs; ■ recognize the differences in representing categorical and numerical data.
Select and use appropriate statistical methods to analyze data	■ describe the shape and important features of a set of data and compare related data sets, with an emphasis on how the data are distributed; ■ use measures of center, focusing on the median, and understand what each does and does not indicate about the data set; ■ compare different representations of the same data and evaluate how well each representation shows important aspects of the data.
Develop and evaluate inferences and predictions that are based on data	■ propose and justify conclusions and predictions that are based on data and design studies to further investigate the conclusions or predictions.
Understand and apply basic concepts of probability	■ describe events as likely or unlikely and discuss the degree of likelihood using such words as *certain, equally likely,* and *impossible*; ■ predict the probability of outcomes of simple experiments and test the predictions; ■ understand that the measure of the likelihood of an event can be represented by a number from 0 to 1.

Number and Operations Standard
for Grades 6–8

Instructional programs from prekindergarten through grade 12 should enable students to—	*Expectations* In grades 6–8 all students should—
Understand numbers, ways of representing numbers, relationships among numbers, and number systems	■ work flexibly with fractions, decimals, and percents to solve problems; ■ compare and order fractions, decimals, and percents efficiently and find their approximate locations on a number line; ■ develop meaning for percents greater than 100 and less than 1; ■ understand and use ratios and proportions to represent quantitative relationships; ■ develop an understanding of large numbers and recognize and appropriately use exponential, scientific, and calculator notation; ■ use factors, multiples, prime factorization, and relatively prime numbers to solve problems; ■ develop meaning for integers and represent and compare quantities with them.
Understand meanings of operations and how they relate to one another	■ understand the meaning and effects of arithmetic operations with fractions, decimals, and integers; ■ use the associative and commutative properties of addition and multiplication and the distributive property of multiplication over addition to simplify computations with integers, fractions, and decimals; ■ understand and use the inverse relationships of addition and subtraction, multiplication and division, and squaring and finding square roots to simplify computations and solve problems.
Compute fluently and make reasonable estimates	■ select appropriate methods and tools for computing with fractions and decimals from among mental computation, estimation, calculators or computers, and paper and pencil, depending on the situation, and apply the selected methods; ■ develop and analyze algorithms for computing with fractions, decimals, and integers and develop fluency in their use; ■ develop and use strategies to estimate the results of rational-number computations and judge the reasonableness of the results; ■ develop, analyze, and explain methods for solving problems involving proportions, such as scaling and finding equivalent ratios.

Algebra Standard
for Grades 6–8

Instructional programs from prekindergarten through grade 12 should enable students to—	*Expectations* In grades 6–8 all students should—
Understand patterns, relations, and functions	■ represent, analyze, and generalize a variety of patterns with tables, graphs, words, and, when possible, symbolic rules; ■ relate and compare different forms of representation for a relationship; ■ identify functions as linear or nonlinear and contrast their properties from tables, graphs, or equations.
Represent and analyze mathematical situations and structures using algebraic symbols	■ develop an initial conceptual understanding of different uses of variables; ■ explore relationships between symbolic expressions and graphs of lines, paying particular attention to the meaning of intercept and slope; ■ use symbolic algebra to represent situations and to solve problems, especially those that involve linear relationships; ■ recognize and generate equivalent forms for simple algebraic expressions and solve linear equations.
Use mathematical models to represent and understand quantitative relationships	■ model and solve contextualized problems using various representations, such as graphs, tables, and equations.
Analyze change in various contexts	■ use graphs to analyze the nature of changes in quantities in linear relationships.

Geometry Standard
for for Grades 6–8

Instructional programs from prekindergarten through grade 12 should enable students to—	*Expectations* In grades 6–8 all students should—
Analyze characteristics and properties of two- and three-dimensional geometric shapes and develop mathematical arguments about geometric relationships	■ precisely describe, classify, and understand relationships among types of two- and three-dimensional objects using their defining properties; ■ understand relationships among the angles, side lengths, perimeters, areas, and volumes of similar objects; ■ create and critique inductive and deductive arguments concerning geometric ideas and relationships, such as congruence, similarity, and the Pythagorean relationship.
Specify locations and describe spatial relationships using coordinate geometry and other representational systems	■ use coordinate geometry to represent and examine the properties of geometric shapes; ■ use coordinate geometry to examine special geometric shapes, such as regular polygons or those with pairs of parallel or perpendicular sides.
Apply transformations and use symmetry to analyze mathematical situations	■ describe sizes, positions, and orientations of shapes under informal transformations such as flips, turns, slides, and scaling; ■ examine the congruence, similarity, and line or rotational symmetry of objects using transformations.
Use visualization, spatial reasoning, and geometric modeling to solve problems	■ draw geometric objects with specified properties, such as side lengths or angle measures; ■ use two-dimensional representations of three-dimensional objects to visualize and solve problems such as those involving surface area and volume; ■ use visual tools such as networks to represent and solve problems; ■ use geometric models to represent and explain numerical and algebraic relationships; ■ recognize and apply geometric ideas and relationships in areas outside the mathematics classroom, such as art, science, and everyday life.

Measurement Standard for Grades 6–8

Instructional programs from prekindergarten through grade 12 should enable students to—	***Expectations*** In grades 6–8 all students should—
Understand measurable attributes of objects and the units, systems, and processes of measurement	■ understand both metric and customary systems of measurement; ■ understand relationships among units and convert from one unit to another within the same system; ■ understand, select, and use units of appropriate size and type to measure angles, perimeter, area, surface area, and volume.
Apply appropriate techniques, tools, and formulas to determine measurements	■ use common benchmarks to select appropriate methods for estimating measurements; ■ select and apply techniques and tools to accurately find length, area, volume, and angle measures to appropriate levels of precision; ■ develop and use formulas to determine the circumference of circles and the area of triangles, parallelograms, trapezoids, and circles and develop strategies to find the area of more-complex shapes; ■ develop strategies to determine the surface area and volume of selected prisms, pyramids, and cylinders; ■ solve problems involving scale factors, using ratio and proportion; ■ solve simple problems involving rates and derived measurements for such attributes as velocity and density.

Data Analysis and Probability Standard for Grades 6–8

Instructional programs from prekindergarten through grade 12 should enable students to—	*Expectations* In grades 6–8 all students should—
Formulate questions that can be addressed with data and collect, organize, and display relevant data to answer them	■ formulate questions, design studies, and collect data about a characteristic shared by two populations or different characteristics within one population; ■ select, create, and use appropriate graphical representations of data, including histograms, box plots, and scatterplots.
Select and use appropriate statistical methods to analyze data	■ find, use, and interpret measures of center and spread, including mean and interquartile range; ■ discuss and understand the correspondence between data sets and their graphical representations, especially histograms, stem-and-leaf plots, box plots, and scatterplots.
Develop and evaluate inferences and predictions that are based on data	■ use observations about differences between two or more samples to make conjectures about the populations from which the samples were taken; ■ make conjectures about possible relationships between two characteristics of a sample on the basis of scatterplots of the data and approximate lines of fit; ■ use conjectures to formulate new questions and plan new studies to answer them.
Understand and apply basic concepts of probability	■ understand and use appropriate terminology to describe complementary and mutually exclusive events; ■ use proportionality and a basic understanding of probability to make and test conjectures about the results of experiments and simulations; ■ compute probabilities for simple compound events, using such methods as organized lists, tree diagrams, and area models.

Index

A

Abacus lesson plan, 57, 59–61
Add 'Em Up game, 85
Addition
 of decimals, 219, 222
 of fractions, 219, 220
 of integers, 288–289
 of whole numbers, 75–109
  alternative algorithms for, 93–95
  basic facts of, 80–88
  computer programs illustrating, 86
  determining underlying structure of
   numbers, 82–86
  front-end estimation, 91
  lattice addition algorithm, 95
  partial sums algorithm, 94–95
  performance-based assessment for,
   86–88, 105
  powers-of-ten blocks and standard
   addition algorithm, 92–93
  for pre-K to 2, 76
  properties of, 82
  rounding, 91
  spreadsheet as problem-solving tool,
   99–102, 103
  teaching estimation and commutative
   and associative properties, 89–91
  using multi-digit numbers, 88–106
 See also Subtraction
Agenda for Action , An (NCTM), 2
Agenda Series, The (NCTM), 3
Algeblocks, 297–300, 301
Algebraic expression, representing
  relationship with, 293–294
Algebraic reasoning, for simple patterns and
  relationships, 277
Algorithms
 addition with powers-of-ten blocks,
  92–93
 alternative
  for whole-number addition, 93–95
  for whole-number division, 136–139
  for whole number multiplication,
   133–136
  for whole-number subtraction, 98–99,
   106
 decomposition, 96–97
 lattice addition, 95
 manipulatives with standard division, 136

 multiplication with powers-of-ten blocks,
  129–133
 partial products, 133
 partial sums, 94–95
 Russian peasant multiplication, 135
 student-created, 88
 subtraction with powers-of-ten blocks,
  95–97
Angles
 exercises measuring, 178–180
 interior, 180
 measuring with protractor, 179
 summing angles of triangle, 179
Anno, Mitsumasa, 20–21, 47, 48
Anno's Counting Book (Anno), 47
Anno's Counting House (Anno), 48
Anno's Hat Tricks (Anno), 21
Apex, 188
Appropriate Education in the Primary Grades
  (NAEYC), 6–7
Area
 of circle, 183–184
 finding, 174, 175
 performance-based assessment of, 177–178
 perimeter and, 174
 relationship between volume and surface,
  186–188
Armstrong, Barbara, 118
Arranging photographs exercise, 282
Arrays as multiplication charts, 117–119,
  120, 121, 122, 123
Arrow arithmetic exercise, 275
Assessment. *See* Performance-based
  assessment
Assessment Standards for School Mathematics
  (NCTM), 3
Associative property of whole-number
  addition, 82
Attribute blocks, 64
Attribute pieces, 48
Attributes
 activity for shared, 63
 developing understanding of numeric,
  62–63
Awesome Animated Monster Maker Myth, 280

B

Bar graphs, 306–308, 336
Base-10 blocks, 55

Bases, chip trading in other, 58
Basic commands in LOGO computer
  language, 192
Basic facts
 of addition and subtraction, 80–88
 strategies for multiplication and division,
  115–122
Bears in their beds exercise, 114
Bicycles and tricycles exercise, 102
Bingo, 85–86, 124
Binomial multiplication, 296–299
Box-and-whisker plots, 345–347
Building
 a flat, 56
 towers exercise, 137
Burns, Marilyn, 17, 308, 310

C

Calculators
 adding fractions with, 208
 constant feature of, 53
 distinguishing between mental
  computations and, 77
 impact on mathematical pedagogy, 46
 mental percents exercise, 250
 need for computational skills with, 75,
  76–77
Calendar math, 62
Cardinal numbers, 48–49, 52
Carle, Eric, 309
Carpenter, Thomas P., 75–76
Cartesian product, 326
Cartland, Patricia, 310–311
Cells, 100
Centimeter ruler, 233
Central tendency, 317–318, 329
CGI (cognitively guided instruction), 40, 42
Chance, 318–320
 cubes in bag exercise, 319
 representing probability of fraction,
  319–320
 See also Probability
Children ages 8 to 13, 16–18, 20–21
Chip trading, 57, 58
Chords and regions exercise, 295
Circle graphs, 339–340, 343
Circles, 183–184
Circles of Learning (Johnson and others), 21,
  24–25

Classifying skills, 48, 50–51, 154–158, 334
Class survey, 316
Closure property
    of whole-number addition, 82
    of whole-number multiplication, 113
Cognitive development, 5–6
Cognitively guided instruction (CGI), 40, 42
Coin exercise, 276
Collective goals, 17
Combinations, 259, 260, 310, 329, 353
Commutative property
    exercise for, 90
    illustrated in exercise, 80
    of whole-number addition, 82
Comparing
    decimals
        direct comparison exercise, 229
        indirect comparison exercise, 229
        using physical model, 218
    fractions, 215
    towers, 81
    volumes, 255
    weights, 252
Comparison model of subtraction, 79
Compensation, 80
Complex patterns and relationships, 277–300
    arranging photographs exercise, 282
    chords and regions exercise, 295
    computer software for, 280, 294
    constructing geometric patterns, 294–295
    cryptarithms, 281
    divisibility, 285–286, 287
    integers, 286–292
    lesson plan
        to represent relationship with algebraic
            expression, 293–294
        on symbolic representation, 278–279
    multiplication of whole numbers and
        binomials, 296–299
    number theory in context, 280
    performance-based assessment of prime
        factors, 281–285
    reptiles exercise, 296
    Sieve of Erathosthenes exercise, 283
    solving equations with one variable,
        299–230
    standards for grades 6 to 8, 279
    worksheet for prime factors assessment,
        284
    See also Patterns and relationships
Computer software
    for addition and subtraction, 86
    for complex patterns and relationships,
        280, 294
    LOGO computer language, 191–198
    for multiplication and division of fractions
        and decimals, 248–250
    for practicing basic facts, 86
    for probability, 327–328
    for teaching geometry, 167–169
    utilities for geometry, 198–199
    for whole number multiplication, 125, 127
Concrete operational stage, 5, 6
Congruency exercise, 166

Conjecture
    defined, 191
    exercises using, 203
Consensus, 126
Consensus Strategies (Robertson, Graves, and
    Tuck), 126
Conserving as developmental signpost, 6, 36
Constant feature of calculator, 53
Constructivism, 39–40, 150
Context
    number theory in, 280
    placing graphs in, 314–315
Continuous model of fractions, 210–211
Control of error, 80
Cooperative learning, 16–18, 20–21, 24–25
Cooperative Learning in Mathematics
    (Davidson), 17
Counting exercise, 54
Counting up subtraction, 99
Cover-up game, 84, 85
*Creative Problem Solving in School
    Mathematics* (Lenchner), 280
Crews, Donald, 40
Cryptarithms, 279, 281
Cubes in bag exercise, 319
Cuisenaire, George, 77, 211
Cuisenaire rods
    adding fractions, 219, 220
    comparing fractions with, 215
    defining fractions with, 214
    described, 12, 77
    dividing fractions with, 241
    exercise using, 12, 13
    identifying relationships with, 270–273
    introducing fractions with, 211, 213
    multiplying fractions with, 240
    rod trains exercise, 79, 80
    subtracting fractions, 221
Cultural influences on assessment strategies,
    38
Curcio, Frances, 310
*Curriculum and Evaluation Standards for
    School Mathematics* (NCTM), 2–3
Curriculum issues, 39
Cylinders and volume, 185–186

D
Dart game, 94
Data analysis, statistics, and probability,
    305–331, 333–357
    chance, 318–320
        cubes in bag exercise, 319
        representing probability of fraction,
            319–320
    graphing and data analysis, 305–318,
        333–348
        bar graphs, 306–308, 336
        box-and-whisker and stem-and-leaf
            plots, 345–347
        circle graph, 343
        combinations exercise, 310
        conducting class survey, 316
        data collection, 334–335
        data collection and representation,
            309–312

describing, classifying, and ordering
    exercise, 334
double bar graphs, 342
double line graph, 343
estimating raisins in box, 309, 311
frequency tally exercise, 335
graphing, 341–344
hanging bar graph, 344
histograms, line graphs, and circle
    graphs, 335–340
lesson plan on statistics, 348–349
line graphs, 317
measures of central tendency, 317–318,
    329
Monte Carlo simulation exercise, 345
performance-based assessment for
    graphs, 340
performance-based assessment for
    plotting, 347
permutations exercise, 310
physical graphs, 306, 307
placing graphs in context, 314–315
for pre-K to 2, 306
simulations, 344–345
using data for solving problems,
    315–316
using data to make decisions, 347–348
using graphs to assess children's
    knowledge, 313–314
very hungry caterpillar exercise, 309
    overview, 305
    probability, 320–329, 348–355
        computer software for, 327–328
        concepts to incorporate, 320–323
        exercise with independent and
            dependent events, 352
        fundamental counting principle, 351
        independent events, 349, 351, 352
        lesson plan on gathering and analyzing
            data, 327–328
        making predictions exercise, 350
        not equally likely events, 320, 326
        Pascal's triangle, 352, 353
        permutations and combinations, 351,
            353–355
        probability fractions, 322–323
        spinners exercise, 321
        standards, 320
        tree diagrams, 325–327
    Web sites for, 330, 356
Data collection
    for grades 6 to 8, 334–335
    representation and, 309–312
Data Explorer, 328
Data sets, 317–318, 329
Davidson, Neil, 17
Decimals, 207–237, 239–265
    adding, 219, 222
    comparing
        direct comparison exercise, 229
        indirect comparison exercise, 229
        using physical model, 218
        volumes, 255
        weights, 252

computer software for multiplication and division of, 248–250
cooperative exercise, for multiplication and division of, 262
creating
    centimeter ruler, 233
    inch ruler, 233
designing a quilt, 261
dividing, 247
eating percents, 249
estimating sums and differences of rational numbers, 225
gelatin dessert exercise, 260
gingerbread people exercise, 260
for grades pre-K to 2, 209
for grades 3 to 5, 209, 219–223, 225
introducing concepts of, 207–209
linear measurement
    cooperative exercise in, 234
    for grades 3 to 5, 230–232
    for grades pre-K to 2, 228–230
making a meter, 234
multiplying, 244, 245
performance-based assessment
    for multiplying, 244, 246–247
    for proportions, 261, 263
subtracting, 219, 223
Web sites for, 236, 264
See also Fractions; Measurement
Decision-making with data, 347–348
Decomposition algorithm, 96–97
Deductive reasoning, 152
Dependent events, 352
Describing skills, 48, 50, 154–158, 334
Dessart, Donald J., 76–77
Developmentally appropriate practice for students, 7
Dienes, Zoltan, 55
Dienes blocks, 55
Dilations exercise, 201–202
Direct comparison exercise, 229
Discrete model of fractions, 213
Distance, estimating, 68
Divide and Conquer (Carraher), 280
Division
    divisibility, 300–301
        by 2, 285
        by 3 or 9, 286
        by 4, 285
        by 8, 285
        by 11, 287
    of fractions and decimals
        computer software for, 248–250
        dividing decimals, 247
        dividing fractions, 223, 225, 241
    of integers, 290–291
    of whole numbers, 111–147
        alternative algorithm for, 136–139
        basic fact strategies for, 115–122
        computer software for, 125, 127
        for grades 3 to 5, 112–113
        for grades 6 to 8, 139–144
        lesson plan for grade 6, 144
        manipulatives with standard division algorithm, 136

multi-digit numbers, 128–139
operations of multiplication and, 111–115
performance-based assessment for basic facts, 127–128
problem solving exercises for, 126, 142–144
subtractive method of division, 137, 139
Web sites for, 146–147
See also Multi-digit multiplication and division; Multiplication
Dominoes, 19–20
Double bar graphs, 342
Double line graph, 343
Doubling numbers, 83

E

Early childhood, defined, 5
Eating Fractions (McMillan), 210
Education goals for teaching mathematics, 3–4
English system of measurement, 230–231
    creating inch ruler, 233
    for volume, 253
    See also Measurement; Metric system
Equal addends subtraction, 98–99
Equally likely events, 320, 323–325
Estimating
    distance and time, 68
    with multiples of ten, 89
    overview, 67
    quantities, 69
    quotients, 141, 245
    raisins in box, 309, 311
    rounding
        with compensation, 140–141
        to multiples of ten, 140
    sums and differences of rational numbers, 225
    teaching, 89–91
Even and odd numbers, 269, 270
Even/odd activity, 119–121
Everybody Counts (National Research Council), 2
Experimental probability, 320

F

Fact families, 40, 41
Family Math, 38
Female students and teacher interaction, 37
Fish in a pond exercise, 78
Flashcard System, The, 86
Folkson, Susan, 310
Formal operational stage, 6
Formulas, 100
Fractions, 207–237, 239–265
    adding, 219, 220
    comparing, 215
        volumes, 255
        weights, 252
    computer software for multiplication and division of, 248–250
    as continuous model, 210–211
    cooperative exercise, for multiplication and division of, 262

creating
    centimeter ruler, 233
    inch ruler, 233
defining fractions, 214
designing a quilt, 261
direct comparison exercise, 229
as discrete model, 213
dividing, 223, 225, 241
eating percents, 249
as equal parts of continuous whole, 212
estimating
    products and quotients, 245
    sums and differences of rational numbers, 225
finding particular weight exercise, 253
function machine exercise, 262
gelatin dessert exercise, 260
gingerbread people exercise, 260
for grades pre-K to 2, 209
for grades 3 to 5, 209, 219–223, 225
indirect comparison exercise, 229
introducing concepts of, 207–209
lesson plans for fractions, 226–228
linear measurement
    cooperative exercise in, 234
    for grades pre-K to 2, 228–230
    for grades 3 to 5, 230–232
    performance-based assessment of, 232–235
making a meter, 234
making lemonade exercise, 255
measurement
    of mass and volume, 250–259
    nonstandard units of, 230
mental percents exercise, 250
metric system, 231–232
models and concepts of, 210–213
multiplying fractions, 223, 225, 240
percent designs, 248
percents on a grid exercise, 251
performance-based assessment
    of equivalent fractions, 216–217
    for identifying appropriate measures, 257–259
    for naming fractions, 213–215
    for proportions, 261, 263
probability of fractions, 319–320, 322–323
rounding rational numbers, 224
subtracting, 219, 221, 223, 225
using tangrams for problem-solving with fractions, 225
Web sites for, 236
See also Decimals; Measurement
Frequency tally exercise, 335
Front-end estimation, 91
Function, 279

G

Gender issues in teaching mathematics, 37
Geoboard, 174
Geometers' Sketchpad, 191
Geometric patterns
    constructing complex, 294–295
    creating simple, 268

Geometric superSupposer, 191
Geometry, 149–171, 173–205
  angle measurements, 178–180
  area, 174, 175
  computer software for, 167–169, 198–199
  conjectures exercise, 203
  connecting to other mathematical ideas, 158, 160
  constructing
    pentagrams, 197
    rectangular prisms, 186–187
  defined, 173
  dilations exercise, 201–202
  exercises measuring triangles, 179–180
  for grades pre-K to 2, 150–154
  for grades 3 to 5, 161–162, 164, 165
  for grades 6 to 8, 173–174, 199
  guided discovery techniques for, 180–186
  interdisciplinary lesson plan for, 189–190
  length of hypotenuse exercise, 175–176
  lesson plan for tangrams, 160–161
  LOGO computer language, 191–198
  medians of triangles, 198
  observation, description, and classification, 154–155
  performance-based assessment
    of area, 177–178
    of combining shapes, 155, 157–158
    of line and rotational symmetry, 167
    of perimeter, 176–177
    of transformations, 202
  perimeter, 174
  reflections exercise, 200
  rotations exercise, 201
  surface area and volume, 186–188
  transformational, 199–203
  translations exercise, 200
  triangles exercise, 195–196
  van Heile levels of development, 150, 152–154
  Web sites for, 204
Geometry Inventor, 199
Geometry World, 199
Geringer, Laura, 308
Get to 24 exercise, 271
Glyphs
  defined, 310
  exercise using, 312
  using, 310–312
Grades pre-K to 2
  addition and subtraction of whole numbers for, 76
  cognitive development of, 5–6
  decimals for, 209
  fractions for, 209
  geometry and spatial sense for, 150–154
  graphing and data analysis for, 306
  linear measurement for, 228–230
  number and numeration for, 45–61
  standards for simple patterns and relationships, 267
  teaching, 6–11, 13–15
  See also Simple patterns and relationships
Grades 3 to 5
  decimals for, 209, 219–223, 225

division of whole numbers, 112–113
  fractions for, 209, 219–223, 225
  geometry and spatial sense for, 161–162, 164, 165
  linear measurement for, 230–232
  multiplication and division for, 112–113
  number and numeration for, 61–64
  probability
    computer software for, 327–328
    concepts to incorporate, 320–323
    lesson plan on gathering and analyzing data, 327–328
    not equally likely event exercise, 326
    performance-based assessments for equally likely events, 323–325
    probability fractions, 322–323
    spinners exercise, 321
    standards, 320
    tree diagrams, 325–327
  relationship between variables and problem solving, 274
Grades 6 to 8
  bar graphs, 336
  box-and-whisker and stem-and-leaf plots, 345–347
  circle graph, 343
  complex patterns and relationships for, 279
  data collection, 334–335
  describing, classifying, and ordering exercise, 334
  division of whole numbers, 139–144
  double bar graphs, 342
  double line graph, 343
  estimating quotients, 141
  frequency tally exercise, 335
  geometry, and spatial sense for, 173–174, 199
  graphing, 341–344
  hanging bar graph, 344
  histograms, line graphs, and circle graphs, 335–340
  lesson plan on statistics, 348–349
  measurement skills, 251–257
  multiplication and division
    of fractions and decimals for, 239–244
    of whole numbers for, 139–144
  number and numeration for, 64–69
  performance-based assessment
    for graphs, 340
    for plotting, 347
  rounding
    with compensation, 140–141
    to multiples of ten, 140
  simulations, 344–345
  using data to make decisions, 347–348
  See also Complex patterns and relationships
Graphers, 328
Graphing and data analysis, 305–318, 329, 333–348
  bar graphs, 306–308, 336
  box-and-whisker and stem-and-leaf plots, 345–347
  circle graphs, 343
  combinations exercise, 310
  conducting class survey, 316

data collection, 309–312, 334–335
  data for solving problems, 315–316, 347–348
  describing, classifying, and ordering exercise, 334
  double bar graphs, 342
  double line graphs, 343
  estimating raisins in box, 309, 311
  frequency tally exercise, 335
  graphing, 341–344
  hanging bar graphs, 344
  histograms, 335–338
  lesson plan on statistics, 348–349
  line graphs, 317, 337–338
  measures of central tendency, 317–318, 329
  Monte Carlo simulation exercise, 345
  performance-based assessment for, 340
  performance-based assessment for graphs, 340
  performance-based assessment for plotting, 347
  permutations exercise, 310
  physical graphs, 306, 307
  placing graphs in context, 314–315
  for pre-K to 2, 306
  simulations, 344–345
  teaching graphing, 341–344
  using graphs to assess children's knowledge, 313–314
  very hungry caterpillar exercise, 309
  weather graphs, 307
Graph Power, 328
Graves, Nancy, 126
Green Eggs and Ham (Seuss), 313
Grifalconi, Ann, 185
Group learning exercise for students, 9
Guess My Rule game, 83
Guided discovery techniques for geometry, 180–186

H
Hanging bar graph, 344
Hembree, Ray, 76–77
Hexomino, 20
Hiebart, James, 75–76
Hindu-Arabic number system, 53–57
Histograms, 335–338
Home life and learning, 38
Hot Dog Stand, 328–329
Hungry caterpillar exercise, 309
Hypotenuse, 175–176

I
Ice Cream Truck, 328
Identity property
  of whole number addition, 82
  of whole number multiplication, 114, 116
"I have . . . Who has . . . ?" game, 83–84
Inch ruler, creating, 233
Independent events, 349, 351, 352
Indirect comparison exercise for fractions and decimals, 229
Individual accountability for students, 17

Inhelder, Barbel, 150
Integers, 286–292, 300
  addition of, 288–289
  multiplication and division of, 290–291
  operations on, 288–291
  performance-based assessment of, 291–292
  subtraction of, 289–290
"Interdisciplinary Learning" (NCTM), 8
"I wish I had . . ." exercise, 81

J

Jigsaw exercise for cooperative learning, 21
Johnson, David, 17
Johnson, Roger, 17

K

Kagan, Spencer, 17–18
Kamii, Constance, 84
King's Rule, The, 294

L

Lattice addition algorithm, 95
Lattice multiplication, 134
Learning centers, 35–36
Learning mathematics before teaching, 1, 42
Lenchner, George, 280
Length of hypotenuse, 175–176
Lesson plans, 32–36
  for Chinese abacus, 57, 59–61
  on division of whole numbers, 144
  for fractions, 226–228
  on gathering and analyzing data, 327–328
  for geometry, 189–190
  for measuring volumes, 257, 258
  for multiplication and division of whole
    numbers, 144
  outline form for, 33
  as pedagogical tools, 32, 69
  for place values, 57, 59–61, 65–66
  representing relationship with algebraic
    expression, 293–294
  for skip counting, 34, 35
  on statistics, 348–349
  for subtraction at grade 1, 104–105
  on symbolic representation, 278–279
  for tangrams, 160–161
Line and rotational symmetry, 167
Linear measurement
  cooperative group exercise in, 234
  direct comparison exercise for, 229
  English standard system of, 230–231
  fractions and decimals in, 208
  indirect comparison exercise for, 229
  metric system of, 231–232
  nonstandard units of measurement, 230
  performance-based assessment of, 232–235
  standards
    for grades pre-K to 2, 228–230
    for grades 3 to 5, 230–232
  See also Measurement
Line graphs, 317, 337–338
  double, 343
Logical Journey of the Zoombinis, The, 328

Logico-mathematical knowledge, 40, 150,
  151
LOGO computer language, 191–198
  basic commands, 192
  cooperative exercise constructing shapes,
    194
  drawing rectangle in, 193

M

Magic squares exercise, 87
Male students and teacher interaction, 37
Mass
  defined, 251
  measurement of volume and, 250–259
  See also Measurement; Volume
Math Ace, 86
Math and Literature (K–3) (Burns), 308, 310
Mathematical reasoning exercise, 162
McMillan, Bruce, 210
Measurement
  English system of, 230–231
    creating inch ruler, 233
    for volume, 253
  estimating distance, 68
  exercise for, 164
  geometry as, 173
  of heights with Unifix cubes, 15–16
  identifying appropriate, 257–259
  lesson plan for, 257–258
  linear
    cooperative group exercise in, 234
    direct comparison exercise for, 229
    English standard system of, 230–231
    fractions and decimals in, 208
    indirect comparison exercise for, 229
    nonstandard units of measurement, 230
    performance-based assessment of,
      232–235
    standards for grades pre-K to 2,
      228–230
    standards for grades 3 to 5, 230–232
  of mass and volume, 250–259
    English standard of measurement for
      volume, 253
    metric standard for volume, 254
  metric standard
    creating centimeter ruler, 233
    for linear, 231–232
    making a meter, 234
    for volume, 254
  nonstandard units of, 230
  of plant growth, 9
  skills for grades 6 to 8, 251–257
Measures of central tendency, 317–318, 329
Medians of triangles, 198
Mental multiplying, 129
Metric system, 231–232
  creating centimeter ruler, 233
  making a meter, 234
  units for volume, 254
  See also English system of measurement;
    Measurement
Mighty Math Astro Algebra, 280
Mighty Math Calculating Crew, 125
Mighty Math Number Heroes, 248

Millie's Math House, 86
Mind or machine exercise, 77
MindTwister Math, 125
Missing addend model of subtraction, 79
Models and concepts of fractions and
  decimals, 210–213
Monte Carlo simulation exercise, 345
Montessori, Maria, 55
Multicultural issues in teaching mathematics,
  37–39
Multi-digit addition and subtraction, 88–106
Multi-digit multiplication and division,
  128–139
  alternative algorithms
    for whole-number division, 136–139
    for whole number multiplication,
      133–136
  estimation and distributive and associative
    properties, 128
  manipulatives with standard division
    algorithm, 136
  performance-based assessment
    of division, 139
    of multiplication, 135–136
  powers-of-ten blocks with standard
    multiplication algorithm, 129–133
Multiples of ten estimation skill, 89
Multiplication
  of binomials and whole numbers, 296–299
  of fractions and decimals, 239–265
    comparing volumes, 255
    comparing weights, 252
    computer software for, 248–250
    cooperative exercise for fractions and
      decimals, 262
    designing a quilt, 261
    eating percents, 249
    estimating products and quotients, 245
    finding particular weight exercise, 253
    function machine exercise, 262
    gelatin dessert exercise, 260
    gingerbread people exercise, 260
    for grades 6 to 8, 239–244
    identifying appropriate measures,
      257–259
    lesson plan for measuring volume, 257,
      258
    making lemonade exercise, 255
    measurement of mass and volume,
      250–259
    mental percents exercise, 250
    multiplying decimals, 244, 245,
      246–247
    multiplying fractions, 223, 225, 240
    percents, 248, 251
    proportional thinking, 259, 261–262
    proportions, 261, 263
    Web sites for, 264
  of integers, 290–291
  of whole numbers, 111–147
    alternative algorithms for whole number
      multiplication, 133–136
    basic fact strategies for, 115–122,
      127–128
    bingo, 124

computer software for, 125, 127
estimation and distributive and associative properties for multi-digit multiplication and division, 128
even/odd activity, 119–121
for grades 3 to 5, 112–113
for grades 6 to 8, 139–144
identity property of whole number multiplication, 114, 116
lesson plan for grade 6, 144
multi-digit numbers, 128–139
multiplication cover-up, 122
operations of division and, 111–115
patterns, 124–125
powers-of-ten blocks with standard multiplication algorithm, 129–133
problem solving exercises for, 126, 142–144
properties of whole-number multiplication, 113–115
salute, 122–123
two over activity, 121
Web sites for, 146–147
zero property of whole number multiplication, 114
See also Division; Multi-digit multiplication and division
Multiplication charts
introducing, 116–117, 118, 119
types of visual arrays, 117–119, 120, 121, 122, 123
Multiplication cover-up, 122

N
NAEYC (National Association for the Education of Young Children), 6–7
Naming fractions, 213–215
National Association for the Education of Young Children (NAEYC), 6–7
National Council of Teachers of Mathematics (NCTM), 2–3, 8
National Research Council, 2
NCTM (National Council of Teachers of Mathematics), 2–3, 8
See also Principles and Standards for School Mathematics
Near-doubles, 83
Neuschwander, Cindy, 185
Nominal numbers, 48–49, 52
Non-proportional place-value model, 55–57
Nonstandard units of measurement, 230
Not equally likely events, 320, 326
Number and numeration, 31–73
cognitively guided instruction, 40, 42
constructivism, 39–40
creating instruction plans, 32–36
exercise for, 163
factors affecting mathematical achievement, 36–39
for grades pre-K to 2, 45–61
for grades 3 to 5, 61–64
for grades 6 to 8, 64–69
performance-based assessment, 43–45
Number boxes, 51

Numbered heads together, 18, 19
Number sense, defined, 46

O
Observation skills, 48, 154–155
Odd and even numbers, 269, 270
One-to-many correspondence, 260
One-to-one correspondence, 47–48
Operations
on integers, 288–291
on number, 162
Ordering skills, 334
Ordinal numbers, 48–49, 52
Origami, 226–228
Outline form for lesson plans, 33

P
Paper plate flowers exercise, 112
Pascal's triangle
applying, 353
exercise using, 352
Pattern blocks exercise, 156
Patterns and functions exercise, 165
Patterns and relationships, 267–303
complex, 277–300
arranging photographs exercise, 282
chords and regions exercise, 295
computer software for, 280, 294
constructing geometric patterns, 294–295
cryptarithms, 279, 281
divisibility, 285–286, 287
integers, 286–292
lesson plan on symbolic representation, 278–279
lesson plan to represent relationship with algebraic expression, 293–294
multiplication of whole numbers and binomials, 296–299
number theory in context, 280
performance-based assessment of prime factors, 281–285
reptiles exercise, 296
Sieve of Erathosthenes exercise, 283
solving equations with one variable, 299–230
standards for grades 6 to 8, 279
worksheet for prime factors assessment, 284
identifying relationships, 270–274
lesson plan to represent relationship with algebraic expression, 293–294
overview, 267
recognizing
basic multiplication patterns, 124–125
patterns in division, 142
relationship between variables and problem solving, 274–277
simple, 267–277
algebraic reasoning, 277
arrow arithmetic exercise, 275
cooperative problem solving for, 269
creating geometric patterns, 268
exercise with coins, 276
get to 24 exercise, 271

odd and even numbers, 269
performance-based assessment for even and odd numbers, 270
performance-based assessment for identifying relationships, 273–274
relationship between variables and problem solving, 274–277
standards for pre-K to 2, 267
Web sites, 302
Pentagrams, constructing, 197
Pentomino, 20
Percent designs, 248
Percents, 249
eating, 249
on grid, 251
mental, 250
percent designs, 248
Performance-based assessment, 43–45
of area, 177–178
for basic addition and subtraction facts, 86–88, 105
for basic multiplication and division facts, 127–128
for cardinal uses of numbers, 52–53
combining shapes, 155, 157–158
cultural influences and, 38
for equally likely events, 323–325
of equivalent fractions, 216–217
evaluating student comprehension with, 44–45
for even and odd numbers, 270
for graphs, 340
for identifying appropriate measures, 257–259
for identifying relationships, 273–274
of integers, 291–292
of line and rotational symmetry, 167
of linear measurement, 232–235
for multi-digit addition and subtraction, 105–106
for multiplying decimals, 244, 246–247
for naming fractions, 213–215
number and operation for grades 3 to 5, 63–64
for one-to-one correspondence, 47–48
of perimeter, 176–177
for plotting, 347
of prime factors, 281–285
for proportions, 261, 263
standardized tests vs., 43–44
of transformations, 202
Perimeter
finding, 174
performance-based assessment of, 176–177
Permutations, 308, 310, 329
combinations and, 351, 353–355
Pet enclosures exercise, 154
Physical graphs, 306, 307
Physical knowledge, 39
pi (π), 183, 184
Piaget, Jean, 5–6, 39–40, 54–55, 150
Place values
lesson plans
for Chinese abacus, 57, 59–61
for grades 6 to 8, 65–66

non-proportional model of, 55–57
placement of numbers, 54
proportional model of, 55, 56
Placing graphs in context, 314–315
Planting a garden exercise, 113
Plotting
  box-and-whisker and stem-and-leaf plots, 345–347
  performance-based assessment for, 347
Polygons, 295
Portfolios of student performance assessments, 88
Pound, defined, 251–252
Powers-of-ten blocks, 55
  Algeblocks versus, 297
  multiplying decimals with, 244
  representing decimal quantities with, 208
  standard addition algorithm and, 92–93
  with standard multiplication algorithm, 129–133
  standard subtraction algorithm and, 95–97
Predictions, 91, 350
Preoperational stage, 5–6
Prime and composite numbers, 67, 68
Prime factors, 281–285
Primitives for LOGO computer language, 192
Principles and Standards for School Mathematics (NCTM), 3, 42
  connection of geometry to other mathematic ideas, 158, 160
  for pre-K to 2
    addition and subtraction, 76
    fractions and decimals, 209
    geometry and spatial sense, 161–162, 164, 165
    graphing and data analysis for, 306
    linear measurement, 228–230
    number and operation sense, 45
    simple patterns and relationships, 267
  for grades 3 to 5
    fractions and decimals, 219–223, 225
    geometry and spatial sense, 161–162, 164, 165
    linear measurement, 230–232
    multiplication and division, 112–113
    number and operation sense, 61–63
    using data for solving problems, 315–316
    variables and problem solving, 274
  for grades 6 to 8
    on complex patterns and relationships, 279
    in data analysis, statistics, and probability, 333–334
    geometry and spatial sense, 173–174, 199
    measurement skills, 251–257
    multiplication and division, 139–144
    on multiplication of fractions and decimals, 239–244
    number and operation sense, 64
Probability, 320–329
  computer software for, 327–328
  concepts about, 320–323
  exercise for, 164

fundamental counting principle of, 326, 351
lesson plan on gathering and analyzing data, 327–328
not equally likely events, 320, 326
performance-based assessments for equally likely events, 323–325
probability fractions, 322–323
spinners exercise, 321
standards for grades 3 to 5, 320
theoretical and experimental, 348–355
  applying Pascal's triangle, 353
  exercise with independent and dependent events, 352
  fundamental counting principle, 351
  independent events, 349, 351, 352
  making predictions exercise, 350
  Pascal's triangle exercise, 352
  permutations and combinations, 351, 353–355
tree diagrams, 325–327
See also Chance
Probability fractions, 322–323
Problem solving
  for equations with one variable, 299–230
  get to 24 exercise, 271
  for multiplication and division of whole numbers, 126, 142–144
  for number and numeration, 43
  relationship between variables and, 274–277
  for simple patterns and relationships, 269
  spreadsheet as tool for, 103
  using data for, 315–316
Products, 245
Professional Standards for Teaching Mathematics (NCTM), 3–4
Proportional place-value model, 55, 56
Proportions
  performance-based assessment for, 261, 263
  proportional thinking and, 259, 261–262
Protractors, 179
Pumpkins, 14
Put and take exercise, 52

Q

Quadrilaterals, 10–11
Quantities, estimating, 69
Quilts
  designing, 163, 261
  patterns and functions exercise, 165
Quotients
  defined, 211
  estimating, 141, 245

R

Random sampling, 316
Ratio, 211
Reader Rabbit's Math, 248
Reasoning
  algebraic, 277
  deductive, 152
  exercise in mathematical, 162

Rectangles, drawing in LOGO, 193
Rectangular arrays for prime and composite numbers, 68
Rectangular prisms, 186–187
Recursive procedure, 196
Reflections exercise, 200
Relationships. *See* Patterns and relationships
Reptiles, 295, 296
Restating problems, 181
Reversal as developmental signpost, 6, 55, 69
Rewriting fractions with like denominators, 219–223
Rigor, 153–154
Robertson, Laurel, 126
Rod trains exercise, 79, 80
Rotational symmetry, 165, 167
Rotations exercise, 201, 202
Rotten apple game, 97
Rounding
  with compensation, 140–141
  to multiples of ten, 140
  rational numbers, 224
Rowe, Mary Budd, 36
Rulers, 233
Russian peasant multiplication, 135

S

Salute, 122–123
Salute game, 84–85
Sand numerals, 8
Sensorimotor stage, 5
Seuss, Dr., 313
Shapes
  analysis of geometric, 152
  combining, 155, 157–158
Sharan, Shlomo, 17
Shared attributes, 63
Sharing paper exercise, 117
Sharing the loot exercise, 138
Show what you hear exercise, 155
Show what you see exercise, 155
Sieve of Erathosthenes exercise, 283
Similarity, 167, 169
Simple patterns and relationships, 267–277
  algebraic reasoning, 277
  arrow arithmetic exercise, 275
  cooperative problem solving for, 269
  creating geometric patterns, 268
  exercise with coins, 276
  get to 24 exercise, 271
  odd and even numbers, 269
  performance-based assessment
    for even and odd numbers, 270
    for identifying relationships, 273–274
  relationship between variables and problem solving, 274–277
  standards for pre-K to 2, 267
  See also Patterns and relationships
Simulations, 344–345
Sir Cumference and the Dragon of Pi (Neuschwander), 185
Sir Cumference and the First Round Table (Neuschwander), 185
Skip counting lesson plan, 34, 35
Slavin, Robert, 17

Social knowledge, 40
Solving equations with one variable, 299–230
Sorting, 49
Spatial Sense, 199
Spatial visualization. *See* Tangrams
Spinners exercise, 321
Spreadsheet as problem-solving tool, 99–102, 103
Standards 2000, 3
Standards for teaching mathematics, 2–3
Statistics
    lesson plan for, 348–349
    See also Data analysis, statistics, and probability
Stem-and-leaf plots, 345–347
"Structural Approach to Cooperative Learning, The" (Kagan), 17–18
Students
    activity-based lessons for, 34–36
    creating portfolios of performance assessments for, 88
    developing and carrying out strategy in problem solving, 182
    developmentally appropriate practice for, 7
    evaluating reasonableness of solutions, 182
    group learning exercise for, 9
    individual accountability and collective goals for, 17
    introducing fractions and decimals to, 207–209
    observation, description, and clarification skills, 48, 154–155
    posing problem-solving questions to, 4–5
    Principles and Standards goals for, 3–4
    restating geometry problems, 181
    theory of geometric development of, 150–154
    time spent on mathematics, 26
    understanding
        magnitude of million, 66–67
        number theory in context, 280
    using graphs to assess knowledge, 313–314
Subitizing, 57
Subtraction
    of decimals, 223
    of fractions, 221, 223, 225
    of whole numbers, 75–109
        alternative algorithms for, 98–99, 106
        basic facts of addition and, 80–88
        computer programs illustrating addition and, 86
        counting up subtraction, 99
        determining underlying structure of numbers, 82–86
        equal addends subtraction, 98–99
        lesson plan for grade 1, 104–105
        missing addend model of, 79
        powers-of-ten blocks and standard subtraction algorithm, 95–97
        for pre-K to 2, 76
        subtractive method of division, 137, 139
        take-away model of, 79
        using multi-digit numbers, 88–106
    See also Addition
Subtraction of integers, 289–290

Surface area and volume, 186–188
Symbolic representation, 278–279
Symmetry, 164–165

T
Take-away model of subtraction, 79
Tangrams
    defined, 157
    exercise with, 159
    lesson plan for, 160–161
    making, 157–158
    as problem-solving strategies for fractions, 225
Teachers
    average "wait time" for answers, 36–37
    awareness of gender issues, 37
    creating portfolios for student assessments, 88
    developing schema for evaluating student problem solving, 127–128
    factoring in cultural influences on teaching, 38
    making performance-based assessments, 43–45
    as mathematics learners, 1, 42
    skills for multicultural classrooms, 37–39
    standards for teaching mathematics, 2–3
    working with Cuisenaire rods, 13
Teaching Children Mathematics (Armstrong), 118
Teaching Children Mathematics (Cartland), 310
Teaching mathematics, 1–29
    for children ages 8 to 13, 16–18, 20–21
    concepts about probability, 320–323
    connecting geometry to other mathematical ideas, 158, 160
    curriculum issues and, 39
    debate over conceptual vs. procedural knowledge, 75–76
    developmentally appropriate practice for children, 7
    education goals for, 3–4
    factors affecting student achievement, 36–39
    guided discovery techniques for geometry, 180–186
    introducing fractions and decimals, 207–209
    learning before, 1, 42
    lesson plans as pedagogical tools, 32, 69
    Piaget's theory of cognitive development, 5–6
    posing problem-solving questions, 4–5
    to primary-grade children, 6–11, 13–15
    standards for, 2–3
    teaching estimation and commutative and associative properties, 89–91
    using activity-based lessons, 34–36
    using glyphs, 310–312
    using numbers in cardinal, ordinal, and nominal sense, 48–49
    See also Principles and Standards for School Mathematics; and specific grades and concepts

Teasers by Tobbs, 248
Ten Black Dots (Crews), 40
Tenth Planet software, 168–169
Tetromino, 19
Theoretical and experimental probability, 348–355
    applying Pascal's triangle, 353
    exercise with independent and dependent events, 352
    fundamental counting principle, 351
    independent events, 349, 351, 352
    making predictions exercise, 350
    Pascal's triangle exercise, 352
    permutations and combinations, 351, 353–355
    theoretical probability, 320
Theory of geometric development, 150–154
Think-Pair-Share exercises, 22–23
Third International Mathematics and Science Study (TIMSS), 39
Three Hat Day, A (Geringer), 308
Time
    estimating, 68
    on task, 36
TIMSS (Third International Mathematics and Science Study), 39
Today Is . . . activity, 61
Transformation, 259, 260
Transformational geometry, 199–203
Transformations, performance-based assessment of, 202
Translations exercise, 200
Tree diagrams, 325–327
Triangles
    constructing medians of, 198
    creating in LOGO, 195–196
    exercises measuring, 179–180
Triangles and quadrilaterals exercise, 151
Triomino, 19
Tuck, Patricia, 126
Two over activity, 121

U
Unifix cubes, 15–16, 36
Usiskin, Zalman, 149

V
Values, defined, 100
Van Heile, Pierre Marie, 150
Van Heile-Geldof, Dina van, 150
Van Heile levels of development, 150, 152–154
    level 0: visualization, 150, 152
    level 1: analysis, 152
    level 2: informal deduction, 152, 153
    level 3: formal deduction, 152
    level 4: rigor, 153–154
Variables
    relationship between problem solving and, 274–277
    solving equations with one, 299–230
Very Hungry Caterpillar, The (Carle), 309
Village of Round and Square Houses, The (Grifalconi), 185

Volume
    of cylinder, 185–186
    English standard of measurement for, 253
    exercise comparing, 255
    lesson plan for measuring, 257, 258
    making lemonade exercise, 255
    measurement of mass and, 250–259
    metric standard of measurement for, 254
    relationship between surface area and,
        186–188
    See also Measurement

W

Wait time, 36–37
Watering plants exercise, 116
Weather graphs, 307
Web sites and resources
    for addition and subtraction of whole
        numbers, 108
    for data analysis, statistics, and probability,
        330, 356
    for fractions and decimals, 236
    for geometry, 204
    for learning and teaching mathematics, 27
    for multiplication and division of whole
        numbers, 146–147
    for NAEYC, 26
    NCTM, 25
    for numbers and numeration, 71
    for patterns and relationships, 302
Weight
    defined, 251
    exercise for finding, 253
Whole numbers, 111–147
    addition and subtraction of, 75–109
    alternative algorithms
        for addition of, 93–95

    for subtraction of, 98–99, 106
    for whole-number division, 136–139
    for whole number multiplication,
        133–136
basic facts
    of addition and subtraction, 80–88
    for multiplication and division,
        115–122
bingo, 124
computer software
    for addition and subtraction, 86
    for multiplication, 125, 127
counting up subtraction, 99
determining underlying structure of
        numbers, 82–86
equal addends subtraction, 98–99
estimation and distributive and associative
        properties for multi-digit
        multiplication and division, 128
even/odd activity, 119–121
front-end estimation, 91
identity property of whole number
        multiplication, 114, 116
lattice addition algorithm, 95
lesson plans
    for grade 6 multiplication and division
        of, 144
    for subtraction at grade 1, 104–105
manipulatives with standard division
        algorithm, 136
multiplication and division
    for grades 3 to 5, 112–113
    for grades 6 to 8, 139–144
    solving problems with, 142–144
    Web sites for, 146–147
operations of multiplication and division,
        111–115
partial sums algorithm, 94–95
patterns, 124–125

performance-based assessment
    for addition and subtraction, 86–88,
        105
    for basic multiplication and division
        facts, 127–128
    of multi-digit multiplication, 135–136
powers-of-ten blocks
    and standard addition algorithm, 92–93
    with standard multiplication algorithm,
        129–133
    and standard subtraction algorithm,
        95–97
problem solving exercises for
        multiplication and division, 126
properties
    of addition for, 82
    of multiplication for, 113–115
rounding, 91
spreadsheet as problem-solving tool,
        99–102, 103
subtractive method of division, 137, 139
teaching estimation and commutative and
        associative properties, 89–91
using multi-digit numbers, 88–106
zero property of whole number
        multiplication, 114
Worksheet for prime factors assessment, 284

Y

*Young Children Continue to Reinvent
    Arithmetic* (Kamii), 84
Young Children Reinvent Arithmetic (Kamii),
    84

Z

Zero
    as identity element in addition, 82
    in whole number multiplication, 114

Notes

Notes

Notes

Notes

Notes